Principles of
Floral Design
An Illustrated Guide

by

Pat Diehl Scace,
AIFD, AAF, CFD

Exhibit Designer, Missouri Botanical Garden, St. Louis, MO
Laureate Member, American Institute of Floral Designers
Member, American Academy of Floriculture
Landscape Architect

James M. DelPrince,
PhD, AIFD, PFCI, CFD

Horticulture Professor, Mississippi State University
Laureate Member, American Institute of Floral Designers
Member, Professional Floral Commentators International

Publisher
The Goodheart-Willcox Company, Inc.
Tinley Park, IL
www.g-w.com

Manufactured in the United States of America.

Library of Congress Catalog Card Number 2014006627

ISBN 978-1-61960-889-4

3 4 5 6 7 8 9 – 15 – 19 18 17

The Goodheart-Willcox Company, Inc. Brand Disclaimer: Brand names, company names, and illustrations for products and services included in this text are provided for educational purposes only and do not represent or imply endorsement or recommendation by the author or the publisher.

The Goodheart-Willcox Company, Inc. Safety Notice: The reader is expressly advised to carefully read, understand, and apply all safety precautions and warnings described in this book or that might also be indicated in undertaking the activities and exercises described herein to minimize risk of personal injury or injury to others. Common sense and good judgment should also be exercised and applied to help avoid all potential hazards. The reader should always refer to the appropriate manufacturer's technical information, directions, and recommendations; then proceed with care to follow specific equipment operating instructions. The reader should understand these notices and cautions are not exhaustive.

The publisher makes no warranty or representation whatsoever, either expressed or implied, including but not limited to equipment, procedures, and applications described or referred to herein, their quality, performance, merchantability, or fitness for a particular purpose. The publisher assumes no responsibility for any changes, errors, or omissions in this book. The publisher specifically disclaims any liability whatsoever, including any direct, indirect, incidental, consequential, special, or exemplary damages resulting, in whole or in part, from the reader's use or reliance upon the information, instructions, procedures, warnings, cautions, applications, or other matter contained in this book. The publisher assumes no responsibility for the activities of the reader.

The Goodheart-Willcox Company, Inc. Internet Disclaimer: The Internet resources and listings in this Goodheart-Willcox Publisher product are provided solely as a convenience to you. These resources and listings were reviewed at the time of publication to provide you with accurate, safe, and appropriate information. Goodheart-Willcox Publisher has no control over the referenced websites and, due to the dynamic nature of the Internet, is not responsible or liable for the content, products, or performance of links to other websites or resources. Goodheart-Willcox Publisher makes no representation, either expressed or implied, regarding the content of these websites, and such references do not constitute an endorsement or recommendation of the information or content presented. It is your responsibility to take all protective measures to guard against inappropriate content, viruses, or other destructive elements.

Library of Congress Cataloging-in-Publication Data

Scace, Pat Diehl
    Principles of floral design: an illustrated guide / by Pat Diehl Scace,
    James M. DelPrince. -- First Edition.
        pages cm.
    Includes index.
    ISBN 978-1-61960-889-4
    1. Flower arrangement. 2. Flower arrangers. I. DelPrince, James M. II. Title.
    SB449.S3582 2015
    745.92--dc23
                                                            2014006627

Cover Images: LiliGraphie/Shutterstock.com; AN NGUYEN/Shutterstock.com; Aprilphoto/Shutterstock.com

Preface

Principles of Floral Design: An Illustrated Guide has been designed for a new generation of students who want to explore career opportunities in floral design or simply want to learn the basics to use floral design as an outlet for their creativity. With hundreds of full-color illustrations, this text covers topics essential for the beginning designer and clearly conveys the theory and practice of floral design to guide students on their way to creating beautiful arrangements of their own.

The authors wrote *Principles of Floral Design* to meet the need for a new textbook that is well-illustrated, practical, and technically accurate. Moreover, the authors recognized the need for new designers to be thoroughly informed on the basics of every aspect of the industry. The textbook was also written with a key goal to support the American Institute of Floral Designers' (AIFD) initiative to engage a younger audience of potential floral designers.

Dozens of Step-by-Step photo sequences have been created for this text by horticulture instructor Janet Gallagher, AIFD. These illustrated procedures are both an effective teaching and learning tool, and form the cornerstone of our highly visual approach. These sequences allow floral design students to learn by doing, creating floral arrangements using commonly available, low-cost materials.

Special care has been taken to introduce topics in *Principles of Floral Design* in a logical, building-block fashion using simple language. Chapter 1 discusses the basis of floral design and the careers people find in, and supporting, this industry. Chapter 2 is a brief history of floral design, revealing how societies have used flowers from ancient times to the modern era.

Chapters 3 to 5 provide additional foundational knowledge. The material covered includes everything from tools and containers, plant structure and functions, to postharvest practices. Chapters 6 and 7 introduce and explain the principles and elements that are basic to *not* only floral design, but design in general.

Chapters 8 and 9 provide the background needed to select flowers and foliage with confidence and with artistic ends in mind. These chapters also include full-color glossaries containing hundreds of images of cut flowers and cut foliage used in floral design. Students participating in FFA Career Development Events (CDE) floriculture competitions will find these glossaries to be an excellent study aid when preparing for plant and flower identification tests.

Chapter 10 puts the principles and elements into action, illustrating types of floral designs from mechanic development and stem placement to finished geometric forms. Chapter 11 guides students into understanding and evaluating the environment into which arrangements will be placed, as well as how to develop themes using color schemes and accessories.

In Chapters 12 through 17, students will learn about creating, customizing, and augmenting basic design forms to suit various occasions. Chapter 12 focuses on flowers as personal adornments. Chapter 13 includes thorough treatment of designing and marketing wedding flowers in a multi-ethnic and multicultural society.

Chapter 14 covers the mainstay holidays of the floral industry as well as a myriad of additional holidays and special occasions. Chapter 15 introduces and covers various flower arrangements for funerals and memorials, as well as proper decorum of floral delivery and setup in funeral homes. In Chapter 16, students learn how to preserve flowers and foliage for use in arrangements created for placement in commercial and residential spaces. Students will also learn how to incorporate silk flowers and foliage into these designs.

Plus69/Shutterstock.com

Live plants, loved for their colorful flowers and interesting foliage, are presented in chapter 17, along with instructions for decorating potted plants. Chapter 18 explains the business of floristry. Students learn about different business areas including entrepreneurship, pricing, sales, customer service, and the use of social media as a means of marketing and sales.

Principles of Floral Design offers an extensive appendix with information on floral design competitions and judging, an illustrated section on state flowers, an anniversary chart including flowers and gifts, and a detailed chart on the meanings of flowers. The appendix also includes illustrations of geometric floral design shapes, cross reference charts (by botanical name) for each of the four illustrated glossaries, and a listing of noteworthy weddings. Extensive postharvest storage charts for flowers and foliage include storage temperatures, storage life, and vase life. A comprehensive glossary rounds out this comprehensive text, helpful for students, professional florists and those with a desire to build knowledge and skills in this creative and profitable industry.

On every page, the authors convey their passion for floral design, extending their message that working with flowers is an exciting profession that allows students to express their creativity and make a lot of people smile.

Special Features

- Dozens of color illustrated *Step-by-Step* procedures help students visualize and create stunning arrangements
- Textbook terminology and techniques aligned with American Institute of Floral Designers (AIFD) standards and practices
- *Safety Notes* appear throughout the text, stressing the importance of developing safe work habits
- *Pro Tips*, *Did You Know?* and *Thinking Green* features include designer advice, interesting facts, and methods of decreasing carbon footprints and increasing environmental awareness
- Emphasis on opportunities for continual advancement and personal evaluation by entering design competitions sponsored by FFA, state organizations, trade magazines, and student chapters of the AIFD

Chapter Pedagogical Aids

- *Objectives* and *Key Terms* identify the knowledge and skills to be obtained and introduce students to industry vocabulary
- *Review Questions*, designed to aid chapter mastery and accessible on our free companion website
- *Activities* to encourage students to learn on their own and with their peers
- *Critical Thinking* questions provide occupational challenges for students

- *STEM Activities and Academics* integrate math, science, social studies, and language arts concepts into topics of floral design
- *Communicating About Floral Design* provides additional writing and language assignments for improving reading, writing, speaking, and listening skills

About the Authors

Jodie Johnson/Shutterstock.com

Pat Diehl Scace currently serves as the Floral Display Supervisor for the Missouri Botanical Garden in St. Louis, Missouri. Pat earned her bachelor's degree in landscape architecture from the University of Illinois in Urbana-Champaign and attended the American Floral Art School in Chicago, Illinois. She has taught Advanced Floral Design at Southwestern Illinois College in Belleville, Illinois; presented for various organizations including state florists' associations, wholesale florists, and garden clubs; and received the Designer of the Year award from the Illinois State Florists' Association. A Laureate Member of the American Institute of Floral Designers, Pat has authored and coauthored several books, including The *Floral Artist's Guide: A Reference to Cut Flowers and Foliages* and *The AIFD Guide to Floral Design*. Pat grew up in the floral industry as part of the third generation to work as florists at Diehl Florist, Inc., a family-owned retail flower shop.

James M. DelPrince is a Professor of Horticulture at Mississippi State University. Jim received his doctoral degree in agricultural and extension education from Mississippi State University, and a master of science degree in agricultural education and a bachelor of science degree in horticulture from The Ohio State University. A Laureate member of the American Institute of Floral Designers, Jim has authored and coauthored several books, including *Interior Plantscaping: Principles and Practices*, *A Centennial History of the American Florist*, and *The AIFD Guide to Floral Design*. He is also the author of dozens of trade press articles for the floral industry.

Reviewers

The authors and publisher wish to thank the following industry and teaching professionals for their valuable input into the development of *Principles of Floral Design: An Illustrated Guide*.

Joshua Anderson
Teacher and Texas Master Florist
James Madison
Agriscience Magnet Program
San Antonio, Texas

Crystal Aukema
CTE Agriculture Teacher
Oxford Academy
Oxford, New York

Eva Crow
Agriculture Science Instructor
Heritage High School
Frisco, Texas

Janet Gallagher AIFD, CFD
Floral Design Instructor
Kishwaukee College
Malta, Illinois

Joyce Grattoni
Owner
Flowers by Grattoni
Hoffman Estates, Illinois

Nan Hamilton
Teacher of Floral Design and
    Advanced Floral Design
Northern Burlington County
    Regional High School
Columbus, New Jersey

Julie Kondoff
Teacher
Liberty High School
Frisco, Texas

Rachel Kostman
Agriculture Science and Technology
    Instructor
Phoenix High School
Phoenix, Oregon

Kimberly Martin
Plant Sciences Design Instructor
University of Missouri
Columbia, Missouri

Lynette McDougald
Instructor of Floral Management
Mississippi State University
Mississippi State, Mississippi

Bill McKinley
Benz Endowed Chair, Director,
    and Senior Lecturer
Texas A&M University
College Station, Texas

Kim New
Agriculture Science Instructor
Manvel High School
Manvel, Texas

Lisa Pieper
Agricultural Science Teacher
Caldwell High School
Caldwell, Texas

Amanda Simmons
Agriculture Science Teacher
Klein ISD/Klein Forest High School
Houston, Texas

Marianne Suess
Coordinator and Professor of
    Floral Design and Fashion Arts
Seneca College
Toronto, Ontario, Canada

Melinda Tague
Horticulture and Agricultural
    Education Instructor
Norman High School
Norman, Oklahoma

Craig Theimer
Floral Design Instructor
Naperville Central High School
Naperville, Illinois

Jack Winterrowd
Agriculture Science Teacher
Cedar Park High School
Cedar Park, Texas

Acknowledgments

The authors and publisher would like to thank the following individuals for their valuable support in the development of *Principles of Floral Design: An Illustrated Guide*.

Janet Gallagher of *Kishwaukee College* and Mary Rose Widmer of *Mary Rose Photography* for the *Step-by-Step* photo sequences

Joyce Grattoni of *Flowers by Grattoni* for her detailed review of the manuscript

June Hutson, supervisor of Kemper Home Demonstration Gardens, Missouri Botanical Garden, St. Louis, MO, for sharing her horticultural expertise

A special thanks to Jenny Scala from Society of American Florists (SAF) for helping obtain many of the beautiful design images.

Baisch & Skinner Wholesale, St. Louis, MO, owners and staff team, for their endless years of floral design support through products, facilities, and continuing educational programs. Particularly, Mike Hellman for his patience and support, allowing access to greenhouse facilities and products for this project

Jack Winterrowd of *Cedar Park High School* for his permission to reproduce lab projects and worksheets

Viola and Ercole DelPrince for supporting my love and education in horticulture

LeRoy Diehl and Ruth (Diehl) Toal for introducing the author to the beautiful world of flowers

The authors and publisher also extend gratitude to the following companies and individuals for many of the beautiful images used throughout the textbook.

aboutflowers.com/SAF
Cindy Anderson, AIFD, PFCI/SAF
Baisch & Skinner Wholesale, St. Louis, MO
Ardith Beveridge, AAF, AIFD, PFCI, CAFA
Blumz by JRDesigns, metro Detroit, MI/SAF
Carol Caggiano, AIFD, PFCI/SAF
Beth Campbell, Bloomtastic Florist, Columbus, OH/SAF
Ceramics and Pottery Arts and Resources
Dr. Delphinium Designs, Dallas, TX/SAF
Farell's Florist, Drexel Hill, PA/SAF
The Flower Studio, Austin, TX/SAF
Lisa Greene, AAF, AIFD, PFCI/SAF
HotHouse Design Studio, Birmingham, AL/SAF
Leanne and David Kesler, Floral Design Institute, Inc. Portland, OR/SAF
Koehler's & Dramm's Institute of Floristry, Minneapolis, MN/SAF
Sharon McGukin, SAF
Monday Morning Flower and Balloon Co., Princeton, NJ and Yardley, PA/SAF
Save On Crafts, www.saveoncrafts.com
Mark Sherouse
Shirley's Flowers & Gifts, Inc., Rogers, AR/SAF
Society of American Florists (SAF)
Bryan Swan, Karin's Florist, Vienna, VA/SAF
Maria Tapia at Shirley's Flowers & Gifts, Inc., Rogers, AR/SAF
Villere's of Metairie, LA/SAF
www.MelzMumz.com, Custom Homecoming Mums and Garters

Using This Textbook

Chapter
12
Flowers to Wear and Carry

objectives

After reading this chapter, you will be able to:

- Describe the design considerations that apply to various types of corsages.
- Create various styles of flowers-to-wear designs, including corsages and boutonnieres.
- Produce a floral jewelry design.
- Apply appropriate techniques to mount flowers and foliage on wires.
- Construct various styles of flowers-to-carry designs, including hand-tied bouquets and bouquets with foam holders.

key terms

arm bouquet	duchess rose
boutonniere	floral jewelry
cascade design	flowers-to-carry design
composite flower	flowers-to-wear design
corsage stem	glamellia
corsage	hand-tied bouquet
crescent design	hand-wired bouquet
double-spray corsage	headpiece

Go to www.g-wlearning.com/floraldesign/ for online vocabulary acti
from the chapter.

Objectives clearly identify the knowledge and skills to be obtained when the chapter is completed.

Chapter
7
Elements of Design

objectives

After reading this chapter, you will be able to:

- Identify the elements of design.
- Compare and contrast major color systems.
- Explain the principles of color harmonies.
- Discuss the application of color psychology to floral design.
- Apply procedures for systemic dyeing and tinting.
- Describe how the elements of form, fragrance, line, pattern, space, size, and texture are applied to floral design.

key terms

achromatic	intensity	space
additive color system	line	spray tint
color harmony	line flower	subtractive color system
color wheel	mass flower	systemic dyeing
design element	partitive color system	tertiary color
filler flower	pattern	texture
form	primary color	tint
form flower	secondary color	tone
fragrance	shade	value
hue	size	visible spectrum

Go to www.g-wlearning.com/floraldesign/ for online vocabulary activities using key terms
from the chapter.

133

Key Terms list floriculture terms from the chapter that are currently used in the industry.

Go to www.g-wlearning.com/floraldesign/ for vocabulary activities using key terms for each chapter.

Thinking Green notes highlight key items related to sustainability, energy efficiency, and environmental issues.

Did You Know? Features point out interesting and helpful facts about the floral industry.

Thinking Green

Eco-Friendly Containers
Although some floral supply companies specialize in eco-friendly containers, any time you reuse a container, you are helping the environment. Do your part by frequenting garage sales, flea markets, and thrift stores to find inexpensive and unusual containers.

Working with Other Types of Containers

Containers made with materials other than glass have advantages and disadvantages. Some are light, others are heavy; some are expensive whereas others are economically priced. The purpose and cost of the arrangement often dictate the type of container used.

Plastic and Ceramic Containers

Plastic containers are popular due to their water-holding ability, the variety of colors, forms, and textures available, and their tendency to be inexpensive. Plastic containers are usually lightweight, but the addition of wet floral foam and water give them the extra weight needed for stability. For permanent botanical designs, plaster, gravel, or a similar material is added to the container to ensure stability.

Ceramic containers are made from clay that has been formed into a shape and fired in a kiln. Ceramic containers are available in a variety of designs, shapes, and sizes. Some containers are decorated after they are fired whereas others are coated with a glaze compound before firing. Ceramic containers are versatile and may be used with all types of floral arrangements.

Metal Containers

Attractive metal containers can support a variety of themes and effects, **Figure 3-8.** Warm colors like copper and golden brass are popular for special occasions and fall arrangements. Cool, silver-colored containers are used for a variety of occasions. Ranging from small bud vases to large, elaborate containers, silver-colored containers are appropriate for the bedside table as well as the lobby of a grand hotel. Most silver-colored containers are not made from silver but are silver plated. Thin metal containers may be made from tin or aluminum and require a plastic liner to prevent leakage and to prevent the metal container from interacting with the preservative.

Did You Know?
By law, solid sterling silver is 92.5% silver and 7.5% copper. The copper is added for strength as pure silver is soft.

ZoneFatal/Shutterstock.com; Image courtesy of Save On Crafts, www.saveoncrafts.com

such as brass or copper make good containers for ...art, well-being, or joy. Metals such as steel are considered ... modern designs.

Miscellaneous Containers

Some containers are not really "containers" at all. For example, decorative birdcages are popular and add a bit of whimsy to the design. Traditional and specially shaped baskets are also popular choices. With the proper planning and materials, even a book can be used as a container.

Ribbon and Bows

Ribbon is used as an accent in floral designs and is a popular way of adding color, texture, and pattern. Ribbons and bows add a festive and sometimes even romantic appearance and enhance the beauty of designs, **Figure 3-9.**

Types of Ribbon

Acetate satin and nylon ribbon are the most commonly used in the floriculture industry. Single-faced acetate satin ribbon is shiny on one side and dull on the other. Double-faced satin ribbon has sheen on both sides and is somewhat thicker than single-faced ribbon. Many designers like to use sheer nylon ribbon because it does not absorb moisture and holds its shape. Velvet ribbon is very popular at Christmastime.

Ribbon is manufactured in varying sizes for the floral industry, **Figure 3-10.** The most popular widths stocked by florists are numbers 3, 9, and 40.

Making Bows

One of the basic skills a floral designer needs is the ability to make an attractive bow. Bows are commonly placed on sympathy pieces, vase arrangements, corsages, and sometimes on delivered and hospital arrangements. Ribbon may also be used as an inexpensive way to "fill" an arrangement. Follow the step-by-step procedure to make a bow.

Pro Tip

If a metal container has a seam, it is usually *not* watertight and will require a plastic liner.

Brian Chase/Shutterstock.com
Figure 3-9. In a corsage, ribbons and bows often serve the practical purpose of securing the flowers while adding beauty to the overall design.

Pro Tips provide students with advice and guidance that is especially applicable for an on-the-job designer.

Ribbon Widths	
Florist Size	**Approximate Measurement**
#1	6/16" (8 mm)
#2	7/16" (11 mm)
#3	5/8" (15 mm)
#5	7/8" (25 mm)
#9	1 7/16" (36 mm)
#40	2 11/16" (68 mm)
#100	4" (100 mm)

Goodheart-Willcox Publisher
Figure 3-10. Ribbon gauges commonly used in floral designs. The gauge, length, and color will be determined in part by the design you are creating.

Thinking Green

Using Raffia
Many floral designers use natural raffia instead of traditional ribbon to tie bouquets and accent arrangements. Raffia, a dried palm fiber, is easy to work with and is recyclable.

Did You Know?
The higher the number of a ribbon, the wider the ribbon.

Step-by-Step

Mother's Day Arrangement

A mother's day arrangement is a great opportunity to decorate a container for a keepsake. *All* moms love something homemade. For this project you will need the following plant materials: 2-3 stems purple larkspur, 8–10 pink spray roses, yellow stock, two lilies, leather leaf, and additional greens. You will also need a large, clean vase, decorative ribbon, a rhinestone buckle, glue dots or hot glue, wet floral foam, water, floral food, scissors, and a floral knife.

1

2   3

Before preparing the floral materials, decorate the vase. Run the decorative ribbon through the rhinestone buckle and wrap the ribbon around the vase. Secure the ribbon with glue dots or hot glue. Secure the soaked floral foam in the decorated vase. Insert the leather leaf first, adding additional greens as desired to add a variety of textures.

Insert the pu... establish the ... arrangement....

4

Group yellow stock on the side opposite to the roses. Grouping the materials adds more visual weight to each flower.

5

Add the lilies to create a focal point in the arrangement.

Mother's Day

The second Sunday in May is Mother's Day in the United States and many other countries. Mother's Day was created to honor mothers and motherhood. It is the busiest weekend of the year for florists. Floral gifts typically include standard arrangements, European gardens, container arrangements, and flowering plants, **Figure 14-2.** The historically popular corsage is still the gift of choice in some regions.

Sunny studio, Igor Yaruta/Shutterstock.com, Goodluz/Shutterstock.com

Figure 14-2. Mother's Day designs may be traditional or contemporary, and often incorporate the colors of spring and early summer.

Step-by-Step Procedures are illustrated and highlighted throughout the textbook to provide clear instructions for hands-on floral design. Both instructors and students benefit from the *Step-by-Step* procedures and can easily refer to these procedures for clarification.

Stem Strippers

Stem strippers are designed primarily for use on roses. They are used to quickly remove foliage that would fall below the water line of the design. When stem strippers are used to remove thorns from rose stems, care must be taken to remove only the sharp tip of the thorn. Water-conducting vessels are present in and near the thorns, but not in the tips. Stem strippers are especially useful when large numbers of flowers are being processed, **Figure 3-14**. Care should be taken to not cut into the epidermis and bark of flower stems. Water-conducting vessels near the outer portion of the stem may be damaged during this process, obstructing water uptake.

Pruners

Designers often use woody plant materials to create large-scale designs. It is difficult to cut stems thicker than 1″ diameter with a floral knife. *Pruning shears*, also called *secateurs*, cut through woody stems safely, **Figure 3-15**. Do *not* use pruners to cut wire.

Pruners have one of three types of blade designs: bypass, anvil, or parrot-beak. The blade alignment of bypass pruners is similar to that of scissors, but the upper blade has a convex shape and the bottom is either straight or concave. Anvil pruners have one sharp blade that closes to meet an unsharpened platform blade. This action may pinch vascular tissues of softer stems, but does not harm woody stems. Parrot-beak pruners have two concave blades designed to trap the stem between them. They are used only on narrow stems.

Some pruning shears have a ratchet action that helps to cut through thick stems a little at a time by squeezing and releasing the handles. After each squeeze, the blades stay in place, successively cutting hard stems with less effort.

Figure 3-14. As illustrated above, the thorns on rose stems vary greatly in size. When using any type of stem stripper, make sure you do not damage the stem or you will shorten the vase life of your roses.

The Naked Eye/Shutterstock.com

Safety Note

Storing Pruning Shears
Pruner blades are sharp and should not be handled carelessly. When pruning shears are not in use, engage the safety catch or loop that holds the handles (and blades) together.

Figure 3-15. Pruners are used to cut thick, woody stems. Make sure your pruners are kept clean and well-oiled.

ik_v_d/Shutterstock.com

Safety Notes alert students of proper procedures and safe use of potentially dangerous materials.

Designers may also use long-handled *loppers* for cutting branches larger than 1″ diameter. Saws used for tree pruning can also be helpful for harvesting and processing branches.

Japanese *ikebana* specialists use *hasami*, a scissor-like tool with highly sharpened, short blades. Hasami can cut through soft, herbaceous stems and small-caliper woody stems. They are used for floral design and for maintenance pruning of *bonsai*, **Figure 3-16**.

Wire Cutters

Wire cutters are used to cut wire lengths, silk flower stems, or premade garland. Do *not* use wire cutters on fresh flowers and foliage. They pinch stems rather than provide a clean cut. The ends of the decorative wire may be finished with pliers. See **Figure 3-17**.

Pins

Pins are used to anchor or hold small arrangements in place. For example, corsage and boutonniere pins are used to secure corsages and boutonnieres. *Greening pins*, also called *fern pins*, are made of heavy gauge wire bent into a U-shape. They are used for many purposes, including pinning moss to floral foam. Other types of floral pins include anchor pins, T-pins, wood picks, and plant stakes.

Figure 3-16. Hasami shears are used to prune and maintain bonsai.

CLM/Shutterstock.com

Did You Know?

In ikebana, withered leaves may be considered a part of the overall design, adding an element of asymmetry.

Figure 3-17. Common wire cutters should be used to cut floral wire. There are different types of handles and sizes so make sure you choose some that are comfortable. This is especially important if you use a lot of floral wire. The boutonniere illustrated here shows a creative use of wire as the stem holder.

Ilya Andriyanov/Shutterstock.com; Image courtesy of Save On Crafts, www.saveoncrafts.com

Tool Identifications introduce students to tools and products used by floral designers both in the shop and on-site for event setup and removal.

Go to www.g-wlearning.com/floraldesign/ for tool identification activities.

Summary feature provides an additional review tool with bulleted sentences that follow the textbook chapter.

Review Questions follow the order of the chapter material and are available in fill-in-form on the G-W Learning companion website.

Activities provided include those that may be done out of or in class, alone, or in groups.

Critical Thinking questions challenge students to apply newly acquired skills to solve real-life activities they may encounter in the workplace.

STEM and Academic Activities are provided in the areas of science, technology, engineering, math, and social studies.

Communicating about Floral Design activities challenge students to apply newly acquired knowledge and skills in groups, or alone. They are designed to help students improve speaking, reading, writing, and listening skills.

Summary

- Design principles define aspects of beauty and are to be recognized and achieved as much as possible.
- Floral designs require both physical and visual balance.
- Visual balance can be created in both symmetrical and asymmetrical floral arrangements.
- The rule of thirds helps designers estimate the amount of space that should be taken up by a floral design for a fixed space.
- Floral designs should be scaled to fit the location where they will be used.
- The elements that are featured in a design are dominant; all other elements are subordinate.
- The focal point is at the base of the design, near the center.
- Large, more fully opened flowers help achieve emphasis when they are used in the focal area.
- A harmonious design is one in which all of the elements work together to create a pleasing effect.
- Unity in a floral design is the sense that all of the elements belong together.

Review Questions

Answer the following questions using the information provided in this chapter. Go to www.g-wlearning.com/floraldesign/ to use the fill-in-form.

1. Identify the aesthetic benefits of floral art.
2. Name eight principles of design.
3. What is the difference between physical balance and visual balance?
4. Explain the importance of including negative space as part of a design.
5. What is the difference between a symmetrical floral design and an asymmetrical design?
6. What is the ideal standard of proportion?
7. How is the concept of scale applied to floral designs?
8. What is the difference between scale and proportion?
9. What is the purpose of dominance in a floral design?
10. How can emphasis be achieved in a floral design?
11. Why is it important to use contrast carefully in a floral design?
12. How does a floral designer create rhythm in an arrangement?
13. Explain how a designer can achieve harmony in a floral design.
14. List the six principles a designer can use to achieve unity.
15. If a customer wants an arrangement to be placed in a pink container, what should the designer do to ensure unity in the design?

Activities

1. Experiment with bala...
2. Research the g... Ancient Greece...
3. Using various p... subordinate elem...
4. Visit a botanical g... parterre, and an E...

Critical Thin...

1. A customer comes... poinsettias and su... could the designer...

130 *Principles of Floral D...*

---

2. How might you unify a holiday arrangement that includes pine cones, tall red candles, and gold-tone sleigh bells?
3. A local college football hero wants to be married on the campus football field. You have been hired to do the floral arrangements, so you accompany the bride to the football field to begin planning. You notice that there is a constant, stiff breeze on the field. What might you suggest to the bride regarding arrangements that will work in this environment? How can you make sure the floral arrangements will stay in place?

STEM Activities and Academics

1. **Math.** As explained in this chapter, the first several numbers in the Fibonacci series are 0, 1, 2, 3, 5, 8, 13, and 21. Do the math to extend the series out to the next 14 numbers. Show your work.
2. **Science.** Design and perform an experiment using a 3″ square block of Styrofoam, a plastic container, and artificial flowers and foliage of various sizes. What is the maximum height that can be supported by the mechanic? Record the steps you use in your experiment. Be sure to write the procedure clearly enough that others can perform the same experiment and verify your results.
3. **Social Studies.** Different societies and cultures have different ideas about how to emphasize or showcase important items. This is true in floral design as in other areas. Conduct research to find out how our principles of design in the United States today are different from those used during the dark ages and the Renaissance. What factors may have caused these differences?
4. **Language Arts.** Write a short chapter for a book that will be used to teach art to sixth-grade students. The chapter should be about the principles of design. Keeping the audience in mind, develop the topic thoroughly. Use concrete details and extended definitions to help the students understand the concepts.
5. **Math.** Many "golden" mathematical concepts have been identified throughout the years. Find out more about the "golden rectangle" identified by the Greeks. Mathematically, how does that concept apply to floral design?

Communicating about Floral Design

1. **Speaking and Listening.** Divide into groups of four or five students. Each group should choose one of the following topics: balance, proportion, scale, dominance, focal point, contrast, rhythm, harmony, or unity. Using your textbook as a starting point, research your topic and prepare a report on how it impacts floral design. As a group, deliver your presentation to the rest of the class. Take notes while other students give their reports. Ask questions about any details that you would like clarified.
2. **Speaking and Reading.** Modify an available arrangement so there are several issues with the design, especially balance. With a partner, role-play the following situation: a floral design judge is discussing physical and visual balance with a contestant. As the judge, ask the contestant questions on balance. Using terminology from your textbook, explain to the contestant why the arrangement does not work. You may use figures in the text for reference. Switch roles and repeat the activity, focusing on a different principle, such as scale.
3. **Speaking and Reading.** Working in groups of three students, create flash cards for the key terms in this chapter. On the front of the card, write the term. On the back of the card, write the pronunciation and a brief definition. Use your textbook and a dictionary for guidance. Then take turns quizzing one another on the pronunciations and definitions of the key terms.

Illustrated Glossaries

include over 400 color images of cut flowers, cut foliage, dried botanicals, and potted green and flowering plants. The glossaries serve as a handy reference tool and include many of the flowers, foliage, and plants included in student competitions.

Foliage Glossary

The cut foliage glossary contains materials commonly available on the wholesale market as well as a few products available from local suppliers. To a beginning designer, the wide variety of plant names can be overwhelming. To help you learn both the common names and botanical names, the foliages are alphabetized by the common name used most frequently in the profession and regional locales. The botanical name is listed below the common name and there is a cross-reference chart in the appendix. For the botanical names, major focus is on the genus name without a specific epithet. Professional florists often use the botanical name as a common name so it is beneficial to learn both. When used in print, the common name is not italicized. *The term botanical name and scientific name may sometimes be used interchangeably. For the sake of consistency, the term botanical name has been used throughout the textbook.*

Go to www.g-wlearning.com/floraldesign/ to use e-flash cards and other activities using the foliages from the illustrated glossary.

Common Name: ...a, African Mask
Botanical Name: ...a amazonica

Common Name: Anthurium
Botanical Name: *Anthurium* sp.

Common Name: ...edium
Botanical Name: ...

Common Name: Aucuba
Botanical Name: *Aucuba japonica*

Chapter 9 Foliage Selection **221**

Flower Glossary

The flower glossary in this text contains materials commonly available on the wholesale market as well as a few products that are available from local suppliers. Because a floral designer is often asked about flowering annuals used in exterior displays, or may have an opportunity to use them in an exhibit or event, some of the familiar flowering annuals have also been included in this glossary.

To a beginning designer, the wide variety of plant names can be overwhelming. To help you learn both the common and botanical (scientific) names, the flowers are alphabetized by the common name used most frequently in the profession and regional locales. The botanical name is below the common name and there is a cross-reference chart in the appendix. For the botanical names, major focus is on the genus name without a specific epithet. Professional florists often use the botanical name as a common name so it is beneficial to learn both. When used in print, the common name is not italicized. *The term botanical name and scientific name may sometimes be used interchangeably. For the sake of consistency, the term botanical name has been used throughout the textbook.*

Go to www.g-wlearning.com/floraldesign/ to use e-flash cards and other activities using the flowers from the illustrated glossary.

Common Name: Ageratum
Botanical Name: *Ageratum* sp.

Common Name: Alstroemeria, Peruvian Lily
Botanical Name: *Alstroemeria* sp.

Common Name: Amaranth Fountain Plant
Botanical Name: *Amaranthus* sp.

Common Name: Amaryllis
Botanical Name: *Amaryllis* sp.

Chapter 8 Flower Selection **177**

Common and Botanical Names

are given with each entry to expand student knowledge of taxonomy and binomial nomenclature. Alphabetized cross reference charts useful for study and locating botanicals by either name are included in the Appendix.

Potted Plants Glossary

Whether you are creating a small scale terrarium or designing the floral and plant décor for a large event, a host of potted plant materials are available. In addition to everyday plants, tropical foliage plants and an assortment of blooming potted plants are commercially grown specifically for holidays or for other special events throughout the calendar year. This illustrated glossary highlights the most common materials available today. As a floral designer you will often be asked about green and flowering plants for the home. To better assist your customers, you should become familiar with the names and availability of these plants and know how to care for them.

To help you learn both the common names and botanical names, the plants are alphabetized by the common name used most frequently in the profession. The botanical name is listed below the common name and there is a cross-reference chart in the appendix. For the botanical names, major focus is on the Genus name without a specific epithet. Professional florists often use the botanical name as a common name so it is beneficial to learn both. When used in print, the common name is not italicized. *The term botanical name and scientific name may sometimes be used interchangeably. For the sake of consistency, the term botanical name has been used throughout the textbook.*

Go to www.g-wlearning.com/floraldesign/ to use e-flash cards and other activities using the potted plants from the illustrated glossary.

Common Name: African Clubmoss, Selaginella
Botanical Name: *Selaginella kraussiana*

Common Name: African Violet
Botanical Name: *Saintpaulia* sp.

Common Name: Agave
Botanical Name: *Agave* sp.

Common Name: Aglaonema
Botanical Name: *Aglaonema commutatum*

Chapter 17 Maintaining and Decorating Potted Arrangements **485**

Dried Botanicals Glossary

The dried botanicals glossary contains materials commonly available on ... market as well as a few products available from local suppliers. To a beginni... the wide variety of plant names can be overwhelming. To help you learn bo... names and botanical names, the dried plant materials are alphabetized by t... name used most frequently in the profession and regional locales. The bot... listed below the common name and there is a cross-reference chart in the ... botanical names, major focus is on the Genus name without a specific epi... florists often use the botanical name as a common name so it is beneficia... When used in print, the common name is not italicized. *The term botanic... name may sometimes be used interchangeably. For the sake of consistency, the term ... used throughout the textbook.*

Go to www.g-wlearning.com/floraldesign/ to use e-flash cards and othe... dried botanicals from the illustrated glossary.

Common Name: Austrian Pine Cone
Botanical Name: *Pinus nigra subsp. austriaca*

Common Name: ...
Botanical ...

Common Name: Billy Balls, Craspedia
Botanical Name: *Craspedia uniflora*

Common Name: Birch Branch
Botanical Name: *Betula* sp.

Chapter 16 Permanent Botanicals **453**

Dried Botanicals Glossary Cross Reference

The following is a cross reference list for the Dried Botanicals Glossary in Chapter 16. It is alphabetized by botanical name whereas the glossary in Chapter 16 is alphabetized by common name. Both botanical and common names are used in the floral industry. Regionally, common names name. Both botanical and common names are used in the floral industry. Regionally, common names vary widely but botanical names are universal. The list is useful for reference and for studying and memorizing both common and botanical plant names and their spellings.

Botanical Name	Common Name
	Okra Pod (dried)
Abelmoschus esculentus	Yarrow
Achillea sp.	Manzanita Branch
Arctostaphylos sp.	Birch Branch
Betula spp.	Moss, Florist Sheet
Callicladium sp.	Cinnamon Sticks
Cinnamomum verum	Moss, Reindeer
Cladina sp.	Pampass Grass
Cortaderia selloana	Clorylus, Contorted Filbert Br
Corylus avellana 'Contorta'	Billy Balls, Craspedia
Craspedia uniflora	Moss, Mood
Dicranum sp.	Millet
Eleusine sp.	Gomphrena
Gomphrena globosa 'Lavender Lady'	Cotton
Gossypium sp.	Strawflower
Helichrysum sp.	Hops
Humulus lupulus	Lichen
Hypogymnia sp.	Bunny tails
Lagurus ovatus	Lotus (large)
Nelumbo nucifera	Lotus (small)
Nelumbo nucifera	Rice
Oryza sativa	Poppy Seed Hea
Papaver sp.	Fountain grass,
Pennisetum setaceum 'Rubrum'	Bamboo, River
Phyllostachys spp.	Chinese Lant
Physalis alkekengi	

Postharvest and Storage Guidelines for Foliage

Florist greens	Botanical Name	Leaf Length	Texture	Storage Temperature	Storage Life	Vase Life
Alocasia	Alocasia amazonica	8"–36"	Coarse	60°F (15.5°C)		7–14 days
Anthurium	Anthurium sp.	8"–12"	Coarse			7–14 days
Aspidistra	Aspidistra elatior	8"–36"	Coarse	55°F–40°F (12.5°C–4°C)	1 week	7–14 days
Bear Grass	Xerophyllum tenax	24"–30"	Coarse	40°F–55°F (4°C–13°C)	2 weeks	14–21 days
Bird's Nest Fern	Asplenium nidus	4'–6'	–			7–21 days
Boston Fern	Nephrolepis exaltata 'Bostoniensis'	20"–8'	–	–		7–14 days
Boxwood	Buxus sp.	6"–18"	–	–		5–10 days
Brake Fern	Pteridium aquilinum	3'	Fine	35°F–40°F (2°C–4°C)	1–2 months	3–5 weeks
Broom Corn	Sorghum sp.	8"–24"	Coarse	33°F–40°F (0.5°C–4°C)	3 weeks	2–5 days
Caladium	Caladium sp.	6"–18"	–	–		7–21 days
Calathea	Calathea sp.	4"–8"	–	–		5 days
Camellia	Camellia sp.	12"–24"	Coarse	–		14–21 days
Cattails	Typha sp.	3'–6'	Leathery	40°F (4°C)	4 weeks	3 weeks
Cedar	Cedrus sp.	18"–30"	Prickly	–		5–14 days
Croton	Codiaeum sp.	6" or more	Smooth	33°F–40°F (0.5°C–4°C)	4 weeks	3–6 days
Crypanthus	Cryptanthus sp.			35°F–40°F (2°C–4°C)	2 weeks	4 weeks
Cycas	Cycas revoluta	4"–24"		–		4 weeks
Cyperus		26"–30"		–		–
Dagger and Wood Ferns		6"–10"	Fine-scaly	–		4 weeks
		10"–24"	Fine	–		7–10 days
Dieffenbachia	Dieffenbachia sp.	6"–24"	Smooth	33°F–40°F (0.5°C–4°C)	2–3 months	10–20 days
Douglas Fir	Pseudotsuga menziesi			55°F (13°C)	1 week	10–22 days
Dracaena	Dracaena sp.	6"–18"	Straplike			–
English Ivy	Hedera helix cv.	12"–24"	Smooth	35°F–40°F (2°C–4°C)	2 weeks	14–21 days
Equisetum	Equisetum hyemale	8"–5'	–	33°F–36°F (0.5°C–2°C)	4 weeks	5–10 days
Eucalyptus	Eucalyptus sp.	Depends on species	Leathery			12 days
				35°F–40°F (2°C–4°C)	1–3 weeks	10 days

(Continued)

State Flowers

A "National Garland of Flowers" created for the 1893 Chicago World's Fair was the inspiration for adopting official state floral emblems. The creators of the garland invited each state to select a flower to represent their state. Minnesota was the first state to choose, followed by Oklahoma. The subject became a heated debate in some state legislatures and few had been chosen by the time of the fair. Some states chose both an official flower and an official wildflower when they could not reach a decision. Some states brought in botany professors to debate on behalf of each candidate and others had school vote when the adults were at a stalemate. Most of the state flowers have remained the same si early 1900s. A few have been changed for various reasons, including the fact that they were fi not be native to the state. This selection of state flowers led to the adoption of the other state recognized today.

State: Alabama
Common Name: Camellia
Botanical Name: *Camellia japonica* L.

State: Alaska
Common Name: Forget-Me-Not
Botanical Name: *Myosotis*

State: Ari
Common
Blossom
Botanical

State: Arkansas
Common Name: Apple Blossom
Botanical Name: *Pyrus coronaria*

State: California
Common Name: Poppy
Botanical Name: *Eschsholtzia californica*

Appendix

Floral Design Competitions

Floral design competitions are held at both student and professional levels. These competitions provide participants an opportunity to increase their knowledge about floral products and design and build professional skills through interaction with peers, coaches, advisors, and judges. Competitions provide a platform to spotlight excellence and quality of floriculture products and floral design.

Participating in competitions is an excellent way for you to build your skills in floral design and boost your confidence. Participating in competitions will also give you a tangible use for the skills you are developing in class. Hopefully, participating in healthy competitions will help create a desire for success that you can carry over into your life.

Rules and Regulations

Each competition has its own set of rules and regulations that are usually available for review as soon as the contest and registration dates are announced. Most organizations also post rules and restrictions on their website as soon as they are available.

You must know and understand the rules and regulations to lessen your chance of costly errors. For example, a maximum height is often given as a restriction for a particular design. If you are working on a centerpiece and your arrangement exceeds the limit, it may be disqualified and eliminated from the competition. Knowing the rules and, in this instance, using a tape measure, would keep the design in the competition. Unless, of course, the use of a ruler or tape measure is not allowed.

Eligibility requirements, fees, and registration deadlines may also be found online and through your instructor.

Tool Kit

Some competitions allow contestants to bring their own tools kits. The restrictions vary by competition and you will be provided with a list of what is allowed. Care should be taken to follow the competition tool box list to the letter. If you bring items that are not allowed, you may be disqualified. Tools are sometimes provided by the organizers of the competition.

Pro Tip
Silence your cell phone before your event begins. Do not use your cell phone during a competition because it suggests dishonesty and is unprofessional.

Postharvest Handling and Storage Charts provide students and instructors with recommended postharvest care and handling procedures of plant materials.

Floral Design Competitions includes instructions and advice to students for successful participation in floral competitions and additional charts with useful information for up-and-coming floral designers.

Student Materials

Workbook

The student workbook provides practice with questions and activities. Each chapter corresponds to the text and reinforces key concepts and applied knowledge.

Online Textbook

An online version of the printed textbook is available at www.g-wonlinetextbooks.com.

G-W Learning Companion Website

Students can use interactive activities in an online environment with G-W's free companion website. The companion website provides vocabulary activities, drill and practice exercises (including e-flash cards for flower and foliage identification), and review and self-assessment activities.

G-W Learning Companion Mobile Website

Smartphones can be used with the G-W Learning companion mobile website for studying on the go. The G-W Learning companion mobile website includes vocabulary activities, flower and foliage e-flash cards, and a self-assessment quiz for each chapter.

Instructor Materials

ExamView® Assessment Suite

Quickly and easily prepare, print, and administer tests with the ExamView® Assessment Suite. With hundreds of questions in the test bank corresponding to each chapter, you can choose which questions to include in each test, create multiple versions of a single test, and automatically generate answer keys. Existing questions may be modified and new questions may be added.

Instructor's Presentations for PowerPoint®

Help teach and visually reinforce key concepts with prepared lectures. These presentations are designed to allow for customization to meet daily teaching needs. They include objectives and images from the textbook and images from the *Step-by-Step* sequences.

Instructor's Resource CD

One resource provides instructors with time-saving preparation tools such as answer keys, lesson plans, correlation charts, and other teaching aids.

Online Instructor Resources

Anywhere, anytime access to all instructional materials is convenient with this resource. Included in the Online Instructor Resources are the Instructor's Resource CD, Instructor's Presentations for PowerPoint®, and ExamView® Assessment Suite for test creation, where applicable.

Brief Contents

Contents

Chapter 7
Elements of Design   133

Chapter 8
Flower Selection   155

Chapter 9
Foliage Selection   207

Chapter 13
Wedding Flowers   321

Chapter 14
Designing for Special Occasions and Holidays   355

Chapter 16

Permanent Botanicals   419

Chapter 17

Maintaining and Decorating Potted Arrangements   461

Procedures

Step-by-Step

2

Chapter

1

Careers in Floriculture

objectives

After reading this chapter, you will be able to:

- Discuss different types of floriculture careers.
- Describe the educational requirements for a career in floriculture.
- Identify continuing educational opportunities for floral designers.
- Explain the AIFD certification and accreditation process.
- Describe the characteristics employers look for in their employees.

key terms

American Institute of Floral Designers (AIFD)
bucket shop
buyers
cash-and-carry
certification
Color Marketing Group (CMG)
commercial grower
continuing education
continuing education units (CEUs)

employability
entrepreneur
floral designer
floriculture
florist
freelance floral designer
full-service flower shop
hard good
horticulture
hybridization

interiorscape
limited-service flower shop
monofloral
portfolio
propagation
résumé
retail florist
specialty shop
wholesale florist
wire service

Go to www.g-wlearning.com/floraldesign/ for online vocabulary activities using key terms from the chapter.

3

introduction

Horticulture (Latin "Hortus" garden + colere "to cultivate") is the branch of agriculture concerned with cultivating, or growing, garden plants. These generally include fruits, vegetables, flowers, and ornamental plants. Some might say, the edibles and the ornamentals. Horticulture has two distinct categories, floriculture and landscape horticulture. Both categories include growing the plants as well as the creative and artistic aspects of design. This textbook is devoted to the floriculture category.

Floriculture includes the production and marketing of floral crops. Growing decorative plants, along with the designing and marketing of floral arrangements, are aspects of floriculture. It is considered both an art and a science. You may hear floriculture referred to as *ornamental horticulture* because it deals with the creative and decorative aspects of horticulture.

Because flowers and plants used in floriculture are often grown in greenhouses in temperate climates, floriculture is called a "greenhouse industry," **Figure 1-1**. The production of cut flowers, blooming, and tropical foliage plants grown under glass for individual sale or use in an exterior landscape are all aspects of floriculture. Whether for indoor or outdoor application, floriculture crops are grown for their decorative uses.

Careers in Floriculture

The floriculture industry includes commercial growers, wholesalers, and retail flower shops. Commercial growers produce the potted blooming

Dervin Witmer/Shutterstock.com

Figure 1-1. Greenhouses are used in the floriculture industry to grow annuals (plants that live only 1 year), perennials (plants that live for multiple years), and flowers for cutting. Flowers for cutting may be annuals or perennials.

plants and cut flowers sold by florists. Wholesalers sell and distribute floral materials and related supplies to retail flower shops. Retail flower shops and other flower vendors combine floral materials into artful designs for sale to individual consumers. All of these facets of the floriculture industry require employees with various skills and specialties.

Commercial Growers

Although they do not deal directly with floral design, *commercial growers* are an important part of the floriculture industry. They produce the plants, cut flowers, and foliage that are used in flower shops. Whether they grow the plants in a greenhouse or in a field, they are responsible for providing healthy, pest-free plants to their customers, **Figure 1-2**. Growers need to know when (at what time of year) to plant them and how to care for them. They use the proper soil mixtures and fertilizers for each type of plant. For those plants that will provide cut flowers and foliage, growers also need to know when to harvest the crops.

All growers need employees with a background in plant science who know how to care for the plants. Growing plants may involve outdoor field work as well as indoor and greenhouse plant care. Some commercial growers have their own *propagation* (growing new plants) and *hybridization* (breeding) programs. These programs help renew existing stock and develop new plants that have different characteristics. For example, a plant may be bred to have larger blooms or stronger fragrance. If you are interested in working directly with plants, you may want to look into being a propagator or a hybridizer.

Did You Know?

The United States now has organic equivalence trade agreements with Japan, the European Union, and Canada that allow the global exchange of organic products.

Thinking Green

LED Greenhouse Fixtures

Many greenhouses have installed specially designed LED (light emitting diode) lights. The new LEDs provide the exact mixture of light needed for rapid flowering, and consume only one-fourth of the energy consumed by older greenhouse fixtures.

Ruud Morijn/Shutterstock.com

Figure 1-2. This greenhouse, full of Gerbera daisies, is in the Netherlands. Harvested flowers may be shipped all over the world.

To a certain extent, the positions available with growers depend on the size of the company. Some commercial growers have facilities in several states. Others are smaller, local businesses. All commercial growers employ sales representatives and production managers. Larger businesses may also need distributors—people who transport the plants and flowers to the wholesale or retail florists.

Wholesale Florists

Wholesale florists buy flowers and plants from commercial growers and sell them to retail flower shops, **Figure 1-3**. Wholesalers buy cut flowers in bulk from local growers around the world. Because wholesale florists keep up with the latest varieties of flowers and offer a large assortment of cut flowers and foliage, they are an important resource for florists.

In addition to perishable products, wholesale florists sell nonperishable materials called **hard goods**, such as glassware, floral foams, wire, packaging products, and tools. They supply all of the products necessary for floral design. Wholesale florists also sell seasonal products and materials that allow retail florists to meet customer demands at different times of the year. For example, in October and November, wholesalers may stock fall items such as ceramic planters in the shape of pumpkins. Retailers purchase these planters and create fall arrangements using the pumpkins as a focal point. Because of their role in supplying the necessary products for florists, wholesale florists are an essential part of the floriculture industry.

Sura Nualpradid/Shutterstock.com

Figure 1-3. This wholesaler provides roses in hundreds of different colors. Buyers for retail flower shops go to wholesalers like this one to purchase the flowers they need for their clientele.

Wholesale floral **buyers** find and purchase the products they offer for sale. Buyers have a solid knowledge of flower varieties, their seasonal availability, and growers who cultivate crops. They understand the needs and wants of their retail customers and arrange to buy suitable products, including plants, cut flowers, and hard goods.

Retail Florists

Retail florists sell directly to individual customers and make up a large part of the floral design industry. Many retail flower shops are run by *entrepreneurs*—people who own their own businesses. They combine business and art to provide exactly what their customers need. Business operations include advertising, pricing, marketing, and accounting. The creative or artistic side of the business includes producing designs for funerals, weddings, everyday celebrations, corporate events, and holidays.

A successful retail flower shop needs to thrive in all facets of the business, **Figure 1-4**. There are several different types of retail florists:

- Full-service flower shops.
- Limited-service flower shops.
- Bucket shops.
- Specialty shops.

Did You Know?

Floristry, as a business, began in the United States on the East Coast following the War of Independence. Nurseries began selling both cut and potted flowers to fill a growing need.

Figure 1-4. A store's location often determines whether or not the business will thrive.

Location, Location, Location
Before starting your own floral business, research real estate in the area in which you are interested. The location you choose may either help your business flourish, or make you close your doors.

Full-service flower shops deal with every aspect of retail floral production, including delivery service, wire service, and wedding and funeral floral designs, **Figure 1-5**.

Some supermarkets contain complete floral operations. Fresh flowers, gift lines, and wire services options are available in larger supermarket floral departments. This type of store hires floral designers to create the wide spectrum of designs typically found in a stand-alone flower shop. When multiple supermarket locations are involved, a central design facility is used. Orders are taken at multiple store locations and produced off-site in the central design facility. Florists with varied skills are needed at both types of locations.

Limited-service flower shops focus on one specialty service. A florist located in a hospital is an example of this type of flower shop. The hospital florist specializes in cheerful arrangements for hospital patients. Although the shop may stock other items such as stuffed animals and children's toys, it does not provide a full range of floral services. These flower shops typically do not offer wire services or delivery outside of their location. They sell to a specific, targeted clientele.

Figure 1-5. A full-service retail flower shop sells premade and custom arrangements and offers a complete range of floral services. This florist is recording a request for delivery later in the day.

A *bucket shop* has an even narrower focus. It provides only cut flowers, either singly (by the stem) or in bunches. Premade floral bouquets of cut flowers for *cash-and-carry* sales are common. *Monofloral* bunches (one type of flower only) or mixed flowers are bundled, then wrapped in decorative sleeves and placed into display buckets for immediate selection. The items are designed to sell quickly and be carried away by customers. Supermarkets and grocery stores can easily display these types of bundles within their existing floor space along with their regular merchandise.

Specialty shops are flower shops that specialize in one particular aspect of the floriculture industry. Examples include wedding florists and caterers. Because specialty shops offer career opportunities unique to their individual focus, they will be addressed later in this chapter. This section concentrates on careers that are common to most retail flower shops.

Pro Tip

Create a name for your flower shop that describes your specialty. For instance, names for an eco-friendly florist could include the word "green."

Owner or Manager

If you are creative and enjoy flowers, you may want to consider becoming a florist and owning or managing your own full-service retail flower shop, **Figure 1-6**. The term *florist* is used for any business that sells flowers, plants, and related supplies, but it also refers to the owner, manager, or employee of these shops. Day-to-day duties of a florist include:

- Helping customers choose the right flowers for a particular occasion.
- Creating bouquets and personalized designs for individual customers.
- Selecting flowers according to freshness, seasonality, and appearance for decoration and displays.
- Conditioning flowers on arrival, and periodically to ensure freshness.

bikeriderlondon/Shutterstock.com

Figure 1-6. Some horticultural enterprises have floral departments as well as a nursery department that sells potted plants and garden supplies. Employees working in such a place must be knowledgeable in floral design, maintaining potted plants, and planting annuals or perennials in a garden.

- Creating eye-appealing displays for merchandise.
- Advising customers on flower and plant care.
- Taking flower orders by phone and arranging delivery.
- Administrative tasks, such as bookkeeping.
- Installing floral displays at special functions and events.

Retail florists are responsible for all aspects of their business, **Figure 1-7**. Ordering and purchasing necessary cut flowers, foliage, blooming plants, and containers and supplies for everyday operations are the florist's responsibility. The florist creates the floral designs or oversees their creation by staff, and often coordinates their delivery to customers. Florists also deal with the necessary paperwork for accounts payable (money the flower shop owes to vendors, such as wholesalers) and accounts receivable (money that customers owe the flower shop for purchases). The owner will also need to consider advertising and marketing through various types of media.

Tyler Olson/Shutterstock.com

Figure 1-7. As the owner of a flower shop, you may have to perform many functions, including ordering, payroll, and bookkeeping.

Floral Designer

All retail flower shops need skilled *floral designers*. The number of designers required to successfully run a business depends on the size of the business. Large businesses and companies with multiple locations hire numerous designers with a variety of skill levels, from basic to advanced.

Floral designers need to be proficient at producing everyday designs, **Figure 1-8**. In addition to being creative, they should have knowledge and understanding of the floral shapes, designs, and styles suitable for a variety

Did You Know?

Extra Special Service
In some parts of the UK, the police often send flowers with an apology when a case can't be solved.

Vaclav Mach/Shutterstock.com

Figure 1-8. Floral designers use plants, live or artificial flowers, containers, wires, and other supplies to create arrangements for special occasions or for everyday use.

of applications. Designers also require a basic understanding of techniques for using living plants, fresh flowers, artificial flowers, and dried materials.

The skill set for a designer includes the ability to create designs using an assortment of materials and mechanics. Designers may use containers made of glass, ceramic, plastic, and wood. Knowledge about a large variety of mechanics such as the gauges of wires, tape varieties, and glues, is crucial. They need a complete understanding of how to use these materials. For example, wiring techniques vary among the types of flowers used in corsages and bridal bouquets. Knowing how to work with ribbon and other accessories is also useful.

Iakov Filimonov/Shutterstock.com

Figure 1-9. A good salesperson greets customers with a smile and pleasant attitude.

Salesperson

Friendly employees with good customer relation skills are prime candidates for sales positions in the retail flower shop, **Figure 1-9**. Florists deal in the expression of sentiment. Employees who can understand what a customer wants to express through flowers can sell the customer the right type of design. A sales position also requires a good understanding of the floral materials being used. Salespeople who can blend their knowledge of materials and supplemental products to grasp what a customer needs can strengthen the business by creating and keeping a strong customer base. It is also necessary for a salesperson to deal with disgruntled customers who are unhappy with the service or an arrangement they received. Effective salespeople have empathy for the customer and know store policies on how to resolve this type of situation. They also know that it is in the shop's best interest to make the customer happy and salvage possible future sales.

Delivery Person

Service is the nature of the floral business, and delivery personnel are a large component of that experience. Whether it is to deliver birthday designs to the home, bridal bouquets to a wedding site, sympathy arrangements to a funeral home, or cheery creations to the hospital, delivery personnel are a critical component. They are often the only representative of the business seen by the recipient of floral gifts. By driving in clean, well-maintained vehicles and dressing in a professional manner, delivery personnel make a good impression. This is important because if the recipients are impressed, they may remember the name of the business and become customers in the future. A good delivery person is priceless for the image of any type of floral business, **Figure 1-10**.

auremar/Shutterstock.com

Figure 1-10. It is important that your delivery people make a good impression because they are the face of the florist shop to the recipient.

Freelance Floral Designer

Highly-skilled floral designers who prefer a more flexible schedule than a retail flower shop provides may prefer to work on a freelance basis. *Freelance floral designers* are another type of entrepreneur. Rather than work for one retail or wholesale business, these designers own their own business. They work for themselves and accept jobs from several different companies. To work on a freelance basis, a designer must have a strong understanding of the fundamentals in design, as well as good oral communication skills.

Freelancing has both advantages and disadvantages. The advantages include being able to set your own hours and choose specific jobs that interest you, **Figure 1-11**. Disadvantages include a lack of company benefits, such as health insurance and paid vacations. As a freelancer, you are responsible for making all of the business decisions. Also, you take the risk that you will be able to generate enough business to make a profit.

Many different types of companies hire freelance floral designers. For example, wholesale florists seek freelance designers for educational programs. They hire highly-skilled designers to show their customers—the retailers—how to use their products in current ways. A freelance designer may present programs or classes to teach applications of design and mechanics using plants, artificial or dried materials, and fresh products.

Specialty gift companies and manufacturers also use freelance floral designers to promote their products. They set up temporary or permanent showrooms to exhibit product lines. A designer assists with *merchandising*, or displaying the company's products in a pleasing and effective way to increase sales. Merchandising requires strong creative and visual display skills. The designer arranges and displays products to entice customers to buy them.

Even some retail flower shops hire freelance designers to assist with production around holidays and at other times when a high order volume is expected. The freelance designer benefits the flower shop by providing "another pair of hands" to ease intensive workloads.

To work in these varied environments, a freelance designer needs to be highly skilled in all aspects of floral design. The ability to work efficiently and well under pressure to meet tight deadlines is a necessity. Having a positive personality and being flexible enough to meet client demands are also critical for freelance designers.

Shestakoff/Shutterstock.com

Figure 1-11. Freelance floral designers have the option to set their own hours and can even work from home. Freelancers often put in long hours to meet customer demands, however.

Pro Tip

Keep a bottle of high quality hand lotion in your tool kit. Using it will not only keep your hands from becoming dry and chapped, it will also make it easier to clean glue or paint from your hands.

Specialty Florists

As explained earlier in the chapter, specialty shops focus on one type or aspect of the floriculture industry. By concentrating on one area, they can offer extended services to meet the needs of their customers more fully.

Event Florist

Large commercial events require florists with the ability and equipment to assist with décor. Event florists, sometimes called *studio florists*, are designers who coordinate an overall look or design for clients based on a suggested theme. They work with catering companies, wedding planners, rental companies, and a variety of clients to achieve the desired effects. Event florists typically have a work space, or studio, and are available to meet with clients by appointment. They understand not only the art of floral design, but also the environmental settings needed for small or large venues. Their strong understanding of spatial relationship and scale helps them provide the most effective application of a thematic style to any event.

Caterer

Floral designers may also find employment with a catering company. Caterers frequently include centerpieces and floral accents on their tablescapes or food buffets, **Figure 1-12**. Serving trays and dinner and buffet tables are frequently decorated with floral materials. Like a floral designer, a good caterer knows how to use the principles and elements of design to present products in a visually exciting manner. If you enjoy both flowers and food and have a passion for visual display, you may find a fulfilling job within the catering business.

Online and Wire Service Florists

With the invention of the Internet, florists also participate in online order filling. A customer can see designs for sale and order them via a website for delivery without verbally communicating with a florist.

Pro Tip

Outdated, unprofessional websites without social media connections will not help your business! Invest in a quality website—it represents you and your business!

MN Studio/Shutterstock.com

Figure 1-12. Floral accents on the tables usually compliment the occasion's color scheme.

Website development and functionality are of high importance to this type of business. High-quality images and easy ordering are the critical components of site development. The web pages must be easy to navigate, and they should look appealing to potential customers. If you enjoy working with computers and developing websites alongside your work with flowers, this career may appeal to you.

Wire services are also an option for Internet sales. Organizations such as Teleflora and FTD (Florists' Transworld Delivery) provide an outlet for florists to target a larger audience than an individual website might reach. A member of the wire services must meet organizational standards and be able to fully participate in the order filling process. National, highly recognizable advertising is included in the annual fees the wire services charge the flower shop. Becoming a member of a well-known wire service is a good option for full-service flower shops because it helps them participate competitively in the Internet markets.

Wholesale florists also offer online ordering. Retail flower shops can order floral materials without spending time on the phone or in person to place the order. However, ordering wholesale products online removes the benefits of personal salesmanship by a wholesale florist staff member. Retailers who want advice or news about the latest floral varieties and trends may prefer to speak with a knowledgeable employee at the wholesale company. Also, when an order is placed over the Internet, a quality control check is critical.

Wedding Florist

Wedding florists are professional florists that deal only with wedding design and installations. Besides strong design skills, a wedding florist needs communication skills to work closely with the bride. The florist meets with the client to discuss the basics of time, place, and venue and to develop a theme for the overall appearance of the event. The florist may assist with choosing colors as well as the flowers and accessories to be used within the arrangements. Decorations for the door, aisles, altar, and ceremonial gestures requiring flowers are discussed. A keen attention to detail is required. Weddings are labor-intensive, so a good understanding of how to price materials and the labor involved to produce them is essential.

A wedding florist usually manages all aspects of floral design for the wedding reception as well as the wedding, **Figure 1-13**. The wedding florist meets with the prospective bride to discuss church or ceremony settings, reception decorations, table décor, and cake decorations. The florist then orders the necessary flowers and materials and produces the requested arrangements. After the event, the wedding florist is also responsible for the removal of the decorations.

Ryan Jorgensen – Jorgo/Shutterstock.com

Figure 1-13. Wedding florists typically help set up the decorations and flowers for the wedding reception as well as the actual wedding.

Adisa/Shutterstock.com

Figure 1-14. Hotels often hire designers to create interiorscapes to make the lobby and other common areas look more comfortable and inviting.

Movie and TV Set Floral Designer

Professional floral designers are often needed on movie sets, especially when a period film is being produced. Designers who work in this field must know the history of floral design in order to produce arrangements that are true to the time period. A set florist must know what types of flowers were available at the time, what time of the year they were available, and what types of containers were used. A floral designer may also be responsible for any gardens and landscaping that appear in the film.

Interiorscape Designer

Some florists specialize in providing plants to enhance indoor environments. These florists use their knowledge of design and decorating skills to create *interiorscapes* that make offices, hotels, and even private homes look more inviting, **Figure 1-14**. These specialty florists work with both live and artificial plant materials, depending on customer preferences. They must have a good sense of scale to decorate both small and large places appropriately.

Other Floral Career Opportunities

Not all of the careers in the floriculture industry deal directly with flowers. Florists rely on manufacturers and supply companies to produce the materials they need. These companies need employees that understand flowers and floral design. Education and research are also viable options.

Product Developer

Containers, baskets, artificial flowers, and holiday decorations are good examples of accessories to floral design. Many kinds of products, both decorative and mechanical, are designed specifically to support the floriculture industry. Product developers and manufacturers of these items need inventive designers who are innovative and enjoy using their creativity.

Experienced designers with strong communication skills and an understanding of the entire floriculture industry are good candidates for product development positions. They can combine their creativity with the practical aspects of an accessory to design a stylish and useful item for production. Designers in this capacity must have flexible schedules for travel and a good eye for design. Most product developers work for the companies that manufacture the accessory items. However, some wholesale florists hire product developers to produce their own product lines. Independent manufacturers of silk or artificial items also need experienced artists for production of their goods. An individual that possesses a strong understanding of color may find the product development track interesting.

As the popularity of interior colors changes, so do the colors of decorative materials being used by consumers. The ***Color Marketing Group (CMG)*** is a nonprofit association that creates color forecast information for professionals who design and market color. The group also provides information about trends in interior colors for manufacturers. Items such as silk flowers, containers, and even decorations for holiday trees, garlands, and themes change with the forecast of trendy new colors.

Education and Research

If you have a strong background in floral design and enjoy teaching others how to do things, you might enjoy employment as a teacher. Floral design is often offered at the high school level in either the agriculture department or the fine arts department. Beyond high school, floral design educators are employed at the community college level and are involved in two-year associate and four-year bachelor's degree programs at many universities.

Do you like to study how things work or how people respond to various situations? If so, you may be surprised to find that you can combine your interest in floral design with a research position. Many types of research in the floral design field are ongoing. A degree in a higher education specialty is generally required for research positions, most of which are available through universities.

For example, a research program at Rutgers, The State University of New Jersey, has studied the effect of flowers on people's moods. In a 10-month study, researchers found a definite link between the presence of flowers and happy emotions. People feel more satisfied and less anxious after receiving flowers. The study indicated that the mood-enhancing effect of receiving flowers is not just a quick sensation. It lasts long enough that study participants reported that they enjoy life more. Therefore, it seems reasonable that flowers can be used as behavioral therapy to help people with chronic depression or anxiety.

Other universities have research programs devoted to developing sturdier plants that are resistant to pests and diseases and can withstand a wider range of temperatures, **Figure 1-15**. The Flower Bulb Research Program at Cornell University, for example, has an ongoing research program dedicated to analyzing new tulip varieties. The plants are evaluated and the results are published to help wholesalers and retailers know which varieties are best for their businesses or customers.

These and other research programs play an important role in floriculture. They provide solid information that can be used by commercial growers, wholesale florists, and retail florists to improve their businesses. The Rutgers study, for example, can be used by retailers to encourage customers to buy flowers for everyday use, rather than wait for a special occasion. The Cornell research helps growers and wholesalers know which tulip varieties are most likely to please their customers.

Vasiliy Koval/Shutterstock.com

Figure 1-15. This research technician is experimenting with new plant hybrids that may improve on the plant's current characteristics.

Training and Education in Floriculture

Through the years, many skills in all aspects of the floriculture industry were learned on the job. Often different parts of a family business were passed on from generation to generation. The skills of a particular greenhouse, wholesale, or retail employee were developed by years of observation and hands-on applications, often without any formal higher education.

Today, education and on-the-job training are both necessities for successful employment in the floriculture industry. Career education has become more available, and there are now many outlets for students to develop their skills. Students can begin to get an understanding of floral design and related careers at the high school level, **Figure 1-16**.

Beyond high school, programs in floral design are offered at the junior and community college level with an associate's degree or certificate of completion. Basic principles are strengthened with an in-depth view into areas of focus, such as bridal designs or sympathy designs. At the four-year university level, students can receive a bachelor's degree. Depending on the structure of curriculum set up by the university, a degree may be available in fine arts (bachelor of fine arts, or B.F.A.) or in floral design itself. Because floral design is a hands-on occupation, both practical and theoretical coursework is required.

Iryna Dzvonkovska/Shutterstock.com

Figure 1-16. High school and college classes offer a foundation in design principles for floral design and other creative uses.

Exhibitions and Competitions

One of the best ways to become a better designer is through practice. Showing your work in exhibitions provides you with an opportunity to practice, design, compose, and produce arrangements that help you grow and refine your skills. Participating in exhibitions also offers you the opportunity to analyze your own design skills as well as those of your peers. As you study designs from professionals or peers, you are evaluating designs and forming precise conclusions about formal qualities, intent, meaning, and historical and cultural influences. The criteria upon which designs are judged may vary slightly between competitions, but they are all based on the basic design principles of floral design which are covered in detail in Chapter 6, *Principles of Design*.

Membership in the FFA is a great way to begin competing in floriculture competitions. High school FFA students can participate in individual and team events referred to as career development events (CDEs). Participation in CDEs provides opportunities for self-assessment and strengthens the skills of all club members. The CDE competition includes testing of student knowledge in all aspects of ornamental horticulture, including growing and harvesting, shipping and packaging, salesmanship skills, job interview skills, job estimating skills, and product display. As a team leader, you can develop your planning, communication, and creative and critical thinking skills and help your teammates learn to work together effectively.

Students can also learn about available career options. Depending on their region, college students may join student chapters of the American Institute of Floral Designers to further hone their skills and compete at a higher level. State floral associations also sponsor competitions at a variety of skill levels.

Portfolios

Exhibitions, competitions, and your class work can help you develop a portfolio, or a collection of your work. As you develop your skills and create both standard and original designs, record pertinent design information to include in your portfolio. Include information such as the type of materials used and the intent and meaning of your design and its influences. You must also include quality photographs of each piece from multiple angles. You should also include your awards and certificates of achievement. Many designers prepare digital portfolios as well as traditional printed portfolios.

Continuing Education

Even after getting a degree and beginning their careers, successful florists continue to learn. *Continuing education* includes classes, presentations, conferences, and other methods of learning, **Figure 1-17**. The purpose of continuing education is to keep your skills current and to learn about the latest breakthroughs and design ideas. High schools, community colleges, trade schools, and independent floral design schools provide continuing education experiences. Professionals who want to excel in the field of floral design continue to seek design education, furthering their knowledge base and expanding their abilities to meet the current markets' needs and trends.

Associations

Participation in a state floral association provides a good source of continuing education. Design panels made up of industry experts present programs on current trends, mechanics, marketing, and design. Hands-on classes are also offered in conjunction with annual association conferences. Association membership provides many opportunities to form business network connections. Networking, or talking to other people in the same field, is a good way to make new business contacts as well

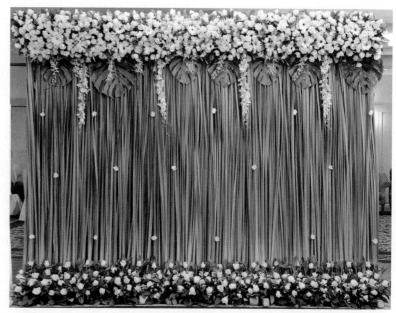

kongsky/shutterstock.com

Figure 1-17. Continuing education programs and floral industry symposiums highlight contemporary styles and help florists stay connected to industry trends. For instance, this stunning wedding backdrop would be reproduced at a convention so designers would not only learn about it, but experience it firsthand.

as learn new concepts, **Figure 1-18**. State floral associations provide design programs, webinars, and seminars by industry experts that can benefit designers at all levels of proficiency. Many state organizations also offer certification programs, as described later in this chapter.

Presentations by Wholesale Florists

In addition to supplying the materials for flower shop operations, wholesale florists provide educational opportunities. Wholesale florists present frequent seminars, lectures, and presentations, on the latest trends and techniques for design applications. These programs are presented by skilled designers and industry leaders. Wholesale florists also offer business and marketing seminars presented by experts in their fields to better equip retail florists to operate their floral businesses.

Certification

Employers throughout the floriculture industry prefer to hire floral designers who have the knowledge, skills, and experience needed to perform their jobs well. *Certification* is one of the best methods of proving to prospective employers that you have the necessary knowledge and skills. By becoming certified, you can greatly increase the probability that you can find a good job within the floriculture industry.

State Certification

Many state floral associations offer certification programs, **Figure 1-19**. For example, the Texas State Florists' Association offers a certification program for high school students in addition to several other certification categories,

Dean Mitchell/iStock/Thinkstock; moodboard/moodboard/Thinkstock

Figure 1-18. Networking is an effective way to make new contacts that may prove valuable when you are job searching or expanding your business. Making new contacts will also help advertise your business and get your name to more people. It is also a good idea to carry business cards, even if you are still a student.

Figure 1-19. In addition to the hands-on work you will do in the lab, you will also have to attend class, study, research, and often work as a team. The skills you acquire in class will carry over to the many student competitions in which you may compete.

including Texas Certified Florist, Texas Master Florist, and Texas Master Florist Advanced certification. The Michigan Floral Association is another example of a state association that provides certification to qualified florists. To be certified, you typically take a test, with or without a hands-on component. Some agencies require that you take a specific course or courses prior to taking the certification test. Contact your individual state association for requirements.

American Institute of Floral Designers

Possibly the best-known certification is offered by the ***American Institute of Floral Designers (AIFD)***. The organization currently has two types of certification, both the (CFD) certified floral designer status and the fully accredited (AIFD) member. The American Institute of Floral Designers is an international nonprofit organization that supports the floriculture industry by establishing high professional standards and supporting those standards with education, certification, and accredited membership. The AIFD has six regions throughout the United States, and supports student chapters in many colleges and universities. Scholarships are available through the AIFD Foundation for talented floral designers who cannot afford the required classes and fees.

Unlike other floral associations, AIFD has strict membership requirements. All of its members are accredited—a status even higher than the CFD certification. The same steps are required for both certification and accreditation, **Figure 1-20**. However, only applicants with top scores in the required hands-on design demonstration are invited to become accredited AIFD members.

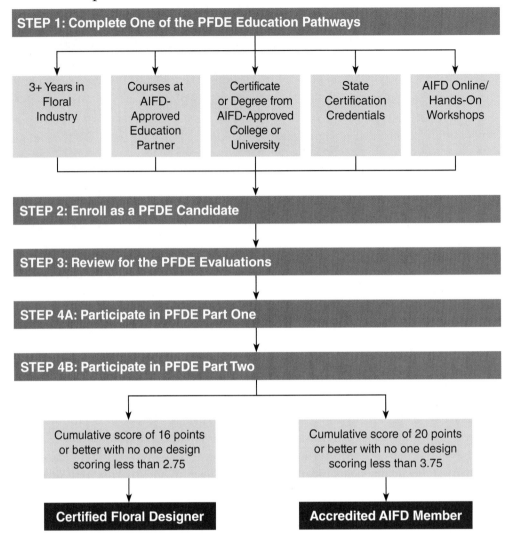

Steps for AIFD Certification and Accreditation

STEP 1: Complete One of the PFDE Education Pathways

| 3+ Years in Floral Industry | Courses at AIFD-Approved Education Partner | Certificate or Degree from AIFD-Approved College or University | State Certification Credentials | AIFD Online/ Hands-On Workshops |

STEP 2: Enroll as a PFDE Candidate

STEP 3: Review for the PFDE Evaluations

STEP 4A: Participate in PFDE Part One

STEP 4B: Participate in PFDE Part Two

Cumulative score of 16 points or better with no one design scoring less than 2.75

Cumulative score of 20 points or better with no one design scoring less than 3.75

Certified Floral Designer

Accredited AIFD Member

Goodheart-Willcox Publisher

Figure 1-20. Both certification and accreditation by the American Institute of Floral Designers require floral designers to follow an "education pathway" and take two exams.

The first step in becoming certified or accredited is designed to ensure that the candidates have the necessary background knowledge, including the principles of floral design and associated concepts and techniques. This step can be met using any of five different pathways, as shown in **Figure 1-20**. The applicant must prove that he or she has a minimum of three years of experience working in the floriculture industry or must take approved courses or programs designed to provide the necessary knowledge. AIFD offers courses, but also accepts state certification, courses provided by AIFD partners, or formal college degrees in floral design to meet this requirement.

Next, applicants enroll in the AIFD Professional Floral Design Evaluation (PFDE) program. This program consists of two tests: an online test (Part 1) and a hands-on evaluation (Part 2). When applicants are accepted into the program, they receive the materials necessary to study for the exams.

The online test is administered first and is based on the *AIFD Guide to Floral Design: Terms, Techniques, and Traditions*. It is a timed test consisting of approximately 55 questions. Upon passing this test with a score of 80% or higher, applicants are eligible to participate in the hands-on evaluation in Part 2. Applicants are required to create five designs in categories specified by the evaluators at the time of testing. Both certification and accreditation depend on the score obtained in the hands-on evaluation.

After becoming a certified floral designer or an accredited member, florists must participate in continuing education to keep their certified or accredited status. AIFD requires members to accumulate 25 *continuing education units (CEUs)* every three years. Five of these CEUs must be in the service/leadership area. The other 20 can be in any approved area of interest to the individual floral designer.

Employment

After studying floral design and possibly becoming certified, the next step is to find a job in the floriculture industry. By this time, you may have a good idea of exactly what type of job you want. You can find job openings by checking with local, state, and national associations, by using an Internet-based search engine, by networking with classmates and friends, or by one of a number of other methods. You will probably want to use more than one method to find several jobs that interest you.

Applying for a Job

Prepare yourself by creating a *résumé* that highlights your education and accomplishments, including any certification or accreditation you have achieved. You can find templates for résumés on several websites. Be sure to choose a style that showcases your talents and achievements.

Also create a *portfolio*, or collection of your work, to show to prospective employers. Fill your portfolio with good color photographs of your best work, as well as copies of any letters of recommendation, certificates of achievement, or other awards you have earned.

Interviewing for a Job

Whichever career you choose, you will probably be offered interviews by companies who are interested in your work. In the interview, the prospective employer will ask questions to help determine whether you are a good fit for the company. Typical questions include:

- Why are you interested in working for this company?
- What do you consider to be your greatest strength?
- What is your greatest weakness?
- What motivates you?
- Why are you considering a career in floral design?
- What are your goals for the next five years?
- How do you plan to achieve those goals?
- Do you prefer to work independently or as part of a team?

Did You Know?

The National FFA Organization has a Job Interview Career Development Event that will help you prepare for a job interview.

 Pro Tip

Interview Practice

To present yourself in the best possible light at an interview, it is helpful to practice ahead of time. Ask a friend to play the interviewer and ask you questions that you may encounter.

You can find many other examples of interview questions on the Internet. Practice answering these questions so that you can answer them smoothly and efficiently during the interview. Always tell the truth. Being untruthful or exaggerating your skills can get you in trouble later.

Be aware, however, that there are some questions interviewers are not allowed to ask. These include questions about your age, race, gender, marital status, or country of origin, unless this information is relevant for the position. If you are asked this type of question, you can politely ask how the question relates to the job, or even refuse to answer the question. If you refuse, be sure to do so courteously.

Be sure to dress appropriately and conservatively for the interview. Arrive on time, and do not forget to bring your résumé and portfolio, **Figure 1-21**. Be self-confident and courteous to the interviewer and to any other employees to whom you are introduced. After the interview, thank the interviewer. You may also want to send a thank-you letter. After a week or two, if you have not heard from the company, you may want to follow up with a phone call to be sure the company knows you are interested. Do not make a pest of yourself, however; some companies, especially larger ones, may take a while to make a decision.

Demonstrating Job Skills

Your *employability* is the sum of your "people skills" and personal characteristics that make you a valuable employee. Employers look for these characteristics when you apply for a job, and if they hire you, they expect you to behave in a manner that benefits their business. In addition to developing these skills, employers expect you to reach a certain level of competency in your understanding and application of the systems of operations used in their business and in the floriculture industry. For example, in a small floral design shop you may be expected to competently process shipments of plant materials to ensure their storage longevity and their longevity after they are placed in arrangements. You may also be expected to record deliveries and payments for the shipments in the business' record keeping program.

Robert Kneschke/Shutterstock.com

Figure 1-21. To make a good impression at your interview, dress conservatively, be polite, and be prepared to show examples of your work.

Work Habits

Work habits include showing up for work whenever you are scheduled, arriving on time every day, and maintaining a positive attitude. Employers depend on their employees to be present and to work efficiently during their shifts. Employees who frequently call in sick are not considered reliable. Some companies may even consider frequent absences from work a cause for terminating your employment.

Being willing to pitch in and help when deadlines are tight is another excellent work habit. During slow times, try to find something productive to do. Ask your supervisor for additional tasks if you run out of work. Do not use the computer or Internet for personal reasons, and turn your phone off during working hours, unless it is necessary for your job. Do not make or accept personal phone calls.

Personal Habits

As in most retail industries, most careers in the floriculture industry involve working face-to-face with the public: your customers. For this reason, having a cheerful, caring attitude is always helpful. You should also pay close attention to personal hygiene. Come to work clean, and keep your hair washed and combed or styled.

Ask your employer if there is a particular dress code, and if there is, stick to it. Even if no dress code is required, you should always dress neatly and conservatively. Wear clothes that are appropriate for your job duties. Whatever your personal tastes, while you are on the job, you should have a neat, clean, and conventional appearance, **Figure 1-22**. Remember that whether you are working with customers or suppliers, you represent your employer. Your appearance, personal hygiene, and attitude have a direct effect on the company's success.

Good Citizenship

Most employers encourage good citizenship. Many people believe that being a good citizen means voting and participating in political efforts. While voting is both a right and a responsibility, this is only a small part of good citizenship. A good citizen respects other people and their property, and willingly helps other people whenever possible. On the job, this means both caring for and about the merchandise, which belongs to the company, and respecting the customers, suppliers, and the employer.

Kinga/Shutterstock.com

Figure 1-22 Having a neat, clean appearance and a cheerful attitude gives customers a good impression of the flower shop.

Other Employability Skills

A good employee demonstrates many other skills as well. These include:

- Teamwork. Your ability to work with and get along with other employees increases shop efficiency and makes the business more profitable.
- Responsibility. When you are responsible and reliable, the employer knows you can be counted on to help with whatever jobs are at hand, even if they are unusual or difficult.
- Self-confidence. If customers see that you are confident, they will more easily trust you to help them with their floral decisions.
- Professionalism. Maintaining a professional appearance and attitude, no matter what happens, is important to the success of the business.
- Honesty and integrity. This means more than just not stealing from your employer; it means giving other people credit when due, and taking responsibility for any errors you make, as well.
- Communication. The ability to communicate your thoughts and ideas, and to understand the thoughts and ideas of others, will benefit the business; it will also help you advance in your career.
- Organization. Being organized allows you to accomplish more in a given amount of time; this productivity can lead to more profits for the business.

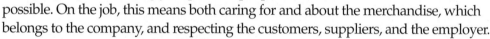

Pro Tip

On the Job Communication

Communicate regularly with your supervisor. Do not be afraid to ask questions or to ask for advice if you encounter difficulty with any task. Your supervisor will respect your willingness to learn.

Chapter Summary

- Commercial growers cultivate the crops to supply wholesalers with plants, foliage, and cut flowers.
- Wholesale florists purchase in bulk from growers and sell to retail florists.
- Retail florists employ managers, floral designers, salespeople, and delivery people.
- Specialty florists concentrate on one aspect of the floriculture industry to provide in-depth service to their customers.
- Other floral career opportunities include product development, education, and research.
- Educational opportunities are available in high schools and colleges, through various floral associations, and organizations such as the FFA.
- Becoming certified in floral design proves to potential employers that you have the knowledge and skills necessary to do a good job.
- Employability skills can help you get and keep a good job within the floriculture industry.

Review Questions

Go to www.g-wlearning.com/floraldesign/ to use the fill-in-form.

Answer the following questions using the information provided in this chapter.

1. What is the difference between horticulture and floriculture?
2. Name three facets, or main categories, of careers in floriculture.
3. Explain the function of a wholesale florist.
4. List the four major types of retail florists.
5. What is an entrepreneur?
6. Describe the products sold in a bucket shop.
7. Name at least five duties a retail florist may expect to have on a day-to-day basis.
8. Why are the conduct and appearance of a delivery person important to a floral business?
9. Describe the advantages and disadvantages of being a freelance floral designer.
10. *True or False?* A caterer may include floral accents on tablescapes or food buffets.
11. Which type of florist typically coordinates an overall look or design based on a suggested theme for large commercial functions?
12. The type of designer that enhances indoor environments by placing live or artificial plants in an attractive manner is referred to as a(n) _____ designer.
13. Explain why it is important for a movie set floral designer to have extensive knowledge of the history of floral design.
14. Explain why it is important for a wedding florist to have good communication skills.
15. Which type of service provides an outlet for florists to target a larger audience than an individual website might reach?
16. *True or False?* Positions as a floral design instructor are available both in high schools and in colleges and universities.
17. *True or False?* Most research career opportunities are offered by retail florists.
18. *True or False?* Continuing education is no longer necessary after a floral designer becomes certified.
19. *True or False?* AIFD certification requires the same steps as AIFD accreditation.
20. *True or False?* Your employability is a measure of how well you perform at a job interview.

Activities

1. Hold a floral arranging competition among classmates using a surprise package of materials for all entrants.
2. Hold a mock competition and take turns leading a team of four students.

3. Attend a state florist association conference.
4. Attend a program sponsored by a local wholesale florist.
5. Tour a supermarket design center facility.

Critical Thinking

1. You have applied to a local grower for a job working with field plants. The company has invited you to come in for an interview. What would you consider appropriate dress for this interview?
2. A customer enters the retail flower shop where you are working. When you ask if you can help him, he says he wants a beautiful arrangement of yellow flowers to surprise his young daughter. You show him a few options, but then he decides he would rather have a smaller, pink arrangement. You show him more options, and then he states that he doesn't like anything you have shown him so far because they don't include a toy that his daughter can keep after the flowers die. How would you handle this customer?
3. You are interviewing for a position as a delivery person for a local retail florist. The interviewer asks, "How old are you?" How should you respond?

STEM Activities and Academics

1. **Science.** Investigate current research programs in floriculture or in botany (plant science). Choose a research program that interests you. Prepare a report on the scientific methods used in this program and how the results affect the floriculture industry.
2. **Technology.** Visit a local commercial greenhouse and ask about the technology used to provide the plants with just the right amount of water and nutrients. If there are no commercial greenhouses in your area, research this topic on the Internet. Write a short report of your findings.
3. **Engineering.** Find out more about plant hybridization and the goals of hybridization programs. Compare the purposes of plant hybridization with engineering research to improve the design of a household appliance. How are they similar? How are they different?

Communicating about Floral Design

1. **Reading and Speaking.** Create an informational pamphlet on how to apply for a job in the floriculture industry. Research résumé strategies and portfolio organization and download a sample job application. Present your pamphlet to the class. After your project has been graded and returned to you, review the instructor's comments. List the type of changes you could make to improve your project.
2. **Reading and Speaking.** Working with two partners, research the type of interview questions you may be asked when applying for a job in the floriculture industry. Look for examples of the best way to reply to interview questions. Create a script with one partner applying for the position and the other two partners performing the interview. Perform the skit for your class.
3. **Writing and Speaking.** Interview a local retail florist, wholesale florist, or wedding florist. Ask the person to describe a typical day at work. Prepare a list of questions similar to the following:

   How long have you been in the floriculture industry? Did you go to school or did you learn as an intern? What is the work environment like? What are your job duties? What other types of professionals do you work with?

   Report your findings to the class, giving reasons why you would or would not want to pursue a career similar to that of the person you interviewed.

Chapter

2

History of Floral Design

objectives

After reading this chapter, you will be able to:

- Summarize the history of floral design.
- Identify design characteristics of historical design periods.
- Explain how flowers were used based upon historical time frames.

key terms

bosom bottle	nesting	stove house
bough pot	orangeries	sustainable
capillary action	physic garden	tulip breaking
conservatory	Society of American Florists (SAF)	tulipmania
cultivar		tussie mussie
mosaic virus		

Go to **www.g-wlearning.com/floraldesign/** for online vocabulary activities using key terms from the chapter.

introduction

Understanding the origins of floral design will help you appreciate the rich history of floristry as a profession. The fleeting nature of flowers makes researching floral design history challenging. However, clues about how flowers have been used over centuries exist in the paintings, writing, and sculptures of the past.

There has not always been an organized floral industry. Florists, floral shops, and the services they perform, began appearing in the nineteenth century. During the latter part of the century, more people had money to spend and could afford to purchase flowers and floral designs for weddings, funerals, and special occasions. That is not to say people from earlier centuries or ancient societies did not use flowers. Flowers have been grown and sold for decorative purposes for thousands of years. The common thread found throughout time is that people have an intrinsic need for beauty and are drawn to beautiful things.

Throughout history, many different periods of design have come and gone, each with their own characteristics and styles. It is impossible to describe all of them in a single chapter, but this chapter covers some of the highlights.

Ancient Civilizations

Much of what we know about the use of flowers in ancient civilizations is derived from their art. For instance, the use of flowers as home décor, wreaths, bouquets, body adornment, and religious offerings is found in Egyptian art from more than 4000 years ago, **Figure 2-1**. In Greek and Roman cultures, people used

Strakovskaya/Shutterstock.com

Figure 2-1. Lotus flowers are displayed prominently on the right side of this ancient Egyptian papyrus.

flowers to adorn their homes and gardens and as body adornments. Flowers were also used to express love and to honor the dead in most ancient societies.

Egypt

Flowers and plants were depicted in art throughout ancient Egypt. The Egyptian period lasted from about 2800 BCE to 28 BCE. Egyptian stone carvings and paintings depict leaves, flowers, and entire plants in vessels, indicating the cultivation of plants was not only for food, but also for beauty. Flowers were used in every aspect of their lives. War carts were adorned with flowers before soldiers headed off to war. Peasants adorned themselves, their animals, and even their dead with flowers. Flowers were given to lovers and to the gods as professions of love and dedication.

The papyrus and lotus flower, both blue and white, are the most symbolic plants throughout Egyptian history, **Figure 2-2**. Both plants were abundant and grew wild throughout the Nile valley. The blue lotus has a more intense fragrance than the white lotus and was often used to make perfume. The Egyptians believed the intense scent of flowers indicated the presence of a god, so the blue lotus was favored and, in many tomb scenes, the deceased is shown with a blue lotus flower held to his nose so he could breathe in the flower's scent.

Between the 16th and 11th century BCE, the Egyptians began providing the deceased with garlands of fresh flowers. They made floral collars and mummy garlands with green leaves, palm leaves, and colorful flower petals. Some mummies have been found with wreath-shaped arrangements on their heads. Bulb leaves were used to cover the eyes, nose, mouth, and mummification incisions. Floral decorations adorned some of the statues and food containers in the tomb. Flowers were also used for large funeral bouquets that were carried in the burial procession and then stood upright in front of the tomb.

Did You Know?

Lotus flowers open in daylight and close at night. The Egyptians probably saw this as an image of rebirth and regeneration, both of which were important concepts in their religion.

Nattapol/Shutterstock.com; foto76/Shutterstock.com

Figure 2-2. Papyrus paper is made from the aquatic plant, *Cyperus papyrus*, that grows on the banks of the Nile River. The papyrus grows up to 15′ (4.5 m) tall and produces flower clusters 10″×20″ (25×50 cm) long. The lotus is consistently used in Egyptian art and is renowned for its ability to grow in water, producing beautiful flowers. The blue lotus has a stronger scent and was often used to make perfume.

Egyptian designs were both simple and highly stylized. Shapes were geometric and often repeated in various patterns. Designs were created in order to keep flowers fresh for extended periods of time using water filled vessels.

Even today, flowers continue to be a large part of the Egyptian culture and economy. There are many flower shops throughout the Egyptian towns and cities, museums with vast collections of flowers from around the world, and public gardens such as the Botanical Island at Aswan and the International Park. The Botanical Island, known for its history and remarkable beauty, also serves as a research center. The International Park presents the plants, flowers, and trees of eight countries. The Egyptian Agricultural Museum in Cairo features a detailed history of flowers and houses one of the most outstanding collections of flowers in the world. Egyptian flowers are also an important trade item for the Egyptian economy with over 600 tons of plants and flowers exported annually.

Greece

In the ancient Greek culture (600 BCE to 146 BCE), people displayed plants and flowers in vessels similar to the one shown in **Figure 2-3**. The portability of the containers allowed for materials to be grown, presented, and traded commercially. Growing flowering plants in containers allowed people to keep them as décor in their homes and to use for special occasions. The containerized plants were also used to decorate places of worship.

The fragrance of the plants and flowers were especially important to the ancient Greeks. Herbs were frequently used in flower arrangements, garlands, and wreaths. During ceremonies and festivities, petals were strewn about the floor to spread the fragrance. Professional wreath and garland makers were commissioned to provide decorations and designs to wear.

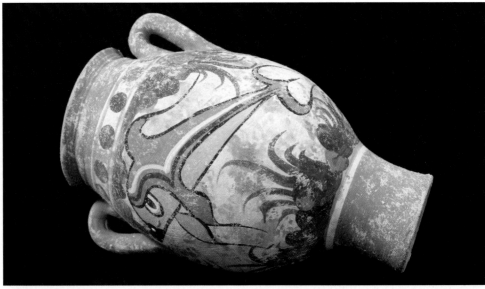

losalex/Shutterstock.com

Figure 2-3. This ceramic vase has another common theme from ancient Greece: the dolphin. Notice the large decorative floral motif both above and below the dolphin.

Garsya/Shutterstock.com; Isantilli/Shutterstock.com

Figure 2-4. Laurel wreaths, symbolizing allegiance and dedication, are still engraved on medals awarded to soldiers, scholars, and athletes. University graduates in the Mediterranean region still wear wreaths or crowns of leaves for their graduation services.

Did You Know?
The Greeks introduced the cornucopia. The cornucopia was filled with flowers, fruits, and vegetables and carried upright in parades as a symbol of abundance, **Figure 2-5**.

Wreaths made with laurel leaves symbolized allegiance and dedication and were given to champion athletes, statesmen, artists, and others to honor their achievements, **Figure 2-4**. It is still possible today to see university graduates in the Mediterranean region wearing palm leaf and other types of foliage crowns during graduation day festivities.

Rome

The Roman period lasted from about 28 BCE to 325 CE. Wealthy Romans used flowers and decorative plants indoors and in their formal gardens. Roman frescoes, tile mosaics, and sculptures depicted floral images such as vines, floral bouquets, and floral arrangements. Aristocrats kept plants as interior accents and enjoyed flowers for their color and perfume. Hair and clothing ornaments were fashioned in the form of leaves and flowers. Flowers were also beautifully rendered in precious metals. Fresh floral decorations were used at parties and events as garlands or in the form of petals thrown on the floor. It is said that at one party thrown by Emperor Nero (37–68 CE), so many petals were thrown from the gallery onto guests that one was asphyxiated, literally drowning in rose petals.

Like the earlier Greeks and Egyptians, the Romans continued to use flowers and foliage in wreaths and garlands. However, their arrangements were more complex than those of the earlier civilizations. They prized large, colorful flowers with bright colors. In addition to wreaths and garlands, they arranged flowers in baskets and used them for table decorations.

neko92vl/Shutterstock.com

Figure 2-5. Achelous was the god of the largest river of Greece, the Achelous River. In this statue, Achelous dons a laurel wreath and holds a cornucopia overflowing with fruits.

Did You Know?
The Romans believed vervain (verbena) held magical properties and used it in love potions.

Middle Ages

Important plants used for medicine, food, and even aesthetics were kept in monasteries throughout the Middle Ages (476 CE to 1450 CE). Monastic architecture often included walled gardens to protect the valuable sources of food and medicine from would-be thieves, **Figure 2-6**. As the feudal system declined, plant cultivation became more important to society. There were more independent farmers growing food to sell as the feudal system fell out of favor and commerce and agriculture increased. Flowering plants were also cultivated and prized for the same reasons we love flowers today: color, pattern, and fragrance.

Flowers were used in the art of the early Christian church as representations of virtue, peace, and loyalty as well as the Holy Trinity. White lilies or blue flowers such as columbine symbolized the Virgin Mary. Red flowers implied martyrdom.

The nobility and the wealthy were soon interested in the commercial production potential of useful plant materials. Ownership of an exotically beautiful, newly-discovered species was enticing to those with means to afford such rarities. The increased interest in exotic species spurred the international trading of plants and flowers, **Figure 2-7**.

Renaissance

The Renaissance began in Italy at about 1400 CE and lasted through 1600 CE. During this era of enlightenment after the "Dark Ages" (Middle Ages), gardens devoted to preservation and science were called *physic gardens*. The first physic gardens were formed in Europe in the 1500s during the

Mark Sherouse

Figure 2-6. Medieval monasteries like this one in Moldavia, northern Romania, grew their crops in gardens hidden inside the high walls of the complex.

Rudra Narayan Mitra/Shutterstock.com

Figure 2-7. A portion of the old silk route, or "Silk Road," that ran from China to India and Europe. There were actually three routes by this name, averaging 4,000 to 6,000 miles and running through both mountains and deserts. Plants, spices, herbs, silks, and other goods were transported by camel along these routes.

Renaissance, **Figure 2-8**. As interest in exotic plants grew, wealthy investors funded expeditions to discover and collect previously unknown plant materials with income prospects. European nations established imperial outposts in tropical regions to pursue new plant discoveries and to increase the flow of exotic plants from native environments to Europe. Plants showing economic medical, culinary, or purely aesthetic promise were cultured in display gardens and buildings that offered protection during harsh weather.

Mark Sherouse

Figure 2-8. The restored gardens at the Villandry Chateau in the Loire Valley of France were designed during the Renaissance period. Notice the highly geometric design that was typical of gardens of this era. Both food crops and flowers were grown in these gardens.

Tulipmania

During the 1630s, northern Europe experienced an economic period now known as *tulipmania*. At that time in the Netherlands, tulip bulbs promising incredible blooms were highly prized and sought after. An obsession with these tulips occurred in part as a result of work by horticulture scientist Charles de l'Ecluse (1526–1609), who catalogued the occurrence of *tulip breaking*. This phenomenon caused the flowers to have vivid colors and unique patterns resembling flames and streaks, **Figure 2-9**. Demand kept driving the price of tulips up until it was all out of proportion and the price of a single tulip exceeded the average working class income. This created a "bubble" of speculation that, when it burst, led to financial ruin of many people involved in the floriculture trade.

At the time, no one knew why some tulips had the beautiful colors and patterns and others did not. About 200 years later, this phenomenon was found to have been caused by a virus, rather than the bulbs' genetic makeup. This virus, called the *tulip breaking virus* or *mosaic virus*, caused the plants to flower brilliantly for a season or two and then die. Despite this history, however, floriculture in the Netherlands flourishes today and results in the employment of many hybridizers, growers, brokers, and shippers, **Figure 2-10**.

Kisialiou Yury/Shutterstock.com

Figure 2-09. The tulip breaking, or mosaic, virus causes tulips to have brilliant colors and patterns, but the virus kills the plants after only a few years.

Did You Know?

The famous flower market in Amsterdam, on the Singel River, is the only floating market in the world! The flower stalls are on houseboats and you walk along the bank to see the wares.

Angelo Giampiccolo/Shutterstock.com

Figure 2-10. A canal view of the Bloemenmarkt, the famous floating flower market on the Singel Canal in Amsterdam. Notice the row of glass-enclosed flower stalls floating along the left side of the canal. The Bloemenmarkt first opened in 1862.

Colonial Period

The Colonial period of floral design, which lasted from roughly 1620 to 1780, reflects the hardships colonists faced as they settled in the New World. Cut flower arrangements were placed in everyday crockery. Particularly in the earlier part of this period, the flowers consisted of wildflowers and flowers grown in and around the house. Arrangements were simple because settlers' livelihood demanded attention to agriculture production or business operation. Later in the Colonial period, as the colonists became more affluent, they began arranging flowers in decorative vases imported from Europe. The *bosom bottle*, a small glass vial with an attached pin, fit into the neckline of the dress and held a few sprigs of fresh flowers and greens. More affluent women wore these with small delicate flowers to help keep them fresh.

Did You Know?

Five-fingered vases, also known as Quintal horns, were popular in colonial America. These vases were used to create a fan-shaped, narrow design.

Classical Revival

The Classical Revival period, which is also known as the Neoclassic period, lasted from 1762 to about 1830. It is called the Classical Revival period because the symmetry of the earlier classical Greek and Roman periods came back into style. This period had different characteristics and was even given different names in different parts of the world. For example, in England, both the late Georgian and the Regency periods were part of the Classical Revival period. In France, the Louis XIV period and Directoire period were included. In America, it included the Federal and Early Republic periods.

Did You Know?

During the early years of the Classical Revival period, people believed flowers could cleanse the air of diseases. This was the reason for the development of nosegays—small bouquets of flowers that were held in the hand and could be brought to the nose and sniffed.

Newly introduced to the continent in the early eighteenth century, citrus plants were prized for their ornamental foliage, fragrant flowers, and delicious fruit. However, they could not withstand the cold temperatures of northern Europe. These tender plants were kept secure and healthy in the winter in *orangeries*, stone and brick structures with large, expensive glass windows, **Figure 2-11**. During cold weather, the windows were closed, allowing sunlight to penetrate and warm the interior. In warmer weather, the windows were raised to cool the interior. Those who could afford to build an orangery used the flowers and fruit for dining and decoration.

In addition to rare and exotic citrus, many types of seasonal plant materials were used to grace elegant dinner tables. Immense lengths of foliage and floral garlands were hung from ceiling corners and gathered at candlelight chandeliers in the center of ballrooms and dining halls. Tables were centered with garlands and floral clusters to provide an elegant welcome to guests.

Shelli Jensen/Shutterstock.com

Figure 2-11. Belton House Formal Gardens and Orangery in Lincolnshire, Great Britain. The huge windows and glass ceiling in the orangery allowed the sun to warm the plants during the winter months when temperatures were too cool to grow citrus outdoors. In the summer, as shown here, the windows could be opened to allow fresh breezes to cool the building.

Victorian Era

When Victoria became Queen of England in 1837, she was only 18 years old. Her reign lasted until her death in 1901. The Victorian era takes both its name and its character from this dynamic figure. It was another time of enlightenment and progress. This era had several distinctive decorative art movements where styles emerged and faded from use. Decorations, including furniture, wallpaper, architecture, and even floral arrangements, were elaborate and highly detailed.

During warm months, the fireplaces of aristocrats' residences were filled with potted plants or containers of cut greenery called **bough pots**. Flowers also adorned the dress apparel of the wealthy. By the late 1800s, women wore flowers in their fanciful hairstyles and on their gowns.

The discovery of new plants by botanical explorers reached its greatest heights in the late 18th and early 19th centuries. Knowledge about these new exotic findings, their availability, and the growing wealth of individuals created a demand for diverse floriculture offerings.

During the Victorian era, the Industrial Revolution led to a new economic class of people referred to as the *middle class*. This class of people had what would be known as *disposable income*, a bit of extra money to purchase items other than food or shelter. In a sense, the Industrial Revolution increased the number of people who appreciated and could afford to purchase flowers and plants strictly for their own enjoyment. People could buy flowers in town and city markets, bring them home, place them in a vase, and enjoy their benefits. Floral gardening became a popular pastime and horticulturists began to publish manuals on topics such as soil fertility, new flower varieties, and flower arrangement. More people began growing and arranging flowers to enjoy in their own homes or to sell.

Victorian London

In 1861, the first table floral competition was held in London, sponsored by the Royal Horticultural Society. The winning entry, with containers designed by Thomas March, consisted of three separate containers. The containers were stacked (largest on bottom) and held in place with a glass rod. Each container had a ball of clay surrounded by wet sand. Flowers were placed into the wet sand and stayed fresh long after the party ended.

In Victorian London, the best place to find fresh flowers and floral decorations was the Covent Garden Market. Land set aside for a fruit and vegetable marketplace by royal decree in the 17th century evolved into a large market with numerous vendors and products. Floriculture products sold there came from nurseries on the outskirts of the city.

In 1870, Covent Garden grew in size with a permanent structure 200′ long × 76′ wide and 70′ tall, allowing more dependable floral vendors to participate. These vendors could be relied upon always to have quality flowers and plants. The Covent Garden Market is still in existence today and is definitely worth a visit. Market hours in the summer were from 4:00 a.m.

until 9:00 a.m.; in the winter, they were from 5:00 a.m. until 9:00 a.m. Many of the cut flowers were imported from nearby European countries, including Belgium, France, and Holland. In less than 10 years, the floral offerings available at Covent Garden grew much broader as demand for flowers and plants increased. **Figure 2-12** lists this more diverse selection of floriculture products.

Victorian Era in the United States

In the United States, floriculture followed population centers in the east and flower shops, as we know them today, began to emerge and prosper. Indeed, the term *florist* came into being in the 19th century. At first, the term referred to floriculture growers. As the popularity and demand of professionally created floral designs rose, growers employed people with a flair for design.

Flowers of Covent Garden, circa 1870		
Abutilon	*Dracaena*	Myrtle
Ardisia	*Epiphyllum*	Narcissi
Arum Lilies	*Eucharis amazonica*	Palms, including *Areca, Rhapis, Kentia,* and *Whaleback*
Aspidistra	*Ficus elastica*	
Aster	Forget Me Not	*Pelargonium*
Azaleas	*Fuchsia*	*Petunia*
Balsam	Gardenias	Poinsettia
Begonia	*Grevillea*	*Rhodanthe*
Bouvardia	Heather	Roman Hyacinths
Calceolaria	*Heliotrope*	Roses
Camellias	Hyacinths	Scented Verbenas
Chrysanthemums	*Hydrangea*	*Solanus*
Cineraria	Ixia	*Sparaxis*
Clematis	*Kalosanthes coccinea*	*Spiraea*
Club Moss	*Laurustinus*	*Spiraea palmata*
Coleus	Lavender	*Stephanotis*
Crocus	Lilac	Stock
Croton	Lilies	*Stokesia*
Cyclamen	Lily of the Valley	Sweet Peas
Cyperus	*Lobelia*	Tuberoses
Cytisus	Maidenhair Fern	*Veronica*
Dahlias	Michaelmas Daisies	Violets
Deutzia gracilis	Mignonette	Wallflower

Figure 2-12. A larger selection of plants and flowers available in Covent Garden in the 1870s.

Those with enough wealth could hire florists to make floral designs for occasions such as funerals, weddings, or parties. Florists could make designs in baskets or other containers for delivery, or could be employed to travel to homes or churches to make designs to client specifications. Florists employed wire workers to make frameworks in shapes such as hearts and crosses. These shapes were stuffed with long-fibered moss or sawdust, overwrapped with wire, waxed tissue paper, or strings, and pierced with flower heads to create specialized floral designs.

As the economy grew and demand for specialized floral designs increased, there was a need for technical information on how to grow flowers, construct designs, and manage commercial floriculture operations. In the latter 19th century, floral writers suggested the use of various *cultivars* of flowers and how they could be prepared and made into floral designs. They also suggested what they considered the appropriate colors to use in their designs. Commercial florists met to discuss business practices and concerns. In 1884, the *Society of American Florists (SAF)*, a trade association for professional florists, was formed.

As for the general public, floral design and floral crafts were explained and illustrated in popular magazines such as Godey's *Lady's Book* (1830–1878). Readers were encouraged to make designs using seashells as flowers when there was a lack of fresh, seasonal flowers. There were also detailed articles on how to use colored tissue paper to make artificial flowers. Flower-drying methods were explained so readers could use the dried plant materials to make permanent displays.

Upper-class households could enjoy year-round use of their own *stove house* that was heated by a wood or coal-burning stove. Wealthier families might have a more elaborate greenhouse referred to as a *conservatory*. A stove house was devoted to the production of flowers, fruit, or plants in general, while a conservatory was often an extension of the interior—a tropical room for the display of exotic plants, **Figure 2-13**.

Figure 2-13. The East Conservatory at Longwood Gardens in Pennsylvania is an example of a Victorian conservatory. The glass roof and walls allow plants to obtain plenty of sunshine while protecting them from extreme temperatures.

Victorian horticulture enthusiasts sought unique plant materials from commercial nurseries or from acquaintances who were also devoted to plant culture. Some estate owners employed gardeners to maintain greenhouses and exterior floral beds. It was often the duty of these gardeners to make up floral designs for daily displays about the house.

Around the middle of the 19th century, when guests were invited to dine at upper-class estates, they experienced the Russian style, or *a la Russe* service. Servers appeared at the left of each guest with platters of food, and the guests served themselves. Prior to this, the French or *a la Francaise* style was used, in which all platters, bowls, and other containers of food were placed on the dining table. The new style freed up space, so the use of floral decorations became important.

Ladies carried small floral bouquets called **tussie mussies** as accessories to balls and fancy dress occasions. The equivalent of the nosegays that were popular in Europe, tussie mussies consisted of fragrant, colorful flowers and greenery formed into tightly gathered bouquets, **Figure 2-14**. They were bound with string or similar binding, then placed in special holders usually made from precious metals,, giving them an elegant handle. Tussie mussies gained their name from the Old English, where the word tussie was taken from "tussock" or grassy hill, referring to the form of the design. Mussie is derived from the dampened moss placed in the cup of the holder to keep flower stems fresh.

During the time when tussie mussies were popular, a floral code or language of flowers was known. Meanings were assigned to different flowers, greenery or even combinations of materials, **Figure 2-15**.

Did You Know?

Varying accounts record that Queen Victoria's bridal bouquet consisted of Snowdrops (Galanthus nivalis) while others state it was White Heather. Some state that the bouquet was edged in English Honiton lace, made from cotton thread.

Figure 2-14. The young woman in this 1913 hand-tinted valentine wears flowers in her hair and holds roses. A Victorian nosegay of delicate garden flowers were generally made by household servants or estate gardeners to contrast or match a woman's formal gown.

Flower	Meaning
Alstroemeria	Devotion, Friendship
Aster	Symbol of Love, Daintiness
Azalea	Take Care of Yourself for Me, Temperance
Baby's Breath	Innocence, Pure of Heart, Festivity
Bells of Ireland	Good Luck
Bird of Paradise	Magnificence
Calla Lily	Magnificent beauty
Carnation	I'll Never Forget You, Capriciousness, Fascination
Chrysanthemum	I Love You, Truth, Slighted Love, You are a Wonderful Friend
Coreopsis	Always Cheerful
Daffodil	Chivalry, The Sun is Always Shining When I'm with You
Dahlia	Dignity, Instability, My Gratitude Exceeds Your Care
Daisy	Innocence, Loyal Love, I'll Never Tell, Purity
Gladioli	Give Me a Break, I'm Really Sincere, Strength of Character
Holly	Defense, Domestic Happiness
Hyacinth	Constancy, Loveliness, I'll Pray for You, Play
Hydrangea	Thank You for Your Understanding, Perseverance
Iris	Your Friendship Means so Much to Me, My Compliments
Lilac	First Love
Lily	Beauty, Elegance, Sweetness, I'm Walking on Air
Myrtle	Emblem of Marriage and Love
Narcissus	Egotism, Formality, Stay as Sweet as You Are
Peony	Happy Life, Happy Marriage, Healing
Petunia	Your Presence Soothes Me
Poppy	Pleasure, Wealth, Success
Ranunculus	I Am Dazzled by Your Charms, Radiance
Red Rose	Love, I Love You, Perfect Love, Respect
Rose	Beauty, Crown or Wreath of Reward, Virtue
Snapdragon	Deception, Presumptuous
Stargazer Lily	Ambition
Statice	Lasting Beauty
Stephanotis	Happiness in Marriage, Desire to Travel
Stock	Bonds of Affection, You'll Always Be Beautiful to Me
Sunflower	Loyalty
Tulip	Perfect Lover, Fame, There's Sunshine in Your Smile
Yarrow	Good Health
Zinnia	Lasting Affection, Constancy, Goodness

Figure 2-15. Flowers were assigned meanings that could not be expressed aloud in Victorian Society. Victorians used floral dictionaries to decipher the meanings of tussie mussies and other types of bouquets. The following chart lists meanings for a few popular flowers. There is a more extensive chart in the appendix.

Art Nouveau and Art Deco

As the 20th century arrived, design movements such as Art Nouveau and Art Deco arrived in the United States from Northern Europe. These movements had an effect on décor as well as design. Most commercial floral design remained conservative, using an abundance of flowers in traditional mass-pattern forms popularized in the Victorian Era. However, many urban florists were inspired by Art Nouveau and, later, Art Deco patterns.

Art Nouveau motifs are characterized by a graceful, sinuous, whiplash line in their design. This same graceful line was used in the design of floral vases made of metal, pottery, and glass, **Figure 2-16**.

Floral designers inspired by architecture and interior design during the 1920s may have desired to use less plant material to express the streamlined elegance of the Art Deco movement. Design and innovation existed, but it was not as prolific during the 1930s due to lack of growth and innovation during the Great Depression. Still, the appreciation of flowers and plants existed as decoration or a way of expressing love and other emotions.

Modern Period

The Modern, or Modernistic, period started around 1930 and lasted through 1960. World War II had a great effect on innovation and manufacturing as the country focused on anything that could help win the war. Floriculture was of less importance than the production of fruits and vegetables, which took over many commercial greenhouses and fields.

As World War II ended, the influx of the armed forces servicemen and servicewomen back to the United States caused a major change unparalleled in American history. Advances in transportation, manufacturing, and technology helped move the nation out of the economic turmoil of the Great Depression. The number of garden clubs grew, allowing more people the opportunity to exchange gardening information and study and practice the art of floral design. Floriculture and professional floristry enjoyed renewal in these prosperous times. New businesses were begun to meet the need for cut flowers and decorative plants for the many occasions surrounding family life. People liked sending and receiving flowers from professional florists.

In 1954, Vernon Smithers of Akron, Ohio, introduced water-absorbent foam that could provide water to cut stems through *capillary action*. This relatively inexpensive foam also provided stem anchorage so that an arrangement could survive motor vehicle delivery and end-user display. From an artistic standpoint, the foam allowed designers to position flowers into seemingly unlimited geometric forms, giving rise to new categories of floral design.

Ceramics and Pottery Arts and Resources

Figure 2-16. This intricate pewter vase by French ceramicist Eugene Baudin illustrates Art Nouveau.

Did You Know?

During the Great Depression, Joseph Hill developed a new red rose that could be grown profitably even in a bad economy. He named it "Better Times." This rose sold well and helped many floral businesses survive the depression.

1960s to Today

Since 1960, styles have changed rapidly. In fact, people might say that there has been no one overriding style. The following sections describe the most prevalent influences on design style.

Postmodernism

Postmodernism was a direct reaction to Modernism and was characterized by cynicism and discontent. Industrialism of the post WWII years was not without its problems. Public awareness about the pollution contaminating our air, water, and ground resources grew. Protests, assassinations, and race riots in the 1960s and 1970s rocked our nation—a nation that was already in turmoil about the U.S. involvement in the Vietnam War. Defiance to authority and protests for peaceful solutions found their way to city streets and college campuses.

On a cultural level, however, people desired an unspoiled environment where love and happiness were the norm. The arts turned toward natural themes and elements. Houseplants became widely popular, not just as room accents, but as entire collections displayed on ledges, hanging in windows, and in glass terrariums. Florists capitalized on this new earthy, "flower-power" style.

Did You Know?

The term flower power was used coined by the American beat poet Allen Ginsberg as a means to transform war protests into peaceful, affirmative events.

Pop Culture and Classicism

At the end of the twentieth century, a large part of media focus centered on *nesting*. Nesting is the tendency to make home life more comfortable through products and practices associated with interior design, foods, cooking, and home gardening. One pioneer on this topic was Martha Stewart. A former caterer and event specialist, Martha integrated the finer elements of living into our daily lives. Her ideas about combining different art styles with the classical beauty of garden-grown flowers and fine dining at home made her a household name, **Figure 2-17**.

Environmentalism

Environmental issues continue to be a primary concern in our everyday lives. Renewable resources, products, and means that are considered environmentally friendly are used by people in the floriculture industry from growers to retailers. "Green" florists strive to purchase locally grown, *sustainable* flowers. During months that are not hospitable to flower growing, florists can purchase materials from third-party growers with certification that assures that they are working toward ecological sustainability and social responsibility. Green florists create floral designs using less floral foam and are more apt to make arrangements in vases of water.

Agnes Kantaruk/Shutterstock.com

Figure 2-17. Casual bouquets for everyday living have become a symbol of happiness and content in our home lives.

Alison Hancock/Shutterstock.com

Thinking Green

Living Walls
Entire walls are now being designed using living plants, **Figure 2-18**. Just as in a floral arrangement, the plants are arranged to create a design or a pleasing appearance. These large areas of plants help remove toxins from the air and produce oxygen.

Figure 2-18. The green wall of this building provides extra insulation for the building and serves as a piece of art that works to clean the air and produce oxygen.

While demand for floriculture continues to rise nationally, the number of wholesale florists and retail flower shops has declined. Our fascination with flowers continues to grow, but the way we buy flowers has changed. Flowers are widely available in grocery stores and farmer's markets. Many people go online and order flowers on the Internet, thus reducing the need for retail shops. Nonetheless, flowers remain an important way to express emotion. From bridal bouquets to prom corsages, from birthday greetings to quiet expressions of sorrow, flowers still say it best, **Figure 2-19**.

Jason Stitt/Shutterstock.com; decathlon/Shutterstock.com; Blend Images/Shutterstock.com

Figure 2-19. Flowers can be used to say many different things. One of the best reasons to give flowers may be "just because."

Summary

- Studying floral design history is important because it gives us insight not only on how flowers were used in the past, but where the industry may be headed.
- We gain historical information about floral use from clues in the art and literature of the past.
- People have been using flowers for thousands of years. The Egyptians, Greeks, and Romans used flowers for decorating their homes and places of worship.
- In the Middle Ages, flowers were grown in protected gardens along with plant materials grown for food and medicinal purposes.
- Personal collections of exotic plant materials became a sign of wealth and status. The exotic plant materials also became an important part of international trade.
- The Industrial Revolution created a middle class with disposable income for the finer things of life, including flowers. Demand for floral products grew as people used flowers to enhance milestone events such as births, weddings, and funerals.
- After WWII, a period of prosperity helped the floral industry grow. Technological innovations aided floristry, advancing the quality and success of products and services.
- Environmental concerns continue to impact the science of floriculture and floral design.
- The landscape of professional floristry is changing. There are fewer floral shops and wholesalers, but people still enjoy the way flowers and plants make occasions special.

Review Questions

Go to www.g-wlearning.com/floraldesign/ to use the fill-in-form.

Answer the following questions using the information provided in this chapter.

1. How do we know details about how flowers were used in ancient cultures?
2. List three ways in which flowers were used in ancient Egypt.
3. Which culture originated the use of laurel leaves in wreaths to honor champion athletes and statesmen?
4. Explain the major purpose of plants and flowers during the Middle Ages.
5. What are physic gardens?
6. Describe the arrangements typical of the Colonial period.
7. What is the purpose of an orangery?
8. What effect did the Industrial Revolution have on floriculture?
9. What is the difference between a stove house and a conservatory?
10. What is the European term for a tussie mussie?
11. Name an identifying characteristic of Art Nouveau motifs.
12. Describe the effect of Vernon Smithers' product on floral design.
13. To what extent did the unrest of the 1960s and 1970s affect floriculture?
14. List three ways in which florists can be environmentally conscious, or "green."
15. How is floriculture changing today?

Activities

1. Use the Internet and your local library to look for period articles on floral design. Choose an illustration or famous painting of a flower arrangement and "dissect" it. List the types of flowers used and determine if the arrangement is realistic. Were all of the flowers available during the same season? Were they all grown in the area? Create a chart with your list explaining what you discovered.
2. Research the art of paper flowers. Find its origin and then make paper flowers of your own. If possible, use different types of paper to see which works best.

3. Write a two-page report on the history of sailor valentines. Explain what they are and where they originated. Plan and design your own sailor valentine. Sketch it out and, if possible, create your design. Make sure to include some flowers in your design.

4. Use seashells, pebbles, beads, beach glass, and other such items to make flowers and/or an arrangement. Plan your design and sketch it out. Decide if it will be standing or placed in a frame. Search the Internet for ideas and how-tos. The different materials may be combined to create your arrangement or individual flowers.

Critical Thinking

1. Consider the characteristics of the Classical Revival period. Why do you think various countries developed their own names for and interpretations of this period?

2. The ancient Egyptian design period lasted almost 3,000 years. In contrast, the ancient Greek period lasted less than 500 years, and the Roman period lasted less than 350 years. What factors might have helped the Egyptian design period last so much longer than any other design period since?

3. Imagine that you were alive and owned a floral shop during and just after World War II. What effects would the war and its aftermath have on you as a shop owner?

STEM Activities and Academics

1. **Technology.** Over the years, many different methods have been used to preserve flowers and floral arrangements. Research the older methods, such as freeze drying, which was used in the early 1800s, and the newer methods in use today. Write an essay explaining the role of technology in the changing methods of flower preservation.

2. **Science.** Research recent tulip cultivars. Choose five cultivars and write a two-page report comparing the differences and similarities of each new variety.

3. **Technology.** Research environmental issues related to floriculture and find out what role technology has played in the advancement of floriculture. Choose two specific topics and write a report explaining how technology has helped (or hurt) efforts to these specific areas to become more environmentally friendly.

Communicating about Floral Design

1. **Reading and Speaking.** Select a historical era that interests you. Using at least three resources, research the history of floral design during that era and write a report. Include how and where flowers and plants were grown and how they were used during that era. Present your report to the class using visuals, such as PowerPoint.

2. **Reading and Speaking.** Using the Victorian Language of Flowers chart in the Appendix, choose at least five types of flowers and two types of foliage to "create" a bouquet or arrangement to convey a personal message. Collect images of the flowers/foliage in your bouquet and attach them to a small posterboard. Explain the message (written or oral) you are conveying and why you chose each particular material.

3. **Reading and Speaking.** With a partner, make flash cards of the key terms listed at the beginning of the chapter. On the front of the card, write the term. On the back, write the phonetic spelling as found in a dictionary. Practice reading the terms aloud, clarifying pronunciations where needed.

4. **Speaking and Listening.** Collect an assortment of wild and garden plant materials (with permission) and create a simple colonial style design. Evaluate your peers' designs in a historical context using material from the text.

3 Containers, Tools, Mechanics, and Safe Work Practices

objectives

After reading this chapter, you will be able to:

- Select appropriate containers for specific floral design styles and display spaces.
- Create a floral bow.
- Use floral design tools properly and safely.
- Properly hydrate, fit and secure fresh floral foam into a container.
- Carry out the procedures for using various types of floral design mechanics.
- Describe safety precautions to be taken in a floral shop.

key terms

armatures	ergonomics	ikebana
bonsai	floral adhesive	mechanic
bowl tape	florist wire	paper-covered wire
chenille stem	greening pin	pruning shears
chicken wire	grids	stem wrap
container	hard good	water pick
decorative wire	hasami	wood pick
dry core	herbaceous plant	

Go to www.g-wlearning.com/floraldesign/ for online vocabulary activities using key terms from the chapter.

introduction

This chapter describes the foundations of floral design: all the things necessary to make a breathtaking design and hold it together successfully. Whether you are creating a gentleman's boutonniere, a table centerpiece, or a grand-scale showpiece for a luxury hotel lobby, the foundation of good design is a stable, secure base. Floral design can be viewed as a series of design questions to be answered. The first question to be answered is "What container should I use?" People who arrange flowers at home often have a favorite floral container. Perhaps it was something handed down in the family or given to them by a special friend. In a flower shop, price usually guides the decisions made by the designer. See **Figure 3-1**.

Once a container is selected, it is time to select the additional *hard goods* and tools necessary to complete the design. Hard goods include adhesives, tape, stem wraps, paints, and other items needed to complete a floral design. Tools include a florist folding knife, wire cutters, scissors, glue guns, and other utensils. Another consideration is how to secure the arrangement. The devices and techniques for keeping floral placements secure and stable in a design are known as *mechanics*. In many ways, the creativity a designer exhibits in his or her work starts with the container and continues with the mechanics.

Containers

The purpose of a *container* is to provide a water source for fresh floral materials and overall stability for any floral design—fresh, dried, or artificial. Fresh flowers must have plenty of water to remain hydrated, so the container must hold the necessary amount of water. The container adds to

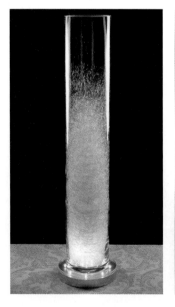

Images courtesy of Save On Crafts, www.saveoncrafts.com

Figure 3-1. An almost endless variety of containers can be used for floral designs. The choice of container sets the stage for the mood of the design. Examples include (left to right): delicate glass for dainty flowers; natural birch vase for a rustic setting; a formal ceramic vase that would work well in a foyer or entryway of a metropolitan home.

the expression of the overall floral arrangement so care should be taken to choose the right container. Repeating the color of the container within the design creates a sense of unity in the arrangement. Keep this in mind to help you tie all the elements of the arrangement together, **Figure 3-2**.

In a flower shop, the cost of the flowers, foliage, container, accessories, and labor must be figured in order for the design to be profitable for the store. Arrangements are usually made in containers that make up only a small part of the total cost. Sometimes, the container is special and becomes a keepsake for the recipient. Containers such as jewelry boxes, high-quality crystal, or ceramics often have a significantly higher value than the floral materials, **Figure 3-3**.

The material and color of a floral container affects its visual weight. Dark colors appear visually weighty, as do handmade pottery, cast iron, or even thick glass. These types of containers can hold flower arrangements that are taller and wider than containers made of delicate porcelain or thin glass.

Working with Glass Containers

Clear glass vases are manufactured in a variety of forms and sizes. Arrangements for occasions such as birthdays, anniversaries, and hospital designs, are sometimes made in glass vases. Because clear and colored glass offers visibility, the stems and water are integral parts of the overall arrangement, **Figure 3-4**.

Rodionov Oleg/Shutterstock.com

Figure 3-2. Choosing a container of the same color as some of the flowers in an arrangement adds to the cohesiveness of the design.

Danshutter/Shutterstock.com

Figure 3-3. An antique bowl or a customers' own heirlooms may be used for high-end floral designs.

Did You Know?

Glass vases date back to as far as the 16th century BCE! For quite some time, only the elite had access to glass products. In some countries, glassmakers were threatened with death if they shared trade secrets.

debr22piocs/Shutterstock.com

Figure 3-4. When clear glass vases are used, the stems become a part of the overall design. Care must be taken to keep the stems and water clean so they do not detract from the arrangement.

No foliage should be allowed to fall below the water line in a floral arrangement because it will decompose and introduce high levels of bacteria into the vase water. The bacteria will proliferate, clouding up the water and making it unsightly. The bacteria will also clog water-conducting vessels of the stems in the container. It is also important to rinse the stems to remove particles of soil, sand, or organic material that can pollute the vase water.

Objects such as marbles, hydrophilic gel beads, seashells, and slices of fruit are often added to glass containers to enhance the beauty of the design, **Figure 3-5**. Since the introduction of organic materials can add to bacterial build-up, this technique is recommended for short-term displays. Less is more with these items, though. They result in additional expense and displace water that would otherwise be available for the cut flowers. They must also be washed and sanitized after every use. They can add substantial weight to the container and can easily break thin-walled glass containers. Too many objects in the vase will compete with stem space and make stems difficult to position. On the other hand, marbles and similar objects can also be used to control and hold them in place. It is best to experiment with this technique so that you can achieve just the right effect.

In contemporary glass container designs, minimal mechanics are used. Vase arrangements rely chiefly on two forms of mechanics: a tape or plastic grid and interlaced stems.

Image courtesy of Save On Crafts, www.saveoncrafts.com

Figure 3-5. Small objects such as beads or stones can add interest to a design. The small pebbles go well with the metal and glass display as well as with the natural feathers.

Grids

Grids, also known as *gridworks*, can be made by stretching waterproof adhesive tape across the container's mouth in a grid pattern, **Figure 3-6**. This mechanical technique works well with glass containers because it is effective and easily hidden, especially if the tape is clear. Grids may also be made with wire or purchased premade. One disadvantage of using a grid is that any leaves or debris below the grid are nearly impossible to remove without having to recreate the design.

Interlaced Stems

The interlaced stem method is a speedy way of designing vase arrangements. Many designers choose to arrange the foliage first and then add flowers. This is often

Goodheart-Willcox Publisher

Figure 3-6. Grids may be purchased premade or can be made with tape. The grid helps keep the individual stems from falling to the side of the container.

the case when arranging a dozen roses. This method allows easy removal of debris that has fallen below the water line. Designers may create the arrangement in one vase and then transfer it to a second, clean vase filled with a fresh flower food solution. This ensures clean and longer-lasting designs. This is a common and recommended practice, especially for vase arrangements made and sold for Valentine's Day and Mother's Day.

Working Safely with Glass

When transporting a glass or ceramic floral container, walk carefully and make sure your hands and the surface of the container are dry. Avoid picking up glass containers, especially bubble bowls, by the rim as the container may be thin and break easily. Careless handling may ruin containers and injure workers. Always place one hand under the container and the other near the neck, sides, or opening of the container, **Figure 3-7**.

Norman Pogson/Shutterstock.com

Figure 3-7. Always carry arrangements in glass vases by supporting the bottom of the vase in one hand, while placing the other hand on the vase.

Step-by-Step

Taping Glass

Some floral tapes are easily torn by hand but using scissors will give you a clean edge and will most likely prevent waste. Periodically, you should wipe any glue that has accumulated on the blades or it will get more difficult to cut or transfer onto the tape.

Wash and sanitize the glass vases. Use a lint-free towel to dry them.

Once your vases are clean and dry, begin applying the tape to the tops.

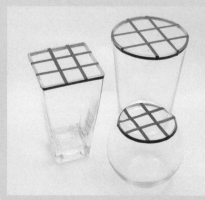

Put tape around the outer edge to keep the strips in place and to neaten the edges.

Did You Know?

By law, solid sterling silver is 92.5% silver and 7.5% copper. The copper is added for strength as pure silver is soft.

Working with Other Types of Containers

Containers made with materials other than glass have advantages and disadvantages. Some are light, others are heavy; some are expensive whereas others are economically priced. The purpose and cost of the arrangement often dictate the type of container used.

Plastic and Ceramic Containers

Plastic containers are popular due to their water-holding ability, the variety of colors, forms, and textures available, and their tendency to be inexpensive. Plastic containers are usually lightweight, but the addition of wet floral foam and water give them the extra weight needed for stability. For permanent botanical designs, plaster, gravel, or a similar material is added to the container to ensure stability.

Ceramic containers are made from clay that has been formed into a shape and fired in a kiln. Ceramic containers are available in a variety of designs, shapes, and sizes. Some containers are decorated after they are fired whereas others are coated with a glaze compound before firing. Ceramic containers are versatile and may be used with all types of floral arrangements.

Metal Containers

Attractive metal containers can support a variety of themes and effects, **Figure 3-8**. Warm colors like copper and golden brass are popular for special occasions and fall arrangements. Cool, silver-colored containers are used for a variety of occasions. Ranging from small bud vases to large, elaborate containers, silver-colored containers are appropriate for the bedside table as well as the lobby of a grand hotel. Most silver-colored containers are not made from silver but are silver plated. Thin metal containers may be made from tin or aluminum and require a plastic liner to prevent leakage and to prevent the metal container from interacting with the preservative.

 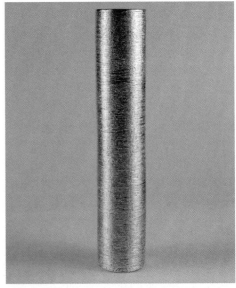

ZoneFatal/Shutterstock.com; Image courtesy of Save On Crafts, www.saveoncrafts.com

Figure 3-8. Warm-colored metals such as brass or copper make good containers for arrangements that express comfort, well-being, or joy. Metals such as steel are considered "cold" and are often used for more modern designs.

Miscellaneous Containers

Some containers are not really "containers" at all. For example, decorative birdcages are popular and add a bit of whimsy to the design. Traditional and specially shaped baskets are also popular choices. With the proper planning and materials, even a book can be used as a container.

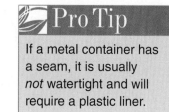

Ribbon and Bows

Ribbon is used as an accent in floral designs and is a popular way of adding color, texture, and pattern. Ribbons and bows add a festive and sometimes even romantic appearance and enhance the beauty of designs, **Figure 3-9**.

Types of Ribbon

Acetate satin and nylon ribbon are the most commonly used in the floriculture industry. Single-faced acetate satin ribbon is shiny on one side and dull on the other. Double-faced satin ribbon has sheen on both sides and is somewhat thicker than single-faced ribbon. Many designers like to use sheer nylon ribbon because it does not absorb moisture and holds its shape. Velvet ribbon is very popular at Christmastime.

Ribbon is manufactured in varying sizes for the floral industry, **Figure 3-10**. The most popular widths stocked by florists are numbers 3, 9, and 40.

Making Bows

One of the basic skills a floral designer needs is the ability to make an attractive bow. Bows are commonly placed on sympathy pieces, vase arrangements, corsages, and sometimes on delivered and hospital arrangements. Ribbon may also be used as an inexpensive way to "fill" an arrangement. Follow the step-by-step procedure to make a bow.

Brian Chase/Shutterstock.com

Figure 3-9. In a corsage, ribbons and bows often serve the practical purpose of securing the flowers while adding beauty to the overall design.

Ribbon Widths

Florist Size	Approximate Measurement
#1	6/16" (8 mm)
#2	7/16" (11 mm)
#3	5/8" (15 mm)
#5	7/8" (25 mm)
#9	1 7/16" (36 mm)
#40	2 11/16" (68 mm)
#100	4" (100 mm)

Goodheart-Willcox Publisher

Figure 3-10. Ribbon gauges commonly used in floral designs. The gauge, length, and color will be determined in part by the design you are creating.

Step-by-Step

Tying a Bow

All floral designers must know how to tie various types of bows as they are used as accents for so many floral design creations. Bows are used to complement everything from floral arrangements, wreaths, and gifts to corsages, bouquets, and boutonnieres. The size of the following bow can be adjusted to suit your needs. Use a floral stem wire that matches your ribbon so it will not detract from the bow.

The materials needed for this bow are floral stem wire (22 gauge), wired ribbon, and scissors. The ribbon used here is 3" wide.

1. Bend a piece of floral stem wire in half so it forms a U shape and set it aside.

2. Starting with the end of the ribbon, measure 18" and hold the ribbon here between the thumb and forefinger of whichever hand is closest to the end of this ribbon. This will be your holding hand.

3. Measure the next 12" and pinch with the thumb and forefinger of your opposite hand. Bring your hands together to form a loop with the ribbon. Grip the loop between the thumb and forefinger of your holding hand.

4. Now measure the next 12" and pinch with the thumb and forefinger of your free hand. Fold the ribbon over (as though you were shutting a book), and pinch with your holding hand.

5. After you have made your first two loops, you should see a figure 8.

6. Measure another 12″ and fold the ribbon over to form another loop. Now you'll have two loops of the same size on one side of your thumb and forefinger, and one loop on the other side. Continue forming new loops in the same way, until you have at least 4 loops on each side.

7. For the final loop that will be in the center of your bow, measure six inches and create a loop where the top of the ribbon curls under the thumb of your holding hand. Insert the floral stem wire through the central loop on top of the bow.

8. Bend the loose ends of the wire around the bottom of the bow and through the U part of the wire to form a knot. Pull to tighten. Separate the loose ends of the wire and pull opposite of each other to tighten. Hold the wire and twist in a clockwise motion several times to secure.

9. Fluff the loops of your bow to create a full appearance. Cut the tails of your ribbon as desired

Tools

In addition to the right hard goods, a floral designer must use the right tools. Using the wrong tools when arranging flowers may decrease the flowers' longevity, make the design process longer, and compromise the designer's safety. Using the right tools for a task makes work easier and extends the lives of your tools. For example, using cutting tools only for the tasks for which they were designed will keep them sharper longer and decrease the likelihood of breakage.

Floral tools can be divided into several categories: cutting, binding, piercing, construction, and tools used to adhere things.

Tools for Cutting

Tools in this category include floral knives, stem strippers, pruners (clippers), wire cutters, folding saw, box cutter, and various scissors or shears.

Folding Floral Knives

Folding floral knives are better than scissors for cutting stems because they make clean cuts and do not pinch the stem's water-conducting vessels. The stems of **herbaceous plants**, cut flowers, and softer woody plant materials should be cut using a sharp knife, **Figure 3-11**. Herbaceous plants are those that have a soft, non-woody stem.

Goodheart-Willcox Publisher

Figure 3-11. A folding floral knife is a designer's most useful tool. Styles vary between manufacturers so you may want to try different types to find one that suits you best. You can sharpen the blade yourself or pay a professional.

Another advantage to using a folding floral knife is that it does not have to be picked up and laid down on the design table between cuts and placements. In busy floral establishments, knife usage saves time because the knife can remain in the designer's hand.

Floral knives should never be used on any materials other than plants. Using them on other materials will quickly dull the blades. A dull blade will damage plant cells. A dull blade also offers more potential for injury. Knife sharpeners are available at hardware stores and should be used regularly.

PRILL/Shutterstock.com

Figure 3-12. A box cutter should be used to open cartons. Do not use a floral knife for this purpose. Keep a fresh blade in the box cutter as a dull blade may snag and slip.

Box Cutters

In addition to floral knives, designers should always stock box cutters with retractable blades, **Figure 3-12**. Box cutters are used to open boxes, cut boxes down for recycling, and sometimes to make boxes useful for transporting arrangements. Keep a sufficient supply of box cutter blades as they dull quickly.

Scissors/Shears

Floral designers use scissors or shears for numerous tasks and, as with floral knives, each pair of scissors should only be used for its intended purpose. *Ribbon shears* have long blades to accommodate wide widths of ribbon and are also used to cut netting, fabric, and other lightweight materials.

Step-by-Step
Using a Floral Knife

The following directions for cutting flowers with a floral knife are for right-handed people. Reverse the directions for the right and left hands if you are left-handed. Floral knives are sharpened on one side of the blade. The opposite side is unsharpened.

Hold knife low in your right hand, the unsharpened side against your fingers. Hold fresh flower stem in your left hand, underhanded.

Place stem between the knife blade and your thumb. Keep your thumb parallel to knife blade at all times, not touching the blade.

Grasping the stem with your left hand, pull the stem through the blade.

Floral shears are made specifically to cut flower stems, but as explained earlier in the chapter, floral knives are preferred for this purpose. *Multipurpose utility shears* have slight serrations on the blades, enabling them to cut light gauges of wire. Although designed for multipurpose use, using multipurpose shears for heavy wire or thick, woody stems may damage the blades, and possibly the stems, **Figure 3-13**. *Floral snips* are used to cut through wire, lightweight woody materials, and wired ribbons.

 Pro Tip

Cutting flower stems on the counter is not recommended because you will not get a clean cut and the knife blade will dull quickly from contact with the counter.

Figure 3-13. Florists use several different types of scissors: ribbon shears; floral scissors; utility scissors.

The Naked Eye/Shutterstock.com

Figure 3-14. As illustrated above, the thorns on rose stems vary greatly in size. When using any type of stem stripper, make sure you do not damage the stem or you will shorten the vase life of your roses.

Stem Strippers

Stem strippers are designed primarily for use on roses. They are used to quickly remove foliage that would fall below the water line of the design. When stem strippers are used to remove thorns from rose stems, care must be taken to remove only the sharp tip of the thorn. Water-conducting vessels are present in and near the thorns, but not in the tips. Stem strippers are especially useful when large numbers of flowers are being processed, **Figure 3-14**. Care should be taken to not cut into the epidermis and bark of flower stems. Water-conducting vessels near the outer portion of the stem may be damaged during this process, obstructing water uptake.

Pruners

Designers often use woody plant materials to create large-scale designs. It is difficult to cut stems thicker than 1″ diameter with a floral knife. ***Pruning shears***, also called *secateurs*, cut through woody stems safely, **Figure 3-15**. Do *not* use pruners to cut wire.

Pruners have one of three types of blade designs: bypass, anvil, or parrot-beak. The blade alignment of bypass pruners is similar to that of scissors, but the upper blade has a convex shape and the bottom is either straight or concave. Anvil pruners have one sharp blade that closes to meet an unsharpened platform blade. This action may pinch vascular tissues of softer stems, but does not harm woody stems. Parrot-beak pruners have two concave blades designed to trap the stem between them. They are used only on narrow stems.

Some pruning shears have a ratchet action that helps to cut through thick stems a little at a time by squeezing and releasing the handles. After each squeeze, the blades stay in place, successively cutting hard stems with less effort.

a_v_d/Shutterstock.com

Figure 3-15. Pruners are used to cut thick, woody stems. Make sure your pruners are kept clean and well-oiled.

Designers may also use long-handled *loppers* for cutting branches larger than 1″ diameter. Saws used for tree pruning can also be helpful for harvesting and processing branches.

Japanese *ikebana* specialists use *hasami*, a scissor-like tool with highly sharpened, short blades. Hasami can cut through soft, herbaceous stems and small-caliper woody stems. They are used for floral design and for maintenance pruning of *bonsai*, **Figure 3-16**.

Wire Cutters

Wire cutters are used to cut wire lengths, silk flower stems, or premade garland. Do *not* use wire cutters on fresh flowers and foliage. They pinch stems rather than provide a clean cut. The ends of the decorative wire may be finished with pliers. See **Figure 3-17**.

Pins

Pins are used to anchor or hold small arrangements in place. For example, corsage and boutonniere pins are used to secure corsages and boutonnieres. *Greening pins*, also called *fern pins*, are made of heavy gauge wire bent into a U-shape. They are used for many purposes, including pinning moss to floral foam. Other types of floral pins include anchor pins, T-pins, wood picks, and plant stakes.

CLM/Shutterstock.com

Figure 3-16. Hasami shears are used to prune and maintain bonsai.

Did You Know?

In ikebana, withered leaves may be considered a part of the overall design, adding an element of asymmetry.

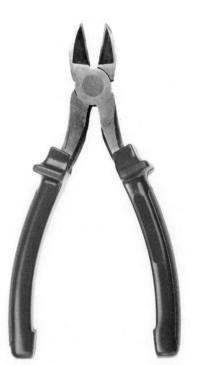
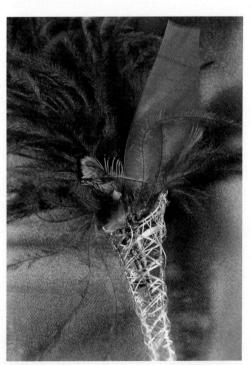

Ilya Andriyanov/Shutterstock.com; Image courtesy of Save On Crafts, www.saveoncrafts.com

Figure 3-17. Common wire cutters should be used to cut floral wire. There are different types of handles and sizes so make sure you choose some that are comfortable. This is especially important if you use a lot of floral wire. The boutonniere illustrated here shows a creative use of wire as the stem holder.

Tools for Binding and Adhering

Except in the most basic floral designs, materials are held together with various types of tape, glues, and adhesives.

Tape Products

The most popular types of tape used in the floral industry are *stem wrap* and *bowl tape*. Stem wrap is made of paraffin-coated crepe paper. This type of tape is used to cover green florist wire for arrangements designed to be worn or carried. When the tape is applied to wire, it is stretched and the paraffin wax helps it to grip and stay attached to the wire. Stem wrap is not an adhesive tape, it sticks only to itself. Stem wrap is also called *floral tape* and is made in a variety of colors. See **Figure 3-18**.

Bowl tape has many other names, including *waterproof tape, anchor tape,* and *bulldog tape*. It is a cloth-based adhesive tape and is primarily used to hold fresh floral foam in a container. It is manufactured in 1/4″ and 1/2″ widths. The process for using tape in a container is explained later in this chapter.

Wire Products

Wire and wire-based mechanics have been used in the floral industry since the nineteenth century. Wire is a tried-and-true construction material that is used for many types of foundations. *Florist wire* is sold in 12″ or 18″ lengths, or on a continuous spool called paddle wire. The wire is manufactured in different gauges (thicknesses). Florist wire ranging from gauges 16 to 32 are used in the floral industry. **Figure 3-19** lists appropriate gauges for mounting flowers and making designs.

Florist wire is annealed, meaning it is heated and then slowly cooled. This makes the wire resistant to breaking. It is painted dark green to help it blend in and to limit rusting when it is exposed to moisture. Cut wire is handy for bracing weak flower stems or for replacing stems for corsages. Designers use spooled or paddle wire when creating garlands.

Chenille stems consist of two wires spun together with short fibers between them. They are used for many tasks, such as replacing natural stems for corsage work, binding stems for hand-tied bouquets, binding ribbon, and hanging holiday decorations. They are available in many colors.

Paper-covered wire is used to tie tender vines and stems to supports. It is also used to bind stems together or to other surfaces. Because of the paper covering, it does not cut into soft stems as easily as bare florist wire. Paper-covered wire is sold in spools.

Glue Guns and Glue Skillets

Glue guns and glue skillets are used to melt solid pieces of plastic glue. Glue guns melt glue sticks and dispense the melted glue in a line or bead.

Images courtesy of Save On Crafts, www.saveoncrafts.com

Figure 3-18. Stem wrap, or floral tape, is used to wrap floral wire or stems.

Did You Know?

The higher the number of a florist wire, the thinner and more delicate the wire.

Floral Wire Gauges	
Flower	**Wire Gauge**
Calla lily	24
Carnation	24
Spray Chrysanthemum	26–28
Full-size Mum	24
Freesia	26–28
Gerbera daisy	26–28
Gladiolus floret	26–28
Orchid	24–28
Rose	24–26
Spray Rose	26–28
Stephanotis	24–28
Tulip	24–28
Application	**Wire Gauge**
Boutonniere	24–28
Bow	24–28
Corsage	24–28
Garland	20–28
Stem	18–24

Goodheart-Willcox Publisher

Figure 3-19. Floral wire has different gauges used for specific purposes. For example, a low-gauge wire like 18 is used to support flower stems, bind florist netting around foam, and secure foam into a container. Whereas 24–28 gauge wires are good-all purpose wires used for securing bows.

Step-by-Step

Using a Glue Skillet to Attach Foam

Before you begin working with the glue skillet, make sure you have a clean, level surface on which to work. Remove any flammable materials from your work area. Place the glue cubes in the skillet and plug it in. Allow the glue to melt completely. *Do not hydrate the foam before gluing it to the container.*

Place the base (the black dish in this case) of the floral design on a level surface. Dip the ends of the items to be glued into the skillet one at a time. *Take care to not get the hot glue on your fingers.*

1

Carefully remove the foam from the glue skillet. Allow excess glue to drip into the pan.

2

Press the glued ends to the base and hold them in place for 10 to 15 seconds. *Do not leave a plugged-in skillet unattended.*

3

Once you are finished with your project, allow the skillet to cool before storing. You do not need to remove the glue from the skillet as it will melt the next time the skillet is used. Store the cooled skillet in its proper location.

4

Hot glue works well for attaching silk flowers or other embellishments but cannot be used on fresh flowers.

Chunks or pillows of solid glue are melted in the heated pan to a thick consistency. Pan glue is moisture and cold resistant so it holds better than the glue from a glue gun.

Adhesives

In addition to glue guns, glue skillets, and tapes, floral designers may use various types of *floral adhesive* to adhere fresh flowers, foliage, ribbon, and dried flowers, **Figure 3-20**. Floral adhesives come in tubes and are dispensed by squeezing the tube from the bottom. Floral adhesive is somewhat runny and will leak if the open tube is placed on its side. This type of cold glue must cure for about a minute before you attach anything.

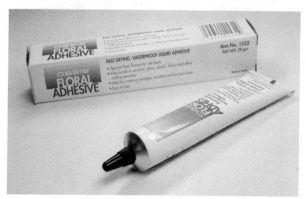

Image courtesy of Save On Crafts, www.saveoncrafts.com

Figure 3-20. Cold glue comes in tubes and must be allowed to cure before it is used to hold items in place. As it cures, its holding power increases.

Pro Tip

Buckets

Use plastic, *not* metal, buckets for transporting and storing flowers. Metal reacts with elements in the water to create rust and it may react with the floral preservative.

Thin strips, circles, and small squares of double-sided adhesives can be used to stick live plant material and hard goods to surfaces. These types of adhesives are commonly used to attach small florets to a mirror or attach sheets of cellophane to contour wrapping on a gift basket.

Stem adhesive is another specialty floral adhesive. Stem adhesive is used after the stem has been inserted into a bouquet holder or wet floral foam. The stem becomes locked in place by the adhesive that has surrounded the insertion point and will help prevent water loss from the top of the foam. If the adhesive is placed on the end of the stem, the stem will not take up water. Placing the adhesive on the side of the stem and then inserting it will ensure adhesion as well as water uptake.

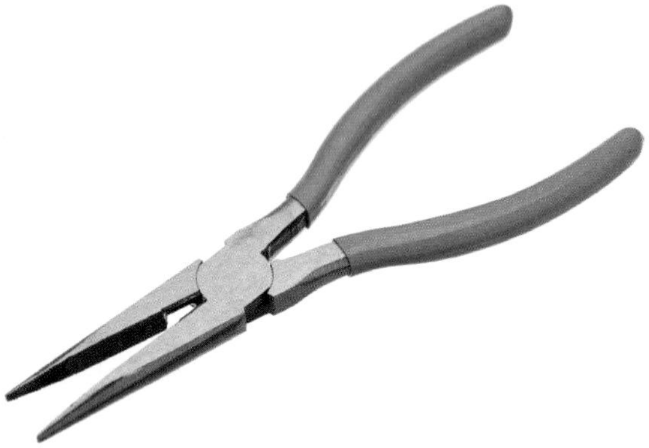

Dan Kosmayer/Shutterstock.com

Figure 3-21. Needle-nose pliers have long, thin jaws that are perfect for bending floral wire.

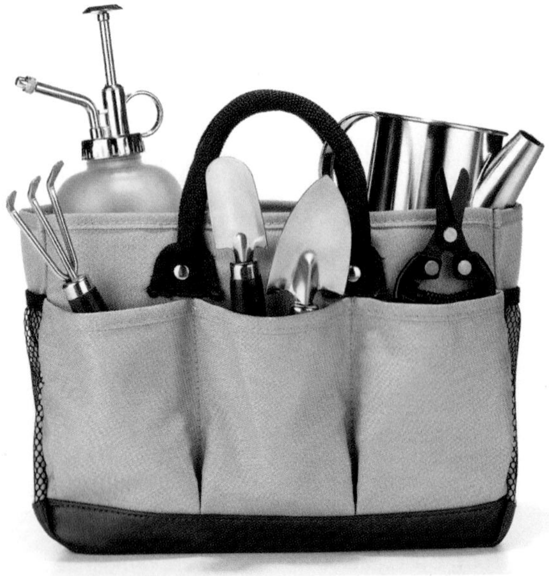

Michael Kraus/Shutterstock.com

Figure 3-22. Choose your toolbox or bag carefully to ensure easy transport as well as quick access to your tools. This garden toolbag is durable and allows easy access to the tools. It also has divided compartments to keep tools and supplies well organized.

Other Useful Tools

Common household tools used in a floral shop include: a hammer, measuring tape, stapler or staple gun, screwdrivers, pliers, and light-colored plastic buckets (they show the dirt better). These tools are used around the shop and most can also be used in designing floral arrangements. For example, needle-nose pliers may be used to curl and crimp wires for special effects, **Figure 3-21**. You should also invest in a durable apron to cover your clothing and keep your tools handy.

Keeping and Caring for Tools

Most designers keep their tools in their work area in drawers, toolboxes, or in a container with commercially prepared sanitizer, but they often have a second set to use when traveling to install floral designs. The tools should be stored in a toolbag or toolbox that protects the tools and is easy to transport, **Figure 3-22**.

Design tools should be cleaned after each use. Dirty tools harbor microorganisms that, when introduced to new, fresh stock, shorten their display life. The regular use of disinfectant sprays or dips, followed by an application of light oil lubricant will keep your tools in working order and bacteria free. Buckets can be kept clean and bacteria free by washing them with a mild bleach and water solution or a commercial product designed for sanitizing floral tools and supplies.

Mechanics

Numerous types of mechanics are used in the floriculture industry. The term mechanics refers to both the objects and methods that are used to fix materials in place. Many of the tools described earlier in this chapter are referred to as mechanics, including wire, adhesives, and pins. As you learn to create more advanced work, you will learn that advanced designs rely on diverse and creative mechanics. Some mechanics are premade and available through wholesalers; others are custom-made by each designer. In many arrangements, the designer often uses a combination of the two.

Mechanics may seem somewhat mysterious because they are, and should be, hidden from view. When looking at a floral arrangement, the viewer should *not* see what is holding the flowers in place. Mechanics may be simple or complicated; they can be quick to install or require several steps. Mechanical instability, and in the case of non-decorative mechanics, lack of concealment, are the two biggest pitfalls in the grading or judging of floral arrangements.

If you are just beginning to study floral design, keep in mind that practicing the most basic methods of mechanics will help you create stable and appealing arrangements. If you find the mechanics of a floral arrangement are unstable, stop and fix the problem before it worsens. This is a common mistake made by beginners. In their anticipation to get to the fun part of adding the flowers and embellishments, they skip practicing the basics and their arrangements may appear stable but tend to fall apart while on display.

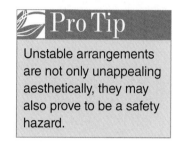

Pro Tip

Unstable arrangements are not only unappealing aesthetically, they may also prove to be a safety hazard.

Floral Foam

Floral foam is one of the most basic mechanics in the floriculture industry. Various types are available but they all serve the same basic purpose—they hold the plant materials in place.

Some floral foams are *hydrophilic*, meaning they readily absorb water and are intended for use with fresh plant materials. Other floral foams are *hydrophobic*, meaning they do not absorb water and are designed for use with silk, plastic, or dried plant materials. Although floral designers may use brand names when referring to different types of floral foam, the most important detail to remember when choosing foam is whether or not you need it to hold water.

Using Fresh Floral Foam

Fresh floral foam is designed to absorb water and to allow the water to pass into fresh cut plant materials, **Figure 3-23**. It is somewhat delicate and should be handled with care. If it is crushed or compressed, it loses its pore space and its capacity to hold water is reduced.

Boxes of floral foam should be handled with care as compression or shock can cause them to lose water-holding capacity.

Fresh floral foam is hydrated by the free-float method. In other words, the foam block is placed in a clean bucket or dishpan filled with water that is deeper than the width of the foam block. The foam block must be allowed to float on the surface where it will quickly absorb enough water to become saturated. Most types of wet floral foam will not sink to the bottom when saturated, but will float just below the surface.

Image courtesy of Save On Crafts, www.saveoncrafts.com

Figure 3-23. Fresh flower foam is the preferred mechanic for arranging fresh flowers.

Sometimes, people try to force foam bricks to take in water quickly. When the dry foam is pushed and held under water, bubbles of air quickly escape from the brick, slowing after a few seconds. This action provides a false sense of completion. What actually occurs is that the outer portion of the foam will become hydrated but the inside of the piece will remain dry. This condition is referred to as *dry core*. If flowers are placed into this brick, some of the stems will hit the dry spots, causing them to wilt. Remember, it takes less than half a minute to fully hydrate a brick of fresh floral foam.

It is better to cut the amount of foam needed for a single project from a dry brick than to soak an entire brick and end up wasting most of the foam. Excess foam can be saved and used in the bottom of larger containers. Excess pieces of foam can also be used on the bottom of a large arrangement—raising the intact brick up and saving money.

Pro Tip

Choose the best foam for your fresh flower arrangement. Fresh floral foam is available in different densities to accommodate soft, medium, and thick flower stems.

Fitting Fresh Floral Foam

When fitting fresh floral foam into a container, leave an adequate amount of space between the foam and the container's inner wall. Water can be added to that space to replace moisture lost from flower stem uptake and evaporation.

Many designers find that a slight sculpting of the fresh floral foam after it is in the container aids in covering the mechanic with foliage. You may also want to remove the corners of the foam, and contour it into a somewhat mounded shape.

Other Types of Floral Foams

Colorful urethane foams can be used with fresh flowers but the water does not move as freely into flower stems as it does through fresh floral foam. If you must use this type of foam with fresh-cut plant materials, use it only for short-term displays.

Hydrophobic foams do not absorb or give water to flowers. Polystyrene is often processed to develop a hard, durable outer skin for wreath forms and other outdoor displays.

Other hydrophobic foams that should *not* be used with fresh-cut plant materials, are Styrofoam™ and trimer foam, simply called silk and dried floral foam. Styrofoam™ is a lightweight, hydrophobic foam that is available in white or green and in various forms, including hearts, rings, and spheres. It is also available in 12″ × 36″ sheets in thicknesses of 1″, 2″, or 3″. It has many purposes, including permanent botanical arrangements, **Figure 3-24**.

Silk and dried floral foam has a lighter density than Styrofoam™. It is used for permanent botanical floral designs and is sold in light green or brown bricks. Dry foam is similar in appearance to fresh floral foam, but it does *not* absorb water. However, its ability to grip silk and dried floral stems makes it popular with many designers.

Images courtesy of Save On Crafts, www.saveoncrafts.com

Figure 3-24. Styrofoam comes in an endless variety of shapes and sizes. Rings are used for wreaths and centerpieces and are specifically designed for indoor or outdoor use. The ball illustrated here could be used for a table decoration or a hanging arrangement.

Step-by-Step

Foam Fitting and Taping Foam

Waterproof tape can be used to attach floral foam to a basket liner or any type of dish. It will not damage the surface of glass, ceramic, or most types of plastic containers. Most waterproof tape can be easily torn and does not require the use of scissors. However, scissors will always leave a nice, clean cut.

The materials needed for foam fitting include a liner, oasis foam cut to size, and waterproof tape.

1

Place the cut, dry foam in the liner and tape from the bottom of the liner, across the floral foam, and onto the other side of the liner. Turn the liner and tape from the bottom of the liner, across the foam, and onto the liner. The pieces of tape should form a cross the center of the foam.

2

Place the liner in the basket.

3

Pour enough water into the liner to thoroughly soak the foam.

4

Taping Floral Foam in Place

Floral foams are adhered to containers in numerous ways and for various reasons:

- To stabilize and hold flower and foliage stems.
- To maintain design integrity during display duration.
- To enable the arrangement to endure transport.

Make sure that the container is clean and dry before waterproof tape is applied. If it is wet, the tape will *not* stick and the foam will have to be remounted. Tape can be applied in an X pattern or in parallel bands over the foam. More tape is applied to the rim of the container to make sure the tape stays in place.

Gluing Floral Foam in Place

Fresh floral foam can be glued into a container, but this should only be done when the container is inexpensive or recyclable. If the foam is being glued to a smooth, plastic surface, use the tip of a knife to scratch up the area where the foam will be glued. The scratches create more surface area, which helps the glue adhere better.

First, cut the dry, fresh floral foam to fit the container. Dip the bottom of the foam into hot glue and place it on the scratched area. The entire container, with the foam glued in place, is then allowed to free-float as a unit.

Safety Note

Do not hydrate fresh floral foam before gluing it to the container. When wet foam is dipped into the hot glue, water droplets will spatter and you may get burned.

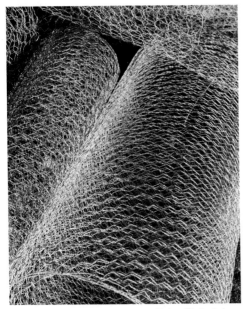

Marbury/Shutterstock.com

Figure 3-25. Chicken wire can add needed support to foam products for heavier arrangements that have thick stems. Make sure the sharp, cut ends do not protrude from the arrangement.

Thinking Green

Floral foam is made with petroleum products and is not considered recyclable. Using chicken wire or decorative wire to hold stems in place reduces the need for floral foam, and the metal is recyclable.

Wire Mechanics

Chicken wire is an old-fashioned mechanic, but still has a place in modern floral design, **Figure 3-25**. It can be cut and formed into a ball or bun shape, secured in a container, and used to hold stems in place. Some designers like to use it on bricks of fresh floral foam as additional support for thick stems. The wire layer helps keep fresh floral foam blocks from splitting and fracturing when the thick stems are inserted.

Decorative wire is popular with floral designers because it is available in various colors, it does not have to be concealed, and it can be used as part of the design. The most popular decorative wires are 10-gauge aluminum wire, 24-gauge copper wire, and a very light gauge wire that is crimped to make it sparkle. It is often called *bullion* and is available in numerous colors.

Bouquet and Corsage Holders

Another common mechanic is the bouquet holder. These holders are usually plastic, but metal holders can also be purchased for use in high-end arrangements. Wrist corsage holders are also used for fresh and artificial arrangements, **Figure 3-26**.

Picks and Other Indispensables

Water picks, also called *water tubes*, provide a small amount of water to sustain flowers for short periods. These plastic or glass vials have snug-fitting rubber or plastic caps with a hole for the flower stem, **Figure 3-27**. Water tubes are used on the stems of loose, cut flowers to minimize stress. They are also used to provide water to fresh flowers when they are added to potted plants and dish gardens.

Goodheart-Willcox Publisher

Figure 3-26. Other kinds of mechanics for floral designs include wet and dry foam bouquet holders.

Four-sided *wood picks* have been used in floral design for more than 100 years. The wood picks are used to secure flowers, ribbon, fruit, and many other objects into mechanics. They are available from wholesalers and are sold plain or with an attached wire.

Many other indispensable design mechanics are used in the floral industry, some that have been used for many years and some that are relatively new. It is important for professional floral designers to keep up with new techniques and products being used in floral mechanics.

Armatures

Many floral designers make customized mechanics to hold stems in place. Decorative frameworks can be made from wire, vines, and combinations of these or other materials. These frameworks are commonly called *armatures* and are used for a variety of purposes including flowers-to-wear, flowers-to-carry, and arrangements. Armatures were the primary floral design mechanics until floral foams were introduced.

Image courtesy of Save On Crafts, www.saveoncrafts.com

Figure 3-27. A water pick will hold enough water for a single stem and may be refilled if necessary.

Step-by-Step

Making an Armature

This armature, created with curly willow and #20 floral wire, will be used to create an arrangement that may be carried as a bouquet and then placed in a vase once the event is over. More decorative branches may also be used to add color or sparkle to your arrangement.

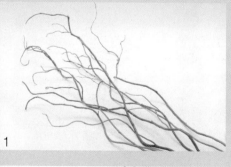

Form the curly willow twigs into a circle.

The curly willow should criss-cross through the center of the circle.

Attach the taped wire in four locations around the perimeter of the armature.

Gather the wire in the middle.

Step-by-Step

Adding Flowers and Greenery to an Armature

The armature created in the previous procedure forms the base of this rustic yet graceful bouquet that may be placed in a vase to extend its life and the recipient's enjoyment. Begin the project by first cleaning your work area and laying out the flowers and greens you will be using.

1

You will be using the armature from the last procedure as the mechanics.

2

Prepare flowers and greenery for this design by cleaning the stems that will be placed beneath the armature.

These stems should be free of greenery and debris so bacteria will not develop in the water.

3

4

Holding the curly willow armature by the handle, begin placing three pieces of leather leaf and three pieces of Israeli ruscus equal distance. Follow this pattern with plumosa on top of the leather leaf to soften and fill in the space with greenery.

Place four carnations (or another mass flower). One in the center and three to follow the same pattern as the greenery. Note the center carnation is upright and the three carnations forming a triangle will have an angle to them. Each stem will meet at the binding point where you are holding the armature by the handle.

5

6

Add three stems of stock forming a triangle directly in between the carnations. Add a filler flower such as statice or button mums forming a triangle around the center carnation, in the same pattern as the bottom carnations. Create a second layer of your filler flower directly below the stock and in between the lower layer of carnations.

The binding point where you are holding the flowers is ready to be bound with binding wire, taped wire, or other binding materials, such as cable ties, chenille stems, or waterproof tape. Cut the flower and foliage stems to the proper length to fit into the desired vase.

Substitute the following recipe to create an alternate arrangement.

4 roses	3 stems of spray roses
3 stems of alstroemeria	Baby's breath or wax flower

Shop Safety

Although the floriculture industry is not considered a dangerous field, ensuring the safety of employees and customers is a high priority for any business. Businesses are required to meet safety standards established by federal, state, and local codes. Owners are required to meet these codes in order to provide and maintain a safe work environment. Some important safety practices include:

- Prominently mark fire exits.
- Keep all fire exits free of obstructions.
- Display a building evacuation plan, **Figure 3-28**.
- Perform regular practice safety drills.
- Keep a certified fire extinguisher(s) easily accessible.
- Install nonskid floors with proper drainage.
- Place antifatigue mats at each workstation.

Ergonomics

Ergonomics is the science of designing equipment and furniture so they fit the human body without causing physical stress and eventual injury. A few areas where ergonomics come into play in a floral shop are counter height, floor surface, and tool size.

Design counters must be at an appropriate height to facilitate good floral design and prevent worker fatigue, **Figure 3-29**. If a designer is bent over a floral arrangement while working, not only will his back be sore, the floral design he is working on may lack a professional finish. An antifatigue mat also helps to reduce sore feet, an aching back, and general fatigue.

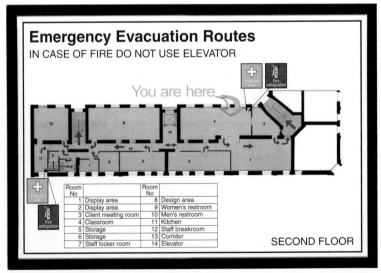

Goygel-Sokol Dmitry/Shutterstock.com

Figure 3-28. The evacuation plan should be posted on a wall where it is clearly visible. Exit signs should also be included by each door.

Floral designers are especially susceptible to carpal tunnel syndrome from repetitive movements with their hands. Properly-sized, quality hand tools help reduce the chance of developing this malady.

Personal Safety

Although the shop owner has a responsibility to maintain a safe work environment, each employee is responsible for working safely. Dressing appropriately and wearing nonskid, closed-toe shoes will help keep you safe while you work. Wear nonskid shoes, because even if the floor is designed to prevent slipping, spilled water or plant material that has fallen to the floor can make it slippery.

During busy periods, there may not be much time to keep floors and work surfaces clean. However, you should still discard plant materials into receptacles rather than dropping them to the floor. In addition to creating a slipping hazard, damaged plant material gives off ethylene gas which is harmful to many types of flowers.

Clean up spills immediately, even if you are busy. Leaving water or other liquids on the floor or workbench creates a hazard. If your shop has walk-in coolers, keep the area inside the coolers clean and dry. This will inhibit the growth of bacteria that may not only harm flowers and foliage, but may also be harmful to your health. Dry floors also help prevent slipping. Establishing proper cleanup procedures and making sure all employees understand the procedures will help keep everyone safe.

Most floral designers rely on aerosol flower paints and sealers to augment or change the natural color of plant materials. When you are using these products, be sure there is adequate ventilation. A sheltered outdoor space helps to minimize spray drift. Use a drop cloth or some barrier underneath objects to be painted. Also wear non-latex gloves to protect your hands. Paint overspray will add color to anything it settles on, including sidewalks, grass, benches, and your skin. When not in use, aerosol paint cans should be stored in cabinets.

First Aid

No matter how careful you are, accidents will happen. Therefore, it is important to keep a fully stocked and, readily available first-aid kit in the shop. Injuries in a floral shop typically include cuts from sharp utensils and burns from hot glue. Small cuts or minor burns are easily treated and usually do not require professional care. If a cut appears to be deep, the injured person should be seen by a medical professional. If the tool that caused the cut had dirt or debris on it, a tetanus shot may be necessary.

For minor burns, hold the burned area under cool running water for several minutes to help remove the heat. Do not apply ointments or creams, because they hold in heat and can actually make the burn worse. If the burn is severe, transport the injured person to a medical facility.

Wiktor Bubniak/Shutterstock.com

Figure 3-29. Working counters and workbenches should be at a comfortable working height. You should also keep an antifatigue mat at each workstation to help reduce back strain and sore feet.

Safety Note

Keeping Floors Safe
Plant stems, leaves, and petals dropped on the floor may cause slippery conditions. Properly dispose of plant materials to keep the work area safe.

Safety Note

Aerosols
It is vital that the area in which you are using an aerosol be well-ventilated! Wear a mask to limit the amount of spray you inhale and wear gloves to protect your hands.

Summary

- Floral designing often begins with the selection of a suitable container.
- Containers should provide an ample water source and physical weight for a floral arrangement.
- Ribbons and bows are used to add color, texture, and pattern to a floral design.
- Specific tools used in floristry include tools for cutting and piercing, tools for binding and adhering, tools for construction, and other miscellaneous and household tools.
- Cut flowers with a knife to ensure that water-conducting vessels remain open.
- Mechanics are devices and techniques used to fix flowers, greenery, and objects within a design.
- Safety in the workplace is important for the welfare of employees and is everyone's responsibility.

Review Questions
Go to www.g-wlearning.com/floraldesign/ to use the fill-in-form.

Answer the following questions using the information provided in this chapter.

1. What are mechanics in a floral design?
2. What precautions must be taken with a glass bubble vase that are *not* necessary with a porcelain or ceramic container?
3. On what two mechanics do most of today's vase arrangements depend?
4. What is the correct way to carry an arrangement made in a fragile container?
5. Name at least two types of ribbon that are used in floral designs.
6. Scissors with long blades that can cut all the way across wide ribbons are called _____.
7. *True or False?* Pruning shears should be used when cutting stems thicker than 1″.
8. Which tool is designed to cut open corrugated packaging?
9. Which tool is designed specifically to remove the sharp tip of the thorns on rose stems?
10. Which tool is ideal for cutting herbaceous plants and flower stems without pinching the water conducting vessels in the stems?
11. List four types of products used to bind or adhere objects in a floral design.
12. What is the purpose of bowl tape?
13. For what tasks are chenille stems used?
14. What common household tools are often needed in a floral shop?
15. List two types of foam commonly used in floral design work.
16. Name three reasons for securing foam to the container in which the design will be built.
17. What is a water pick?
18. What is the purpose of an armature?
19. Describe the features of an evacuation plan.
20. Explain the principal of ergonomics and how it applies to a floral shop.

Activities

1. Design symmetrical bows using #3, #9, and #40 ribbon.
2. Practice using a floral knife with various types of stems.
3. Create a floating floral design suitable for a pool or pond using the proper type of foam.
4. Demonstrate how to free-float soak fresh floral foam.
5. Devise alternative mechanical techniques using two or three types of mechanics in the same design.

Critical Thinking

1. You are creating a fresh flower arrangement for a client using fresh floral foam. You have placed all of the flowers and are adding foliage and embellishments when you notice that a couple of the flower stems are starting to droop. What could be the cause of this, and how can you fix it?

2. You have been asked to do the table centerpieces for a wedding reception. There will be three round tables, each seating eight people. The client has asked you to make the arrangements tall, but slender, so people can see around them. The bride is environmentally conscientious and has requested that no floral foam be used in the arrangements. What mechanics will you use in these centerpieces?

3. You are hurrying to finish a design for a rush job and have just begun to hot-glue the embellishments in place. Your employer calls from the other room, asking you to come quickly and to bring the first-aid kit, because your coworker has cut himself badly. What should you do, and in what order?

4. While working for a wholesaler, you walk into the design area and find that water containing floral preservative has spilled from a walk-in cooler onto the tile floor. Determine and write the most appropriate solution to the problem while addressing the following points: using personal safety precautions, using proper safety procedures in cleaning up the situation, properly disposing of waste materials, and using proper follow-up procedures.

STEM Activities and Academics

1. **Science.** Investigate the physical properties of fresh floral foam. Write a report explaining how these properties allow the foam to mimic the natural water uptake of fresh plant stems.

2. **Technology.** A floral frog is a mechanism that is similar to a grid in that it holds stems in place, but the frog is placed inside the container. Conduct research to find out more about floral frogs, their history, and how technology has improved them in recent years. Write an essay explaining your findings.

3. **Engineering.** Create an armature of your own design that will support an arrangement that is 24″ tall and 36″ wide. Choose the materials for the armature, build it, and then test it by adding floral materials or weights. Analyze how well the design works, and summarize your findings in a three-paragraph report.

4. **Math.** Determine how much ribbon you will need to make 22 bows and how much it will cost per bow. You have three rolls, each with 12 yards of ribbon. Each roll costs eight dollars. Each bow requires 3.5′ of ribbon. How much ribbon do you need to make six bows? How much does each bow cost? How much ribbon do you have left?

Communicating about Floral Design

1. **Speaking.** Working in groups of three, create flash cards for the key terms in this chapter. Each person in the group chooses six terms and makes flash cards for those six terms. On the front of the card, write the term. On the back of the card, write the pronunciation and a brief definition. Use your textbook and a dictionary for guidance. Take turns quizzing one another on the pronunciations and definitions of the key terms.

2. **Reading and Writing.** Working in groups of two or three, read the section and procedure on how to make a bow and practice tying one. Once each member of the group is able to tie a bow, compare bows and discuss issues and/or problems you each encountered.

3. **Reading and Speaking.** Choose the three main topics in the chapter that you would like to understand better. Reread the section on each topic, stop, and write a three to four sentence summary of what you just read. Be sure to paraphrase and use your own words.

Chapter

4

Plant Structures and Functions

objectives

After reading this chapter, you will be able to:

- Explain the system used to classify plants.
- Understand how the binomial plant naming system works.
- Identify the families of flowers and leaves that are often used in floral design.
- Describe the anatomy of flowers and leaves.
- Summarize plant physiology.

key terms

anther	genus	photosynthesis	stamen
binomial nomenclature	incomplete flower	pistil	stigma
blade	inflorescence	plant anatomy	stipules
calyx	internode	plant morphology	stomata
cambium	kingdom	plant physiology	style
carpel	leaf base	propagated	taxonomy
chlorophyll	margin	receptacle	transpiration
complete flower	meristem	rhizome	vascular bundle
corolla	node	root hair	vegetative
domain	pedicel	rooting hormone	reproduction
family	petal	powder	venation
filament	petiole	sepal	xylem
floret	phloem	species	

Go to www.g-wlearning.com/floraldesign/ for online vocabulary activities using key terms from the chapter.

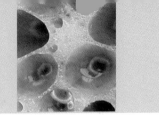

introduction

In floral design, we have the opportunity to work with living, growing, and changing materials. The stages of development from a bud to a fully open flower help determine how we may choose to use a particular type of flower. For instance, a gladiolus bud with its florets barely open is a slender and linear design material. As each flower along the stem begins to develop and open, it changes to a dense and visually heavy material. Other flowers, such as lilies, change shape from a bud to a fully open flower. The bud takes up less space within a design, while the fully open flower demands attention and adds visual weight to an arrangement, **Figure 4-1**.

All artists need to know the characteristics of the items they use to create designs. Sculptors, for example, often work with metal, clay, wood, or glass. They know how to use the natural qualities of their materials to achieve a desired effect in their designs. The same applies to floral designers. They must understand the characteristics of the flowers, leaves, and stems of the plants they use. Younger branching materials, such as young willow branches, can be bent very easily. They can be used to create curved lines, or bent over the top of a focal area to create a sheltering effect. Older, more mature stems are not as flexible and cannot be used in this manner. The floral designer determines which material works best for the situation and desired effect. A designer who completely understands the materials can use them to their fullest potential.

Star of Bethlehem buds just opening

Ranunculas not fully open

Ranunculas, just opening and full bloom

Anemone fully open and almost fully open

Baby's Breath

Oleg Rodionov/Shutterstock.com

Figure 4-1. This design contains both fully open flowers and flower buds. When the buds open, they will change the dynamics of the design, making it heavier and fuller.

To begin this process of understanding, you must first identify the basic qualities of each floral material. Does it have color? If so, how can the color be used in the design? Does the flower have large or small leaves? Are they round or lobed? Do they have smooth or spiny edges? Which type will work best? See **Figure 4-2**.

The study of the physical form and external structure of plant material is called *plant morphology*. It deals with the exterior appearance of a plant. It is different from *plant anatomy*, which is the internal structure of plants. A thorough knowledge of plant morphology and plant anatomy gives designers insight into each plant's characteristics and allows them to choose materials that will be most effective in their designs.

Taxonomy

Whether speaking with a customer, teaching a class of students, or ordering materials from the wholesale grower, a designer must know the names of the vast number of plants used in floral design. *Taxonomy* is the science of classification of all organisms, both living and extinct. Carl Linnaeus (1707–1778), a Swedish botanist, naturalist, physician, and explorer, is considered the father of modern taxonomy. He believed that humans should discover, name, count, understand, and appreciate every living thing on earth.

> ### Did You Know?
> Plant morphology, as a scientific discipline, is over 200 years old. The biological concept of morphology was developed by Johann Wolfgang von Goethe in 1790.

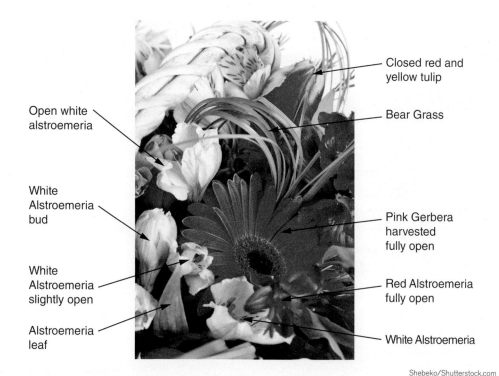

Open white alstroemeria

White Alstroemeria bud

White Alstroemeria slightly open

Alstroemeria leaf

Closed red and yellow tulip

Bear Grass

Pink Gerbera harvested fully open

Red Alstroemeria fully open

White Alstroemeria

Figure 4-2. Basic characteristics of items used in floral design include the shape, size, and color of both the flowers and the leaves. These elements are combined to make the finished design.

To create a uniform system of classification, Linnaeus introduced a hierarchy, or ranking, system. His system had two major classifications for living things: the Animal Kingdom and the Plant Kingdom. ***Kingdom*** was the highest category in the original ranking system. In the 1960s, scientists revised the model based on molecular research. They identified six different kingdoms that fall into three ***domains*** based on an organism's cellular characteristics. **Figure 4-3** shows the entire ranking system. For practical purposes in floral design, you need only be familiar with the family, genus, and species levels in this hierarchy.

Plant Families

At the *family* level, one main characteristic links plants together. For instance, the Euphorbiaceae family, or Euphorbia family, is a group in which all family members have a milky sap. The poinsettias *Euphorbia pulcherrima* and *Euphorbia punicea* are both members of this family, **Figure 4-4**. Although they are quite different, they are both members of the Euphorbia family. The family name always ends in the 'ae', as in Euphorbiac*eae*.

The broad classification of plants into a family helps floral designers understand how plants relate to each other. It provides information about the care and handling of plants with similar needs. For example, plants in the mint family share several characteristics, including square-shaped stems, opposite leaves, tiny flowers, and volatile oils in their leaves and stems. Their fragrance and flavors are derived from the plants' oils.

How Plants Are Classified

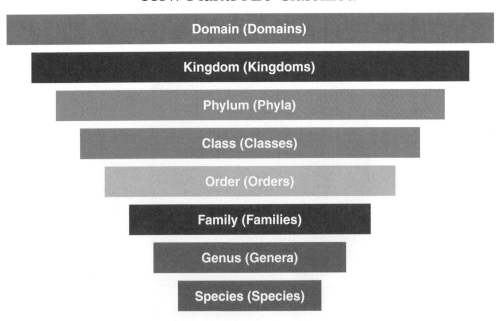

Domain (Domains)

Kingdom (Kingdoms)

Phylum (Phyla)

Class (Classes)

Order (Orders)

Family (Families)

Genus (Genera)

Species (Species)

Goodheart-Willcox Publisher

Figure 4-3. The taxonomy first developed by Carl Linnaeus. Classification allows scientists and students a way to sort and group organisms according to similar characteristics.

Sasimoto/Shutterstock.com; Malgorzata Litkowska/Shutterstock.com

Figure 4-4. Although they may look considerably different, *Poinsettia pulcherrima* and *Euphorbia punicea* (Jamaican poinsettia) are both members of the Euphorbiaceae family because they both have a milky sap. Poinsettias are very popular for the winter holidays and they are available in a variety of colors.

Genus and Species

Plants within each family are given a **genus** (plural *genera*) and **species** name to identify them individually. The genus name is similar to human last names, and the species name is similar to first names. The species name (sometimes referred to as the specific epithet) refers to notable characteristics of a specific plant. For example, *hirsute* indicates a plant that has hairy surfaces. It can also describe a place of origin, like *californicus* for something native to California. Sometimes the species name reflects the person who first cataloged it. For example, *Opuntia englemanii* is named for George Englemann, a scientist who journeyed west from St. Louis in search of new species.

The genus and species names are used as the short form of the plant's scientific name. Together, they distinguish a specific type of plant from all others. This usage of the genus and species names is known as **binomial nomenclature**. *Binomial* means "two names," and *nomenclature* means "naming system," or "taxonomy." Genus and species names are always italicized, and the genus name is capitalized. Sometimes the genus is abbreviated so that only the first letter is used, especially in lists, charts, and tables. For example, you may see *Euphorbia pulcherrima* listed as *E. pulcherrima*.

Both genus and species names are usually rooted in Latin (or sometimes Greek) words. Knowing the specific meanings will make using the names a more fun and comfortable practice. For example, *zebrinus*, meaning "zebra striped," is easily recognizable.

In the floral business, both scientific and common names are used to identify materials, so designers should become familiar with both. Regionally, common names can vary widely. Since scientific names are universal, the designer who understands them is better prepared to compete in the global workforce.

Did You Know?

Sneezewort Yarrow, which is also known as sneezeweed, earned its name because it was once used as a sneezing powder to get people to clear out their sinuses.

Plant Anatomy

Although plants in each family have major differences, they have some basic structures in common. Knowing the name of each structure can help you understand lectures and instructions given by growers and educators. This, in turn, can help you care for the plants and cut flowers you use in your designs.

Flowers

The parts of a flower are shown in **Figure 4-5**. At the end of a flower stalk, or *pedicel*, all of the parts of a flower, including the petals, are attached to the *receptacle*. This forms the basis for the flower and supports the reproductive structures.

Reproductive Structures

When you think of flowers, you probably think of brightly colored blossoms. While this is often the case, the flower is also the reproductive mechanism of many plants. Its *petals* are modified leaves that surround the reproductive parts of the flower. The petals often have bright colors or distinct scents that are designed to attract pollinators. The Gongora orchid is a prime example. It looks similar to its pollinators, the Euglossini bees (also called *orchid bees*). It also has a scent that attracts these bees.

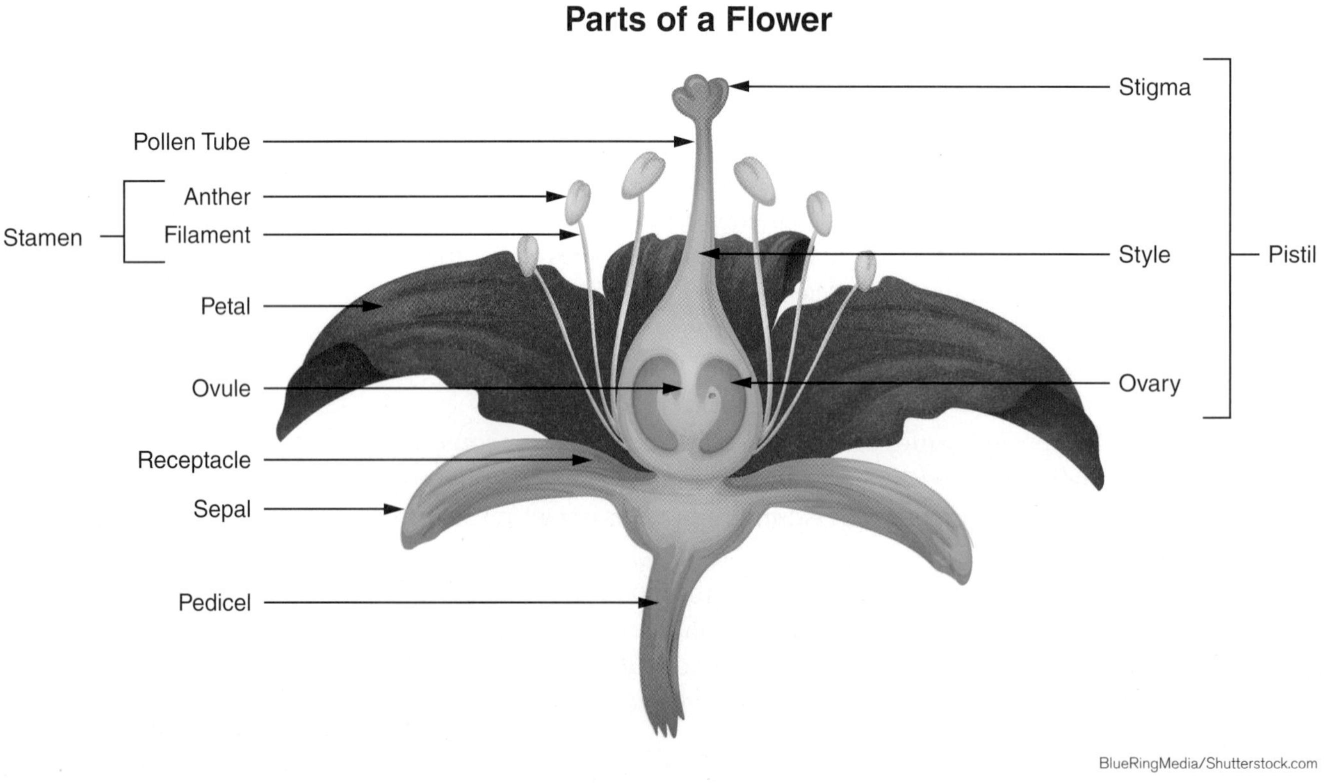

Did You Know?

William Harvey, the great 17th century plant physiologist, thought plants had a circulatory system like ours. He abandoned the idea after plant dissection failed to reveal a heart.

Parts of a Flower

BlueRingMedia/Shutterstock.com

Figure 4-5. The anatomy of a flower.

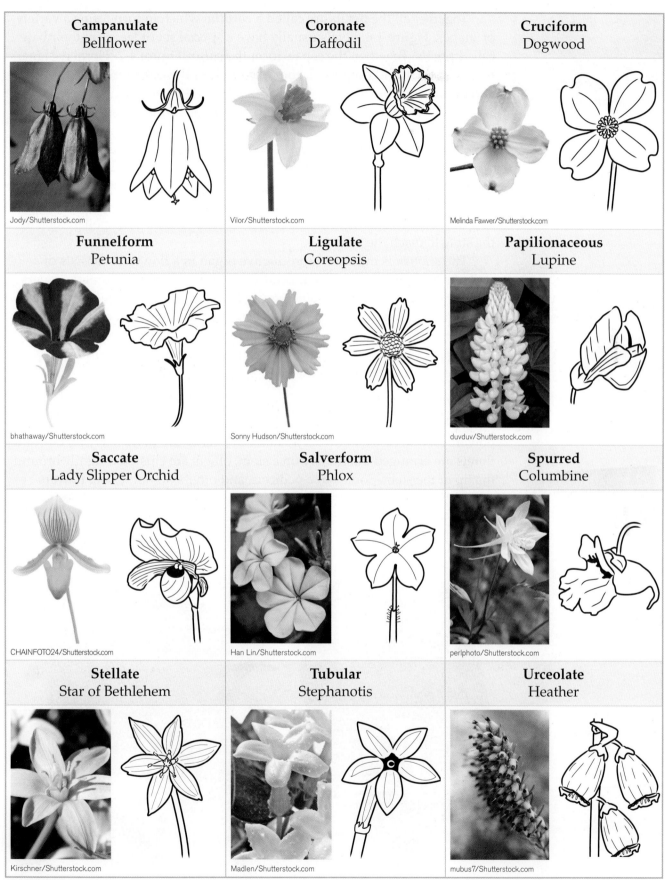

Figure 4-6. The images above are a very small selection of the many types of corollas.

Goodheart-Willcox Publisher

Together all the petals are called a *corolla*, which in turn forms a variety of shapes, **Figure 4-6**. Petals usually have a special set of leaves at their base called *sepals*. Together, the sepals form the *calyx*, **Figure 4-7**. Floral designers refer to the calyx of both roses and carnations as the insertion point for wiring and taping.

Many flowers have both male and female reproductive structures. These flowers are called *complete flowers*. Flowers that are missing some of the structures are *incomplete flowers*. The female reproductive organ is the *pistil*, which includes the carpel, stigma, and style. The *carpel*, or ovary, is the female reproductive organ. It encloses the ovules that develop into seeds after fertilization. It consists of the *stigma* and usually a *style*. The stigma collects the pollen to fertilize the ovules. The pollen travels down the pollen tube in the style to reach the carpel.

The *stamen* is the male reproductive organ in a flower. It consists of a stalk, or *filament*, with a pollen-producing *anther* at its tip. Floral designers may remove the anthers in some types of flowers. For example, the anthers are frequently removed from lilies, because the heavy pollen on the anthers can discolor the petals and surrounding surfaces. Removing the anthers from heavy pollinators will also prevent reproduction, which ultimately will increase the vase life of the flowers.

Inflorescence Patterns

Inflorescence refers to the characteristic development and arrangement of flowers on a stem. The flowers in an inflorescence are known as *florets*. Some florets are arranged alternately on a stem; others are clustered tightly around the tip of the stem. Some have pedicels, and others do not. Using flowers with different inflorescence can add beauty and interest to a floral design. **Figure 4-8** shows various forms of inflorescence.

Figure 4-7. Cross section exposing the flowers' reproductive structures.

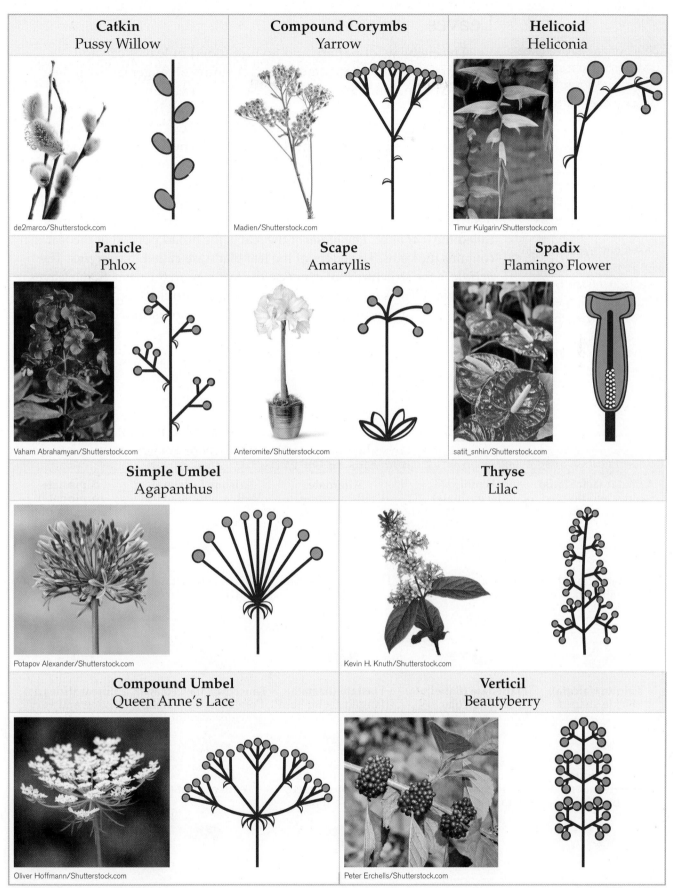

Figure 4-8. Inflorescence patterns.

Leaves

The elements of pattern and texture found in leaves can add focal interest to an arrangement. In fact, entire arrangements can be designed using only leaves. Leaves can have a variety of colors and *venation*, or patterns of veins. They can be round, oval, heart-shaped, or bladelike, **Figure 4-9**. They may attach to the stem of a plant opposite each other or in an alternate or whorled pattern. Sometimes many small leaflets make up one larger leaf. Leaves can be rough or smooth, shiny or dull, or soft or rigid.

In spite of their differences in appearance, most leaves have the same basic parts, **Figure 4-10**. The point at which the leaf attaches to a stem is called the *leaf base*. The *blade* of the leaf is the broad portion of the leaf that contains the veins. The edges of the leaf blade are called its *margins*. The *petiole* is the structure that connects the leaf base to the stem. Some leaves also have *stipules* on each side of the base. The stipules help protect the leaf bud. As the leaf matures, some stipules become thorns, and others retain their original shape.

Shape and Arrangement

Acicular (acicularis) Slender and pointed, needle-like 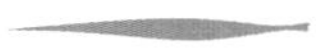	Acuminate (acuminata) Tapering to a long point 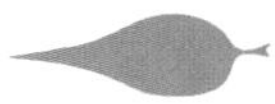	Alternate Leaflets arranged alternately 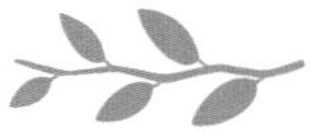	Aristate (aristata) With a spine-like tip 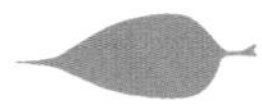	Bipinnate (bipinnata) Each leaflet a pinnate 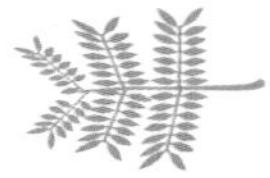
Cordate (cordata) Heart-shaped, with petiole attached to cleft 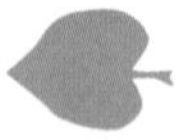	Cuneate (cuneata) Wedge-shaped, stem attaches to point 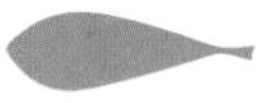	Deltoid (deltoidea) or deltate Triangular, stem attaches to side 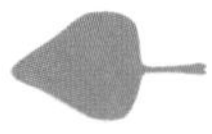	Digitate (digitata) Divided into finger-like lobes 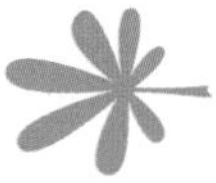	Elliptic (elliptica) Oval, with a short or no point 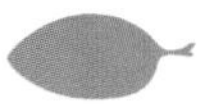
Falcate (falcata) Sickle-shaped 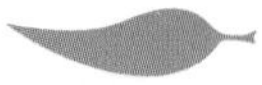	Flabellate (flabellata) Semicircular, or fan-like 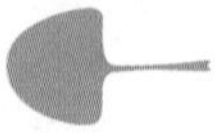	Hastate (hastata) Triangular with basal lobes 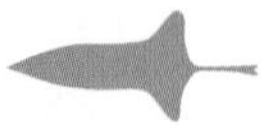	Lanceolate (lanceolata) Pointed at both ends, wider in middle 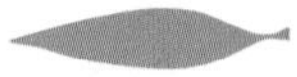	Linear (linearis) Long and very narrow 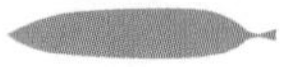
Lobed (lobata) Deeply indented margins 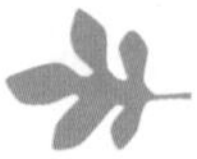	Obcordate (obcordata) Heart-shaped, stem attaches to point 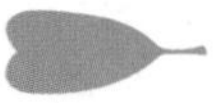	Obovate (obovata) Teardrop-shaped, narrow at base 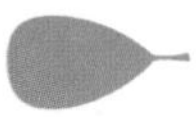	Obtuse (obtusus) With a blunt tip 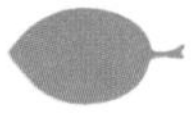	Opposite Leaflets in adjacent pairs 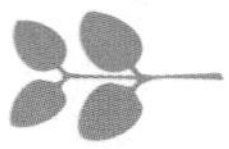

McSush/Debivort

Figure 4-9. Leaves have many different shapes and textures that can be used to add interest to a design.

Parts of a Leaf

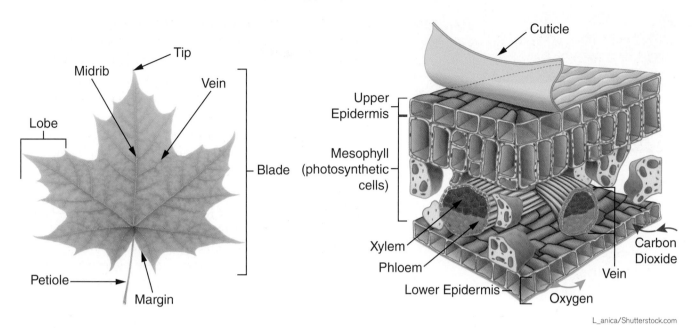

Figure 4-10. Parts of a leaf.

L_anica/Shutterstock.com

Shape and Arrangement				
Orbicular Circular	**Ovate (ovata)** Oval, egg-shaped, with tapering point	**Palmate (palmata)** Resembles a hand	**Pedate (pedata)** Palmate, divided lateral lobes	**Peltate (peltata)** Rounded, stem underneath
Perfoliate (perfoliata) Stem seeming to pierce leaves	**Odd-pinnate (imparipinnate)** Leaflets in rows, one at tip	**Even-pinnate** Leaflets in rows, two at tip	**Pinnatisect (pinnatifida)** Deep, opposite lobing	**Reniform (reniformis)** Kidney-shaped
Rhomboid (rhomboidalis) Diamond-shaped	**Rosette** Leaflets in tight circular rings	**Spatulate (spathulata)** Spoon-shaped	**Spear-shaped** Pointed, barbed base	**Subulate (subulata)** Awl-shaped with tapering point
Trifoliate/Ternate (trifoliolate/trifoliata) Leaflets in threes	**Tripinnate (tripinnata)** Leaflets are bipinnate	**Truncate (truncata)** With a squared off end	**Unifoliate (unifoliata)** With a single leaf	**Whorled** Rings of three or more leaflets

(Continued)

McSush/Debivort

sakhorn/Shutterstock.com

Figure 4-11. A cross section of lotus stems showing the xylem and phloem.

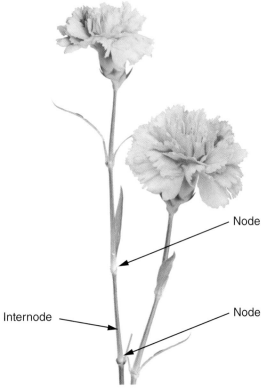

Node

Internode

Node

Quang Ho/Shutterstock.com

Figure 4-12. Carnations are cut above or below a node so that the slender internodal part of the stem can be inserted into the design.

Did You Know?

The largest stem in the world, the trunk of the giant sequoia tree, is up to 136 yards (115m) tall and 9 yards (8m) wide.

Stems

Stems are the structures that support the leaves and buds. They also contain the vascular system of the plant, carrying minerals, water, and sugar to the leaves and buds. *Xylem* vessels conduct water and minerals, and *phloem* vessels conduct food, **Figure 4-11**. These vessels are surrounded by the *cambium* or *meristem*, which is the site of active plant growth. Together, the xylem, phloem, and cambium are known as the *vascular bundle*. Stems can be long or short. They can be in unexpected places like underground as will tulips or potatoes. However, they must have leaves or buds to be classified as a stem.

The places along a stem where leaves, flowers, or branches are attached are called *nodes*. Nodes are an area of growth, where new leaves or flowers are produced. The area between the nodes is called the *internode*. Floral designers frequently cut the stem of a flower in the internode region, just above or below a node. A carnation, for example, has bulbous nodes. When cutting a carnation, the designer cuts off the node so that the narrower internode can be inserted into the floral foam, **Figure 4-12**.

Floral designers use many types of stems for a variety of applications, depending on their inherent qualities of strength or flexibility. For example, equisetum, or scouring rush, has a hollow stem between every node. The hollow stem allows a sturdy floral wire to be inserted to create bends. This is especially useful in contemporary style arrangements.

A *rhizome* is a stem that grows horizontally underground. The nodes of the stem put down roots and then form new plants. Water lilies and some irises are examples of flowering plants that have rhizomes.

Roots

Roots are the foundation of plants. They can take many forms, as shown in **Figure 4-13**. They have four major functions:

- Support and anchor the plant.
- Absorb and carry water and minerals.
- Store food and minerals.
- Provide a source of vegetative reproduction in certain types of plants.

| **Bulb,** Tulip | **Corm,** Freesia | **Tuber,** Dahlia | **Tuberous,** Daylily |

Denise Kappa/Shutterstock.com Stockbyte/Brand X Pictures/Thinkstock photowind/Shutterstock.com ID1974/Shutterstock.com

| **Rhizome,** Ginger | **Tap Root,** Dandelion | **Fibrous Root,** English Daisy |

Reika/Shutterstock.com Brzostowska/Shutterstock.com vilax/Shutterstock.com

Goodheart-Willcox Publisher

Figure 4-13. Root types.

Some plants can produce roots from a cutting taken from a leaf and or stem. This method of plant reproduction is called *vegetative reproduction*. African violets, mother-in-law's tongue, peperomia, and pothos can be *propagated* (reproduced) by leaf cutting. Willow branches can be propagated this way as well. A water-filled glass vase with cut willow branches eventually develops root systems.

Plant Physiology

Whereas plant anatomy describes the internal structures of a plant, *plant physiology* describes to the functions of the various parts of the plant. Plant functions include how the plant receives and processes nutrients and water, as well as how it receives the energy needed for growth.

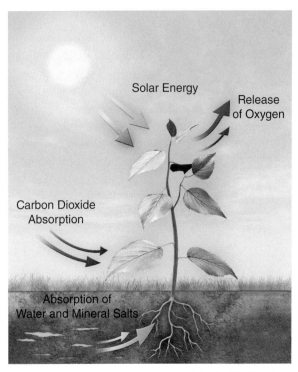

Andrea Danti/Shutterstock.com

Figure 4-14. Photosynthesis is the process plants use to make the food they need. During the process of photosynthesis, plants release oxygen into the atmosphere.

Leaf Functions

Leaves are the primary site of *photosynthesis*, the process by which green plants transform light energy into chemical energy for food. This process requires three main ingredients: light, water, and carbon dioxide. When the *chlorophyll* (the green pigment) in leaves is exposed to these ingredients, it combines them to produce the carbohydrates, or sugars, the plant needs to live. In the process, it releases oxygen into the environment. *Respiration* is the cellular process in which stored food reserves are converted into useful energy for the plant. See **Figure 4-14**.

Leaves are also involved in *transpiration*, a process by which water is transported from the roots to all parts of the plant and then evaporates from the leaves, **Figure 4-15**. When the water reaches the *stomata* (pores) on the underside of the leaves, the water evaporates. Temperature extremes, darkness, or internal water loss cause the stomata to close in order to prevent moisture loss. When conditions are more favorable, the stomata open and increase transpiration. See **Figure 4-16**. Floral designers need to know about transpiration to maximize the life of the cut leaves they use in designs.

Thinking Green

Oxygen Machines

Plants are natural air cleaners because they remove carbon dioxide from the air and release oxygen in its place. Aside from aesthetics and fresh produce, oxygen production is another good reason to plant roof gardens and green areas in cities.

Did You Know?

Studies indicate that about 10% of the moisture in earth's atmosphere comes from transpiration. The other 90% comes from evaporation from large bodies of water.

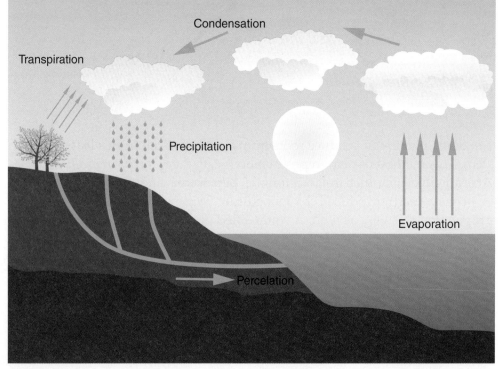

wawritto/Shutterstock.com

Figure 4-15. The transpiration process.

Stem Functions

One of the functions of a plant stem is to provide a framework to support the flowers and leaves. The stem also contains the vascular bundle described earlier in the chapter. The xylem is the part of the bundle that provides the stiffness needed to support the flowers and leaves. This is why, when a cut stem does not receive enough water, the flowers and leaves droop. The phloem absorbs the carbohydrates manufactured in the leaves and distributes them throughout the plant.

Green stems can also serve as secondary sites of photosynthesis. In addition, they can store some of the carbohydrates manufactured during photosynthesis.

Root Functions

Probably the most important function of roots is to absorb water and minerals from the surrounding soil. The vascular bundle in the stem extends down into the roots, where it picks up the water and nutrients and distributes them throughout the plant. Roots also anchor the plant in the ground. They can store carbohydrates, which is important for perennial plants (those that live more than one year). During the winter, those plants that lose their leaves have no way to make food. The carbohydrates stored in the roots allow the plants to survive until spring, when the leaves bud out.

Roots absorb water and minerals through tiny, hair-like projections called *root hairs*, **Figure 4-17**. The root hairs are only one cell thick, so they absorb the water and minerals readily. However, their extremely small size makes them fragile. They can easily be destroyed during transplanting.

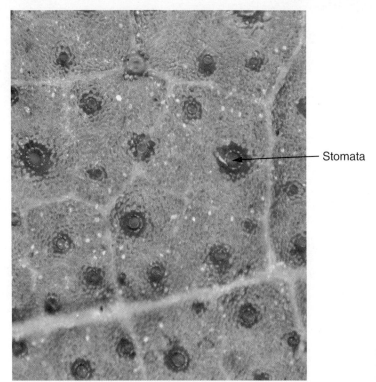

defun/iStock/Thinkstock

Figure 4-16. All above ground parts of a plant, including the flower petals, petioles, soft herbaceous stems, and leaves, have stomata. The stomata are located on the outer skin layer. Each one has two guard cells that surround the opening, or pore, called a stoma. The guard cells control the size of the stoma, opening the stoma more when conditions are favorable.

Tompet/Shutterstock.com

Figure 4-17. Roots absorb minerals and water through tiny root hairs. Carefully look for the smallest hair roots of this aloe vera plant.

Summary

- Understanding the characteristics of the flowers, stems, and leaves of plants helps floral designers make good choices for specific designs.
- Plant morphology is the study of the physical form and external structures of plants.
- Plant anatomy is the study of the internal structures of plants.
- Taxonomy is the classification of organisms and is used to assign the scientific names of plants.
- Plants are commonly identified by their genus and species names (binomial nomenclature).
- Flowers are often the reproductive mechanism of plants.
- Plant physiology is the study of how the internal structures, or anatomy, of plants function.

Review Questions

Go to www.g-wlearning.com/floraldesign/ to use the fill-in-form.

Answer the following questions using the information provided in this chapter.

1. What is the difference between plant morphology and plant anatomy?
2. List at least five families of plants that are commonly used in floral design, and give an example of a flower or plant in each family.
3. The science of classification of all organisms, both living and extinct, is _____.
4. What two levels of classification are used to identify plants for floral design purposes?
5. Briefly describe why plants produce flowers.
6. Briefly explain the difference between complete flowers and incomplete flowers.
7. *True or False?* The anthers are frequently removed from lilies because the pollen on the anthers can discolor the petals and surrounding surfaces.
8. *True or False?* The carpel is the male reproductive organ of a flower.
9. *True or False?* Together, the sepals of a flower form the corolla.
10. What is inflorescence?
11. List and briefly describe five parts of a leaf.
12. What purpose(s) does a plant stem serve?
13. Name four functions of roots.
14. *True or False?* Plant physiology describes the internal structures of a plant.
15. Briefly explain the process of photosynthesis.
16. Briefly explain the process of transpiration.
17. What purpose does the stomata of a leaf serve?
18. *True or False?* The phloem absorbs the carbohydrates manufactured in the plant and distributes them to the leaves.
19. *True or False?* Carbohydrates stored in the roots of perennials allow the plants to survive until spring.
20. *True or False?* The root hairs of plants are fragile and can easily be destroyed.

Activities

1. Create a seasonal journal by pressing 25 different flower or leaf forms throughout the semester.
2. Propagate African violets by leaf cuttings.
3. Study the vascular intake of nutrients in celery stems by conducting a dye test using water-soluble food dyes.
4. Dissect pieces of an aloe vera, calla lily, or other flower to study vascular tissues. Draw the dissected pieces and label them correctly.
5. Visit a botanical garden or arboretum and identify 25 different species of trees.

Critical Thinking

1. Why is it important for floral designers to understand the anatomy and physiology of the plants they use?
2. Plant morphology has little to do with keeping a plant or cut stem healthy. Why, then, do floral designers also need to know the morphology of the plants they use?

STEM Activities and Academics

1. **Science.** Find out more about flower pollination. Why do some plants need neighboring plants in order to produce blooms or fruits? Write a report summarizing your findings.
2. **Science.** Choose four different plants in your neighborhood that interest you. Find out the common name and the scientific name of each, using binomial nomenclature. Make a table with three columns: Common Name, Scientific Name, and Example. In the Example column, either draw a picture of each plant, or attach a photograph of the plant.

Communicating about Floral Design

1. **Speaking and Reading.** Create an informational report on taxonomy as it relates to plants. Explain how the hierarchy system is set up for the Plant Kingdom. Explain how the original ranking system was modified due to molecular research. Choose one plant family and list all of its plants and flowers. List the common characteristics that link these plants together. Include drawings or photographs of the most common family members. Present your report to the class.
2. **Speaking and Listening.** Visit a nearby arboretum, botanical garden, or a large flower growing operation. Ask to interview their botanical expert. Prepare a list of questions before your interview. Here are some questions you might ask: What is your work environment like? What are your job duties? What type of research are you currently doing? What type of facilities do you use for your research? What impact will your research have on the floriculture industry?

    Ask if you can have a tour of their facilities. Report your findings to the class, giving reasons why you would or would not want to pursue a career similar to that of the person you interviewed.
3. **Speaking and Listening.** Make a collage. Using pictures from magazines or free online resources, create a collage that helps you remember the function of each part of a flower and each part of a leaf. Show and discuss your collage in a group of four to five classmates. Are the other members of your group able to determine the system and functions that you tried to represent?

Chapter

5 Postharvest Processing, Conditioning, and Storage

objectives

After reading this chapter, you will be able to:

- Describe the grower's role in harvesting, pretreating, packing, and shipping cut flowers.

- Identify the characteristics retail florists look for when they are purchasing flowers from growers or wholesale florists.

- Carry out the procedure for processing floral shipments.

- Discuss the storage requirements of various types of cut flowers and foliage.

- Describe common techniques for working with specific species of flowers and foliage.

key terms

acidifier	ethylene inhibitor	pulsing
air embolism	ethylene scrubber	rehydration
biocide	geotropic	senescence
Chain of Life	grading	tropism
citric acid	phototropic	vase life
conditioning	precooling	
dry-packed	preservative	
ethylene	pretreatment	

Go to www.g-wlearning.com/floraldesign/ for online vocabulary activities using key terms from the chapter.

introduction

Proper handling of cut flowers begins long before they are harvested and continues through retail sale. In many cases, the flower shop even provides post-sale instructions to help consumers maximize the life of cut flowers. Different types of flowers and foliage have different needs, so the florist needs to understand the needs of specific types of flowers.

For instance, the preferred water level in a storage container holding calla lily stems is different than that for roses. The soft, pithy stem of the calla lily begins to weaken when it is placed in water. Therefore, the water level for calla lilies should be high enough to allow adequate water absorption but not high enough to cause stem decay.

Water is only one of many factors that affect the life span of cut flowers and foliage. Temperature, relative humidity, and preservatives are also important. By becoming proficient in the care and handling of plant materials, florists can prolong their freshness and maximize profits.

This chapter presents the basics of handling, processing, and caring for cut flowers and foliage. The Society of American Florists has a more detailed program called *Chain of Life*® that addresses every aspect of the care and handling of cut flowers, from harvest through final consumer. By paying close attention to conditions throughout the "chain of life," growers and florists can achieve longer-lasting flowers and higher quality.

Hongqi Zhang/iStock/Thinkstock

Figure 5-1. The care a plant receives before the flowers are harvested affects the quality and endurance of the blooms.

Harvesting and Shipping

Growers play an important part in the process of keeping cut flowers fresh. Proper irrigation, fertilization, and pest control tend to produce healthier flowers that last longer, **Figure 5-1**. The timing of harvest makes a difference, as well. Research has shown that flowering plants have the highest levels of water and carbohydrates (stored energy) in the late afternoon and early morning. Therefore, many flowers are harvested during the morning hours. An early-morning harvest is also preferred over late-afternoon harvest because a morning harvest leaves the rest of the day for processing and packing the flowers for shipment.

The stage at which the flowers are harvested varies depending on the type of flower and the intended market. Iris, for example, are harvested when buds are swollen and showing color, **Figure 5-2**. Flowers harvested for use in a local market can be cut when the flowers are more mature or fully open. **Figure 5-3** provides the best harvesting stage for several species. For a more extensive list, refer to the *Appendix*.

Goodheart-Willcox Publisher

Figure 5-2. Flowers like iris are harvested just as they begin to show color. Once processed and placed in water, they open quickly.

Common Name	Scientific Name	Harvest	Storage Life	Storage Temperature	Ethylene Sensitive	Vase Life
Alstroemeria	–	First flowers fully colored	2 weeks wet	38°–40°F (3.3°–4.4°C)	Yes	12–14 days
Anthurium	*Anthurium*	Spadix is 50%–75% mature	2–4 weeks	53°–63°F (12.5°–17.2°C)	No	10–25 days
Aster, China	*Callistephus chinensis*	Fully open flowers	1–3 weeks	36°–40°F (2.2°–4.4°C)	No	5–10 days
Baby's Breath	*Gypsophila* spp.	Flowers open but not overly mature	1–3 weeks	40°F (4.4°C)	Yes	5–11 days
Bachelor's Button	*Centaurea* spp.	Flowers beginning to open	5–14 days	36°–38°F (2.2°–3.3°C)	Yes	5–7 days
Bells of Ireland	*Moluccella laevis*	Bells are fully open	2 weeks	36°–38°F (2.2°–3.3°C)	Yes	7–14 days
Bird of Paradise	*Strelitzia reginae*	Just beginning to open	2 weeks	55°–70°F (12.8°–21.1°C)	No	7–14 days
Calla Lily	*Zantedeschia* sp.	Mostly open	1 week	50°–70°F (10.0°–21.1°C)	No	4–8 days
Carnation	*Dianthus* sp.	In the bud stage when being stored	2–4 weeks	36°–40°F (2.2°–4.4°C)	Yes	7–14 days
Chrysanthemum	*Dendranthema* sp.	Mostly open, depends on use	2–4 weeks	36°–40°F (2.2°–4.4°C)	No	6–12 days
Cone Flower	*Echinacea*	Petals expanding; 50% of globe is blue	2 weeks	40°F (4.4°C)	Yes	7–10 days
Daffodil	*Narcissus* cvs.	Goose neck stage	1–3 weeks	36°–40°F (2.2°–4.4°C)	Yes	5–12 days
Dahlia	*Dahlia* cvs.	Fully open flowers	3–5 days	40°F (4.4°C)	No	7–14 days
Daisy, Marguerite	*Anthemis* sp.	Just opening	1–2 weeks	36°F (2.2°C)	Depends on species	5–10 days
Delphinium	*Leucanthemum*	One-half florets open	1–2 days	40°F (4.4°C)	Yes	5–7 days
Gladiolus	*Gladiolus* cvs.	1 to 5 buds showing color	5–8 days	35°–42°F (1.7°–5.6°C)	Yes	6–10 days
Hyacinth, Common Grape	*Muscari botryoides*	One-half florets open	3 days	35°–41°F (1.7°–5.0°C)	Somewhat	3–7 days
Iris	*Iris* sp.	Showing color	1–2 weeks	36°–40°F (2.2°–4.4°C)	Yes	3–6 days
Larkspur	*Delphinium* sp.	Half florets open	2 weeks	36°–38°F (2.2°–3.3°C)	Yes+	4–10 days
Lily	*Lilium* sp.	Buds in color	2–3 weeks	36°–40°F (2.2°–4.4°C)	Yes	7–12 days
Lupine	*Lupinus* cvs. Russell	One-half to three-quarters buds open	3 days	40°F (4.4°C)	Yes	7 days
Peony	*Paeonia* sp.	Buds just in color	2–6 weeks	36°–40°F (2.2°–4.4°C)	Very	4–10 days
Ranunculus	*Ranunculus asiaticus*	Buds beginning to open	7–10 days	36°–41°F (2.2°–5.0°C)	Yes	5–7 days
Snapdragon	*Antirrhinum majus*	One-third florets open, buds at top showing color	1–2 weeks	40°F (4.4°C)	Very	5–7 days
Statice	*Limonium* spp.	Almost fully open flowers	2–4 weeks	35°–40°F (1.7°–4.4°C)	Yes	4–8 days
Stephanotis	*Stephanotis floribunda*	Fully open flowers	1 week	40°F (4.4°C)	Yes	3–4 days
Stock	*Matthiola incana*	One-half florets open	3–5 days	40°F (4.4°C)	Yes	5–8 days
Sunflower	*Helianthus annuus*	Fully open flowers	1 week	36°–41°F (2.2°–5.0°C)	Depends on species	5–14 days
Tulip	*Tulipa* cvs.	Half-colored buds	2–3 weeks	36°–40°F (2.2°–4.4°C)	Yes	3–6 days
Zinnia	*Zinnia elegans*	Fully open flowers	5 days	37°–39°F (2.8°–3.9°C)	No	6–10 days

Goodheart-Willcox Publisher

Figure 5-3. Harvest stage, storage life, and other characteristics of flowers commonly used in floral design.

Goodheart-Willcox Publisher

Figure 5-4. Lisianthus are harvested and shipped with a few flowers open, and several buds showing color along the stem. The unopened buds of this flower are mature enough to also be used individually in designs.

Pro Tip

Cutting Garden Processing
Because flowers contain the highest amount of carbohydrates in the morning and evening, it is preferred to cut materials in the morning hours.

Goodheart-Willcox Publisher

Figure 5-5. Cymbidium orchids packaged for wholesale markets are stored in a separate and warmer tropical cooler while awaiting purchase. Tropical plant materials at the retail level should also be stored at the appropriate temperature.

Flowers that will be shipped to markets at distant locations are often harvested at the bud stage. Flowers in bud stage are less difficult to transport because they retain moisture better, are less likely to be damaged, and take up less space than more mature flowers. Flowers in bud stage are also less sensitive to ethylene gas and handle dry storage very well. Lisianthus are good examples of flowers that are sold in bud form at the wholesale level, **Figure 5-4**.

Foliage, on the other hand, is generally harvested after all of the leaves are fully formed and expanded. This practice helps prevent wilting of underdeveloped leaves after harvest.

Pretreatments

Although the flower shop is responsible for the care and processing of flowers after they arrive, growers may apply *pretreatments* to help extend the life of cut flowers. For example, many growers use a technique called *pulsing* immediately after harvesting some types of flowers. Pulsing consists of placing the cut flowers into a sugar solution, usually at a low temperature, for a few hours. This provides a food source for the flowers and typically extends their useful life span, or *vase life*.

Some types of flowers, including mums, gerberas, and roses, benefit from pretreatment with a *citric acid* solution. The stems are dipped into the citric acid solution before they are placed in any other type of hydration or pulsing pretreatment. Citric acid is an *acidifier*. It adjusts the acidity of the stems to a level that encourages the uptake of water and nutrients.

Another important requirement is cooling the flowers as soon as possible after harvesting. Most cut flowers should be cooled to a temperature between 1°C and 2°C (33°F and 35°F) and maintained at that temperature throughout transportation or distribution. The only exceptions are tropical flowers, which must be maintained at temperatures above 10°C (50°F) to avoid damage. Examples of flowers that may be damaged by cooler temperatures include bird of paradise and tropical orchids such as cymbidium, **Figure 5-5**.

Grading

Another activity that may occur before the products are shipped is *grading*. Certain flowers, including roses, carnations, and gladioli, are classified in grades. A flower's grade is usually based at least partially on stem length. Grades can also be assigned according to characteristics such as flower size, petal count, stem straightness, uniformity, foliage quality, number of defects, and expected vase life. Descriptions of the grades differ globally, but in the United States, grades of roses by size include short, medium, long, fancy, and extra-fancy categories.

Packing and Transportation

The primary needs of a cut flower are water, nutrients, and refrigeration. All along the harvesting chain, water is a critical component. Ironically, many flowers are *dry-packed*, or dry-shipped, and are transported at low temperatures without water. See **Figure 5-6**. Cut flowers are placed in specially designed cardboard boxes that have holes in the ends to allow air circulation. In most cases, the boxes are long and flat to avoid crushing the flowers. Growers use various methods to hold the flowers in place. Cleats, or spacers, can be made of wood, padded metal, or plastic and are often stapled directly to the box to secure the flowers. Newspaper and plastic netting are often used to protect the blooms.

When flowers are removed from refrigeration for packing, their temperature begins to rise as a result of respiration. The rising temperature as may cause water condensation inside the plastic sleeves, which can decrease vase life. To help minimize this process, packing boxes are designed with holes. Openings in the packing boxes allow the temperature of the packed flowers to be reduced quickly through a process called *precooling*. In this process, the boxes are placed with the holes in line with a forced air flow in a refrigerated storage area. When they have reached

Pro Tip

Flowers stored in water continue developing and maturing. Flowers stored in water instead of being dry-packed will be more mature on removal from storage.

Pro Tip

The circulation fans in storage coolers should be positioned to pull air through rather than push it through. Pushing the air results in dead spaces where there is little air movement.

Did You Know?

To help keep the humidity in shipping boxes near 100%, foliage is wrapped in plastic sheeting and the inside surfaces of the boxes may be coated with wax.

hansenn/iStock/Thinkstock; Erik Ferkranus/iStock/Thinkstock

Figure 5-6. For long-distance shipping, cut flowers are often dry-packed in heavy cardboard boxes. The flowers may also be wrapped in cellophane to aid in moisture retention and protect them from damage.

Baisch & Skinner Wholesale, St. Louis MO

Figure 5-7. Most buckets used for transporting flowers in water are rectangular- or square-shaped to fit efficiently in refrigerated truck trailers. Standard shapes also make moving materials on pallets easier throughout the wholesale warehouse.

the required temperature, they are kept in refrigerated storage and ideally shipped in refrigerated units to maintain the low temperature during transport. If refrigeration is not possible during transport, they are packed in insulated containers or are surrounded by ice or cooling packs. Note, however, that tropical flowers are not precooled.

A newer system allows flowers to be transported vertically in water packs, which are sturdy, water-holding containers that fit compactly into refrigerated tractor-trailers. This system allows the flowers to remain hydrated at all times, limiting the risk of damage to vascular tissues by water loss. Procona™ buckets are an example of containers made specifically for the transport of cut flowers in water, **Figure 5-7**. Newer brands of water packs are made from recyclable corrugated cardboard produced domestically.

Purchasing

When purchasing flowers, the florist examines the products closely. The *quality* of material is key. The florist analyzes the health of the leaves, the size of the buds, and the stage of development, because these factors help determine the life expectancy of the plant material. Wholesalers, as well as retailers, need to conduct quality checks on a regular basis, **Figure 5-8**. Any type of damage can shorten the life of any perishable material.

Knowing the life expectancy of various materials helps florists get the best return on their investment.

Wholesale florists, growers, and retail florists price their products according to quality and, if the product has been graded, according to grade. Florists purchase the grade and quality needed for their intended designs. For example, corsage work does not require a rose graded extra-long, because the stem length is not necessary. A rose graded as short would be more appropriate and more cost-effective.

> **Pro Tip**
>
> Flower quality will not improve beyond the moment they arrive from a supplier or grower. Always select the highest quality materials to begin your designs.

Baisch & Skinner Wholesale, St. Louis MO

Figure 5-8. Quality control checks are performed at every level of transportation. Entire bundles suspected of possible injury or damage are often checked by hand to ensure a salable product.

Step-by-Step

Processing Floral Shipments

When a shipment arrives from the grower or wholesale florist, retail florists should follow this sequence of events:

1. Open the boxes upon arrival to allow for air circulation.
2. Prepare the containers in advance. Fill containers to an appropriate water level and add flower preservative as prescribed.
3. Unpack the flowers and examine them for damages; remove broken pieces.
4. Remove all foliage that will be below the water level.
5. Depending on flower variety and stem length, cut 2″–3″ off the bottom tip of the stems using a clean knife or pruners; cut on an angle. Quickly dip stems into hydrating solution (if being used).
6. Place the stems into a clean container and keep them at room temperature until materials are rehydrated. Hydration may take 30 minutes or more depending on the type of flower.
7. Place the container into a cooler or refrigerated storage facility with controlled temperature, humidity, and air circulation.

Post-Shipment Processing and Conditioning

Inspection upon Delivery

When inspecting a shipment of cut flowers, the florist should note any of the following problems:

- Freezing or extremely high temperatures outside or within delivery vehicles
- Browning tips
- Pale color
- Wilting
- Pale or yellow leaves

Minimal problems may be expected upon delivery. See **Figure 5-9**. However, if a third party delivered the flowers, there is a chance they were exposed to warm or extremely cold temperatures before they reached the shop. If the boxes are damaged or have water stains on them, flower stems may be broken or the flowers may be smashed. There may even be mold in the box if it was extremely wet at some point of

Goodheart-Willcox Publisher

Figure 5-9. You should always review products upon arrival for damages during shipping. Stems may be broken or flowers may be smashed. Other problems may be present due to age or improper handling.

Goodheart-Willcox Publisher

Figure 5-10. Stems are placed in water containing hydrating solution immediately after cutting.

Goodheart-Willcox Publisher

Figure 5-11. Recutting the stems upon arrival removes the clot or scab at the cut end and allows the xylem to take up water for efficient rehydration.

its journey. If a substantial percentage of the shipment is damaged or not as expected, the florist should contact the grower or wholesale florist immediately to discuss the quality of the shipment.

Rehydration

Water is the single most important element to keep flowers fresh after delivery from a supplier. *Rehydration* is therefore a top priority, especially when flowers are dry-packed. Stems are placed in water that contains a hydrating solution, **Figure 5-10**. This solution is formulated to encourage the stems to take up water, so they recover more quickly. The process is usually performed at room temperature. Many people refer to this process of rehydrating and providing nutrients to the cut flowers as *conditioning*.

Water Uptake

When a flower is harvested, it forms a scab-like seal at the cut end. When a shipment of cut flowers arrives at the flower shop, stems should be recut at an angle 2"–3" above the cut end to remove the scab and provide a new, clean entry for water through the xylem. Materials purchased bundled from the wholesaler may be cut initially with a commercial cutter, **Figure 5-11**. This should be done before the stems are rehydrated to maximize rehydration and minimize the time the cut flowers are without water.

Even after the stem is recut, clogging of the xylem may prevent it from taking up water. One of the most common causes of clogging is bacteria and other microorganisms that flow into the xylem along with the water. Bacteria that are present on the knife, in the containers, or even the water itself when decaying leaves are left below the waterline can enter the xylem. As the bacteria multiply, the stem becomes clogged.

For this reason, containers and tools must be cleaned and checked on a regular basis. Scrubbing the containers with small amounts of a bleach solution helps prevent bacteria from growing. Commercial cleaners are also available. Plastic containers are preferred. They are lightweight and easy to keep clean. Tools can be cleaned by scrubbing with soap and water.

Step-by-Step

Proper Hydration

Keep in mind that the water balance of a fresh-cut flower will determine its level of hydration, turgidity, vase life, and freshness. Properly preparing and hydrating your flowers and foliage will keep your inventory fresh, and give customers the best product possible.

1 Clean your buckets with a product that will remove any bacteria left behind from the last bunch of flowers. *The importance of cleanliness cannot be stressed enough.* A properly-treated flower placed in a dirty bucket may die from the microbes in the dirty bucket.

2 Fill the buckets 1/3 full with warm water and floral food solution to the specifications of the manufacturer. Warm water will dissolve the rehydration chemical more easily and enhance water uptake in the first 24 hours.

3 Gently remove the plastic sleeve and remove the foliage on the stems that may fall below the waterline of the bucket. Cut the flowers with a floral knife on an angle. Dip the end of the cut stem into a citric acid solution for 3 to 5 seconds to aid in water uptake.

4 Immediately place the cut flowers in the prepared bucket. Do *not* recut the flowers. Leave the flowers out of the cooler for a minimum of one hour. This time will vary based on the flowers that are being processed.

Michaela Stejskalova/Shutterstock.com

Figure 5-12. Special processing is necessary to keep stems straight and maximize water absorption with gerberas. The result of bacterial stem clogging is bent neck, then wilting of petals.

Pro Tip

You may have heard to use aspirin or copper pennies as homemade floral preservatives. The best option is a commercial fresh flower food.

Another cause of clogged stems is an *air embolism*—a bubble of air that enters the xylem. Water cannot move past the air bubble, so the stem cannot transport water and nutrients to the flower, **Figure 5-12**. For this reason, underwater cutters are often used to process flowers. Research has shown that although underwater cutters are effective in theory, stems and debris left in the cutting water solution introduces bacteria into the freshly cut stem. It is best to use a sharp knife and plunge stems into flower food solutions immediately after cutting.

Water Quality

The quality of the water is also important to the vase life of cut flowers. They need pure, clean water. Tap water is easily accessible and always available to process flowers. However, tap water often contains chemical compounds that are detrimental to flowers. Fluoride, for example, can shorten the vase life of gerberas, freesia, gladiolus, and some types of roses. Sodium, typically present in soft water, is toxic to roses and carnations. Hard water contains minerals that can raise the pH, or alkalinity, of the water. Minerals can be removed from tap water using a commercial deionizer, but the cost of the equipment and upkeep outweigh the slight disadvantage of using municipal water.

Preservatives

Flower foods, or *preservatives*, are used to prolong the life of cut flowers. Fresh flower foods should be used during the entire postharvest period. The grower, wholesale florist, retail florist, and consumer can all benefit from using a flower food.

The three primary ingredients in floral preservatives are sugar, biocide, and an acidifier. Some manufacturers use dextrose, which does not clump; or sucrose, which is more soluble than dextrose. The sugars (carbohydrates) provide a source of food and nutrients for the cut flower. A *biocide*, or germicide, is included in the preservative to kill bacteria, fungi, yeast, and mold.

An acidifier, as discussed earlier in the chapter, reduces the pH of the water. Acidifiers produce the ideal level of acidity, with a pH level between 3.0 to 4.5. Citric acid is one of the most effective acidifiers. Aluminum sulfate is effective in water that is high in salts. Any brand of commercial preservative should be used as directed. The acidifier also stabilizes the flowers' pigment, helping them keep their bright colors.

At this point, give flowers about an hour to completely rehydrate. After rehydration, they are placed into a cooler or refrigeration unit, as described in the next section. Both dry-packed and flowers in water are stored in temperature- and humidity-controlled coolers, **Figure 5-13**.

Goodheart-Willcox Publisher

Figure 5-13. In this walk-in cooler, a wholesaler displays dry-packed bunches of flowers and flowers in water that have already been processed. Florists select their materials from the wholesaler's inventory displayed in these walk-in coolers.

Storage Considerations

It is critical for flowers to be kept at the correct temperature to maximize their life span. When temperatures begin to rise, some flowers develop more rapidly, and others do not develop at all. In either case, vase life is reduced. Maintaining proper postharvest storage conditions includes paying attention not only to temperature, but also to humidity and air circulation.

Temperature

At the flower shop, refrigerated storage units are used to maintain the proper conditions. More than one storage unit is usually needed. For example, the florist may want a refrigerated display case to showcase premade floral designs, as well as a storage cooler to maximize the life span of flowers that have not yet been used, **Figure 5-14**. Also, if the florist carries tropical flowers, these flowers must be maintained at a different temperature than most other flowers.

Storage units have controls to set the temperature, relative humidity, and air circulation at optimum levels for the flowers being stored. Temperature requirements are the same as those used immediately after harvest and during transport. Cut flowers and foliage should be stored at 33°F and 35°F (1°C and 2°C), except tropical or subtropical flowers, which should be stored at temperatures above 50°F (10°C). Although some people may use regular refrigeration units to store flowers, it is best to invest in a floral cooler. Floral coolers are designed to keep a much higher humidity level than a regular refrigerator and the airflow is baffled so it doesn't dry out the flowers. Floral coolers may also have an ethylene filtration system.

bst2012/Shutterstock.com

Figure 5-14. Presentation storage cases maintain proper conditions while allowing customers to view floral products.

Goodheart-Willcox Publisher

Figure 5-15. Placing boxes of dry-packed flowers slightly apart in a storage cooler improves airflow, helping to lower respiration and increasing heat removal.

Pro Tip

Ripening rooms in a warehouse should be vented to the outside to prevent the accumulation of ethylene around the cut flowers.

BW Folsom/Shutterstock.com

Figure 5-16. When stressed or exposed to ethylene, carnations show signs of wilting.

Relative Humidity and Circulation

The relative humidity is important because the process of transpiration does not end when the flower is cut. In a dry environment, transpiration speeds up, so flowers lose water faster. Refer to Chapter 4, *Plant Structures and Functions*, for more information about transpiration. To reduce water loss due to transpiration, the relative humidity in the storage area should be maintained between 95% and 99%.

You might think that air circulation speeds up transpiration, and that is partly true. However, moderate air circulation is important for another reason. As flowers age, they produce chemicals and waste gases that, if not removed, can cause the aging process to speed up dramatically. To remove them, floral storage units have low-speed fans that draw air out of the unit and replace it with fresh air periodically. Most experts agree that there should be a full air exchange in the cooler at least once every hour.

In storage coolers, it is important to remember that air must be able to flow through the stored boxes as well as around them. Place the boxes slightly apart so that airflow is maximized, **Figure 5-15**.

Ethylene Sensitivity

Ethylene is a naturally occurring plant hormone that is often used in agriculture to force the ripening of fruit. It is also called the "aging hormone," because it triggers the *senescence*, or biological aging, of flowers, plants, and fruit. Ethylene is produced naturally by damaged, stressed, or old plant materials. Non-plant sources, such as vehicle exhaust, heater fumes, and cigarette smoke also produce ethylene.

Even the smallest amount of ethylene can damage some cut flower species. The chart in **Figure 5-3** includes a column listing flowers that are sensitive to ethylene. The visual result of ethylene exposure includes yellowing leaves or pale flower color, unopened buds, and prematurely dropped petals, **Figure 5-16**. Carnations, in particular, develop a "sleepiness" or wilted appearance when exposed to ethylene gas. Fruits, especially pieces damaged in some way, produce high levels of ethylene. This is why fruit should never be stored openly in a cooler with cut flowers.

It is necessary for growers, wholesale florists, and retail florists to develop strategies for preventing ethylene damage. Three main strategies are used to prevent damage from ethylene: prevention, removal, and inhibition.

Ethylene pollution can be prevented by:

- Removing diseased and dying plant material.
- Having good sanitation practices.
- Storing flowers separately from fruits and vegetables.
- Making sure gas heaters in greenhouses and handling areas are working properly.

Ethylene can be removed from the atmosphere by:

- Maintaining good air circulation and ventilation in handling and storage areas.
- Using *ethylene scrubbers* or filtration systems in cold storage areas, **Figure 5-17**.

Finally, the effect of ethylene on flowers can be inhibited using *ethylene inhibitors*. In the past, the chemical most commonly used to inhibit the effect of ethylene was silver thiosulfate (STS). STS acted on the flower's ethylene receptors and production sites to protect it from ethylene in the environment. It also prevented the flower itself from producing ethylene. This was typically done at the grower level. Now, however, STS has been banned in The Netherlands and some other countries because it poses an environmental threat. Although it is still legal in the United States, research continues into replacement chemicals and it is no longer widely sold or used by florists.

The most widely used antiethylene agent is 1-Methylcyclopropene (1-MCP). 1-MCP is an organic chemical similar in make up to ethylene, so it binds to ethylene receptor sites. In this way, ethylene molecules cannot take hold and age plant tissues toward senescence. Mixed with water, 1-MCP becomes a gas and is released into the air. It must be used in closed spaces such as tightly-closed greenhouses and cut flower coolers. Because of these restrictions, it is mostly used at the grower level. It is safe to use and not harmful to the environment.

Flowers

Customers will remember how long the flowers in an arrangement lasted even though they may not recall anything about the design. Even a novice flower-giver and flower-receiver can easily distinguish between

Thinking Green

Recovering Silver from STS

The environmental objection to STS is related to concerns about silver disposal. A system has been developed that allows the silver from STS to be recovered and recycled. Many florists in the United States are now using this method to reduce the environmental impact of STS.

Goodheart-Willcox Publisher

Figure 5-17. Most florists either use storage units that include ethylene filtration systems or add freestanding units that can remove up to 99% of the ethylene produced by the flowers. The ethylene scrubbers pictured above are a part of the filtration system.

Goodheart-Willcox Publisher

Figure 5-18. Buckets of red, white, and pink ranunculas have been cut and placed into water. Flowers that are water stressed may be incorrectly judged by consumers as old.

a wilting and non-wilting flowers. See **Figure 5-18**. This chapter contains many excellent recommendations for handling flowers and prolonging vase life. The following sections describe a few special techniques that apply to specific species.

Working with Roses

As described earlier in this chapter, all foliage that would fall below the water level in a vase must be removed. This is particularly difficult when working with roses because of their thorns, **Figure 5-19**. The thorns on a rose stem are typically pointed downward to discourage predators from climbing up the stems. To minimize injury when removing the foliage, pull the leaves off in a downward motion.

Commercial rose thorn and leaf strippers are also available. Typically constructed of metal, the spring-loaded tool has a V-shaped channel that allows the rose stem to move through the clasped stripper while the thorns and leaves are stripped away, **Figure 5-20**. Caution should be used to avoid damaging the exterior tissue of the stem. Removing the sharp tips is preferred to peeling the entire thorn from the stem. This practice helps avoid damaging the exterior stem surface, making the rose more susceptible to disease.

Synthetic hand grippers are also available for removing rose thorns, **Figure 5-20**. The flat, hand-sized material provides a protective surface between the thorns and the flower processor. This method works best when thorns and leaves are removed from one rose at a time. Each florist and flower shop uses the method that works best with its processing system.

The Naked Eye/Shutterstock.com; Hemerocallis/Shutterstock.com; Aphichart/Shutterstock.com

Figure 5-19. Leaving the thorns on the rose stem do not detract any beauty from the flower, but if the roses are being presented individually and not in an arrangement, people are likely to get scratched.

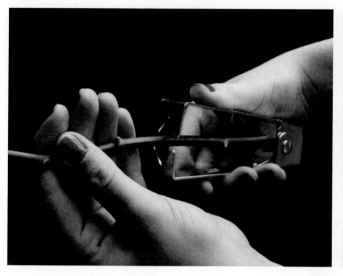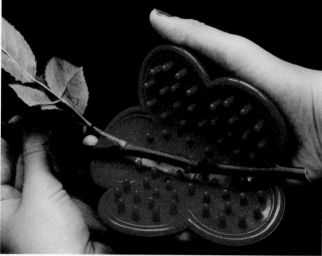

Goodheart-Willcox Publisher

Figure 5-20. Commercial rose thorn and leaf strippers should be used with care to avoid damaging the exterior of the stem. Synthetic hand grippers protect the hands from thorns.

Dealing with Tropisms

Tropisms, or growth curvatures, are the involuntary response of a cut flower toward or away from a stimulus, such as heat, light, or gravity. Gladiolus, for example, are *geotropic*—they bend away from the ground or gravity. Never store containers of gladiolus or other geotropic flowers horizontally. Store them vertically against a wall or a vertical support. This keeps the tips from turning upward or away from gravity, which distorts their form. Snapdragons are also geotropic, needing to be stored in vertical boxes when transported from the grower to the wholesaler and while stored in the cooler of a wholesale distributor in order to keep the stems straight, **Figure 5-21**.

 Pro Tip

Calla lilies may arrive bent. Simply turn the box over and leave it for 12 hours before processing the flowers. Tying the flowers in a bundle while hydrating will also prevent them from bending.

Goodheart-Willcox Publisher

Figure 5-21. Geotropic flowers bend away from gravity. Snapdragons are shipped and stored vertically in the wholesale cooler to deter curvature of the flower tips.

Marta Teron/Shutterstock.com

Figure 5-22. Phototropic flowers bend toward a light source. In some species, such as tulips or daffodils, this bending can be fairly dramatic as the flowers follow the path of sunlight throughout the day.

Goodheart-Willcox Publisher

Figure 5-23. Certain foliage, like plumosa fern, only needs a light misting and an air-tight bag with cool storage.

Phototropic flowers use light as a source of energy, so they always bend toward the light. Anemones and tulips are an example of flowers with phototropic behavior. They can create unusual lines of curvature within designs but should always be used with caution. They will continue to bend toward light sources, even after a design shape is completed, **Figure 5-22.**

Foliage

Although the leaves of some flowering plants are used in floral design, many are not because they do not keep as long as the flower. If leaves are thin and soft, they will wilt rapidly. Sturdy, strong-veined foliage such as magnolia, salal, and galax, has a much longer vase life.

The care and handling of cut foliage is different from that of cut flowers. Floral preservatives may or may not be used, and many materials are not stored in water containers. However, the issue of transpiration must still be addressed. Recall that transpiration continues even after the flower or foliage has been cut from the plant.

As with cut flowers, increasing the relative humidity of the storage environment helps reduce water loss from foliage due to transpiration. Some types of foliage require placement in water containers, but the majority only require processes to minimize the amount of transpiration. For example, pittosporum and other woody stem foliages do well when stored in water. With other types of cut greens, florists maintain the humidity by storing the foliage in plastic bags or boxes with a light plastic wrap, **Figure 5-23.** Processing involves spraying water on the foliage surface and tightly sealing the bag before refrigerating.

Most greens should be stored at the same temperature level as cut flowers and with proper air circulation. **Figure 5-24** provides storage temperatures for commonly used foliage.

Florist Greens	Length	Texture	Storage Temperature	Storage Life	Vase Life
Alocasia	8″–36″	Coarse	60°F (15.5°C)	–	7–14 days
Anthurium	8″–12″	Coarse	55°F–40°F (12.5°C–4°C)	1 week	7–14 days
Asparagus, plumose	8″–36″	Fine	35°F–40°F (2°C–4°C)	2–3 weeks	6–14 days
Asparagus, sprengerii	8″–36″	Fine	35°F–40°F (2°C–4°C)	2–3 weeks	6–14 days
Aspidistra	8″–36″	Coarse	40°F–55°F (4°C–13°C)	2 weeks	14–21 days
Boxwood	6″–18″	Fine	35°F–40°F (2°C –4°C)	1–2 months	3–5 weeks
Brake fern	3′	Coarse	33°F–40°F (0.5°C–4°C)	3 weeks	2–5 days
Camellia	12″–24″	Leathery	40°F (4°C)	4 weeks	3 weeks
Cedar	18″–30″	Prickly	33°F–40°F (0.5°C–4°C)	4 weeks	3–6 days
Croton leaves	6″ or more	Smooth	35°F–40°F (2°C–4°C)	2 weeks	4 weeks
Dagger and wood ferns	10″–24″	Fine	33°F–40°F (0.5°C–4°C)	2–3 months	10–20 days
Dieffenbachia	6″–24″	Smooth	55°F (13°C)	1 week	10–22 days
Dracaena	6″–18″	Straplike	35°F–40°F (2°C–4°C)	2 weeks	14–21 days
Eucalyptus	Depends on species	Leathery	35°F–40°F (2°C–4°C)	1–3 weeks	10 days
Galax	3″–6″	Smooth	33°F–40°F (0.5°C–4°C)	4 weeks	5–10 days
Ground pine	3″–6″	Needles	33°F–40°F (0.5°C–4°C)	4 weeks	5–7 days
Hedera	stems 12″–36″ leaves 1″–6″	Smooth	35°F–40°F (2°C–4°C)	2–3 weeks	7–28 days
Huckleberry	18″–30″	Fine	33°F–40°F (0.5°C–4°C)	1–4 weeks	7–14 days
Ilex (holly)	18″–30″	Prickly	33°F–36°F (0.5°C–2°C)	3–5 weeks	5–14 days
Ivy, English	12″–24″	Smooth	33°F–36°F (0.5°C–2°C)	4 weeks	5–10 days
Juniper	12″–24″	Needles	33°F–40°F (0.5°C–4°C)	1–2 months	7–14 days
Laurel, Mountain	20″–30″	Smooth	33°F–40°F (0.5°C–4°C)	2–4 weeks	7–10 days
Leatherleaf fern	10″–24″	Lacy	34°F–40°F (1°C–4°C)	1–2 months	7–15 days
Leucothoe, Drooping	12″–40″	Lacy	35°F–40°F (2°C–4°C)	4 weeks	7–21 days
Magnolia	18″–36″	Smooth	35°F–40°F (2°C–4°C)	2–4 weeks	5–8 days
Maidenhair fern	8″–20″	Lacy	33°F–40°F (0.5°C–4°C)	1 week	3–7 days
Mistletoe	6″–12″	Fine	33°F–36°F (0.5°C–2°C)	3–4 weeks	5–14 days
Palm, Commodore	18″–40″	Palm	45°F (7°C)	3 weeks	5–7 days
Philodendron	10″–30″	Smooth	35°F–40°F (2°C–4°C)	1 week	10–14 days
Podocarpus	18″–40″	Large needles	45°F (7°C)	4 weeks	7–21 days
Pothos	6″–12″	Smooth	35°F–40°F (2°C–4°C)	1 week	–
Rhododendron	12″–24″	Smooth	33°F–36°F (0.5°C–2°C)	2–4 weeks	–
Sago palm	18″–40″	Needles	40°F–50°F (4°C–10°C)	4 weeks	21–30 days
Salal, Lemon Leaf	2″–4″	Leathery	35°F–40°F (2°C–4°C)	2–4 weeks	7–21 days
Scotch Broom	24″–40″	Grassy	40°F (4°C)	2–3 weeks	7–21 days
Smilax	36″–72″	Vining	40°F (4°C)	3 weeks	5–14 days
Staghorn fern	12″–40″	Smooth	55°F (13°C)	1 week	3–7 days
Strelitzia	–	Smooth	55°F (13°C)	1 week	7–14 days
Ti leaves (Palm Lily)	10″–40″	Smooth	40°F (4°C)	1 week	10–14 days
Woodwardia	18″–48″	Lacy	33°F–40°F (0.5°C–4°C)	1 week	7–21 days

Figure 5-24. Storage temperatures and vase-life expectancies for common foliage.

Summary

- Proper care of cut flowers and foliage begins with the grower, who is responsible for producing healthy flowers and foliage, harvesting and pretreating them, packaging them appropriately, and transporting them to the wholesale florists or distributors.
- Quality is the most important element florists look for when they are purchasing flowers.
- When a shipment of cut flowers or foliage arrives at a flower shop, it is processed immediately, including conditioning as necessary and adding preservatives to maintain the freshness of the material.
- Three important factors for the storage of fresh flowers and foliage are temperature, humidity, and air circulation.
- Ethylene is produced naturally by flowers and fruits as they age, but must be removed in order to prolong the vase life of the plant materials.
- Tools are available to remove the thorns or the tips of thorns on roses without damaging the stem.
- Flowers that are geotropic or phototropic must be stored and used in specific ways to minimize or make use of these effects.

Review Questions

Go to www.g-wlearning.com/floraldesign/ to use the fill-in-form.

Answer the following questions using the information provided in this chapter.

1. Explain the benefits of the "chain of life" method of handling cut flowers.
2. What can growers do before a flower is harvested to help ensure healthy, long-lasting flowers?
3. Briefly describe the process of pulsing and explain its benefits.
4. At what temperature should most nonexotic cut flowers be stored?
5. Name five characteristics on which flowers may be graded.
6. Why do growers generally pack cut flowers for dry-shipping in long, flat boxes?
7. What factors might a florist consider when shopping for flowers from a wholesale florist or distributor?
8. What is the purpose of the hydrating solution that is added to the water when cut flowers are being rehydrated?
9. Why are the stems of dry-packed flowers recut when they arrive at the flower shop?
10. Why is underwater floral cutting equipment often used to recut dry-packed flower stems?
11. What are the three primary ingredients of a floral preservative?
12. What is the ideal level of acidity for cut flowers?
13. What is the optimal level of humidity for storing cut flowers and foliage?
14. Why is it important to remove ethylene from storage units on a continuing basis?
15. Which chemical has been widely used in the past to inhibit ethylene production?
16. How does 1-MCP reduce or impede damage from ethylene?
17. When removing leaves from a rose stem by hand, what is the proper technique to use?
18. Why are geotropic flowers stored in a vertical position?
19. Give an example of a phototropic flower.
20. Briefly describe how florists maintain the high humidity needed to reduce water loss in cut foliage.

Activities

1. Find out more about the benefits of the Chain of Life® program by the Society of American Florists.
2. Research shipping methods used by growers in the United States, The Netherlands, and China. Create a table that shows the most common transportation methods in each country.

3. Obtain floral shipping boxes and practice packing flowers to avoid damage while they are being transported. Use the methods described in this chapter to protect the flowers.

4. Practice using thorn strippers or stem strippers on roses.

Critical Thinking

1. Yesterday your flower shop received a shipment of dry-packed flowers. Your coworker rehydrated the flowers using tap water, a hydrating solution, and then placed them in water containing a floral preservative. Today you notice that some of the flowers are starting to wilt. What might be the cause of this, and what can you do to reverse it?

2. Why are cut flowers typically precooled before being stored in refrigerated storage units?

STEM Activities and Academics

1. **Science.** Go to a local park or public garden on a sunny weekend. Try to arrive early in the morning and find a flower that appears to be leaning toward the morning sun. Take a photo of the flower. Return at least three times during the same day and take additional photos from the same viewpoint. Is the flower phototropic?

2. **Technology.** Use your imagination and creativity to design a technological system that would notify a florist if cut flowers are receiving too little water or nutrients. Sketch your ideas and use your sketches to support a written description of your idea. If possible, build your system and perform a demonstration to show how it helps maintain the freshness of flowers and foliage.

3. **Science.** Design and perform an experiment to determine how much longer cut flowers last when a flower preservative is used, compared to placing the flowers in plain tap water. Document the method you used and your results.

4. **Math.** Suppose a wholesale florist sells 60 gerbera daisies to a retail florist for $82. The retail florist returns 12 of the daisies because the flowers were pale and the tips were turning brown. How much did the florist originally pay per flower for the 60 daisies? If the wholesale florist refunded the full purchase price for the returned flowers, how much was the total refund?

5. **Science.** Design and perform an experiment to verify the optimum acidity level for a specific type of flower. Use different concentrations of citric acid, and use pH strips to document the specific acidity levels. Document the method you used and your results.

Communicating about Floral Design

1. **Speaking.** Debate the topic of floral preservatives and synthetic chemicals. Divide into two groups. Each group should gather information in support of either the pro argument (preservatives are necessary for the floriculture industry) or the con argument (the chemicals used in preservatives are toxic and can be dangerous for the environment and the workers that handle the flowers). Use definitions and descriptions from this chapter, as well as other resources, to support your side of the debate and to clarify word meanings as necessary. Do additional research to find expert opinions, costs associated with floral chemicals, and other relevant information.

2. **Listening.** As classmates deliver their presentations, listen carefully to their arguments. Write down any questions that occur to you. Later, ask questions to obtain additional information or clarification from your classmates as necessary.

Chapter

6 Principles of Design

objectives

After reading this chapter, you will be able to:

- Explain the difference between design principles and design elements.
- Compare physical and visual balance in a floral design.
- Apply the concept of scale to floral arrangements and costs.
- Explain how dominance can be used to create a focal point.
- Discuss reasons for the careful use of contrast.
- Describe ways to introduce rhythm into a floral design.
- List ways to make a floral design harmonious.
- Describe methods of achieving unity in a floral design.

key terms

accent	gradation	rule of thirds
asymmetrical floral design	harmony	scale
balance	inverse proportion	subordinate
central vertical axis (CVA)	negative space	symmetrical floral design
contrast	proportion	transition
design principle	proximity	unity
dominance	radiation	visual balance
emphasis	repetition	visual weight
focal point	rhythm	

Go to **www.g-wlearning.com/floraldesign/** for online vocabulary activities using key terms from the chapter.

introduction

Floral art is the presentation of expression through the use of flowers as a medium. A floral design can create a sense of calm or excitement, or merely stand as a simple object of beauty. As with any art medium, creating these effects does not happen by accident. Floral designers plan the effect of their work using design elements and design principles. *Design elements* are the things that make up the design. Chapter 7 describes design elements in more detail. This chapter describes the principles of floral design.

Design principles are considered the "laws of beauty." They provide guidelines for organizing floral materials and elements in pleasing ways. Floral design students do not always appreciate the design principles and may initially fail to see the importance of their accurate application. However, these principles, or "laws of beauty," are the objective standards by which floral design competitions are judged. So, as a floral design student, it is in your best interest to study and know how to properly apply and evaluate these principles on any design. Floral designers often attempt to copy the beauty found in nature, **Figure 6-1**. In fact, many floral designers agree nature is one of the best teachers of floral design. All we have to do is use our senses to experience it.

The principles of design include:

- Balance.
- Proportion.
- Scale.
- Dominance.

- Contrast.
- Rhythm.
- Harmony.
- Unity.

Figure 6-1. Many floral designers are influenced by the natural beauty of our surroundings. Notice the tree's branch gently arching and hanging downward. This image could easily be the inspiration behind an ikebana design.

Safety Note

Ensuring Stability

To ensure the stability of arrangements during the delivery run, florists may use a grid system with movable pegs or sandbags that can be "molded" to a box or vase. Newer products include foam-holding systems that have premade holes that fit various vase sizes. For maximum safety, delivery vans should be equipped with a divider between the cargo area and the driver.

Balance

In floral design, **balance** refers to a sense of stability. Designs must be balanced both physically and visually.

Physical Balance

When a design is physically balanced, it is able to stand on its own. A design that falls apart or can be knocked over easily lacks stability. If an object is unstable, it has the risk of falling over. There are many reasons why this may occur, including:

- Unstable footing.
- Excessive force.
- Lack of anchorage.
- Inadequate support.
- Poor mechanics

An unstable footing allows even the smallest movement to topple an otherwise well-balanced floral design. An exertion of force caused by the wind or someone accidentally bumping into the design may cause an unstable display to move or topple over, **Figure 6-2**. It is critical to make certain the stand or column being used to display an arrangement is steady. If the design mechanics become unstable, they were most likely not properly anchored in the first place.

Placing top-heavy materials above the mechanics may cause an arrangement to lose stability. This may happen regardless of how well the stems are anchored in the foam. The loss of stability may then cause the mechanics to fail, **Figure 6-3**.

Floral placements have specific insertion points that help maintain the physical balance of the design regardless of its size. Well-constructed mechanics, solidly anchored into containers, and physical balance help ensure that floral designs will endure transport and remain stable throughout the duration of their display.

Sometimes, the design construction is not entirely at fault. Designs may be subjected to harsh weather at events held outdoors. Sudden storms or gusty breezes can take their toll on designs. The designer must keep this in mind when designing and building floral arrangements for outdoor events.

jannoon028/Shutterstock.com

Figure 6-2. Beautiful designs using lightweight plastic stands can easily topple if a gust of wind occurs or a wedding guest bumps into them.

bikeriderlondon/Shutterstock.com

Figure 6-3. With lightweight glass or plastic vases, the amount of water used becomes critical to add physical weight to the design, especially for those holding tall flowers such as these Delphinium.

Zadorozhnyi Viktor/Shutterstock.com

Figure 6-4. The large size and physical weight of these garden sunflowers can visually overpower the container, depending on the viewer's vantage point.

Pro Tip

Visual balance should not only be evident from the front of the design, it should be visually balanced when viewed from front to back, side to side, and top to bottom.

Did You Know?

A piece of plant material used low and close to the CVA of a design may seem lighter than the same piece of plant material used higher or further away from the CVA.

Visual Balance

Visual balance refers to the optical stability of a design: does the arrangement *appear* to be balanced? Visually unbalanced designs may appear to be top-heavy or leaning to one side, even though they may be physically balanced. They give the viewer a sense of unease and the feeling the design may fall over even though the arrangement is upright and secure, **Figure 6-4**. *Visual weight* is the perceived lightness or heaviness of a design. The strategic placement of "heavy" and "light" materials determines the visual weight of a floral arrangement.

The perceived lightness or heaviness of a flower or type of foliage is based on its color, shape, size, and pattern.

Color

The color of each piece of plant material is very important to the overall visual weight and balance of a design. Most people would agree that dark colors appear heavier than light colors, and pale colors appear lighter than bright colors. Using these perceptions, a designer may create visual balance by using lighter-colored materials toward the outside of an arrangement and heavier-colored materials toward the center. Visual balance may also be achieved, in part, by placing larger, darker flowers that appear heavy, low in an arrangement. Be careful not to use too much dark material at the base, or the design may look bottom heavy and weighed down.

Shape and Size

Placing larger flowers with darker colors and bold shapes low in an arrangement help "weigh down" the design, making it look more balanced and stable. Placing larger or darker flowers or foliage in the center, right above the container, will also help create visual stability.

Smaller flowers tend to have lighter colors, delicate textures, and "timid" shapes that make them seem lighter in weight. By using lighter materials and colors toward the outside of an arrangement, the designer can manipulate the visual balance of the design. If theses lighter materials were used in the center, and the darker materials were used on the outer edges, the dark materials would appear to be "pulling down" on the arrangement, making it appear unstable.

Pattern

Just as the color and shape of a flower or piece of foliage contribute to visual balance, the pattern of the plant material also affects visual balance. Bold, overpowering shapes with strong patterns may seem heavier than plant material with less contrast and smaller patterns. Designers tend to avoid placing flowers in exactly the same positions on either side of the *central vertical axis (CVA)*. The CVA divides the design vertically at the point where the stems come together. Instead of making opposite placements on either side of the CVA, designers often create alternating placements, **Figure 6-5**.

Negative space is a planned space within a design that contains no flowers or foliage; it is an open area that is integral to the overall design. See **Figure 6-6**. Often, designers do not think about arranging space, only flowers, greens and accessories. Negative space between materials is quite important because it allows the materials (positive space) to be seen without obstruction and enjoyed to the fullest.

Central Vertical Axis

All floral designs have a central vertical axis (CVA) that divides the design into two visually balanced parts. However, the balance can be either symmetrical or asymmetrical. In *symmetrical floral designs*, equal visual weight is placed in similar positions on both sides of the CVA, and the focal point is in the center of the arrangement, near the base of the CVA. In *asymmetrical floral designs*, the weight is equal on both sides of the CVA, but the distribution of flowers and materials is different.

Symmetrical Floral Designs

In symmetrical floral designs, equal visual weight is placed in similar positions on both sides of the CVA, creating an almost mirror image between each side of the arrangement, **Figure 6-7**. This mirrored-type of design makes symmetrical floral designs seem more formal than asymmetrical designs. Asymmetrical designs create the feeling of the more natural flow one would find in the outdoors.

edography/Shutterstock.com

Figure 6-5. The alternating pattern of leaves, from largest to smallest at the very top, provide a pattern of floral placement beyond the usual *opposite*.

Richard Schramm/Shutterstock.com

Figure 6-6. The negative space within this Ikebana design emphasizes its simplicity.

Dr. Delphinium Designs, Dallas, TX/SAF

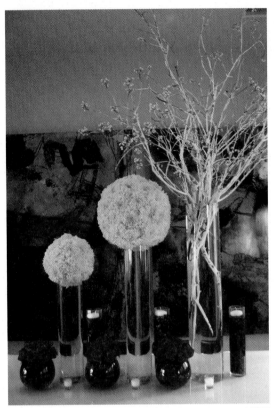

Figure 6-7. The round, symmetrical design is created by precisely inserting the stems at the proper depth.

Visual balance is created in symmetrical designs through the repetition of foliage, flowers, buds, and accessories on either side of the central vertical axis. This repetition is what makes the two sides nearly mirrored images. Some examples of floral designs that use symmetry are vertical arrangements, oval, round, and fan arrangements, triangle-shaped designs, and the inverted T design. Symmetrical, or formal, designs may be considered "easy" because of the repetition involved, but they still require skill and a keen eye for plant materials that will work well together.

Formal arrangements are traditionally used for church, funeral, memorial, and award services. It is also typical to find identical formal arrangements gracing either side of an entrance. Whether it's the entrance to a hotel or presidential ball, many people may find this type of order more "proper" for the occasion or location.

Asymmetrical Floral Designs

As stated earlier, in asymmetrical floral designs, the weight is equal on both sides of the CVA, but the distribution of flowers and materials is different. This type of balance creates a more natural appearance where materials may be used on both sides but not in exactly the same space or manner. The CVA in an asymmetrical design may be off center. For instance, a tall vertical line may be on one side of the design, and a low horizontal line may be used on the other side. There is a great deal of difference between these two sides but, when done properly, they will be visually balanced, **Figure 6-8**.

Visual balance is created in asymmetrical designs by using materials that vary in size but are still proportionate. For example, an asymmetrical design with gladiolas and 4′ tall sansevieria leaves on one side, may *not* be balanced with a sprig of baby's breath and a few miniature carnations on the other side. However, an asymmetrical design with gladiolas and 4′ tall sansevieria leaves on one side *could* be visually balanced with a low horizontal line created with hydrangea at the focal point and a grouping of roses or carnations on the other.

Blumz by JRDesigns, metro Detroit, MI/SAF

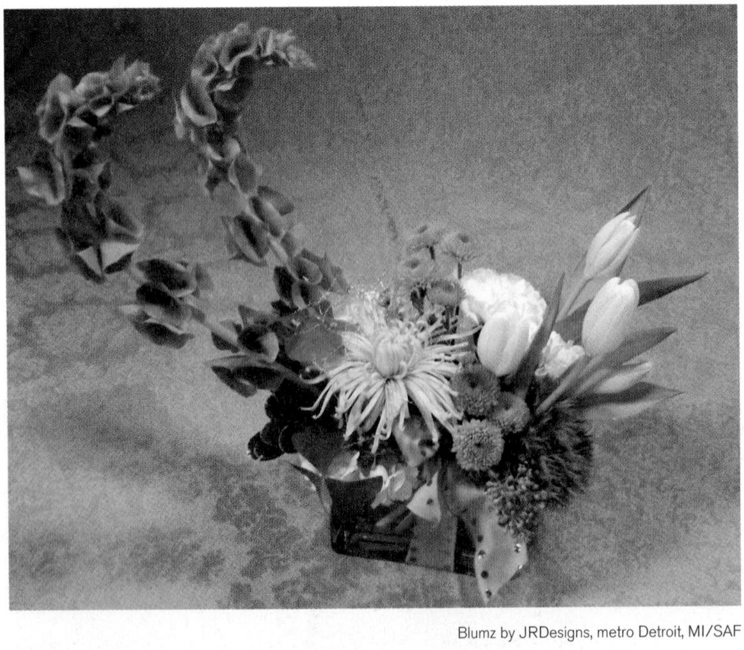

Figure 6-8. This St. Patrick's Day asymmetrical arrangement is visually balanced. The green Bells of Ireland on the left create dynamic lines that curve back toward the white tulips on the right.

Creating effective asymmetrical designs requires a great deal of ability to counterbalance the materials. When creating visual balance in an asymmetrical, or informal, arrangement, the designer must use plant materials based on their color, shape, size, and patterns as well as the color, shape, size, and pattern of the container. Since they will not be creating a set pattern, they must also consider how to use these factors so both sides of the arrangement complement each other. Common floral designs that are asymmetrical are the scalene and right triangles, crescents, and the Hogarth curve, **Figure 6-9**.

Both symmetrical and asymmetrical balance can be used in all types of floral designs, including tabletop merchandising displays, church altars, dish gardens, bridal bouquets, and even boutonnieres.

Proportion

A floral arrangement is made from combining many kinds of materials, including the container, foliage, flowers, and accessories. Each of these components must be proportionate to each other in size to achieve the desired effect. For example, if a designer creates a small floral arrangement, but then overshadows the design by adding a large greeting card, the flowers cannot be seen until the card is removed. The card, as a design component, is disproportionate to the petite design, **Figure 6-10**. *Proportion* refers to the relative sizes and amounts of elements within a design and to the design as a whole.

Cindy Anderson, AIFD, PFCI/SAF

Figure 6-9. The crescent design is an asymmetrical arrangement.

Did You Know?

In ancient Egyptian art, political figures and gods were shown much larger than ordinary people because proportion was used as an indication of importance.

Photodisc/Photodisc/Thinkstock; Peredniankina/Shutterstock.com

Figure 6-10. Most florist enclosure cards are about the size of a flower, thus fitting well into an arrangement without overpowering the design.

WhiteTag/Shutterstock.com

Figure 6-11. Daisy Chrysanthemums work well with babies' breath.

The design must also be in proportion to where it is going to be displayed, be it a room, a patio, or someone's lapel. For example, a centerpiece designed for a dining table in a one-bedroom apartment would be dwarfed in the formal dining room of a five-bedroom home with cathedral ceilings.

Every part of a floral design contributes to good proportion. For example, in an arrangement using twelve large sunflowers with four stems of solidago, the materials would be disproportionate and there would be an imbalance of both physical and visual weight. In this case, the large sunflowers would also overpower the solidago if the stem count was equal. The same is true of foliage. Large flowers, such as sunflowers, will look better with larger-leafed foliage than with small-leaved greenery. The same goes for smaller flowers using small-leaved greenery as opposed to larger-leafed foliage. See **Figure 6-11.**

Floral designers use the following general rule of thumb in order to keep the main elements of their designs in proportion to the rest of the materials being used. The plant material (flowers and greenery) should be 1.5 to 2 times the height, length or width of the container. See **Figure 6-12.** This proportion is taken directly from nature. For example, the average human face is about 1.5 times long as it is wide. In some cases, exceptions must be made. For instance, the height of the arrangement may be increased to create proper proportion to the dimension of the room in which it will be placed. The type of materials being used may arrive taller and fuller than anticipated, requiring an increase in height.

IgorGolovniov/Shutterstock.com; Society of American Florists

Figure 6-12. The upright line of the vase on the left suggests a design 1.5 times taller than the vase while the washbasin to the right could be filled with flowers 1.5-2 times taller than the container's width. Note the floral portion of this design is about twice the height of the vase. The entire design is about 1.5-2 times the height of the floral mass.

Rule of Thirds

When planning a floral design for a defined space, you can get a rough estimate for arrangement sizes by dividing the space into thirds. For example, a table centerpiece should take up no more than one-third of the length and width of a table in order to leave space for china, flatware, and stemware, **Figure 6-13**. Conversely, a floral design placed on a hall table may take up two-thirds of the space. This guideline is known as the *rule of thirds*.

This same rule of thirds can be used to visually divide larger spaces, such as tall-ceilinged ballrooms. Arrangements, ornamental trees, props, or other objects can occupy a dominant (two-thirds) or subordinate (one-third) proportion of the space, **Figure 6-14**. The event designer who uses the rule of thirds to work with proportional use of space should keep a tape measure and take notes in order to make designs the appropriate scale for a space, whether making a holiday design for a coffee table or church designs for a high-profile wedding.

Proportion applies not only to design principles, but also to design elements. Color, light, fragrance, and all the other elements must be used in correct proportions in order to achieve a physically and visually balanced design.

Society of American Florists

Figure 6-13. The foot of this vase centerpiece takes up approximately one-third the space of the tabletop.

 Pro Tip

When plant material runs down over the container, instead of standing upright, the designer is using *inverse proportion*. A tall vase may be used, so that the arrangement flows downward to cover the top two-thirds of the vase.

Dallas Events, Inc./Shutterstock.com; Konstantin Goldenberg/Shutterstock.com

Figure 6-14. These tall centerpieces are two-thirds the height of the reception space.

LeS/Shutterstock.com

Figure 6-15. If you place a golden rectangle over the front of this ancient Greek temple, the temple fits almost perfectly. Once you draw the usual subdivisions of the golden rectangle, you will notice the major architectural features align perfectly.

Good   Poor

Goodheart-Willcox Publisher

Figure 6-16. The illustrations above illustrate how important balance is in a piece of art, be it a painting, sculpture, or floral composition.

The Golden Ratio

A discussion on proportion would not be complete without the mention of the golden ratio, along with the *golden section*, *golden rectangle*, *golden mean*, and even the *golden rule*. Take note that these terms are often used interchangeably but they all use the same ratio. The golden ratio is a ratio of 1:1.5 or 2:3. This ratio was first applied to art and architecture by the Greeks to create designs that were well-proportioned and aesthetically beautiful, **Figure 6-15**. Today, this ratio is applied to art, architecture, all types of media, and for our purposes, floral design. It is believed that this ratio naturally appeals to the human eye and people have been drawn to it throughout time. The golden ratio occurs throughout nature, even the human face follows it.

The golden section is also a Greek rule of proportion based on the golden rectangle and/or the golden ratio. The golden section involves the division of a form or line so that the ratio of the smaller portion to the larger portion is the same as that of the larger portion to the whole. For instance, when applied to a floral arrangement, the ratio of the container to the flowers is the same as the ratio of the flowers to the entire arrangement, **Figure 6-16**. This ratio could be 3:5 or 5:8 as these ratios are roughly the same as 2:3.

The sides of the golden rectangle or oblong, are at a ratio of 2:3 and the golden mean is a rule of proportion that refers to the division of a line or form between one-half and one-third of its length. These rules of proportion all use the ratio of 2:3 to create a division that is pleasing to the eye. The golden rule may also be applied to determine the width of an arrangement as well as the height of the flowers.

Scale

When an architect creates a rendering of a building, she often includes a few humans in the picture to indicate the actual size of the building. This works because the viewer understands the size relationship, or *scale*, between humans and the building. What seems to be a mansion may actually be a storage shed. See **Figure 6-17**. This same idea can be applied to floral designs. When planning the design, the designer must take into account the setting in which the design will be used. For example, an arrangement designed to fit on an occasional or end table is likely to be too small to work on a dining room table. An arrangement designed for a table in a large hotel lobby, however, will probably be far too large for a dining room table in someone's home.

Scale Adjustments

Scale is a relative concept that must sometimes be adjusted to meet a customer's specifications. For example, if a bride states that she does not want her bouquet to be too small or too large, the designer could ask her to demonstrate the dimensions with her hands. The designer can then measure the space with a ruler to determine the scale the bride is specifying.

Cost and Scale

Floral designs are often scaled according to cost. Many customers have a general idea of what they want, as well as a price range. For customers who do not know exactly what they want, a sales staff member may explain that arrangements are available in small, medium, and large sizes, and that the prices range from $30 to $150 depending on the size or scale of the arrangement. The floral designer must then make appropriate, cost-effective decisions to create the design at the scale chosen by the customer, **Figure 6-18**.

Sven Hoppe/Shutterstock.com

Figure 6-17. A piggy bank is available in many sizes, but a penny is a standard size. In this image, the coin gives scale to various piggy banks.

Fransesco83/Shutterstock.com

Figure 6-18. A professional florist should fill each order for full value and every design beautiful for the customer and profitable for the business.

Dmitry Strizhakov/Shutterstock.com

Figure 6-19. Both hands are the same, just their sizes are different.

Artjazz/Shutterstock.com

Figure 6-20. The repetition of purple flowers in this trio of vases dominates the composition.

Scale vs. Proportion

Scale is closely related to proportion, but the two are different. If a design is scaled upward, the amounts and sizes of all of the materials increase, but the proportions between the materials stays the same. See **Figure 6-19**. For example, suppose you have made a coffee mug design for Boss's Day (October 16). The design includes 3 carnations, 5 daisy spray chrysanthemums and 5 purple statice placements. To scale the design upward for a higher dollar value, you could use a soup bowl with 6 carnations, 10 daisies, and 10 statice placements.

Dominance

If the proportions of all the elements in a design are the same, the design may appear to lack cohesion. *Dominance* is an emphasis on one or more elements that provides a focus, theme, or overall "feeling" for the design. It helps the viewer make sense of what the design portrays. For instance, in a monochromatic design, one color is used repeatedly throughout the materials. Color is the dominant element in these designs, **Figure 6-20**. When one element becomes dominant, all of the other elements in the design are said to be *subordinate*.

Any element of form, fragrance, texture, color, and space can also create dominance. Holiday arrangements of mixed evergreens are a good example of dominance by texture. Soft and flexible pine needles with spikey juniper tips, flowing incense cedar, and spiny spruce branches play well against each other. The arrangement is pleasing to the eye because the dominant use of texture helps tie the variety of plant material together.

Focal Point

The *focal point* of a floral design is the area of dominance within the design. In a successful design, it holds the strongest concentration of elements. It is the area of the design that captures the eye's attention first.

When dominance is used to direct the viewer's attention to a particular part of the design, usually the focal point, it creates *emphasis*. Emphasis can be created by making one area of the design denser, visually heavier, or darker in color, or simply by using larger materials in that area. See **Figure 6-21**. To create a strong focal point in a design, make sure the most focal flower (or flowers) face the viewer. Flowers should be closer together at the focal area of the design, helping the eye to focus in this part of the arrangement first. The focal area should hold the greatest concentration of plant material. The further away from the focal area, a greater the amount of space should be used between flowers.

In general, larger, more fully opened flowers help to achieve emphasis when they are used at the focal area. Smaller materials and buds have less impact and are more useful at the outer edges of the design. Spiky line materials form the skeleton of the design and if used, are often placed first in the arrangement. (*Skeleton flowers* are the first few placements, regardless of flower type, that form the skeleton of the arrangment.) They should not only be used on the outside edge of a design, resembling a turkey's tail feathers, but also worked through the central vertical axis, or trunkline, of the design.

longsky/Shutterstock.com

Figure 6-21. The viewer's eye is automatically drawn to the white flower in the arrangement.

Mass flowers help provide emphasis at the focal area and through the heart of the design. They may also be used to form the skeleton of the arrangement. Filler flowers like *Solidago*, statice or Baby's Breath help to connect the different materials, adding more visual interest as well as fill a pattern with more positive space. New designers often have difficulty achieving even distribution of filler flower throughout the design. For example, they may add statice to the upper half of the design and not add any to the focal area, which should have the largest and most plentiful placements of flowers.

Bright advancing colors get the most attention, so designers can use this aspect to their advantage. When using varying colors of flowers, reserve those with the highest values and chroma for the focal area because they will pull the viewer's attention.

Accents

Many floral designs include interesting details, or *accents*, that add character to the overall design. Accents are completely different from the other materials in the design and are used primarily to add interest, **Figure 6-22**.

Maria Tapia at Shirley's Flowers & Gifts, Inc., Rogers, Arkansas.

Figure 6-22. The bass in this design is made from polystyrene foam and hand painted to achieve a realistic appearance. Lines and lures promote the fisherman's theme.

Figure 6-23. Purple and yellow are direct opposites on the color wheel, thus are in strong contrast to each other.

Figure 6-24. The eye lingers on the portion of the dried floral potpourri with more color and detail. It tends to move more quickly over the objects that are dull and spaced further apart.

To be effective, they should not overpower the rest of the design. When chosen carefully, they can highlight or even help emphasize the dominant features of the design.

Contrast

Emphasis can also be achieved through *contrast*. Rather than point to a focal area, as dominance does, contrast adds interest to an arrangement through difference or opposition. Contrast can be used to emphasize the characteristics of flowers and foliage. For example, using purple flowers next to yellow ones punches up both the richness of the purple and the brightness of the yellow, **Figure 6-23**.

Contrast adds interest to a design by creating tension, or a sense of energy. It can also be used to bring variation to a design. It must be used carefully, however. Too many contrasting elements can cause a sense of conflict or even make the design look messy and uncoordinated.

Rhythm

In floral design, *rhythm* is a sense of movement created visually by the placement of floral materials. A regular, equally spaced pattern of insertions using the same type of material creates visual "beats." It provides ordered movement leading the eye. Rhythm can be slow or smooth, fast or jagged, depending on the elements used.

Rhythm is accomplished using spacing or intervals between similar elements in the design. Repetition of textures, lines, colors, or shapes is an easy way to create rhythm. One of the advantages of repeating these elements is that it helps to increase the cohesiveness of the arrangement while providing a sense of movement.

Items that are placed in close proximity to each other slow down the speed at which the eyes move through an arrangement. Items placed farther apart speed up the movement. See **Figure 6-24**. The pace for observing the complete design is established by this deliberate pattern of insertions. The goal is to make the entire rhythm pleasing while leading the eye to a final resting spot at the focal point.

In some arrangements, the rhythm changes as the eye moves through the design. These designs have transitions, or gradually changing elements, that alter the pace while leading the eye from one part of the arrangement to another. The transition can be a gradual change in color, size, texture, or any other design element.

Unity

Unity is a celebration of similarities. A floral design with a strong sense of unity shows an organization of elements so they appear to belong together. Unity indicates the arrangement as a whole is more important than its individual pieces. When you feel that your design is not coming together, review and apply the established techniques of proximity, repetition, and transition to help you achieve unity in your design. Using these techniques as guidelines can help new designers make a design look professional instead of appearing as an unkempt composition.

Proximity

Sometimes, by merely placing flowers or objects in *proximity* (next to each other), they appear to build a relationship. Therefore, when we look at a well-planned floral arrangement, our brain groups the flowers and we perceive them as a unified design. This is how a floral arrangement using a variety of seasonal garden flowers in numerous colors can look so beautiful.

Repetition

Cindy Anderson, AIFD, PFCI

Figure 6-25. The repetition of the anthurium flowers mimicked by the monkey grass below them, works well. The parallel and vertical insertions of equisetum also create repetition.

Repetition can be used to contribute to the harmony of the arrangement. A floral designer can repeat similar elements throughout a composition to help unite all the material in the design, **Figure 6-25.** Using repetition in a design does not restrict the designer to one piece being used in the same manner throughout the design. The repetition can be:

- Irregular or regular; using materials in a slightly different or the same manner throughout the composition.
- Uneven or even; each element can be used an even or odd number of times (even numbers of items are more formal whereas odd numbers are more natural).
- *Radiation*; the repeated elements spread out from a central point (stems radiate from center/foam/container). See **Figure 6-26.**
- *Gradation*; the repeated elements slowly decrease or increase in size.
- Similar elements (shapes, colors, lines) used more than once. (When repeating colors, use varying values and intensities to keep the composition from becoming dull and boring.)

sarsmis/Shutterstock.com

Figure 6-26. Notice how the different flowers radiate from the base of the arrangement. Each element forms a part of the "arc" across the top.

Illadam36III/Shutterstock.com

Figure 6-27. Dried and preserved plant materials are at home when arranged in a vine or willow basket.

Transition

Much like a term paper, a floral arrangement without smooth transitions does not make sense. For example, if the first paragraph in a term paper introduces the concept of indoor gardening and the second discusses bird identification, there is no harmony or unity. It doesn't make sense. *Transition* is the smooth gradual change from one material to another. It creates a flow that takes the viewer from one area of the arrangement smoothly to the next. Just as repetition is not limited in its form, transition can be achieved in more than one way. Transition can be achieved by:

- Using the size of filler flowers to transition from large flowers to smaller ones.
- Using color to transition from lighter-colored flowers, to medium-colored, and to darker-colored ones.

Smooth transitions are also important in a florist's store displays. If the displays flow smoothly from one section to another, the customer is more likely to look at all of your merchandise. If there are obstructions between displays, the customer is more likely to skip areas of the store and just tend to their business or worse, just leave.

These principles also apply to the container being used. When you need to create designs for an upscale hotel, a rustic, willow-woven basket will not work. The container would need to first, match or complement its surroundings. Secondly, the plant materials would have to complement both the container and its surroundings. The rustic, willow-woven basket with locally growing grasses and flowers would be right at home in a mountain resort. The container and plant materials would be in harmony with each other and with the surroundings, **Figure 6-27.**

Harmony

Harmony can be considered a celebration of differences. The pleasing interaction of the different elements of a design creates *harmony* for the viewer. This is typically accomplished by the use of unique materials, colors, or shapes. Flowers of the same color, but in different shades, are harmonious. They blend with each other and provide a sense of order. They work together as a whole.

Similarity

The principle of similarity is things that look similar are assumed to be related in some way and can grouped together. Three elements used to convey similarity are shape, size, and color. When your eyes are on visual information overload, your brain tries to simplify the information by grouping items that look alike. The designer should use this principle when creating emphasis and harmony in floral designs. The more alike the flowers are, the more likely your brain will form them into groups and help direct you to the focal point of the design. The less the flowers look like each other, the more your brain will resist grouping and recognize the individual flowers or, the point of emphasis instead. **Figure 6-28**.

Envision a beautiful display made using a variety of vintage glassware holding diverse types of flowers. The flowers may be vastly different, but the glassware is perceived as a group that unites the design and creates harmony. Now envision the display with nothing but roses in a rainbow of colors. Which element unites the design? Is there harmony in the design? Can you see this same display with gladioli, poppies, *Godetia* and *Gerbera* in variations of pale orange? This combination of flowers in the same color family creates similarity and the viewers' eyes will group them together into a unified, harmonious design.

Theme

Adherence to a particular theme also helps bring about harmony. For example, for a couple celebrating their wedding anniversary and whose favorite music is jazz, the designer could suggest they use a New Orleans theme for the party. Floral pieces could use Mardi Gras colors and accents such as beads and other French Quarter type props. The floral designer could continue the theme on everything from corsages and boutonnieres to lavishly decorated masks being worn by the guests.

Simplicity

There is a lot to be said about the often forgotten technique of keepings things simple. When fewer elements are combined, there is less chance of complication. Sometimes, the most memorable and distinctive floral designs are made from one flower in a modest vase, accented by a fresh, green leaf, **Figure 6-29**. Encrusting an event design with lots of crystals, pearls and shiny objects may look great in some venues, yet terrible in others. When in doubt, the adage "less is more" should apply to your work. Keeping a design simple and uncluttered allows the beauty to shine through.

Mr. Mitr Srilachai/Shutterstock.com

Figure 6-28. As each grouping of flowers is separated by type and color, your eye begins at the focal point and travels from group to group.

Agnes Kantaruk/Shutterstock.com

Figure 6-29. Sometimes the simplest things can bring the biggest smile.

Summary

- Design principles define aspects of beauty and are to be recognized and achieved as much as possible.
- Floral designs require both physical and visual balance.
- Visual balance can be created in both symmetrical and asymmetrical floral arrangements.
- The rule of thirds helps designers estimate the amount of space that should be taken up by a floral design for a fixed space.
- Floral designs should be scaled to fit the location where they will be used.
- The elements that are featured in a design are dominant; all other elements are subordinate.
- The focal point is at the base of the design, near the center.
- Large, more fully opened flowers help achieve emphasis when they are used in the focal area.
- A harmonious design is one in which all of the elements work together to create a pleasing effect.
- Unity in a floral design is the sense that all of the elements belong together.

Review Questions
Go to www.g-wlearning.com/floraldesign/ to use the fill-in-form.

Answer the following questions using the information provided in this chapter.

1. Identify the aesthetic benefits of floral art.
2. Name eight principles of design.
3. What is the difference between physical balance and visual balance?
4. Explain the importance of including negative space as part of a design.
5. What is the difference between a symmetrical floral design and an asymmetrical design?
6. What is the ideal standard of proportion?
7. How is the concept of scale applied to floral designs?
8. What is the difference between scale and proportion?
9. What is the purpose of dominance in a floral design?
10. How can emphasis be achieved in a floral design?
11. Why is it important to use contrast carefully in a floral design?
12. How does a floral designer create rhythm in an arrangement?
13. Explain how a designer can achieve harmony in a floral design.
14. List the six principles a designer can use to achieve unity.
15. If a customer wants an arrangement to be placed in a pink container, what should the designer do to ensure unity in the design?

Activities

1. Experiment with balance by stacking different sizes and shapes of wooden blocks.
2. Research the golden ratio to learn how it was discovered and applied to architecture in Ancient Greece.
3. Using various pictures of floral arrangements, determine the following: the dominant and subordinate elements, the focal point, and rhythm.
4. Visit a botanical garden and identify various landscape designs, such as formal gardens, formal parterre, and an English woodland garden. Sketch floral designs based on the landscape designs.

Critical Thinking

1. A customer comes to your flower shop and requests a custom arrangement that includes poinsettias and sunflowers. Why might a designer want to avoid this combination? What could the designer say to the customer?

2. How might you unify a holiday arrangement that includes pine cones, tall red candles, and gold-tone sleigh bells?

3. A local college football hero wants to be married on the campus football field. You have been hired to do the floral arrangements, so you accompany the bride to the football field to begin planning. You notice that there is a constant, stiff breeze on the field. What might you suggest to the bride regarding arrangements that will work in this environment? How can you make sure the floral arrangements will stay in place?

STEM Activities and Academics

1. **Math.** Research the Fibonacci series. The first several numbers in the Fibonacci series are 0, 1, 2, 3, 5, 8, 13, and 21. Do the math to extend the series out to the next 14 numbers. Show your work.

2. **Science.** Design and perform an experiment using a 3″ square block of Styrofoam, a plastic container, and artificial flowers and foliage of various sizes. What is the maximum height that can be supported by the mechanic? Record the steps you use in your experiment. Be sure to write the procedure clearly enough that others can perform the same experiment and verify your results.

3. **Social Studies.** Different societies and cultures have different ideas about how to emphasize or showcase important items. This is true in floral design as in other areas. Conduct research to find out how our principles of design in the United States today are different from those used during the dark ages and the Renaissance. What factors may have caused these differences?

4. **Language Arts.** Write a short chapter for a book that will be used to teach art to sixth-grade students. The chapter should be about the principles of design. Keeping the audience in mind, develop the topic thoroughly. Use concrete details and extended definitions to help the students understand the concepts.

5. **Math.** Many "golden" mathematical concepts have been identified throughout the years. Find out more about the "golden rectangle" identified by the Greeks. Mathematically, how does that concept apply to floral design?

Communicating about Floral Design

1. **Speaking and Listening.** Divide into groups of four or five students. Each group should choose one of the following topics: balance, proportion, scale, dominance, focal point, contrast, rhythm, harmony, or unity. Using your textbook as a starting point, research your topic and prepare a report on how it impacts floral design. As a group, deliver your presentation to the rest of the class. Take notes while other students give their reports. Ask questions about any details that you would like clarified.

2. **Speaking and Reading.** Modify an available arrangement so there are several issues with the design, especially balance. With a partner, role-play the following situation: a floral design judge is discussing physical and visual balance with a contestant. As the judge, ask the contestant questions on balance. Using terminology from your textbook, explain to the contestant why the arrangement does not work. You may use figures in the text for reference. Switch roles and repeat the activity, focusing on a different principle, such as scale.

3. **Speaking and Reading.** Working in groups of three students, create flash cards for the key terms in this chapter. On the front of the card, write the term. On the back of the card, write the pronunciation and a brief definition. Use your textbook and a dictionary for guidance. Then take turns quizzing one another on the pronunciations and definitions of the key terms.

132

Chapter

7 Elements of Design

objectives

After reading this chapter, you will be able to:

- Identify the elements of design.
- Compare and contrast major color systems.
- Explain the principles of color harmonies.
- Discuss the application of color psychology to floral design.
- Apply procedures for systemic dyeing and tinting.
- Describe how the elements of form, fragrance, line, pattern, space, size, and texture are applied to floral design.

key terms

achromatic	intensity	space
additive color system	line	spray tint
color harmony	line flower	subtractive color system
color wheel	mass flower	systemic dyeing
design element	partitive color system	tertiary color
filler flower	pattern	texture
form	primary color	tint
form flower	secondary color	tone
fragrance	shade	value
hue	size	visible spectrum

Go to www.g-wlearning.com/floraldesign/ for online vocabulary activities using key terms from the chapter.

introduction

Design elements are all of the things that go into creating a floral design. They are similar to ingredients used to prepare a meal: various ingredients are blended together to create a successful outcome. The selection and blending of elements of floral design are guided by the principles of floral design, explained in Chapter 6, *Principles of Design*. The elements of floral design are:

- Color
- Form
- Fragrance
- Line
- Pattern
- Size
- Space
- Texture

Pro Tip

Remembering Design Elements

Use this acrostic tool to help you remember the elements of floral design: Cool, Flashy Ferrets Love Perfectly Sized Silk Toupees.

Color

Color is one of the most important elements in floral design and is often the deciding factor for consumer purchases. When people shop for clothing, furniture, or flowers, they are looking for just the right colors to suit their needs. In fact, color is the first element most people recognize in an object.

To understand color, you need to know a little about what it is and what causes it. Scientifically, colors are formed by light energy of different wavelengths bouncing off an object. All objects absorb some or all of the wavelengths of energy. The wavelengths the object does not absorb are reflected, and it is this reflected light energy that we perceive as color. Natural white light from the sun contains all of the colors. When that light is refracted (bent) through a prism, you can see all of the colors that make up the white light. This is the *visible spectrum*, **Figure 7-1**.

You may have noticed that the visible spectrum does not include white, black, or gray. Technically, these are not colors. They are neutral or *achromatic*, which means "without color." White is the combination of all of the individual colors in the spectrum. White objects do not absorb any wavelengths of light; they reflect all of the wavelengths. Black is the absence of any colors in the spectrum; black objects absorb all of the light energy and do not reflect any wavelengths. Gray is a combination of black and white or diminished light.

The colors of the spectrum are also called *hues*. A pure hue is a color that has not been darkened, lightened, or grayed. When white, black, or gray is added to a pure hue, it changes the *value*, or purity, of the color, making it lighter or darker. See **Figure 7-2**. This helps to define objects in a painting or in a floral design.

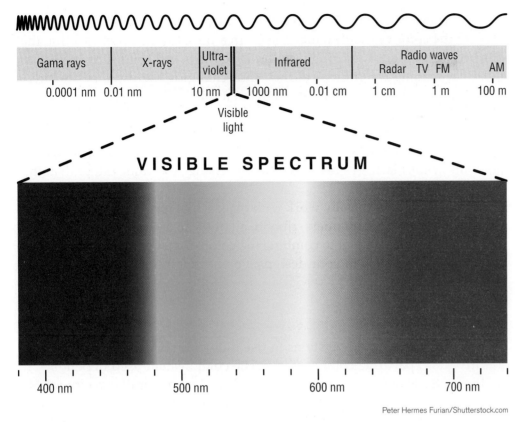

Peter Hermes Furian/Shutterstock.com

Figure 7-1. The wavelengths of light that are responsible for the visible spectrum are only a small portion of energy emitted by the sun.

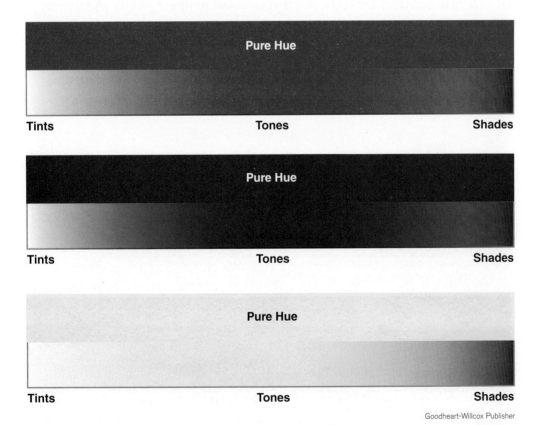

Goodheart-Willcox Publisher

Figure 7-2. Tints, tones, and shades are created by adding white, gray, or black, respectively.

A *tint* is a hue that has been lightened by mixing it with white. Mixing the color red with white results in a pink tint. A *shade* is a hue that has been darkened by mixing it with black. Tints and shades change color by either making it lighter or darker, thus changing the value of the hue. When gray is added to a hue, it results in a *tone*. Adding gray to a hue also lessens its intensity.

Intensity (sometimes called *chroma*) refers to the brightness or dullness of a hue. A color's intensity can be changed by mixing it with other colors, but not with white, black, or gray, which would change the value rather than the intensity. See **Figure 7-3**.

Floral designers usually work with objects that already possess color. Cut flowers, foliage, containers, ribbon; all of these items arrive in color. The role of the designer is to combine the colors for a desired effect. To use colors most effectively in your designs, you need to understand how color can be made.

Pro Tip

Remember, color *intensity* is changed when a hue is mixed with another hue or hues. Color *value* is changed when a hue is mixed with white, gray, or black.

Color Systems

The three basic color systems in use today are the subtractive, additive, and partitive color systems. The color system used depends on the materials used to create it. Floral designers generally work with partitive color, but they need to understand the subtractive and additive systems as well.

Subtractive Color

Thinking back to the days when you mixed tempera paints together in art class, you may have noticed that as you mixed more colors together, the developing color got darker and darker until it was eventually black. It was not a true black, but it was close. When the paints are mixed together, they absorb more light and reflect back less color. For this reason, this system is known as the *subtractive color system*. See **Figure 7-4**.

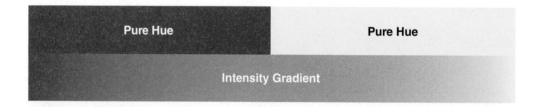

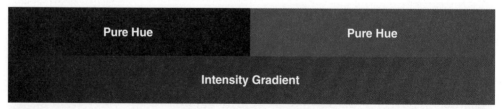

Goodheart-Willcox Publisher

Figure 7-3. A color's intensity, or brightness, is changed by adding various amounts of another color.

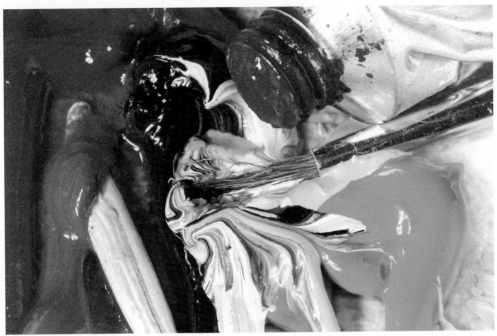

Figure 7-4. In a subtractive color system, the more colors you mix together, the darker the overall color becomes.

Additive Color

Designers sometimes have the opportunity to work with colored light, such as in visual merchandising, lighting for special events, photography, television, or cinema. Flowers look very different under varying colors of light. Sometimes their color is enhanced, but with the wrong lighting, colors can become muddy, washed-out, or unattractive. As colors of light are mixed together, the resulting color becomes lighter and lighter. This system of mixing colors is called the *additive color system*.

A light wheel is used to show the effects of additive color, **Figure 7-5**. Additive colors have a different set of primary colors: red, blue, and green. Combinations of red, blue, and green lights yield these results:

- Red + green = yellow
- Green + blue = cyan (a greenish-blue color)
- Blue + red = magenta (a purplish-red color)

If all the primary additive colors are combined, as shown in the center of the light wheel, the light color will be white. Recall that black is the absence of color, so to achieve black, simply turn off the lights.

Figure 7-5. Lights are additive and behave differently from partitive and subtractive colors, as shown in this light wheel.

Partitive Color

A *partitive color system* does not add or subtract color. Instead, it is based on the way the viewer perceives or reacts to the colors when they are placed near each other. This is especially important to floral designers because they work with established colors more often than with paints, dyes, and lighting. When designers combine flowers, containers, and accessories together in a composition, the final effect is due to the relationships of the colors within the arrangement.

One of the easiest ways to see the effects of partitive color is to use a *color wheel*, which shows the colors in a logical order according to the spectrum, **Figure 7-6**. Red, yellow, and blue are called the *primary colors*, because no other colors can be mixed to achieve these colors. All of the other colors on the wheel can be created using red, yellow, and blue. *Secondary colors* are created by mixing two primary colors together. The secondary colors are orange (red + yellow), green (yellow + blue), and violet (blue + red). A third level of colors, the *tertiary colors*, are created by combining one primary and one secondary color:

Other Color Systems

The color systems we recognize today are the result of hundreds of years of theory and research by philosophers, scientists, and inventors. The Greek philosopher Aristotle wrote the first known publication on color, *De Coloribus*.

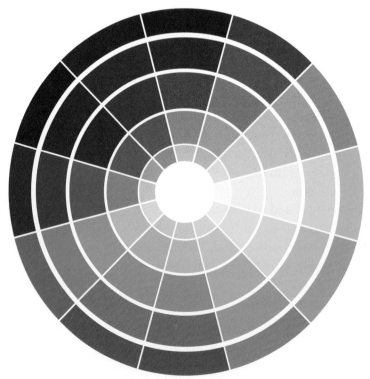

Figure 7-6. A color wheel showing the relationships among the primary, secondary, and tertiary colors. The warmer colors are shown on the right side of the wheel, and the cooler colors are on the left.

One color theorist whose ideas are often used by floral designers is Albert Munsell. He built on Chevreul's work with afterimages to devise a color wheel containing the principal colors of red, yellow, blue, green and purple. The afterimage colors, which he called *secondary hues*, are aligned opposite the principal colors and make up the Munsell color wheel. Later, Munsell added different values of each color and organized them into the *Munsell color tree*. The colors on the outside of the tree are the pure hues, and the "trunk" of the tree consists of the achromatic white, gray, and black.

Color Harmonies

Color harmonies, also called color schemes, are guidelines for combining colors and color values in design. Used in professions such as floral design, clothing and textiles, interior design, and photography, they give designers a plan for how to use color and how to make color choices.

Monochromatic Colors

A monochromatic color scheme consists of one hue that varies in value (from light to dark) or intensity (from intense to dull). See **Figure 7-7**. Monochromatic combinations provide a sense of unity, peace, and order.

Analogous Colors

Three colors that are adjacent on the 12-slice color wheel are *analogous*. These will only include one primary color. The primary color is usually dominant, with the other colors filling in and adding interest. Extended-analogous groups of colors consist of four or five colors that are adjacent on the color wheel.

ortis/Shutterstock.com; Kieren Welch/fotolia

Figure 7-7 Examples of monochromatic color occur all around us. The leaves are an example of a naturally occurring monochromatic color scheme with varying shapes and textures. The wedding bouquet is an example of a monochromatic color scheme.

Analogous and extended-analogous schemes provide similarity without being repetitive. Autumn colors often fall into the category of analogous schemes. See **Figure 7-8**.

Complementary Colors

Made up of two hues on opposite sides of the color wheel, complementary color schemes offer the greatest contrast of colors. Perhaps this is because they are as far apart on the color wheel as possible. Different color wheels are used for different color theories, and complementary colors can be different according to the theory being used.

Color Manipulation

Successful color usage allows one color to dominate within a floral design and throughout a composition, such as a living room interior design or a dining room table set for dinner. Repetition is an important aspect of working with color. When a hue is repeated, it gives the design a sense of unity. In general, a composition of a few hues of varying values is usually more pleasing than a composition of many hues. If the arrangement has only one hue, use many different values of it to add interest.

Remember that certain colors give the impression of coolness, while others seem to be warmer. However, the "temperature" of a color can be modified to a certain extent. Darkening a hue can make it appear warmer, while a lighter value appears cooler. Blacks can be warm or cool in appearance, because it often has a hint of a warm or cool color.

Maksim Shmeljov/Shutterstock.com; desert trends/fotolia

Figure 7-8 Leaves in the fall create beautiful analogous colors. The different shapes, sizes, colors, and textures all contribute to a wonderful, natural analogous color scheme. A designer may take clues from nature to create autumnal bouquets.

The viewer will notice white and light-value colors first, middle values next, then dark values and black last. Designs with black or dark values at the bottom and light values at the top are often more pleasing to people.

Systemic Dyeing

Today's breeders and producers of cut flowers have all but eliminated the need to dye flowers to achieve a certain effect. Colors that used to be unavailable or difficult to obtain, have been cultivated into production. Lime green anthurium and deep purple carnations are examples. However, florists occasionally receive requests for a particular color, such as a school spirit color, that is not available in a flower staple such as carnations. In these cases, *systemic dyeing*, or stem dyeing, is an option.

To dye white carnations, for example, you can use commercial food dyes. The carnations should be open and in good condition. As the flower loses water through transpiration, it takes up the dyed water. As transpiration continues, the water evaporates, leaving behind the dye pigment. Once the desired color is achieved, remove the flowers from the dyed solution and place them in clear water with preservative. Monitor the process to avoid too much concentration of color along the flower margins. The entire process may take up to 24 hours. Some florists recommend using flowers that have been shipped dry and have not been hydrated. When they are placed in water containing the dye, the dye is absorbed quicker and more evenly.

Spray Tinting

Fashion color trends generally follow home interior, gift item, and other consumer product lines, but flowers don't always naturally match the popular color. *Spray tints*, or paints, can be used to change a flower's color to match popular trends, **Figure 7-9**.

Trendy colors tend to transform rapidly as they follow fashion changes. Considering the research, science, and time involved in cultivating flowers of a certain color, spray tinting to create popular colors makes sense. Paint colors can be developed much more easily and quickly than a new flower. Some companies even produce transparent floral spray paints that provide a hint of color without hiding the natural beauty of the floral products. In addition to dyeing or painting flowers and foliage, spray tints can be used on ribbon, containers, and many types of accessories. *It is not recommended for use on candles.*

Pro Tip
Systemic Dyeing
If the exact shade of a dyed flower is critical, begin the dyeing process early in the morning so that you can monitor the color during the day.

Pro Tip
White flowers, such as carnations and daisy pompons, work well with systemic dyeing since the flowers have no other color that will affect the color of the dye.

Safety Note
Spray Tinting
Always wear gloves to protect your hands when using spray tints. Also, work in a well-ventilated area to minimize paint fume inhalation.

Elena Pominova /Shutterstock.com
Figure 7-9. Some flowers grow with their tips a different color, others need to be tinted or painted. The effect above can be achieved by holding the flower ever so lightly closed, and spraying the edges with special floral spray tint or paint. Wear gloves and an old shirt so you don't get paint on yourself or your clothes.

Step-by-Step

Systemic Dyeing

A florist will dye fresh flowers to match school colors, the color scheme for a wedding, or for another special event. A florist may also dye flowers before drying them. Preparing the flowers with a surfactant, if it isn't included in the dye itself, before dyeing will enable the flowers to take the dye more evenly and quickly.

Fill your vase with clear water and add the dye as indicated by the manufacturer.

1

Allow the dye to dissolve completely.

2

3

Give the flowers to be dyed a fresh cut and place them into the vase containing the water and dye solution. Systemic dyeing works best if the flowers have been dry packed or have not already been hydrated.

4

Flowers will begin to take up the solution and change color.

5

When the desired concentration of color has been reached, remove the flowers and place them into a solution of water and floral food.

Before using these sprays:
- Make sure the room has adequate ventilation.
- Make sure the surface of the object you are painting is clean and dry.
- Make sure your work area is protected from the overspray.
- Line the nozzle opening up with the small black mark on the rim of the can.
- Shake the can vigorously to thoroughly mix the contents.

When you begin spraying, maintain a distance of 12"–18" from the object being painted. As with any type of paint, it is better to use several thin coats than a single, thick coat which may cause runs and puddling on the surface. When using spray paint dyes, concentrate on the process and be methodical in order to achieve the best effects. Rushing the process will result in waste and added expense.

Carnations and roses are good candidates for a spray tinting technique known as tipping. To add color only to the tips or margins of petals, hold the flowers tightly, exposing only their margin, and apply the spray tint lightly to the tips.

Safety Note

The propellant used in spray tints becomes very cold when it hits the air and can cause injury to plant tissues. *To prevent damage, hold the nozzle about a foot away from fresh flowers and leaves when applying spray tints.*

Form

In floral design, *form* refers to the shape of an overall arrangement, as well as the shapes of the individual plant materials used in the arrangement. Some floral designs, such as a sphere of flowers or an angular line-mass design, stress the overall design. The form of the flowers becomes subordinate to the form of the design. These are said to be *closed-form arrangements*. The form outlines are solid and there is not a lot of airspace between the flowers, **Figure 7-10**. Conversely, *open-form arrangements* have more open space around the flowers. The form of the individual materials is more visible and important in open form arrangements.

Flower forms can be classified into four material categories: line, mass, filler, and form. A *line flower* is one that has a long stem, a spike or linear form, or both. Liatris, gladiolus, bells of Ireland, snapdragons, and delphinium are line flowers. Cattails and branches are also line materials. When creating an arrangement, designers often arrange line materials first to form the "bones" or framework for a geometric design.

Next, mass flowers go into the design. *Mass flowers* are closed-form, single flowers that have a dense, rounded shape. They form the "muscle" of the arrangement, filling spaces around the linear materials. Chrysanthemums, peonies, sunflowers, roses, daffodils, and carnations are considered mass flowers.

The final placements are usually the *filler flowers*. These are fine, often frilly materials such as Monte Cassino aster, statice, and baby's breath. They have an open-form inflorescence and are often clustered or branched. They form a visual connection between the line and mass flowers, enabling a designer to fill or complete a geometric form.

Farell's Florist, Drexel Hill PA; Leanne and David Kesler, Floral Design Institute, Inc.

Figure 7-10. In closed-form arrangements, emphasis is on the overall shape of the arrangement instead of the individual flowers. In this composition, the tightly-spaced flowers contribute to the ball-shaped form. In an open-form arrangement, emphasis is on the form of the individual elements that make up the design.

Stephen B. Goodwin/Shutterstock.com; Moon Light PhotoStudio/Shutterstock.com; Susi/Shutterstock.com; Dan Kosmayer/Shutterstock.com

Figure 7-11. Linear or line materials like this reddish snapdragon often form the basis for a design. Mass flowers, like carnations, fill out the design and give it character. Filler flowers such as baby's breath, form visual connections between the other types of flowers and help fill spaces. Form, or distinctive, flowers are best used in open-form designs to highlight their unique forms.

Form flowers are those having a distinctive or unusual shape. They do not necessarily fit into the other categories. They are often exotic and may be sold at a premium. A few distinctive flowers include bird of paradise, anthurium, and cattleya orchids. While these flowers can be placed very close together to create a design, most designers keep a lot of space between these flowers so their unique forms can be recognized and enjoyed. See **Figure 7-11**.

Fragrance

Flowers are appreciated the world over for their sweet perfumes. In nature, flowers have scents to attract specific pollinators. Some flowers give off *fragrances*, or specific aromas, at night because their pollinators are nocturnal moths. Others have terrible aromas, smelling like rotting meat to attract their preferred pollinators: flies.

Many commercially grown flowers have attractive fragrances, including stephanotis, stock, lilacs, freesia, gardenias, and carnations. Some floral designers take this into consideration when making a floral design, creating arrangements that have both fragrance and beauty. **Figure 7-12** lists fragrant flowers foliage that are commonly used in floral designs.

Did You Know?

Linalool is the chemical compound in mint, cinnamon, and citrus identified as giving a pleasing fragrance. Japanese researchers have found that stress in laboratory rats is reduced when they smell these fragrances.

Fragrant Flowers and Greenery	
Acacia	Easter Lily
Amaryllis (some varieties)	Lily of the Valley
Bouvardia	Oriental Lily
Carnations	Myrtle foliage
Cattleya (some varieties)	Paperwhites
Eucalyptus foliage	Peonies (some varieties)
Freesia	Rosemary
Gardenia	Roses (some varieties)
Scented Geranium foliage	Stephanotis
Ginesta	Stock
Hyacinth	Sweet Pea
Jasmine	Tuberose
Lavender	Waxflower
Lilac	

Goodheart-Willcox Publisher

Figure 7-12. The chart lists examples of fragrant flowers and foliage.

The use of fragrant flowers in floral designs can help people remember an occasion. Memories associated with fragrance are among the strongest memories people can experience. For example, suppose a bride chooses to use gardenias in her bridal bouquet. Decades after her wedding, she may be reminded of her wedding day whenever she smells gardenias.

Care must be taken when sending highly-perfumed flowers to places such as hospital rooms or small spaces. Too many fragrant flowers can be offensive, especially to those who are sensitive to fragrances.

Line

In floral design, *line* is the visual path that creates the foundation for an arrangement's style and form. It can be straight or curved, static or dynamic. *Static lines* appear rigid. Horizontal and vertical lines are typically considered static.

Dynamic lines are formed by bending, contorting, cascading, and zigzagging materials that make the eye move. They create energy and excitement. They direct the eye along the stronger vertical and horizontal static lines of the axis. When used correctly, the combination of static and dynamic lines is pleasing to the eye. See **Figure 7-13**.

Physical lines such as the stem of a flower, the stalk of a piece of wheat, or the branch of a tree, are called *actual lines*. These lines help build the structure of the design. However, not all lines are physically present in a design. Materials placed close together that visually connect to one another create an *implied line*. The mind's eye combines the similar elements into one visual stroke or line, **Figure 7-14**.

Different types of lines create a sense of mood or feeling from a design. Horizontal lines put emphasis on width rather than height. They create a sense of foundation and stability. Horizontal materials may be inserted along the rim of a container to create a resting place for the eye parallel to the surface of a table. Horizontal lines are often used in sympathy pieces because of their soothing, restful nature.

leungchopan/Shutterstock.com

Figure 7-13. Static lines often form the basic structure of a design, while dynamic lines create interest by adding movement. In this natural example, the tree bark forms static lines while the vine creates the dynamic line.

TaiChesco/Shutterstock.com

Figure 7-14. The mind's eye combines similar elements into one visual stroke or line. These rocks leading to the open water create a line that your eyes follow until the end.

An arrangement with a dominant vertical line suggests strength and stability. As one of the first insertions into most container arrangements, the vertical center establishes height and sets the stage for balance, proportion, scale, and design style. Whether combined with other vertical lines or with materials of other shapes, the vertical line is a critical element for motion in any design. It can direct a person's eye upward to the top of a design or down toward a focal point, creating intense energy.

Diagonal lines are effective for creating dramatic effects. Their slanting appearance creates motion. If not used correctly, using diagonals in combination with horizontal and vertical lines can create a sense of chaos. This type of design should be avoided by the beginning designer.

Pattern

In the most basic sense, a *pattern* is an element that is repeated to form a decorative design. Any of the design elements described in this chapter can be repeated to form a pattern. Artists and designers use patterns to create emphasis. The conscious use of repetition of a pattern sets up rhythm within a design.

When thinking about pattern as an element of floral design, it is hard not to take notice of the wonderful examples of patterns found in nature. Patterns are all around the natural world. Whether it's in the veins of a leaf, the stripes of a zebra, or the beautiful scales of a monarch butterfly, repetition can create dramatic effects. See **Figure 7-15**.

In another sense, pattern can refer to the overall shape or silhouette of a floral design. For example, a floral designer who duplicates a centerpiece for a reception with many tables is mimicking the pattern of flower insertions in each arrangement to make them look uniform.

Sombra/Shutterstock.com

Figure 7-15. Patterns and repetition can be found almost everywhere in nature. In these leaves, notice how perfectly the vein pattern is repeated.

sspopov/Shutterstock.com

Figure 7-16. Negative space is an integral part of this Ikebana design.

Steve Mann/Shutterstock.com

Figure 7-17. Determine the size of the design before choosing the flowers. The size of the arrangement should be proportionate to the overall size of the space.

Space

Floral designers determine the height, width, and depth of designs based on an arrangement's final destination and application. This requires a good understanding of space. *Space* is the three-dimensional area that is occupied by a floral design and may also include the area immediately surrounding it.

Floral designs contain two types of space. *Positive space* includes all of the space that is actually taken up by design materials. Flowers, foliage, vases, accessories—all of these things take up positive space. *Negative space* is the opposite. It is an intentionally empty area, skillfully left without objects and floral materials in order to emphasize a focal point or design feature. Negative space is a critical component of many design styles. The use of negative space is common in contemporary and Ikebana designs, **Figure 7-16**.

Size

The element of *size* works with the elements of line, form, and space to help determine the physical dimensions of an arrangement. The floral designer considers many factors when making decisions about the size of an arrangement.

- Where will the arrangement be used? Is it for a large room or a small tabletop?
- How much space is available?
- What form is best suited to the available area?

The arrangement's location is the biggest determining factor for size. In a large church or office space with high ceilings, a large design and a large container are needed. The floral materials used in the design also need to be big. Small materials would be dwarfed by the space. Delicately small flowers and foliage would get lost.

On the other hand, if the design will be placed in a bud vase, the flowers and foliage must be small enough to match the size of the container. Materials that are too large will overpower the vase and be out of scale. If the materials are not an appropriate size, the design will have neither physical nor visual balance. Select flowers based on the final size of a design, **Figure 7-17**.

Texture

Texture is both the visual and tactile surface quality of a material. It can be seen and touched. For example, the sharp spines of the leaves on a holly tree give the eye a sense of dark, dense, and coarse texture and provide a prickly poke when touched. The soft surfaces and rounded edges of a lamb's ear plant provide both the appearance and physical touch of softness. In floral design, the word texture refers to both the visual qualities and physical attributes of materials—most often focusing on a material's dominant trait. See **Figure 7-18**.

Every part of a floral arrangement, including the foliage, flowers, container, and accessories, add texture to the overall composition. This combination of textures makes the arrangement more interesting by creating excitement for the viewer. When an arrangement is not interesting, it usually lacks a focal point and textural interest within the focal area. The arrangement may appear flat or dull. By varying the concentration or percentages of texture, the designer may create contrast by using different types of textures, or create unity by using similar types of textures. The well-designed stairway garland in **Figure 7-19** is a good example of how materials complement each other and create a pleasing, natural design.

Vizual Studio/Shutterstock.com; Vaide Seskauskiene/Shutterstock.com

Figure 7-18. When a floral arrangement is to be viewed at close range, a variety of textures can add interest to the design. The lamb's ear provides a soft, fuzzy texture, whereas the holly has a prickly, shiny surface.

Zigzag Mountain Art/Shutterstock.com; Carol Caggiano AIFD PFCI/Society of American Florists

Figure 7-19. This natural evergreen wreath uses hanging incense cedar, blue-berried juniper, pine cones, and, fir to create exciting textural interest. This arrangement uses accents in addition to the plant material to create texture and interest.

Pro Tip

Using too many textures will make an arrangement look busy and overly done whereas using too few textures may make an arrangement look dull and incomplete.

Daniela Pelazza/Shutterstock.com

Figure 7-20. This white bridal bouquet has an interesting variety of flower shapes, colors, and textures. The green leaves and buds provide good contrast to prevent it from looking flat.

In order to create a successful design using contrast, a designer may use a combination of materials with the same color but different textures. For example, if a bride wants an all-white bouquet, you can still make a bouquet with impact by using materials such as freesia, roses, and bouvardia. Each material in the bouquet has its own evident texture which helps create exciting contrast. Using foliage with shiny, dark green leaves or leaves with distinct shapes, really makes the white flowers "pop." See **Figure 7-20**.

A good rule of thumb to follow when choosing foliage, is to use three types within a design. For example, the popular trio of ruffled leatherleaf fern, smooth salal, and soft plumosa fern adds three distinct colors, shapes, and textures to the arrangement, **Figure 7-21**. The dark green leather leaf is smooth with quite a few small leaflets on each leaf. The salal leaves have a smooth surface with a very distinct shape and may vary slightly in color. The plumosa fern appears soft and adds a very light and springy texture. Always keep in mind that using more pattern, shape, and texture within the leaves can draw interest, improve focal points, and create a more professional arrangement, **Figure 7-22**.

When creating a floral design, using a variety of materials in moderation is the key to success. Whether it is foliage or filler flowers, care should be taken to avoid over use of any one type of material.

chungking/Shutterstock.com; Madlen/Shutterstock.com; Madlen/Shutterstock.com

Figure 7-21. Following the three-texture guide, feathery plumosa, round salal, and multi-leaflet leatherleaf are often used together. Each one of these examples has a distinct shape and texture. Most designers recommend using three different greens to create more interest.

Figure 7-22. Collection of winter greens for holiday designs include juniper, holly, and pine. There are quite a few different cones available for use in arrangements and wreaths. The umbos (individual scale tips) vary in size, texture, and color. A variety of berries may also be used to contribute to the overall design of a piece.

While working with the concepts of texture and contrast, you may want to keep the following ideas in mind:

- The container and embellishments add texture to the arrangement. Keep the types of flowers and foliage to be used in mind when choosing these materials.
- Varying textures have a greater impact in one-color designs because they are not competing with a busy color theme.
- Each type of flower in a design should have a different texture. For example, if you are using two fillers, do not choose two fillers with the same texture. The same rule applies to mass flowers and line flowers.
- Each type of foliage in a design should have a different texture.
- When using contrasting textures, use a pattern of flower types to create a smooth transition between the different textures.
- Creating a repetitive pattern with extreme contrasts adds interest to an arrangement.
- Texture varies with a plant's surface and the arrangement of its petals and florets. When using one type of flower, turning the buds, stems, and blooms will help take advantage of the flower's varying textures.

Pro Tip

The environment in which the arrangement will be placed also contains textures. The arrangement should complement, not compete with its surroundings.

Summary

- Color is reflected light.
- Value is the lightness (tint) or darkness (shade) of a color.
- Intensity or chroma changes when a bright, pure hue is gradually dulled with gray.
- The primary colors are red, yellow, and blue, and the secondary colors are green, violet, and orange.
- Color harmonies are color schemes based on colors that work well together.
- The color of flowers can be changed using systemic dyeing or spray tinting.
- Flower forms can be categorized as line, mass, filler, or form.
- Floral fragrance appeals to the sense of smell and is closely linked to memory.
- Lines in a floral design can be static or dynamic, actual or implied.
- Most floral arrangements contain some type of pattern that gives unity and rhythm to the design.
- Floral designers need to develop a good sense of space to determine the size of a floral design.
- The use of various textures is more effective when an arrangement will be viewed up close.

Review Questions

Go to www.g-wlearning.com/floraldesign/ to use the fill-in-form.

Answer the following questions using the information provided in this chapter.

1. Name the eight design elements that are used in floral design.
2. Which colors are considered achromatic?
3. Which color system is based on the effect a color has on nearby colors?
4. Explain how the "temperature" of a color can be modified to a certain extent.
5. In which type of color harmony are colors adjacent on the color wheel combined in a floral design?
6. Briefly describe the process for dyeing white carnations.
7. Explain why spray tinting might be a better idea than cultivating a new color flower?
8. What is the difference between a closed-form arrangement and an open-form arrangement?
9. Why might a customer want to include fragrant flowers in an arrangement made for a special occasion?
10. Compare the uses for static and dynamic lines in a design.
11. Describe the two uses of the word *pattern* in floral design.
12. What is negative space and why is it often included in a floral design?
13. What other elements work together with size to determine the physical dimensions of an arrangement?
14. Explain why it is important to use different textures in a design.
15. Compare and contrast the use and application of design elements in floral design.

Activities

1. Locate a large selection of clothing articles such as hats, gloves, and scarves, all in black. Can you identify which are warmer in color and which are cooler?
2. Using a mixed floral arrangement as the subject, observe and record the varying effects of different types of light and light levels on the flowers within the design.
3. Stem-dye white carnations to make them green for St. Patrick's Day.
4. Form groups of four students and, using real student-designed floral arrangements or images from your portfolios, analyze your peers' designs in terms of the formal design qualities covered in the text. What type of conclusions did you reach about the use of formal design qualities?

Critical Thinking

1. The parents of a 15-year-old girl come to your flower shop to order a floral arrangement for her birthday. The parents tell you that they recently moved to the area and their daughter has been depressed because she does not know anyone at school. What colors might you suggest for the arrangement, and why?

2. Your flower shop has been commissioned to create an altar arrangement for a local church. You visited the church to get an idea of the space. You found that the building itself is fairly small, but it has a deep cathedral ceiling in an inverted V shape. The seating area for the congregation is decorated in blue. Describe the flowers, colors, and form you would use for this arrangement.

STEM Activities and Academics

1. **Social Studies.** Choose a color that was described in this chapter and research ways the color has been used throughout history. What concepts or beliefs are associated with the color? Prepare an oral report on the subject and deliver it to the class.

2. **Language Arts.** Patterns and repetition are found everywhere in nature. Go for a nature walk and find three natural items, such as flowers, leaves, trees, or even insects that have a pattern of some kind. Think about items made by people that have those same patterns. Write an essay comparing the natural items to the corresponding human-made items.

3. **Science.** Set up an experiment to determine how long it takes a white carnation to become completely dyed. The flower is considered "completely dyed" when leaving it for a longer time in the dye solution does not result in a darker shade. Take detailed notes, and record your method and results.

4. **Math.** A customer has asked you to design a floral arrangement that features ten roses for a ten-year wedding anniversary. Determine what filler materials you will need and the type of vase you will use. Go to a wholesale florist site online and find the quantity and prices for all of the items you will need for the arrangement. Estimate the time you will need to create the arrangement and include a charge for your time.

   A. What is the total cost of the arrangement, including materials and time?

   B. How much would you need to charge the customer in order to make a profit of $12.50?

   C. If your combined local and state sales tax is 6%, how much would the total be, including tax?

5. **Technology.** Today, many fragrances found in perfumes are artificial. Conduct research to find out how a flower scent can be incorporated into a perfume without using flowers. Write a report on your findings.

Communicating about Floral Design

1. **Speaking and Listening.** Working in small groups, create a poster illustrating the elements of design applied to floral arrangements. Decide what type of arrangement you are going to use. Second, draw and color the arrangement, keeping the element of color in mind. Use crayons, markers, colored pencils, or paint to create the arrangement. Label the following: form of arrangement (open or closed); line flowers, mass flowers, form flowers, and filler flowers; static and dynamic lines; any patterns used; negative and positive space; and various textures used. As you work with your group, discuss the meaning of each element. If time allows, present and explain your poster to the class.

2. **Speaking and Listening.** In small groups, discuss with your classmates—in basic, everyday language—your knowledge and awareness of the elements of design in your everyday surroundings. Take notes on the observations expressed. Review the points discussed, factoring in your new knowledge of the elements of design. Develop a summary of what you have learned about the elements of design and their presence in our everyday surroundings. Present your findings to the class, using the terms that you have learned about the elements of design in this chapter.

3. **Speaking and Writing.** Working in groups of three, create flash cards for the key terms in this chapter. Each student chooses four terms and makes flash cards for those four terms. Quiz one another on the pronunciations and definitions of the key terms. Using your textbook and dictionary for guidance, write the term on the front and the pronunciation and definition on the back.

Chapter

8

Flower Selection

objectives

After reading this chapter, you will be able to:

- Define the application for a design to narrow the choices of floral materials.
- Choose colors for a floral design using color harmonies and palettes.
- Determine when it is appropriate to use flowers with fragrance.
- Describe ways to reduce allergens in floral arrangements.
- Explain the traditional meanings of common flowers.
- Discuss the role of cost in selecting flowers for a design.
- Discuss the role of form in selecting flowers for a design.
- Identify flowers used in floral design.

key terms

application
color palette

color story
ROYGBIV

Go to **www.g-wlearning.com/floraldesign/** for online vocabulary activities using key terms from the chapter.

introduction

Flower selection is critical to the success of any floral design. Flowers chosen wisely not only produce the best results, but also minimize the cost to achieve those results.

Every flower, berry, branch, or leaf has natural qualities that make it different from all the others. Analyzing materials for their strongest trait can help you loosely group materials into categories for easy selection. Does the flower have a round shape or a star shape? Does it have single or multiple stems? Is it long and thin or short and dense? Designers use these special traits to create a desired effect, **Figure 8-1**. This chapter focuses on choosing the right flowers to create a successful design.

Application

As you know by now, hundreds of different flowers are available commercially for floral design work. How do you begin to choose which flowers to use for your designs? Base your selections on the "W" principle: *who*, *what*, and *where*. Answer these questions to determine the *application* for each design, which in turn will narrow your choice of options. For whom is the arrangement being created? Is the design for an adult or a child? For a male or a female? What is the occasion? Is it for a birthday celebration in someone's home or a visit to the hospital to see a sick friend? Is it for a business? Is it for a one-night event?

Mayabuns/Shutterstock.com

Figure 8-1. Floral designers choose materials with specific characteristics to achieve a desired outcome.

Next, you need to understand where the design will be used. Will the completed arrangement be placed in the center of a table or at the side of a hospital bed? Smaller materials are generally used in hospital arrangements because of the limited available space. These designs are viewed up close, so select products with a small scale and textural interest, **Figure 8-2**. Hefty flowers should be reserved for large designs in big spaces.

You must also consider the longevity of the flowers. If the flowers are for a one-night event, they are not expected to last two weeks. However, if the arrangement(s) is for a business account where the customer wants them changed every two weeks, they have to last two weeks. One compliment a florist loves to hear is that the "flowers lasted so long." The recipient usually remembers that the flowers were pretty, but they always remember how long they lasted. This complement is often followed with a new customer.

Another important aspect of flower selection is selling flowers from existing stock. Whether the customer is in your store or on the phone, suggest flowers that you have in stock. If the customer is in the store, take him or her to see live specimens from your flower cooler. Seeing and smelling the flowers may help sway them to your suggestions and away from flowers you do not have in stock.

One more consideration is the role the mechanical design or water source plays in flower selection. Depending on the type of arrangement your customer desires, the type of flowers they like may not work because of the mechanics. Flower stems that turn the water cloudy, daffodils for example, may not be the best selection for a design using a clear glass vase. There are flowers that do well in foam and others that do not. Combinations of flowers that do not like the same type of water will not work well either.

Be sure to take the customer's preferences into account when planning a floral design. What are the recipient's favorite colors? Does the recipient have a favorite type of flower? Incorporating favorite materials makes a design more personal and, therefore, seem more special to the customer and recipient.

Susan Fox/Shutterstock.com

Figure 8-2. Hospital rooms typically do not have much counterspace for floral arrangements. Hospital arrangements are, therefore, typically fairly small, depending on texture and contrasts for interest.

Color

After you have determined the application, select a ***color story***, or color theme, based on the information you have gathered. Base your material selections on the overall look of the event, or perhaps the honoree's favorite color. This is especially important when the job requires more than one arrangement. With the overwhelming types and colors of floral materials available, you can narrow your selection options by sticking to your color story, **Figure 8-3**. Take care that all arrangements, large or small, coordinate with the color selections.

Red/pink hues

Achillea	Celosia	Erica	Leptospermum	Phlox
Alstroemeria	Centaurea	Gerbera	Leucadendron	Protea
Amaranthus	Chamelaucium	Gladiolus	Lilium	Prunus
Anemone	Chrysanthemum	Gloriosa	Limonium	Rosa
Anigozanthus	Cosmos	Gomphrena	Malus	Schinus
Anthurium	Costus	Heliconia	Monarda	Sedum
Antirrhinum	Cymbidium	Hippeastrum	Nerine	Tulipa
Astilbe	Cytisus	Hypericum	Nigella	Xeranthemum
Bouvardia	Dianthus	Ilex (verticellata)	Paphiopedilum	Zantedeschia
Capsicum	Eremurus	Ixia	Pentas	Zinnia

Orange hues

Anthurium	Calendula	Dianthus	Hippeastrum	Rosa
Antirrhinum	Carthamus	Euphorbia	Ixia	Sandersonia
Asclepias	Celastrus	Freesia	Lilium	Strelitzia
Banksia	Chrysanthemum	Gerbera	Papaver	Tagetes
Bracteantha	Crocosmia	Gladiolus	Physalis	Zinnia

Yellow hues

Acacia	Centaurea	Digitalis	Gladiolus	Narcissus
Achillea	Chrysanthemum	Eremurus	Heliconia	Oncidium
Alstroemeria	Craspedia	Euphorbia	Iris	Rosa
Anigozanthus	Cymbidium	Forsythia	Lilium	Tulipa
Antirrhinum	Cytisus	Freesia	Limonium	Zantedeschia
Bracteantha	Dianthus	Gerbera	Matthiola	Zinnia

Green hues

Amaranthus	Bupleurum	Dianthus	Molucella	Viburnum
Angiozanthos	Chrysanthemum	Euphorbia	Paphiopedilum	Zantedeschia
Anthurium	Cymbidium	Gladiolus	Sarracenia	Zinnia
Banksia	Dendrobium	Malus	Triticum	

Blue/Indigo hues

Aconitum	Centaurea	Echinops	Iris	Nigella
Agapanthus	Delphinium	Hydrangea	Limonium	

Violet/Purple hues

Allium	Chamelaucium	Eryngium	Liatris	Syringa
Alstroemeria	Chrysanthemum	Freesia	Limonium	Tulipa
Anthurium	Delphinium	Gladiolus	Matthiola	
Aster	Dendrobium	Hydrangea	Phlox	
Callicarpa	Dianthus	Iris	Rosa	
Cattleya	Echinacea	Lavandula	Scabiosa	

White

Agapanthus	Chrysanthemum	Gardenia	Leptospermum	Prunus
Anemone	Convallaria	Gerbera	Lilium	Rosa
Anthurium	Cymbidium	Gladiolus	Limonium	Stephanotis
Aster	Delphinium	Gomphrena	Malus	Syringa
Astile	Dendrobium	Gypsophila	Matthiola	Tulipa
Bouvardia	Dianthus	Hippeastrum	Ornithogalum	Zantedeschia
Cattleya	Eremurus	Hydrangea	Phalaenopsis	
Chamelaucium	Freesia	Iris	Protea	

Goodheart-willcox Publisher

Figure 8-3. This chart includes many of the most common flowers listed by color.

Working with Color Harmonies

Chapter 7, *Elements of Design*, introduced the various color harmonies. This section explains how to use the color harmonies to develop a color story for any occasion. Adhering to a single color harmony, whether it's monochromatic, complementary, or analogous, to develop your color story eliminates floral choices that are not necessary to portray a theme. No matter how beautiful, unique, or appealing a flower may appear, if it does not work with your color story, it should be avoided.

Complementary Arrangements

As you may recall, flowers that are opposite each other on the color wheel are complementary. The traditional Christmas colors of red and green are an example of complementary colors used in floral design. The combination of red flowers and seasonal evergreens is often a customer's first choice for designs created for this holiday, **Figure 8-4**.

Analogous Arrangements

Colors that appear next to each other on the color wheel tend to look pleasant together because they are closely related. Choose one color to be the dominant color, and another to be the secondary color. Use a third color as an accent, along with gray, black, or white, **Figure 8-5**. A fall centerpiece can be beautiful in analogous colors. For example, you could use red rover mums, orange lilies, and light bronze spray chrysanthemums. Adding seasonal accents of small orange pumpkins or gourds and preserved bronze leaves makes a strong statement of fall.

Monochromatic Arrangements

As the name implies, monochromatic arrangements contain one dominant color. Secondary neutral materials support the primary color. For example, you might use pink and white miniature carnations for a newborn baby girl. In this case, pink is the primary or

Keybrite/Shutterstock.com

Figure 8-4. When placed next to each other, complementary colors like the blue and orange above create a high level of contrast and excitement. Many schools use complementary colors for their school's colors.

Sergey Andrianov/Shutterstock.com

Figure 8-5. Many autumn arrangements use analogous colors. The colors used in this bouquet can be seen in the foliage and flowers of the fall season.

ElenaKor/Shutterstock.com

Figure 8-6. In this arrangement for a baby girl, the pink ranunculus dominate the arrangement and are supported by the smaller white flowers.

dominant color, and the white supports it. The arrangement in **Figure 8-6** is a monochromatic arrangement featuring pink as the primary or dominant color.

Color Palettes

A good starting point for choosing flower colors is to use one of the many *color palettes*, or selection tools, that have been developed over the years. Tools that can be used for this purpose include the 12-hue color wheel, the Munsell color system, and the Munsell color tree.

Another color wheel, devised by Sir Isaac Newton, includes seven colors in order of their appearance in a rainbow. Today it takes the form of either a wheel or a color chart called ***ROYGBIV***, which stands for Red-Orange-Yellow-Green-Blue-Indigo-Violet, see **Figure 8-7**. Several mnemonics, or memory devices, have been developed to help people remember the order of the colors. Some of the more popular ones include:

- Roy G. Biv
- Rinse Out Your Granny's Boots In Vinegar
- Richard Of York Gave Battle In Vain
- Rowntree Of York Gave Best In Value
- Read Out Your Good Book In Verse

R   O   Y   G   B   I   V

Skylines/Shutterstock.com; kubais/Shutterstock.com; Anettphoto/Shutterstock.com; Vorobyeva/Shutterstock.com; Vorobyeva/Shutterstock.com; Kubais /Shutterstock.com

Figure 8-7. The colors of the rainbow are not the separate bands we see. The colors actually flow into each other with gradations we may not see. If desired, flowers like the roses above, may be dyed to create "rainbow" arrangements or to cover an arch for a school dance or birthday party.

Psychology of Color

Most people see colors the same way—light reflecting off of objects is taken in through the eye and processed in the brain. However, color means different things to different people. Emotional and psychological responses to color vary among people from different cultures, geographies, and backgrounds. Even personal experiences can affect a person's response to color.

Colors can also affect human behavior. Blues and greens are calming and restful, while red is active and passionate. Yellow is considered cheerful and orange has been documented to increase appetites. The following information about the effects of color may help you use it more effectively when creating floral designs for holidays, for various occasions, or for the places where people live and work.

Blue

In general, blue is a tranquil, calming hue, **Figure 8-8**. Blue is the color of the sky and ocean; various shades and tints of blue are used for nautical applications. Sometimes, people say they are "blue" when they are feeling depressed. Blue flowers include Delphiniums, Dutch iris, Agapanthus, and bachelor buttons.

Green

When something is green, it is usually part of the environment. With today's focus on sustainability and using natural resources wisely, being "green" is important. This color is youthful, robust, and reminds people of growth. Green flowers include chrysanthemums, bells of Ireland, Dianthus and just as important, the incredibly wide variety of cut foliage available to us for use in floral design, **Figure 8-9**.

Sherjaca/Shutterstock.com; mubus7/Shutterstock.com

Figure 8-8. These blue bachelor buttons or delphiniums could be used in an arrangement to create a sense of peacefulness or calm. The bachelor buttons are vibrant and add a great deal of texture whereas the delphiniums are more petite with rounded petals.

Dirk van der Walt/Shutterstock.com; NH/Shutterstock.com

Figure 8-9. The color green can evoke a sense of youthfulness or environmental responsibility. The Bells of Ireland flowers are line flowers that are often used to add height or create the form of an arrangement. The button spray mums, as depicted here, can be mass flowers in small designs or filler flowers in medium and large designs.

Figure 8-10. The color lime green draws attention. Both the larger mum and button mums are naturally lime green. These flowers go especially well with purple and violet.

In recent years, lime green has become popular in both flowers and foliage. Breeders have developed numerous flowers, such as chrysanthemums and carnations, to be naturally colored lime green. This strong and bright color makes a good companion for dark purple, hot pink, deep red, and orange flowers. Foliage is also available in lime green.

Because of its vibrant color, lime green draws attention, **Figure 8-10**. The eye perceives lime green as an advancing color whereas other shades of green are perceived as receding colors. It can be used for contrast against colors opposite on the color wheel, or as a colorful element in a focal zone. Examples include Bupleurum, some types of Leucadendron, and the berry-type Hypericum.

Orange

Warm is usually the first word people use to describe orange. It is the color of sunset and sunrise, and it is a healthy color because of its association with the vitamin C in oranges and the sun. Sometimes, orange may seem aggressive, and it is often used in construction to warn of potentially dangerous sites. Gerbera daisies, calendula, zinnias, tulips and many other flowers are naturally orange. The leaves of croton cultivars also have a lot of orange in them, **Figure 8-11**.

Figure 8-11. Orange, as in the zinnias above, is a warm color that can be used to bring a sense of cheerfulness or happiness to a floral arrangement. As illustrated by the croton cultivar on the right, color may also be found in foliage.

Pink

Softer than red, pink is sometimes thought of as a feminine color, although many men also enjoy wearing it. A pink ribbon has become the symbol for breast cancer awareness. The expression "being in the pink" means that someone is healthy. Pink is most often thought of as a spring color, but it is widely used in the summer months because it is not as warm as the color red. The color pink is also used as an alternative color to red in the winter months through the use of pink poinsettias. Roses, carnations, lilies, and Phalaenopsis orchids are just a few of the myriad variety of pink flowers, **Figure 8-12**.

Purple

Deep violets and purples hold the eye a bit longer than many colors. Throughout history, purple has been considered primarily as the color of royalty. It has also been used to symbolize magic and mystery, power, nobility, and ambition. Some studies indicate that almost 75% of young children prefer purple to all other colors. Purple is the color of fresh violets, statice, and lavender. Lisianthus and the Moon Series™ carnations provide a dose of vibrant purple to fresh floral designs. Velvety, showy purple hairs grow on the leaves of *Gynura aurantiaca*, a popular houseplant, **Figure 8-13**. Some people think purple is overpowering if used in dominant proportions in designs while others cannot get enough of this rich color.

Ilya Mikhaylov/Shutterstock.com; natuska/Shutterstock.com

Figure 8-12. Phalaenopsis orchids and pink gerbera daisies are examples of two very distinct pink flowers that can add color and a feminine touch to an arrangement.

Scisetti Alfio/Shutterstock.com; hd connelly/Shutterstock.com

Figure 8-13. Lavender is favored not only for its soft, purple color, but also for its soothing scent. The *Gynura aurantiaca*, or Purple Passion is a popular houseplant because of its beautiful leaves.

Red

Arguably the color with the most emotional impact, red is at the top of the rainbow. It is used to get attention, and is an effective color for sports cars, lipstick, and roses. Red can symbolize anger, blood, debt, and fire, but it also suggests love, life, and happiness. Poinsettias, Anthurium, amaryllis, Ranunculus, and dahlias are just a few of the flowers available in variations of red, **Figure 8-14**.

Yellow

Yellow is possibly the most vibrant, recognizable color on the planet, **Figure 8-15**. It shows well from a distance and is often seen in nature as a warning when placed next to black (think snakes and bees). Humans also use this combination in safety signs to remind people to be cautious. Search for yellow daffodils, yarrow, and euonymus foliage for floral designs.

Gold and Silver

Although gold and silver are not naturally found in plant material, they are often used as accessories or accents in floral designs. Metallic gold appears warm, while matte or flat gold is somewhat cooler in appearance. Gold is highly reflective, especially when used with black or dark colors. It appears cooler when placed on white because it loses some of its reflectivity. Silver is a cool metal and takes on the hues reflected into it, like a mirror. When using metallic backgrounds, rely on shadow to provide a layering of black between the background and the floral materials.

William Milner/Shutterstock.com; Chaowalit Seeneha/Shutterstock.com

Figure 8-14. Red poinsettias are always a favorite for the winter holidays. The bold, red salvia will add vibrant color, height, and interesting texture to any garden.

Loskutnikov/Shutterstock.com; Michael Solway/Shutterstock.com

Figure 8-15. Yellow is one of the happiest and enthusiastic colors. Tulips have quickly gone from a common garden flower to a favorite addition to stylish arrangements. Yarrow is popular in both traditional and modern floral arrangements. It is also an excellent choice for dried floral arrangements.

Earthy Colors

Earthy colors such as browns are made by mixing unequal proportions of primary colors. Artists refer to these as *broken hues*, and they are warmer and less intense than other hues. In floral designs, earthy colors are found in flowers, stems, leaves, roots, and fruits. They work well with all colors because their parent hues are the primary colors red, yellow, and blue.

White

White flowers are often associated with heaven and bridal bliss, therefore floral designers often use various white flowers for sympathy designs and bridal bouquets. The color itself is clean because it is pure light. When used without contrasting colors, it may seem like the flag of surrender to some people. Others may find it too bland or too cold. Baby's breath, Shasta daisies, Easter lilies and larkspur are just a few of the flowers that are available in white. See **Figure 8-16**.

Gray

Gray can be a strong support color or, depending on the material's form, it can highlight a focal area, as with eryngium, **Figure 8-17**. The weeping habit of seeded eucalyptus can provide both physical and visual "movement" to a design. Placed along the lip of a container, the downward droop can visually connect a holiday centerpiece to the table on which it is placed.

Middle values of gray make hues adjacent to it appear stronger, and a hue surrounded by gray seems more colorful.

Nina B/Shutterstock.com; MARKABOND/Shutterstock.com

Figure 8-16. Shasta daisies are often used in arrangements to achieve a clean, uncomplicated effect. For many people, daisies are a "happy flower." White hybrid delphinium will complement almost any type of floral arrangement.

Sebastian Knight/Shutterstock.com; arka38/Shutterstock.com

Figure 8-17. Gray flowers and foliage with interesting shapes, such as this *Eryngium*, can form the focal point of an arrangement. Succulents often have a gray tint and are popular in bouquets and other arrangements.

The gray will appear to be tinged with the complement of the hue. Mixing gray-toned plant material such as limonium can tone down the colors of a design if used in increasingly dominant quantities.

Black

Black is the color of the deepest part of the night. It is mysterious and quietly intense. Apparel designers often choose to wear black because it shows authority, yet blends with all other colors. Black is the absence of light and may be depressing to some people. It is sometimes considered the color of death and mourning in American culture, but this is a holdover from the Victorian period and not always followed. It is often considered a sophisticated, powerful color. Some plant materials can be dyed black and accessories can be painted. Fresh flowers that are close to black are usually dark purple or very dark red, **Figure 8-18**.

The importance of color in floral design is indisputable. Color helps tell a story, set a theme, or support a mood. Floral designers should always consider the appropriate use of color and continue to experiment with its effects throughout their careers.

Form

As explained in Chapter 7, *Elements of Design*, form refers to both the shapes of the individual plants and flowers used in an arrangement as well as the arrangement itself. Closed-form arrangements do not have much open space in or around the composition. Open-form arrangements use open space around the flowers as part of the design.

marionhassold/Shutterstock.com; Henk Vrieselaar/Shutterstock.com

Figure 8-18. Although these "black" calla lilies are actually a deep purple, they are commonly used as black flowers in bouquets and table arrangements. Most people do not think of the color black when they think of flowers, but these black tulips would make a striking and beautiful display, especially when paired with a white flower.

Liatris Line flower	Mum Mass	Baby's Breath Filler	Gloriosa Form
Brzostowska/Shutterstock.com	nelea33/Shutterstock.com	Natasha Breen/Shutterstock.com	ntdanai/Shutterstock.com

Figure 8-19. Examples of the four flower forms. Liatris comes in various colors and is a favorite line flower for many floral designers. Mums are also available in many colors and varieties and is one of the standard mass flowers in floral design. Baby's breath can be used to fill in bouquets and arrangements. Many exotic flowers have distinctive forms and colors and often demand attention when used in a composition.

When choosing flower forms, remember the four classifications: line, mass, filler, and form or distinctive, **Figure 8-19**.

- Line flowers may have a long stem, a spike or linear form, or both; often used to form the "bones" of the design.
- Mass flowers are closed-form, single flowers that have a dense, rounded shape; used to fill out around the linear materials.
- Filler flowers are materials such as baby's breath; used to form a visual connection between the line and mass flowers or to add visual weight.
- Form flowers usually have a strong or unusual shape; often set somewhat apart from other flowers in a design.

As you can see, both form and color play major roles in flower selection.

Fragrant Flowers

Although many people enjoy the fragrance of flowers, fragrance is not always appropriate. Think carefully about how the arrangement will be used before including fragrant flowers in the design. For example, materials with low fragrance, or no fragrance at all, should be chosen for hospital rooms, **Figure 8-20**. If possible, find out whether the customer enjoys the fragrance of flowers before including heavily fragrant flowers in a design.

Did You Know?

The brightest flowers are often fragrance-free. Some birds have a poor sense of smell and are attracted to bright flowers because of their color.

Carnation	Sunflower	Dahlia
Drozdowski/Shutterstock.com	Ian 2010/Shutterstock.com	apiguide /Shutterstock.com
Anemone	**Poppy**	**Calla**
InavanHateren/Shutterstock.com	Vladimira/Shutterstock.com	limages/Shutterstock.com
Ranunculus	**Chrysanthemum**	**Lisianthus**
Kantaruk/Shutterstock.com	Vincent Roy/Shutterstock.com	kiya-nochka/Shutterstock.com

Figure 8-20. Because hospital rooms are typically small and are often filled with guests, flowers with fragrance may be overpowering. Choose flowers with little or no fragrance for this setting. As you can see by the flowers illustrated here, little or no fragrance does not diminish natural beauty.

In many cases, however, fragrance can add another dimension of beauty to a floral design. Some flowers, such as roses and gardenias, have distinctive, easily recognizable fragrances. Many others also have interesting fragrances that may add character to a floral design. Examples include:

- Lilac—purple clusters that have a sweet, fruity odor with a hint of vanilla.
- Chocolate cosmos—reddish-brown flowers with a light fragrance.

- Tuberose—white flowers, sometimes with a blush of pink, that have a strong, candy-like fragrance.
- Freesia—flowers of various colors that have a sweet, fruity fragrance with a hint of mint or citrus.
- Wisteria—purple or white clusters that have a mild, sweet scent.
- Lily of the valley—small white or pink flowers with a sweet fragrance.
- Strawberry-scented geranium—pink flowers with a light strawberry-lemon fragrance.
- Stock—single or double flowers with a pleasing clove-like scent.

Flower Pollen

Once in a while, consumers may shun cut flowers because they feel as though they may cause allergies to flare up. Goldenrod (*Solidago*) is a cut flower that often gets a bad rap. Its natural blooming time is late summer, which just happens to coincide with the time Ragweed is in bloom. While Ragweed and other windborne pollens cause many people discomfort, Solidago's pollen is too heavy to be borne on the wind. It must be carried by pollinators like honeybees, thus, it is not usually a trigger for allergy problems.

Lily pollen tends to be messy. The pollen is on the anthers at the tip of the stamens, which extend beyond the flower petals. The sticky pollen transfers to anything it touches, including clothing and skin, and pollen stains are difficult to remove, **Figure 8-21**. If you buy lilies that do have anthers, remove them as soon as the lily bloom begins to open. At this point, the pollen is not dry and messy. Simply pluck the anthers and discard them. Do not remove the stamens, because doing so will reduce the vase life of the flower.

Ruth Peterkin/Shutterstock.com; Elliotte Rusty Harold/Shutterstock.com

Figure 8-21. Pollen from lilies stains everything it touches, including your hands. It is best to remove the anthers as soon as the flower opens to prevent getting the pollen on your hands or clothes. A honeybee gathering pollen on Goldenrod. This pollen is too heavy to be blown by the wind.

Step-by-Step

Removing Lily Pollen

Follow these tips to avoid staining the flower petals, your fingers, or the working surface when you remove the anthers from lilies:

Anthers

- Remove anthers as soon as the lilies begin to open.
- Do not spread lily pollen to the stigma. This hastens fertilization and ethylene synthesis, thus speeding senescence.
- If lily pollen attaches to your clothing, do not brush it away with your fingers. Natural oils in your skin will help set it deeper, making it more difficult to remove.
  Use a soft brush or chenille stem to lift lily pollen from your clothes. If possible, leave the stained material in strong sunlight for a few days. After a few days, the pollen will dry and you can brush it away.
- If pollen accidentally falls on a flower petal, use a pipe cleaner to gently dust off the pollen. An antitranspirant spray may also be used to gently wash it away.

Meanings of Flowers

Traditionally, specific meanings have been attached to various types of flowers. In fact, in Victorian times, flowers were often used to express coded meanings. For example, acacia meant friendship, but yellow acacia meant secret love. Baby's breath and daisies symbolized innocence or purity, and jasmine stood for grace and elegance. Carnations could have many meanings, depending on their color. Pink carnations symbolized gratitude, but red carnations meant deep love or passion.

Some people still enjoy using the traditional meanings of flowers when they choose the flowers for an arrangement. In Great Britain, brides often choose their wedding flowers according to their meanings. For example, Princess Kate Middleton's bouquet consisted of lily of the valley, hyacinth, myrtle, ivy, and Sweet William. To see what these and other flowers mean, see **Figure 8-22**. For a more detailed table of suggested flower meanings, refer to the *Appendix*. Knowing the traditional meaning of various types of flowers can help you inform customers who want their arrangements to represent a certain thought or sentiment. For example, if a young man comes in and wants to propose and present a bouquet to his girlfriend that expresses his feelings using the perceived meanings of flowers, as a florist, you could make a bouquet conveying his thoughts. He could explain what each of the flowers means to him as part of his proposal.

Flower	Meaning
African Violet	Faithfulness
Ambrosia	Your Love Is Reciprocated
Bronze Mums	Joy, Long-life, Truth, Wonderful Friend
Cactus	Endurance
Cattail	Peace, Prosperity
Dandelion	Faithfulness, Happiness
Gardenia	You're Lovely, Secret Love, Remembrance, Strength
Ivy	Wedded Love, Fidelity, Friendship, Affection
Lily of the Valley	Sweetness, You've Made My Life Complete
Orchid	Love, Beauty, Refinement, Beautiful Lady, Chinese Symbol for Many Children, mature charm
Pink Camellia	Longing for You
Pink Rose	Perfect Happiness, To My Friend
Red and White Roses	Unity
Red Camellia	You are a Flame in My Heart
Sweetpea	Good-bye, Departure, Blissful Pleasure, Thank You for a Lovely Time
White Rose	Purity, You're Heavenly
Yellow Rose	Joy, Gladness and Friendship

Goodheart-Willcox Publisher

Figure 8-22. The chart above is a small example of flowers and their perceived meanings. Refer to the appendix for a more extensive list.

Identifying Flowers

Because floral designers can choose from literally hundreds of different types of flowers for their designs, there is no easy way to learn or remember all of the options available. You will learn the most common flowers through experience, but it is a good idea to become familiar with as many choices as possible. This will allow you to create a variety of beautiful designs with confidence. The illustrations at the end of this chapter will help you get started. You may also choose to visit the websites of wholesale florists and growers occasionally to find out about any new and exciting cultivars that have become available.

Cost

Lastly, but also importantly, floral designers choose flowers based on their cost. When flowers are purchased during their standard growing season, they are less expensive. This is why the price of a particular design may change throughout the year.

Methods of pricing floral designs will be discussed in Chapter 18, *Floriculture Marketing, Pricing, and Sales.* However, before you begin selecting flowers for your designs, you should know a little about how your choice of materials affects the price of an arrangement.

Design Costs

Before you select the flowers for a design, consider both the customer and the application. Many customers have a price range in mind when they come to the flower shop. That price range has a definite effect on the materials you choose. The profit you make on an arrangement equals the price you charge the customer minus the cost of materials, overhead costs like rent and utilities, and your labor. Therefore, if a customer gives you a low price range, you will need to choose less expensive materials than if the customer gives you a high price range.

For example, suppose a young woman comes to your flower shop wanting an arrangement for her sister, who just had a baby girl. She wants a pretty arrangement with pink roses, but she does not have much money to spend. You agree on a price of $50 for the arrangement. This price includes a labor charge of $15.00 (many florists charge a 30% labor fee), a $10.00 vase, and $12.00 for filler materials and accessories. In your shop, you have the following flowers available:

- Pink and white carnations, for which you paid $1.00 per stem
- Pink spray roses (two to three roses per stem), for which you paid $1.37 per stem
- Pink sweetheart roses (one rose per stem), for which you paid $1.75 per stem

Obviously, the carnations are the least expensive choice, but the customer wants roses. **Figure 8-23** shows several different options for this arrangement. As you can see, the obvious choice is not always the best choice. The "Total Cost for Flowers" column represents the combined total of the different types of flowers in each of the other columns.

Carnations		Spray Roses		Sweetheart Roses		Total Cost for Flowers
No. of Flowers	Cost	No. of Flowers	Cost	No. of Flowers	Cost	
7	$ 7.00					$ 7.00
4	$ 4.00	2	$ 2.74			$ 6.74
				7	$ 12.25	$ 12.25
		3	$ 4.11	2	$ 3.50	$ 7.61

Figure 8-23. Options for a low-cost arrangement.

To find the total cost of the entire arrangement, first add all of the other expenses:

$	15.00	labor
	10.00	vase
+	12.00	fillers/accessories
$	37.00	total other expenses

Suppose your shop policy is that you must make at least $4.00 in profit on every arrangement. The agreed-upon price of the arrangement is $50.00, so you have $50.00 – $37.00 – $4.00 = $9.00 left to spend on the flowers. Right away, you can see from **Figure 8-23** that you cannot afford to use all sweetheart roses in the arrangement, and you cannot afford to use a combination of spray roses and sweetheart roses. Both of these options cost more than $9.00.

For $9.00, you could do an arrangement using all carnations. However, a nicer option would be mix in two stems of the pink spray roses with four white carnations. This would actually cost a little less than using all carnations, and it would provide four to six roses in the arrangement. As you can see, it pays to think about the various design options before settling for the most obvious choice. Be creative, do the math, and determine which option will be the best for both the flower shop and the customer.

Practice

The "workhorse" flowers such as chrysanthemums and carnations are used consistently for a reason. Practically the entire spectrum of color is available in these two types of flowers. They are durable, long-lasting, versatile, and reasonably priced. For this reason, you may choose to practice on these flowers before moving on to more expensive design materials, **Figure 8-24.**

Eky Studio/Shutterstock.com; joloei/Shutterstock.com

Figure 8-24. Chrysanthemums are available in a variety of colors and may be dyed to match themes for special events, such as weddings and homecoming dances, and for Texas mums. Carnations are versatile and are often used for school fund raisers and in the construction of corsages in school colors.

Summary

- One way to narrow the many choices of flowers for a floral design is to determine the intended application for the arrangement.
- Floral designers use color harmonies and color palettes to plan arrangements with pleasing colors.
- Different colors affect people in different ways psychologically, so colors can be used to evoke specific feelings.
- Many flowers have a nice fragrance that can enhance a floral design, but the designer must be aware of occasions and places where fragrance should not be used.
- Knowing the traditional meaning of various types of flowers can help you inform customers who want their arrangements to represent a certain thought or sentiment.
- Choosing the best material for an arrangement requires a basic knowledge of the flowers used in floral design.
- The cost of flowers should be appropriate for the price range of a design.

Review Questions   Go to www.g-wlearning.com/floraldesign/ to use the fill-in-form.

Answer the following questions using the information provided in this chapter.

1. What questions should you ask to determine the application for a design?
2. Why should you usually stick to a single color harmony when you develop the color story for an arrangement?
3. Name a holiday for which monochromatic color schemes are often used, and specify the usual colors.
4. What is ROYGBIV?
5. From the information in this chapter, identify three line flowers, three mass flowers, three filler flowers, and three form flowers. (You may choose flowers from the Flower Glossary.)
6. Describe a situation in which fragrant flowers should *not* be used in a floral design.
7. Name five flowers that can be used to add fragrance to a floral design.
8. Explain how a designer should handle potential problems caused by lily pollen.
9. Explain how knowing the traditional meanings of flowers can help a floral designer.
10. Explain why it is important to keep the cost of the flowers in mind when you are designing an arrangement for a customer.

Activities

1. Play "flower form" jeopardy using 100 top flower and foliage options for designs with students.
2. Create your own mnemonic for ROYGBIV.
3. Design a bud vase using flowers that have a specific meaning of your choice.

Critical Thinking

1. A customer tells you he wants an arrangement for his 7-year-old daughter that is "full of fun, cheerfulness, and giggles." Using the information in this chapter, in the Appendix, and online resources, plan a design that includes flowers with these meanings.
2. A young boy comes to your flower shop and explains that he wants to buy flowers for his mother, who is "very sick." He has saved up his money and proudly shows you his savings of $15. Go online to research the cost of various flower types and accessories. What can you do for this customer?

STEM Activities and Academics

1. **Language Arts.** Complete an oral history by interviewing a floral designer. If you are unable to interview someone, read one or more case studies about floral designers from reliable Internet or library resources. How does the information you learned from the interview or reading compare to information presented by the authors of this textbook? Write a detailed summary of your interview or reading, describing how floral design affected the person's life.

2. **Math.** A wholesale florist sells 50-yard rolls of satin ribbon at $19 per roll, or at $16 per roll if you purchase three or more rolls. Answer the following questions:

   How much would you pay per yard if you bought one roll?

   How much would you pay per yard if you bought 12 rolls?

   What would the total cost be, before taxes, if you bought two rolls?

   What would the total cost be, before taxes, if you bought 15 rolls?

3. **Science.** Conduct research to find out more about why extensive hybridizing tends to breed the pollen out of plants. Write a report of your findings.

4. **Math.** Many wholesale florists give *quantity discounts*: The more you buy, the lower the price per stem. Find a wholesale florist online that gives quantity discounts. Research and record the prices for different quantities of red roses and red carnations. If necessary, do the math to determine the price per stem at each quantity for each type of flower. Then create a graph showing your results. Your graph should show how the price per stem changes depending on the quantity purchased.

5. **Social Studies.** Conduct research to find out more about how flowers were used during the Victorian era. If you were a flower shop owner in Victorian England, what types of designs would you be making? For example, would the majority of your work be creating tabletop designs, flowers to wear, or other types of arrangements? What types of flowers might you use most?

6. **Technology.** Search the Internet for new technologies related to floral design. Choose one of interest and determine the following: What are the benefits of using the technology to enhance productivity? What are some disadvantages or risks of using the new technology? What actions could you take to reduce the disadvantages or risks? In your opinion, for what applications will this new technology most likely be used?

Communicating about Floral Design

1. **Writing and Listening.** Divide into groups of four or five students. Have each person choose a person in the group to whom they would like to give flowers. Using the charts with flower meanings and colors, design (on paper) a monochromatic flower bouquet for that person. Present the bouquet to the recipient and ask them to decipher its meaning. Share your interpretations with the rest of the group or class. If time permits, create an analogous bouquet and repeat the activity.

2. **Reading and Speaking.** Using real or silk plant materials, create a bouquet that goes against every color harmony rule. Use a container that is also contrary to the design and color harmony. Write a list of questions to ask your fellow students how they would fix the arrangement. Include at least one of each type of flower (line, mass, filler, form).

3. **Reading and Writing.** The ability to read and interpret information is an important workplace skill. Presume you work for a well-known, successful floral designer. Your employer is considering pitching a proposal to the White House to supply the floral arrangements for the inaugural ball. He wants you to evaluate and interpret some research on past designers and the arrangements that were used. Locate three reliable resources for the most current information on designs from an inaugural ball. Read and interpret the information. Write a report summarizing your findings in an organized manner.

paula french/Shutterstock.com

Flower Glossary

The flower glossary in this text contains materials commonly available on the wholesale market as well as a few products that are available from local suppliers. Because a floral designer is often asked about flowering annuals used in exterior displays, or may have an opportunity to use them in an exhibit or event, some of the familiar flowering annuals have also been included in this glossary.

To a beginning designer, the wide variety of plant names can be overwhelming. To help you learn both the common and botanical (scientific) names, the flowers are alphabetized by the common name used most frequently in the profession and regional locales. The botanical name is below the common name and there is a cross-reference chart in the appendix. For the botanical names, major focus is on the genus name without a specific epithet. Professional florists often use the botanical name as a common name so it is beneficial to learn both. When used in print, the common name is not italicized. *The term botanical name and scientific name may sometimes be used interchangeably. For the sake of consistency, the term botanical name has been used throughout the textbook.*

Go to www.g-wlearning.com/floraldesign/ to use e-flash cards and other activities using the flowers from the illustrated glossary.

AlessandroZocc/Shutterstock.com

Common Name: Ageratum
Botanical Name: *Ageratum* sp.

cre250/Shutterstock.com

Common Name: Alstroemeria, Peruvian Lily
Botanical Name: *Alstroemeria* sp.

feawl/Shutterstock.com

Common Name: Amaranth Fountain Plant
Botanical Name: *Amaranthus* sp.

ntdanai/Shutterstock.com

Common Name: Amaryllis
Botanical Name: *Amaryllis* sp.

satit_srihin/Shutterstock.com

Koroffka/Shutterstock.com

| Common Name: Anthurium | Common Name: Aster |
| Botanical Name: *Anthurium* sp. | Botanical Name: *Aster* sp. |

Vahan Abrahamyan/Shutterstock.com

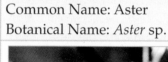

schankz/Shutterstock.com

| Common Name: Aster, Novae Belgii | Common Name: Aster, China |
| Botanical Name: *Aster novae belgii* | Botanical Name: *Callistephus chinensis* |

Maria Meester/Shutterstock.com

Natasha Breen/Shutterstock.com

| Common Name: Astilbe, Plume Flower | Common Name: Baby's Breath |
| Botanical Name: *Astilbe* sp. | Botanical Name: *Gypsophila* sp. |

val lawless/Shutterstock.com

Common Name: Bachelor's Button, Cornflower
Botanical Name: *Centaurea cyanus*

hwongcc/Shutterstock.com

Common Name: Balloon Flower
Botanical Name: *Platycodon grandiflorus*

Lily Zdilar/Shutterstock.com

Common Name: Banksia
Botanical Name: *Banksia* sp.

islavicek/Shutterstock.com

Common Name: Beard Tongue
Botanical Name: *Penstemon* sp.

dashingstock/Shutterstock.com

Common Name: Beauty Berry
Botanical Name: *Callicarpa* sp.

Vahan Abrahamyan/Shutterstock.com

Common Name: Bee-Balm, Fragrant Balm
Botanical Name: *Monarda didyma*

Fogflow/Shutterstock.com

Common Name: Bellflower, Chimney Bells
Botanical Name: *Campanula* sp.

Bayanova Svetlana/Shutterstock.com

Common Name: Bells of Ireland
Botanical Name: *Moluccella laevis*

photomatz/Shutterstock.com

Common Name: Bird of Paradise
Botanical Name: *Strelitzia reginae*

Skorpionik00/Shutterstock.com

Common Name: Bittersweet
Botanical Name: *Celastrus* sp.

Fogflow/Shutterstock.com

Common Name: Black-Eyed Susan
Botanical Name: *Rudbeckia* sp.

oksana2010/Shutterstock.com

Common Name: Blanket Flower
Botanical Name: *Gaillardia* sp.

Mary Terriberry/Shutterstock.com

Common Name: Blue Bells, Virginia Blue Bells
Botanical Name: *Mertensia virginica*

haru/Shutterstock.com

Common Name: Bouvardia
Botanical Name: *Bouvardia* sp.

Ruud Morijn Photographer/Shutterstock.com

Common Name: Brunia
Botanical Name: *Brunia* sp.

prizzz/Shutterstock.com

Common Name: Bupleurum
Botanical Name: *Bupleurum rotundifolium*

LianeM/Shutterstock.com

Common Name: Butterfly Bush
Botanical Name: *Buddleja davidii*

limages/Shutterstock.com

Common Name: Calla
Botanical Name: *Zantedeschia* sp.

Bildagentur Zoonar GmbH/Shutterstock.com noppharat/Shutterstock.com

eurobanks/Shutterstock.com

Common Name: Camellia
Botanical Name: *Camellia* sp.

Common Name: Candytuft
Botanical Name: *Iberis* sp.

Gertjan Hooijer/Shutterstock.com

Darkkong/Shutterstock.com

Common Name: Carnation
Botanical Name: *Dianthus* sp.

Common Name: Carnation, Spray Carnation
Botanical Name: *Dianthus* sp.

kenjii/Shutterstock.com

Baisch & Skinner Wholesale, St. Louis MO

Common Name: Chinese Rose
Botanical Name: *Camellia* sp.

Common Name: Clematis
Botanical Name: *Clematis* sp.

Alexander A. Kataytsev/Shutterstock.com

Common Name: Clivia, Kaffir Lily
Botanical Name: *Clivia miniata*

noppharat/Shutterstock.com

Common Name: Cockscomb
Botanical Name: *Celosia argentea* var. *cristata*

Teri Virbickis/Shutterstock.com

Common Name: Columbine
Botanical Name: *Aquilegia* sp.

Alekcey/Shutterstock.com

Common Name: Cone Flower
Botanical Name: *Echinacea* sp.

lynea/Shutterstock.com

Common Name: Coral Bells
Botanical Name: *Heuchera* sp.

Madlen/Shutterstock.com

Common Name: Cornflower, Bachelor's Buttons
Botanical Name: *Centaurea cyanus*

Keattikorn/Shutterstock.com

Common Name: Cosmos
Botanical Name: *Cosmos* sp.

Baisch & Skinner Wholesale, St. Louis MO

Common Name: Crabapple
Botanical Name: *Malus* sp.

Susii/Shutterstock.com

Common Name: Craspedia, Billy Balls
Botanical Name: *Craspedia* sp.

Ian Grainger/Shutterstock.com

Common Name: Crocosmia
Botanical Name: *Crocosmia* sp.

guppys/Shutterstock.com

Common Name: Daffodil
Botanical Name: *Narcissus* sp.

luckypic/Shutterstock.com

Common Name: Dahlia
Botanical Name: *Dahlia* sp.

JCox/Shutterstock.com

Common Name: Daisy, Marguerite
Botanical Name: *Argyranthemum* sp.

Noind40/Shutterstock.com

Common Name: Daisy, Ox-Eye
Botanical Name: *Heliopsis* sp.

Lijuan Guo/Shutterstock.com

Common Name: Daisy, Shasta
Botanical Name: *Leucanthemum* sp.

JBDesign/Shutterstock.com

Common Name: Dianthus, Pinks
Botanical Name: *Dianthus* sp.

Kitch Brian/Shutterstock.com

Common Name: Eucalyptus Pods
Botanical Name: *Eucalyptus* sp.

Ussr79/Shutterstock.com

Common Name: Eucharis
Botanical Name: *Eucharis* sp.

MAFord/Shutterstock.com

Common Name: Euphorbia
Botanical Name: *Euphorbia* sp.

Baisch & Skinner Wholesale, St. Louis MO

Common Name: False Dragonhead,
Gooseneck Flower
Botanical Name: *Lysimachia* sp.

Peter J. Kovacs/Shutterstock.com

Common Name: Feverfew
Botanical Name: *Parthenium* sp.

Tissiana Kelley/Shutterstock.com

Common Name: Flame Tip, Leucadendron
Botanical Name: *Leucadendron* sp.

Ligak/Shutterstock.com

Common Name: Flowering Plum
Botanical Name: *Prunus* sp.

Meiqianbao/Shutterstock.com

Common Name: Flowering Quince
Botanical Name: *Chaenomeles* sp.

Graeme Dawes/Shutterstock.com

Common Name: Flowering Stock
Botanical Name: *Matthiola incana*

CHRISTOPHE ROLLAND/Shutterstock.com

Common Name: Forget-Me-Not
Botanical Name: *Myosotis sylvatica*

LiliGraphie/Shutterstock.com

Common Name: Forsythia, Golden Bells
Botanical Name: *Forsythia* sp.

urbanlight/Shutterstock.com

Common Name: Foxtail Lily
Botanical Name: *Eremurus* sp.

Oleksii Sagitov/Shutterstock.com

Common Name: Freesia
Botanical Name: *Freesia* sp.

Ivonne Wierink/Shutterstock.com

Common Name: French (Florist's) Hydrangea
Botanical Name: *Hydrangea macrophylla*

Yongkiet jitwattanatam/Shutterstock.com

Common Name: Fuchsia
Botanical Name: *Fuchsia* sp.

RATCHANAT BUA-NGERN/Shutterstock.com

Common Name: Gardenia
Botanical Name: *Gardenia jasminoides* 'Fortuniana'

Sonny Hudson/Shutterstock.com

Common Name: Gayfeather, Liatris
Botanical Name: *Liatris* sp.

Artens/Shutterstock.com

Common Name: Gerbera, African Daisy
Botanical Name: *Gerbera* sp.

Africa Studio/Shutterstock.com

Common Name: Gladiola, Sword Lily
Botanical Name: *Gladiolus* sp.

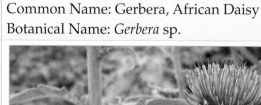

T.W. van Urk/Shutterstock.com

Common Name: Globe Artichoke
Botanical Name: *Cynara* sp.

paula french/Shutterstock.com

Common Name: Globe Thistle
Botanical Name: *Echinops* sp.

kukuruxa/Shutterstock.com

Common Name: Globeflower
Botanical Name: *Trollius* sp.

ntdanai/Shutterstock.com

Common Name: Gloriosa, Glory Lily
Botanical Name: *Gloriosa* sp.

Baisch & Skinner Wholesale, St. Louis MO

Common Name: Godetia
Botanical Name: *Clarkia* sp.

Le Do/Shutterstock.com

Common Name: Grape Hyacinth
Botanical Name: *Muscari* sp.

Imageman/Shutterstock.com

Common Name: Green or Red Tassel Flower
Botanical Name: *Amaranthus caudatus*

krasky/Shutterstock.com

Common Name: Heather
Botanical Name: *Erica* sp.

Baisch & Skinner Wholesale, St. Louis MO

Common Name: Heather Boronia
Botanical Name: *Boronia* sp.

Eugene Sergeev/Shutterstock.com

Common Name: Helen's Flower
Botanical Name: *Helenium* sp.

FomaA/Shutterstock.com

Common Name: Hosta, Plantain, Funkia
Botanical Name: *Hosta* sp.

Allison Herreid/Shutterstock.com

Common Name: Iris, Bearded
Botanical Name: *Iris* sp.

MIGUEL GARCIA SAAVEDRA/Shutterstock.com

Common Name: Iris, Dutch
Botanical Name: *Iris x xiphium*

spline_x/Shutterstock.com

Common Name: Japanese Thistle
Botanical Name: *Cirsium* sp.

18042011/Shutterstock.com

Common Name: Kangaroo Paw
Botanical Name: *Anigozanthos* sp.

David Steele/Shutterstock.com

Common Name: King Protea
Botanical Name: *Protea cyanoides*

Gucio_55/Shutterstock.com

Common Name: Lady's Mantle
Botanical Name: *Alchemilla mollis*

Warren Price Photography/Shutterstock.com

Common Name: Larkspur
Botanical Name: *Delphinium* sp.

Vladimira/Shutterstock.com

Common Name: Lavender
Botanical Name: *Lavandula* sp.

Tamara Kulikova/Shutterstock.com

Andrey Kozyntsev/Shutterstock.com

Common Name: Lepto
Botanical Name: *Leptospermum* sp.

Common Name: Lilac
Botanical Name: *Syringa* sp.

Michael Shake/Shutterstock.com

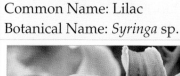
kukuruxa/Shutterstock.com

Common Name: Lily, Asiatic Lily
Botanical Name: *Lilium* sp.

Common Name: Lily, Oriental Lily
Botanical Name: *Lilium* sp.

Vickie Szumigala/Shutterstock.com

Liz Van Steenburgh/Shutterstock.com

Common Name: Lily, Star Gazer Lily
Botanical Name: *Lilium* 'Star Gazer'

Common Name: Lily, Trumpet (Easter) Lily
Botanical Name: *Lilium longiflorum*

JPL Designs/Shutterstock.com

Common Name: Lily of the Nile
Botanical Name: *Agapanthus* sp.

Nataliia Melnychuk/Shutterstock.com

Common Name: Lily of the Valley
Botanical Name: *Convallaria majalis*

Alexander Demyanenko/Shutterstock.com

Common Name: Lisianthus
Botanical Name: *Eustoma grandiflorum*

mypokcik/Shutterstock.com

Common Name: Lobster Claw
Botanical Name: *Heliconia* sp.

ekina/Shutterstock.com

Common Name: Loosestrife
Botanical Name: *Lysimachia* sp.

Skorpionik00/Shutterstock.com

Common Name: Love-in-a-Mist
Botanical Name: *Nigella damascena*

Geoffrey Kuchera/Shutterstock.com

Common Name: Lupine
Botanical Name: *Lupinus* sp.

ultimathule/Shutterstock.com

Common Name: Marigold, Pot, Calendula
Botanical Name: *Calendula officinalis*

Artem and Olga Sapegin/Shutterstock.com

Common Name: Marigold, African
Botanical Name: *Tagetes erecta*

SF photo/Shutterstock.com

Common Name: Masterwort
Botanical Name: *Astrantia major*

Mark Herreid/Shutterstock.com

Common Name: Milkweed, Butterflyweed
Botanical Name: *Asclepias* sp.

axyse/Shutterstock.com

Common Name: Milkweed Balloon Plant
Botanical Name: *Gomphocarpus brasiliensis*

Iakov Filimonov/Shutterstock.com

Common Name: Mimosa, Acacia
Botanical Name: *Acacia* sp.

vaivirga/Shutterstock.com

Common Name: Monkshood, True
Botanical Name: *Aconitum* sp.

Cosmin Manci/Shutterstock.com

Common Name: Mum, Button Mum
Botanical Name: *Chrysanthemum* sp.

isak55/Shutterstock.com

Common Name: Mum, Cushion Mum
Botanical Name: *Chrysanthemum* sp.

Lyudmila Suvorova/Shutterstock.com

Common Name: Mum, Daisy Mum
Botanical Name: *Chrysanthemum* sp.

Mary Lane/Shutterstock.com

Common Name: Mum, Spider Mum, Fuji Mum
Botanical Name: *Chrysanthemum* sp.

mubus7/Shutterstock.com

Common Name: Nerine Lily
Botanical Name: *Nerine* sp.

Denys Dolnikov/Shutterstock.com

Common Name: Onion flower
Botanical Name: *Allium* sp.

Decha Thapanya/Shutterstock.com

Common Name: Orchid, Butterfly Orchid
Botanical Name: *Phalaenopsis* sp.

kajornyot/Shutterstock.com

Common Name: Orchid, Cattleya Orchid Hybrid
Botanical Name: *Cattleya* sp.

aodaodaodaod/Shutterstock.com

Common Name: Orchid, Cymbidium Orchid
Botanical Name: *Cymbidium* sp.

Yongkiet jitwattanatam/Shutterstock.com

Common Name: Orchid, Dendrobium Orchid
Botanical Name: *Dendrobium* sp.

Holly Kuchera/Shutterstock.com

Ru Bai Le/Shutterstock.com

Common Name: Orchid, Ladyslipper Orchid
Botanical Name: *Paphiopedilum* sp.

Common Name: Orchid, Oncidium Orchid
Botanical Name: *Oncidium* sp.

Donjly/Shutterstock.com

Laitr Keiows/Shutterstock.com

Common Name: Orchid, Vanda Orchid
Botanical Name: *Vanda* sp.

Common Name: Ornamental Kale
Botanical Name: *Brassica oleracea*

ermess/Shutterstock.com

Nicholas Toh/Shutterstock.com

Common Name: Ornamental Pepper
Botanical Name: *Capsicum annuum*

Common Name: Ornamental Pineapple
Botanical Name: *Ananas bracteatus*

KIM NGUYEN/Shutterstock.com

Common Name: Pansy
Botanical Name: *Viola x wittrockiana*

daffodilred/Shutterstock.com

Common Name: Peony
Botanical Name: *Paeonia* sp.

Elena Schweitzer/Shutterstock.com

Common Name: Persian Buttercup
Botanical Name: *Ranunculus* sp.

Olga_Phoenix/Shutterstock.com

Common Name: Phlox
Botanical Name: *Phlox paniculata*

Leah-Anne/Shutterstock.com

Common Name: Pink Mink Protea
Botanical Name: *Protea* sp.

Vladimira/Shutterstock.com

Common Name: Poppy, Oriental
Botanical Name: *Papaver orientalis*

Taiftin/Shutterstock.com

Common Name: Prince's Feather
Botanical Name: *Amaranthus cruentus*

David Steele/Shutterstock.com

Common Name: Protea, Pincushion Protea
Botanical Name: *Leucospermum* sp.

Allison Hays - Allicat Photography/Shutterstock.com

Common Name: Purple Foxglove
Botanical Name: *Digitalis purpurea*

2bears/Shutterstock.com

Common Name: Pussy Willow
Botanical Name: *Salix discolor*

Irina Fischer/Shutterstock.com

Common Name: Queen Anne's Lace
Botanical Name: *Ammi majus*

Malgorzata Kistryn/Shutterstock.com

Common Name: Rose, Sweetheart
Botanical Name: *Rosa* sp.

Kisialiou Yury/Shutterstock.com

Common Name: Rose, Spray Rose
Botanical Name: *Rosa* sp.

Jeanne McRight/Shutterstock.com

Common Name: Rose, Tea Rose
Botanical Name: *Rosa* sp.

yumehana/Shutterstock.com

Common Name: Safflower
Botanical Name: *Carthamus tinctorius*

Chaowalit Seeneha/Shutterstock.com

Common Name: Sage, Salvia
Botanical Name: *Salvia splendens*

Missouri Botanical Garden

Common Name: Saltbush
Botanical Name: *Atriplex hortensis*

Alastair Wallace/Shutterstock.com

Common Name: Saponaria
Botanical Name: *Saponaria ocymoides*

Eric Krouse/Shutterstock.com

Common Name: Sarracenia, Pitcher Plant
Botanical Name: *Sarracenia* sp.

V.J. Matthew/Shutterstock.com

Common Name: Scabiosa, Pincushion Flower
Botanical Name: *Scabiosa* sp.

DementevaJulia/Shutterstock.com

Common Name: Sea Holly
Botanical Name: *Eryngium* sp.

muratart/Shutterstock.com

Common Name: Snapdragon
Botanical Name: *Antirrhinum majus*

haraldmuc/Shutterstock.com

Common Name: Snowdrop
Botanical Name: *Galanthus* sp.

Le Do/Shutterstock.com

Common Name: Solidaster
Botanical Name: *Solidago* sp.

Baisch & Skinner Wholesale, St. Louis MO

Common Name: Speedwell
Botanical Name: *Veronica* sp.

Marius Rudzianskas/Shutterstock.com

Common Name: Star of Bethlehem
Botanical Name: *Ornithogalum* sp.

noppharat/Shutterstock.com

Common Name: Statice, Sea Lavender Statice
Botanical Name: *Limonium* sp.

Tusumaru/Shutterstock.com

Common Name: Stephanotis
Botanical Name: *Stephanotis floribunda*

Emily Goodwin/Shutterstock.com

Common Name: Stonecrop
Botanical Name: *Sedum* sp.

Marbury/Shutterstock.com

Common Name: Strawflower
Botanical Name: *Xeranthemum* sp.

Common Name: Sunflower
Botanical Name: *Helianthus* sp.

Common Name: Sweet Pea
Botanical Name: *Lathyrus* sp.

Common Name: Sweet Violet
Botanical Name: *Viola odorata*

Common Name: Tickseed
Botanical Name: *Coreopsis* sp.

Common Name: Toad Lily
Botanical Name: *Tricyrtis* sp.

Common Name: Torch Ginger
Botanical Name: *Alpinia* sp.

Common Name: Torch Heliconia
Botanical Name: *Heliconia* sp.

Common Name: Torch-Lily, Red hot poker
Botanical Name: *Kniphofia uvaria*

Common Name: Tuberose
Botanical Name: *Polianthes tuberosa*

Common Name: Tulip
Botanical Name: *Tulipa* sp.

Common Name: Turtlehead
Botanical Name: *Chelone* sp.

Common Name: Valerian
Botanical Name: *Centranthus rubra*

haru/Shutterstock.com

Common Name: Waxflower
Botanical Name: *Chamelaucium uncinatum*

Hong Vo/Shutterstock.com

Common Name: Windflower, Anemone
Botanical Name: *Anemone* sp.

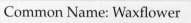
Michael Solway/Shutterstock.com

Common Name: Yarrow
Botanical Name: *Achillea* sp.

ZanozaRu/Shutterstock.com

Common Name: Yarrow
Botanical Name: *Achillea* sp.

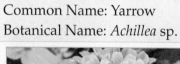
vaivirga/Shutterstock.com

Common Name: Yarrow
Botanical Name: *Achillea* sp.

Wutthichai/Shutterstock.com

Common Name: Zinnia
Botanical Name: *Zinnia elegans*

Chapter

9 Foliage Selection

objectives

After reading this chapter, you will be able to:

- Identify the application for the foliage in an arrangement.
- Explain how the color and texture of foliage can be used to enhance a floral design.
- Choose foliage according to its form to achieve its intended purpose in a design.
- Describe how foliage can be used to create rhythm in a floral design.
- Identify types of foliage that are commonly used in floral design.
- Match the cost of foliage material to its intended use in a floral design.

key terms

foliage	variegated
compatible	vine

Go to www.g-wlearning.com/floraldesign/ for online vocabulary activities using key terms from the chapter.

introduction

Foliage is a general term that refers to the leaves of a plant. It is sometimes referred to as *greenery*, but this is a less accurate term because not all foliage is green. In floral design, foliage is used to establish form, amplify a design style, hide the mechanics of construction, and supply elements of color, texture, or pattern. The process of selecting foliage is therefore just as important as choosing flowers for a design.

Foliage selection is based on both the design application and the mechanical needs of the design. Because foliage is commonly used as a tool to cover mechanics such as floral foam, it is often not the first thing designers think about when selecting materials. Today, however, the variety of foliage readily available presents great opportunities to use the greenery as a pronounced part of the design. See **Figure 9-1**.

Application

When you choose the foliage for a design, the questions of *who*, *what*, and *where* apply, just as they do for flowers. Gather information to narrow the options of design style and material. Is the arrangement going to an individual or a business? What is the occasion for the flowers, everyday enjoyment, or a special event with a theme? Will the arrangement be seen from all sides or only viewed from the front? Once these questions are answered and the options are narrowed, you can begin purchasing the foliage and floral materials.

emin kuliyev/Shutterstock.com

Figure 9-1. Predominantly foliage, the hypericum berries, seeded eucalyptus, and syngonium leaves in this bouquet provide strong textural interest.

Compatibility

The type of foliage used also depends on the flowers chosen for the arrangement. The foliage should be *compatible* with, or suited to, the flowers. For example, the long, stiff sleekness of the flax leaf works best with flowers of the same exotic look, such as tropical anthurium. See **Figure 9-2**. Flax would not be as compatible with a garden-style design that features delicate baby's breath and small filler flowers. Foliage should be chosen with the flowers, or at least at the same time as the flowers, to ensure proper form and compatibility.

Purpose

Since foliage can serve several functions in a design, designers also consider the application of the foliage *within* the design. For example, because flax has such a strong line appearance, it can establish the size of a piece and serve as the vertical or horizontal lines of the design. However, it does not fill a large space within the design, nor can it hide the mechanics, **Figure 9-3**. Therefore, flax is best used to establish form and add color. Other foliage or methods are used to hide the mechanics in this type of arrangement.

Bridget Lazenby/iStock/Thinkstock; LazingBee/iStock/Thinkstock

Figure 9-2. To avoid a chaotic look, choose the foliage to blend well with or complement the flowers used in the design. Flax is available in an assortment of colors and varieties.

Craig Hanson/Shutterstock.com; c12/Shutterstock.com

Figure 9-3. Flax is a strong line foliage that can provide the vertical or horizontal lines to form the basis of a design. The ikebana design uses three full flax leaves to establish height and line. Slender, smaller and pliable bear grass pieces can easily be curved to add visual movement to a design.

Heidi Brand/Shutterstock.com

Figure 9-4. Leather leaf is a staple in flower shops because it is attractive, inexpensive, and can be used to hide mechanics and to add interest to the design. The basic arrangement above is the type of design a beginner would make. Note the use of leatherleaf.

Leather leaf, on the other hand, is a multi-leaflet greenery that is extremely versatile. The small lateral divisions of the leaflets provide pattern and interest. Leather leaf can be used as a design shape or to cover the surface of floral foam. For years, leather leaf has been used in everyday design work, including round or oval centerpieces. Today, because of its versatility and competitive cost, leather leaf is used both by beginners to practice as well as by flower shops for everyday designs, **Figure 9-4.**

Color and Texture

When you select foliage for an arrangement, think beyond the basic color green. In addition to the many shades of green, foliage can be red, purple, blue-green, yellow, whitish-gray, or even brown. Some leaves are *variegated*, or have multiple patches, stripes or marks of different colors; these can add interest to a design as well. See **Figure 9-5**.

apiguide/Shutterstock.com

Figure 9-5. Leaves of various colors, shapes and textures can be used to enhance an arrangement. Not all flowers are used in floral design and some plants are used only for their interesting foliage. The leaves of the croton plant illustrated above are very colorful and would be a beautiful addition to a bouquet.

The color of the foliage you choose should fit within the color story you have created. Refer to Chapter 8, *Flower Selection*, for more information about color stories and color harmonies. Consider the color of the flowers in the arrangement. The color of the foliage should work well with the flower colors. Even among green foliage, some shades of green enhance certain flower colors more than others. **Figure 9-6** lists common floral foliage according to its color.

Foliage can also add texture to a design. Some leaves, such as magnolia leaves, are glossy, shiny, and thick. Others, such as lamb's ear, have a soft, velvety texture. Some, including many of the ferns, have a lacy or airy feel. Others are rough (begonia), or smooth (salal). Some, like holly, have prickly leaf margins. The branches and vines supporting the leaves of these plants can also be interesting to use in designs. When chosen well, the texture of the plant materials can support the mood or purpose of the entire arrangement, **Figure 9-7**.

Color of Foliage			
Red/Yellow/Purple/Blue Hues or Variegated Colors	**Green**		**Gray**
Acalypha	Abies	Hosta	Acacia
Acer	Acer	Ilex	Artemesia
Atriplex	Anthurium	Laurus	Eryngium
Aucuba	Asparagus	Liriope	Eucalyptus
Buxus	Aspidistra	Lycopodium	Leucadendron
Caladium	Atriplex	Magnolia	Limonium
Calathea	Buxus	Mahonia	Perovskia
Codiaeum	Calathea	Miscanthus	Stachys
Eucalyptus	Camellia	Monstera	Tillandsia
Grevillea	Chamaecyparis	Myrtus	
Hedera	Chamaedorea	Nephrolepis	
Hosta	Cordyline	Phormium	
Ilex	Cycas	Pinus	
Maranta	Cytisus	Pittosporum	
Miscanthus	Equisetum	Podocarpus	
Phormium	Fagus	Rumohra	
Protea	Galax	Ruscus	
	Gaultheria	Salix	
	Hedera	Thuja	

Figure 9-6. Colors of foliage commonly used in floral design work.

Jill Lang/Shutterstock.com

Figure 9-7. Foliage may be chosen for its texture as well as its color. This holiday arrangement has Norfolk Island pine, English ivy, and maidenhair fern complementing the red and green of the poinsettias. The rustic basket also contributes texture to the arrangement.

Form

The form of foliage includes both its shape and its configuration. Some leaves are rounded; others are pointed or have complex leaf margins. Review the dominant traits of each material, just as you would for flowers. What qualities does the item possess? Consider one or more of the following characteristics:

- Shiny vs. dull leaves
- Dotted vs. striped leaves
- Sleek vs. ruffled leaves
- Large vs. small leaves
- Venation vs. no venation
- Broadleaf vs. needle-like leaves

Changing the Form of Foliage

With a little imagination, a good designer can change the form of foliage to create special effects. For example, galax leaves (*Galax urceolata*) can be used to create a flower-like form known as a galax rose. Beginning with a single, tightly rolled galax leaf, the designer can add subsequent leaves in layers around the first leaf to create a rose-like effect. This accent piece can be placed as a focal point just as any form flower might be, as shown using flax leaves like ribbon, **Figure 9-8**.

Zygotehaasnobrain/Shutterstock.com

Figure 9-8. The bouquet of foliage roses is a good example of how the shape and purpose of foliage can be modified.

Rhythm

Many floral designers also use vines for foliage accents. *Vines* are leaves arranged naturally along a stem to form a chain. The use of vines in a design can create a dynamic line that adds rhythm or movement to an arrangement, **Figure 9-9**. Examples of vines commonly used in floral design include:

- English ivy
- Grape vine
- Hoya vine
- *Vinca major*

Foliage can also be used in other ways to create rhythm. Galax leaves, for example, are round, flat, and have a single strong stem for insertion. A single leaf may not seem exciting. However, when numerous leaves are overlapped into a scale-like pattern in a design, the rhythm created by the leaves becomes more exciting. See **Figure 9-10**. Galax can be used to create a collar on the edge of a bud vase, or it can be wrapped around the outside of a nosegay bouquet as a finishing collar. The leaves can be glued with waterproof adhesive to the surface of a utilitarian container to give the container a completely different look.

Malgorzata Kistryn/Shutterstock.com

Figure 9-9. Carefully chosen vines can add rhythm and movement to a design, in addition to color and texture. The English Ivy on this heart adds movement to the arrangement but does not detract from the overall design.

Jon Gorr/iStock/Thinkstock

Figure 9-10. The galax leaves are placed at the base of the arrangement.

When foliage combinations are used, thoughtful placement is required. Three distinct forms are most effective, for example, leaves with dominant lines, distinctive form, and mass shapes. When textures are too similar and overused, a design can appear too messy for the eye to focus, **Figure 9-11**.

Identifying Foliage

As you may have realized by now, foliage selection can be a complex process. Foliage is available in many different colors, textures, and forms, so choosing just the right material for a design requires a basic knowledge of foliage types. The Foliage Glossary at the end of this chapter includes over 100 types of cut foliage. Some types are common and inexpensive whereas others may be rare and very costly. As you go through the illustration, take note of the different colors, textures, and forms.

Beginning floral designers typically use basic greens, such as leatherleaf, jade, emerald, and salal leaves, to support the flowers and hide the mechanics. Today's advanced designers use foliage as they would use flowers. They apply line, form, filler, and mass plant materials within designs using the wide variety of foliage available, **Figure 9-12**.

Figure 9-11. Too much greenery incorrectly placed can be detrimental to your design. Foliage is not used to its best advantage in this design.

ilogic27/Shutterstock.com; Foto by M/Shutterstock.com

Figure 9-12. The designs above were created by using mostly foliage. The different green colors, textures, and forms of the arrangements have been combined to create interesting monochromatic color schemes.

Harvesting Wild Foliage

Some beginning floral designers may choose to harvest wild foliage to use for practice. If you do this, you should be aware of two possible pitfalls. First, harvesting foliage is illegal in some areas. For example, in the southern Appalachian Mountains, harvesting galax leaves is a crime that may result in fines of up to $5,000 and even a possible jail sentence.

Second, some attractive foliage is poisonous. **Figure 9-13** shows poison ivy and poison oak. Be sure you know how to identify these plants and take care to avoid them.

Tim Mainiero/Shutterstock.com; Tom Grundy/Shutterstock.com; Melinda Fawver/Shutterstock.com; Dwight Smith/Shutterstock.com

Figure 9-13. Be aware of poison ivy and poison oak if you are outdoor looking for wild foliage to use in your designs. Both the poison ivy and poison oak vary in color, shape, and size and may appear to be a vine or a bush. If you suspect something is any of the above, do not take chances using the foliage in class or at home.

Step-by-Step

Cutting Emerald or Jade Foliage

Tailoring pinnately compound leaves such as this Bamboo Palm, called Emerald in the floral industry, is easily accomplished with a pair of sharp scissors dedicated to the task.

You will need a sharp pair of scissors and the leaves you are going to cut. As the leaflets are cut, take care to follow the desired geometric form.

Begin with a single piece of Emerald or Jade foliage and a sharp pair of shears. Begin at the base trimming the outside 1/2" to 1" of the leaf tips.

Work towards the tip of the foliage. Flip the foliage over and repeat on the other side.

Cost

When purchasing foliage, cost should always be a factor. Apply the correct material for the right use, and understand that more is not necessarily better. When the only purpose of the foliage is to cover the mechanics, use less expensive materials. Reserve the more expensive choices for higher-priced designs and focal applications. Beyond the practical function, it is the combination of color, form, and textural interest that make foliage use successful. Combining three or more different forms is most effective, even in small amounts. It doesn't have to be expensive… just exciting. See **Figure 9-14**.

Thinking Green

Socially Responsible Purchasing

Many types of foliage are imported to the United States from around the world, including third-world countries. In some of these countries, little attention may be paid to environmental damage caused by pesticides and fertilizers. Many florists today purchase foliage and flowers only from "socially responsible" sources. These sources guarantee that the farms that grew the materials comply with strict guidelines for labor and environment-friendly practices.

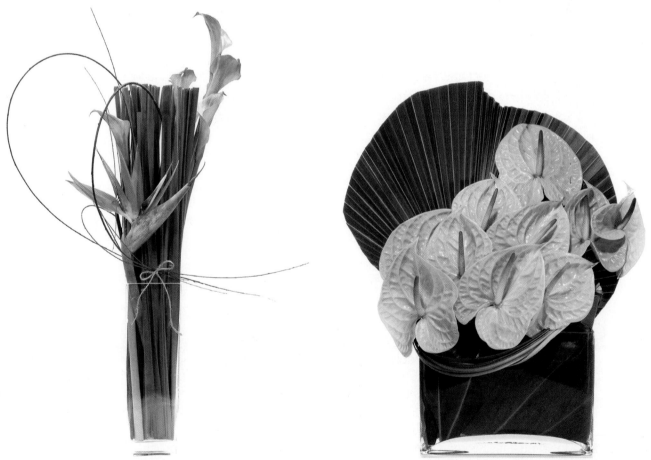

Susii/Shutterstock.com; Michael Kraus/Shutterstock.com;

Figure 9-14. For the beginner, experimenting with foliage shapes by cutting leaves and stems for a design idea can be fun.

Summary

- Foliage can be used to establish form, amplify a design style, hide mechanics, and supply elements of color, texture, or pattern.
- Foliage should be compatible with the flowers chosen for the arrangement.
- The type of foliage chosen should be able to achieve its purpose in the design.
- Careful selection of foliage of different colors and textures can enhance a floral design.
- The form of foliage includes both its shape and its configuration.
- Vines can be used to create rhythm in a floral design.
- Choosing the best material for a design requires a basic knowledge of foliage types.
- The cost of foliage should be proportionate to its purpose in a design.

Review Questions

Go to www.g-wlearning.com/floraldesign/ to use the fill-in-form.

Answer the following questions using the information provided in this chapter.

1. Name three uses for foliage in a floral design.
2. Why does the type of foliage used depend on the flowers chosen for the arrangement?
3. What type of foliage is commonly used in everyday designs because of its versatility and competitive cost?
4. Identify at least four colors, other than green, that can be added to a design using foliage.
5. What is a variegated leaf?
6. Name at least three types of foliage that add texture to an arrangement, and identify the texture of each.
7. List four options that may be considered in deciding on the form of the foliage for an arrangement.
8. Why do many designers incorporate vines in their floral designs?
9. Explain how floral designers determine how much to spend on foliage for an arrangement.
10. Identify four types of foliage that are commonly used by beginning floral designers.

Activities

1. Play 'foliage form' jeopardy using 100 top foliage options for designs.
2. Create a journal entry to sketch 10 leaves with different forms, including the correct name of each form.
3. Make a rosette using galax leaves.
4. Make a bear grass braid and incorporate raffia to demonstrate how the form of a leaf can be changed or used creatively.

Critical Thinking

1. Your flower shop has just received an order for six matching corsages to be used for a local homecoming "court." The homecoming game is tonight, and the customer wants to pick up the corsages in 2 hours. Your usual practice is to use leather leaf in this type of arrangement, but due to an unexpected number of orders, you have run out of leather leaf. What other material could you use to create a similar effect?
2. A local businesswoman is planning a formal dinner at her home for prospective customers. She tells you that her home is "modernistic" with stark white walls, chrome-and-glass furniture, and abstract paintings. She wants three arrangements: one for the dining room, one for the living room, and one for the foyer or entry. Plan three coordinating arrangements using flowers and foliage that will work well in her home.

3. A customer has brought in an antique silver vessel in the shape of a Victorian women's boot. The boot is about 8″ from toe to heel, and the opening at the top of the boot is about 3″ and is roughly oval. He wants you to create an arrangement in the vessel as a surprise for his parents. He realizes the arrangement cannot be large, but he says he wants "one or two flowers and a lot of green stuff." What factors should you consider in planning this arrangement? Is there anything you should advise the customer before beginning? What type of flowers and foliage could you use to overcome the obstacles?

STEM Activities and Academics

1. **Math.** Find two different wholesale florists online and record the prices for each of the following types of foliage: jade green filler, leather leaf, galax, bear grass, and foxtail. Since these items are generally sold by the bunch, find out how many stems or leaves are included in a bunch and calculate the price of one stem or leaf. Create a graph showing the cost of each type of foliage at each wholesale florist.

2. **Language Arts.** Imagine that you are the marketing director for a large company that grows and sells flowers and foliage. One of your job responsibilities is to write articles for the grower's information center. Write an article about how to choose the best quality foliage. Focus on the characteristics of at least three different types of foliage.

3. **Social Studies.** Foliage has been used for many different purposes throughout history. Conduct research to find out how olive leaves, bay (laurel) leaves, and acanthus have been used by different societies in the past. What social impacts or implications did these leaves have?

4. **Science.** Many fall arrangements make use of leaves that have turned brilliant autumn colors. Conduct research to find out why these color changes occur. Why do some leaves turn yellow, while others turn red or orange?

5. **Math.** A flower shop owner has estimated that the shop will need about 150 stems of aspidistra leaves, 50 stems of variegated pittosporum, and 300 stems of leather leaf during the next week. Visit at least three wholesale florists online that sell these items. Compare their prices, including any discounts for the number of stems needed. Make a chart listing the name of each company and its price for each item. Identify the lowest price for each item and calculate the total cost for the items.

Communicating about Floral Design

1. **Reading and Speaking.** After reading chapter 9, you should have a good understanding of the difference between the types of foliage used in floral design. Create an arrangement, draw a picture with labels, use photos, or write an essay in which you describe how specific types of foliage and combinations of foliage, affect a design. Show and explain how changing the color or size of the foliage will affect the design. Explain how foliage can be used to establish height, form, and rhythm.

2. **Listening and Speaking.** Search online for local garden clubs that have floral design workshops, guest speakers, or presentations on floral design by professional designers. Also look for online videos on floral design and foliage selection. Your local library may also have various media covering floral design topics. Watch several videos, attend a presentation, and take notes. Listen for floral design terms that you have learned from your textbook. Write a short summary and be prepared to present your findings to the class.

Foliage Glossary

The cut foliage glossary contains materials commonly available on the wholesale market as well as a few products available from local suppliers. To a beginning designer, the wide variety of plant names can be overwhelming. To help you learn both the common names and botanical names, the foliages are alphabetized by the common name used most frequently in the profession and regional locales. The botanical name is listed below the common name and there is a cross-reference chart in the appendix. For the botanical names, major focus is on the Genus name without a specific epithet. Professional florists often use the botanical name as a common name so it is beneficial to learn both. When used in print, the common name is not italicized. *The term botanical name and scientific name may sometimes be used interchangeably. For the sake of consistency, the term botanical name has been used throughout the textbook.*

Go to www.g-wlearning.com/floraldesign/ to use e-flash cards and other activities using the plant materials from the illustrated glossary.

TeeraPhoto/Shutterstock.com

Common Name: Alocasia, African Mask
Botanical Name: *Alocasia amazonica*

Baisch & Skinner Wholesale, St. Louis MO

Common Name: Anthurium
Botanical Name: *Anthurium* sp.

DENIS KHVESHCHENIK/iStock/Thinkstock

Common Name: Arrowhead
Botanical Name: *Syngonium podophyllum*

Alxpin/iStock/Thinkstock

Common Name: Aucuba
Botanical Name: *Aucuba japonica*

Baisch & Skinner Wholesale, St. Louis MO

Common Name: Bear Grass
Botanical Name: *Xerophyllum tenax*

BHKang/Shutterstock.com

Common Name: Bird's Nest Fern
Botanical Name: *Asplenium nidus*

Baisch & Skinner Wholesale, St. Louis MO

Common Name: Boston Fern
Botanical Name: *Nephrolepis exaltata* 'Bostoniensis'

Firelia/Shutterstock.com

Common Name: Bottle-Brush Plant
Botanical Name: *Callistemon* sp.

Lipowski Milan/Shutterstock.com

Common Name: Boxwood
Botanical Name: *Buxus* sp.

Missouri Botanical Garden

Common Name: Boxwood, Variegated
Botanical Name: *Buxus sempervirens* 'Variegata'

Baisch & Skinner Wholesale, St. Louis MO

Common Name: Bracelet Honey Myrtle
Botanical Name: *Melaleuca armillaris*

Sergio Schnitzler/Shutterstock.com

Common Name: Broom Corn
Botanical Name: *Sorghum* sp.

sevenka/Shutterstock.com

Common Name: Buddhist Pine
Botanical Name: *Podocarpus* sp.

niceregionpics/Shutterstock.com

Common Name: Caladium, Fancy-Leaved
Botanical Name: *Caladium* sp.

Baisch & Skinner Wholesale, St. Louis MO

Common Name: Caladium, Miss Muffet
Botanical Name: *Caladium* sp.

Baisch & Skinner Wholesale, St. Louis MO

Common Name: Caladium, Pink
Botanical Name: *Caladium* sp.

Baisch & Skinner Wholesale, St. Louis MO

Common Name: Calathea
Botanical Name: *Calathea* sp.

Daimond Shutter/Shutterstock.com

Common Name: Calathea
Botanical Name: *Calathea* sp.

kajornyot/Shutterstock.com

Common Name: Calathea, Rattlesnake Plant
Botanical Name: *Calathea lancifolia*

Zigzag Mountain Art/Shutterstock.com

Common Name: California Incense Cedar
Botanical Name: *Caleocedrus decurrens*

francescocarniani/iStock/Thinkstock

Common Name: Camellia
Botanical Name: *Camellia* sp.

Malgorzata Litkowska/Shutterstock.com

Common Name: Cattails
Botanical Name: *Typha* sp.

Common Name: China Doll, Emerald Tree
Botanical Name: *Radermachera sinica*

Common Name: Coontie Fern
Botanical Name: *Zamia pumila*

Common Name: Croton
Botanical Name: *Codiaeum* sp.

Common Name: Croton, Yellow
Botanical Name: *Codiaeum* sp.

Common Name: Croton, 'Icetone'
Botanical Name: *Codiaeum variegatum* 'Icetone'

Common Name: Croton, 'Red Bananas'
Botanical Name: *Codiaeum variegatum* 'Red Bananas'

Moolkum/Shutterstock.com

Baisch & Skinner Wholesale, St. Louis MO

Common Name: Cryptanthus
Botanical Name: *Cryptanthus* sp.

Common Name: Crypanthus
Botanical Name: *Cryptanthus* sp.

Waddell Images/Shutterstock.com

Baisch & Skinner Wholesale, St. Louis MO

Common Name: Cutleaf Philodendron
Botanical Name: *Monstera deliciosa*

Common Name: Cutleaf Philodendron, 'Variegata'
Botanical Name: *Monstera deliciosa* 'variegata'

Artesia Wells/Shutterstock.com

Noah Strycker/Shutterstock.com

Common Name: Cycad, Sago Palm
Botanical Name: *Cycas revoluta*

Common Name: Douglas Fir
Botanical Name: *Pseudotsuga menziesii*

asharkyu/Shutterstock.com

Common Name: Dracaena, Lucky Bamboo
Botanical Name: *Dracaena sanderiana*

Calvste/Shutterstock.com

Common Name: Dracaena, Tricolor
Botanical Name: *Dracaena marginata* 'Tricolor'

Inna Fischer/Shutterstock.com

Common Name: Dusty Miller
Botanical Name: *Senecio* sp.

Alexander Bark/Shutterstock.com

Common Name: Dusty Miller Diamond Frost
Botanical Name: *Senecio cineraria* 'Diamond'

Mirco Vacca/Shutterstock.com

Common Name: English Ivy
Botanical Name: *Hedera helix*

Baisch & Skinner Wholesale, St. Louis MO

Common Name: English Ivy, Variegated
Botanical Name: *Hedera helix* 'variegata'

Common Name: Equisetum, Horsetail, Scouring Rush
Botanical Name: *Equisetum hyemale*

Common Name: Eucalyptus
Botanical Name: *Eucalyptus* sp.

Common Name: Eucalyptus, Knifeblade
Botanical Name: *Eucalyptus* sp.

Common Name: Eucalyptus, Silver Dollar
Botanical Name: *Eucalyptus* sp.

Common Name: Eucalyptus, Willo
Botanical Name: *Eucalyptus* sp.

Common Name: Euphorbia, Snow-on-the-Mountain
Botanical Name: *Euphorbia marginata*

Baisch & Skinner Wholesale, St. Louis MO

Common Name: Fern Fiddleheads
Botanical Name: *Dicranopteris linearis*

Mason Vranish/Shutterstock.com

Common Name: Flat Fern
Botanical Name: *Polystichum munitum*

GOLFX/Shutterstock.com

Common Name: Foxtail Fern
Botanical Name: *Asparagus densiflorus* 'Meyeri'

Matjoe/Shutterstock.com

Common Name: Foxtail Millet
Botanical Name: *Setaria italica*

Tim Mainiero/Shutterstock.com

Common Name: Galax
Botanical Name: *Galax urceolata*

Denys Kushchaiev/Hemera/Thinkstock

Common Name: Green Wheat
Botanical Name: *Triticum* sp.

apple2499/Shutterstock.com

Common Name: Guzmania
Botanical Name: *Guzmania* sp.

Shahril KHMD/Shutterstock.com

Common Name: Hala
Botanical Name: *Pandanus* sp.

Baisch & Skinner Wholesale, St. Louis MO

Common Name: Hen and Chicks, Echeveria
Botanical Name: *Echeveria* sp.

colognephotos/Shutterstock.com

Common Name: Holly, American
Botanical Name: *Ilex opaca*

Phillip Minnis/Shutterstock.com

Common Name: Holly, Variegated
Botanical Name: *Ilex* sp.

Baisch & Skinner Wholesale, St. Louis MO

Common Name: Hoya, Wax Plant
Botanical Name: *Hoya* sp.

Baisch & Skinner Wholesale, St. Louis MO

Baisch & Skinner Wholesale, St. Louis MO

Common Name: Israeli Ruscus
Botanical Name: *Ruscus* sp.

Common Name: Italian Ruscus
Botanical Name: *Ruscus* sp.

osoznanie jizni/Shutterstock.com

Illzia/Shutterstock.com

Common Name: Juniper
Botanical Name: *Juniperus* sp.

Common Name: Juniper, Berried
Botanical Name: *Juniperus* sp.

Vizual Studio/Shutterstock.com

de2marco/Shutterstock.com

Common Name: Lamb's Ear
Botanical Name: *Stachys byzantina*

Common Name: Laurel
Botanical Name: *Laurus nobilis*

Madlen/Shutterstock.com

Common Name: Leatherleaf Fern
Botanical Name: *Rumohra adiantiformis*

alybaba/Shutterstock.com

Common Name: Leucadendron
Botanical Name: *Leucadendron* sp.

Baisch & Skinner Wholesale, St. Louis MO

Common Name: Lily Grass, Liriope
Botanical Name: *Liriope* sp.

Baisch & Skinner Wholesale, St. Louis MO

Common Name: Lily Turf Grass, Variegated
Botanical Name: *Liriope* sp.

Robyn Mackenzie/Shutterstock.com

Liane Matrisch/Hemera/Thinkstock

Common Name: Magnolia
Botanical Name: *Magnolia* sp.

Common Name: Mahonia, Oregon Grape
Botanical Name: *Mahonia* sp.

OrganAlle/Shutterstock.com

Common Name: Maidenhair Fern
Botanical Name: *Adiantum raddianum*

s74/Shutterstock.com

Common Name: Mint
Botanical Name: *Mentha* sp.

Baisch & Skinner Wholesale, St. Louis MO

Common Name: Mother-in-Law Tongue
Botanical Name: *Sanseveria* sp.

Baisch & Skinner Wholesale, St. Louis MO

Common Name: Mother-in-Law Tongue
Botanical Name: *Sanseveria* sp.

Baisch & Skinner Wholesale, St. Louis MO

Common Name: Mother-in-Law Tongue
Botanical Name: *Sanseveria* sp.

IHervas/iStock/Thinkstock

Common Name: Myrtus, Myrtle
Botanical Name: *Myrtus communis*

Melissa E Dockstader/Shutterstock.com

Common Name: Nandina, Autumn-colored
Botanical Name: *Nandina domestica*

Ruth Peterkin/Shutterstock.com

Common Name: Nandina, Berried
Botanical Name: *Nandina* sp.

Baisch & Skinner Wholesale, St. Louis MO

Common Name: Nandina, Green
Botanical Name: *Nandina domestica*

LazingBee/iStock/Thinkstock

Common Name: New Zealand Flax
Botanical Name: *Phormium* sp.

Calvsle/Shutterstock.com

Common Name: Orange Jessamine
Botanical Name: *Murraya paniculata*

Jaochainoi/Shutterstock.com

Common Name: Ornamental Cabbage, Kale
Botanical Name: *Brassica oleracea*

Madlen/Shutterstock.com

Common Name: Palmetto
Botanical Name: *Sabal* sp.

Nuttapol Noprujkul/Shutterstock.com

Common Name: Papyrus
Botanical Name: *Cyperus* sp.

noppharat/Shutterstock.com

Common Name: Papyrus
Botanical Name: *Cyperus* sp.

Missouri Botanical Garden

Common Name: Peperomia, Variegated
Botanical Name: *Peperomia obtusifolia* 'Variegata'

White Tag/Shutterstock.com

Common Name: Philodendron Xanadu
Botanical Name: *Philodendron* 'Xanadu'

Chris Curtis/Shutterstock.com

Common Name: Pittosporum
Botanical Name: *Pittosporum tobira*

Missouri Botanical Garden

Common Name: Pittosporum, Variegated
Botanical Name: *Pittosporum tobira* 'Variegatum'

Missouri Botanical Garden

Common Name: Plumosa Fern
Botanical Name: *Asparagus setaceus*

Solomiya Trylom/Shutterstock.com

Common Name: Port Orford Cedar
Botanical Name: *Chamaecyparis lawsoniana*

Scisetti Alfio/Shutterstock.com

Common Name: Rosemary
Botanical Name: *Rosmarinus officinalis*

Adam Lu/Shutterstock.com

Common Name: Sage, Tricolor
Botanical Name: *Salvia* sp.

Baisch & Skinner Wholesale, St. Louis MO

Common Name: Sagebush
Botanical Name: *Artemisia* sp.

Madlen/Shutterstock.com

Common Name: Salal, Lemon Leaf
Botanical Name: *Gaultheria shallon*

Paul van Eykelen/Shutterstock.com

Common Name: Schefflera
Botanical Name: *Schefflera arboricola*

Missouri Botanical Garden

Common Name: Schefflera, Australian Ivy
Botanical Name: *Schefflera actinophylla*

Baisch & Skinner Wholesale, St. Louis MO

Common Name: Scotch Broom
Botanical Name: *Cytisus scoparius*

cameilia/Shutterstock.com

Common Name: Selloum
Botanical Name: *Philodendron pinnatifidum*

Missouri Botanical Garden

Common Name: Skimmia
Botanical Name: *Skimmia japonica*

herreid/iStock/Thinkstock

Common Name: Smokebush
Botanical Name: *Cotinus* sp.

Baisch & Skinner Wholesale, St. Louis MO

Common Name: Spider Plant, Airplane Plant
Botanical Name: *Chlorophytum* cosmosum

Missouri Botanical Garden

Common Name: Sprengeri Fern
Botanical Name: *Asparagus densiflorus* 'Sprengeri'

joloei/Shutterstock.com

Common Name: Staghorn Fern
Botanical Name: *Platycerium bifurcatum*

Susii/Shutterstock.com

Common Name: Strelitzia, Bird of Paradise
Botanical Name: *Strelitzia reginae*

Sarun T/Shutterstock.com

Common Name: String of Hearts
Botanical Name: *Senecio* sp.

Baisch & Skinner Wholesale, St. Louis MO

Common Name: String of Pearls
Botanical Name: *Senecio rowleyanus*

Baisch & Skinner Wholesale, St. Louis MO

Common Name: Syngonium
Botanical Name: *Syngonium* sp.

Baisch & Skinner Wholesale, St. Louis MO

Common Name: Syngonium
Botanical Name: *Syngonium* sp.

Leena Damle/Shutterstock.com

Common Name: Ti Leaves
Botanical Name: *Cordyline* sp.

Sanit Fuangnakhorn/Shutterstock.com

Common Name: Tillandsia
Botanical Name: *Tillandsia* sp.

Baisch & Skinner Wholesale, St. Louis MO

Common Name: Tillandsia
Botanical Name: *Tillandsia* sp.

Baisch & Skinner Wholesale, St. Louis MO

Common Name: Tillandsia
Botanical Name: *Tillandsia* sp.

joloei/Shutterstock.com

Common Name: Triostar Stromanthe
Botanical Name: *Stromanthe sanguinea* 'Triostar'

Elmar Langle/Shutterstock.com

Common Name: Vaccinium, Green Huckleberry
Botanical Name: *Vaccinium ovatum*

kredo/Shutterstock.com

Common Name: Viburnum berries
Botanical Name: *Viburnum* sp.

Srdjan111/Shutterstock.com

Common Name: White Pine
Botanical Name: *Pinus strobus*

Martina Roth/Shutterstock.com

Common Name: Wintercreeper
Botanical Name: *Euonymus* sp.

objectives

After reading this chapter, you will be able to:

- Create floral designs in various geometric shapes and styles.
- Evaluate where a floral arrangement falls on the line-mass continuum.
- Describe traditional floral design styles with Oriental, European, and American origins.
- Classify floral design styles developed in the 20th century.
- Summarize current trends in floral design styles.

key terms

abstract design	geometric design	parallel systems design
Biedermeier design	hedgerow design	phoenix design
cascade design	Hogarth curve	traditional design
della Robbia design	ikebana design	underwater design
double-ended triangle design	landscape design	vegetative design
early colonial design	line design	waterfall design
English garden design	mass design	Williamsburg design
flob	massing	zoning
formalinear design	millefleur design	
freestyle design	new convention design	

Go to **www.g-wlearning.com/floraldesign/** for online vocabulary activities using key terms from the chapter.

introduction

Over the years, floral designers have developed and documented various styles of arrangements that fall in and out of fashion. Some design styles have stood the test of time, categorized by the types of plant materials used to make them or by specialized patterns or effects. A versatile floral designer is adept at creating beautiful designs from all classifications and styles. See **Figure 10-1**.

This chapter describes ways to classify floral design styles. For example, floral designs can be classified according to their shape or geometry. Floral designs also reflect the cultural styles of the civilizations in which they develop. Because the eastern (oriental) and western (European) cultures through the centuries have been quite different from one another, their floral design traditions are also different. Within each of these broad cultural backgrounds, individual countries and cultures have developed their own variations and design styles, often called *design movements*.

Geometric Design

One practical way to classify floral designs is according to their geometry. Most floral designs have at least some geometric elements, and many have a definite geometric shape. *Geometric design* refers to arrangements that are based on geometric forms such as the circle, triangle, and square. Most of the design styles described in this chapter are geometric. See *Appendix* for complete chart of geometric design shapes.

Floral designers often refer to designs according to their geometric shapes, so it is necessary to understand the basic geometric terms and what they mean in floral design. Some of the geometric shapes that are commonly used in floral design include circles, various triangles, ovals, and crescents.

Blumz by JRDesigns, metro Detroit; Society of American Florists

Figure 10-1. Floral designers may use basic geometric shapes as the basis for their designs, or expand on those basic shapes to make more elaborate compositions.

Circular Styles

The most common design shape is the circle. Centerpieces, nosegays, and vase arrangements are typically produced using the circle or round form as a guide. Variations on the basic circular form include the fan design, which is semicircular, and the elongated oval and pointed oval designs. A pointed oval design is an oval shape that is rounded at the bottom, but narrows to a gentle point at the top. See **Figure 10-2.** The crescent and the Hogarth curve are also variations of a circular design style. See **Figure 10-3.**

Figure 10-2. The circular style is rounded when viewed from the side and circular when viewed from the top.

Hogarth Curve

Crescent

Figure 10-3. A Hogarth curve is a variation of the crescent shape in which two crescents face opposite directions. The crescent style may be configured curving down, up, or to the side like a crescent moon.

Step-by-Step

Round Arrangement

For this project you will need the following plant materials: nine purple carnations, nine white daisy pompons, leatherleaf, statice, and limonium. You will also need a floral knife, a utility container, 1/3 of a block of soaked floral foam, water, scissors, and anchor tape.

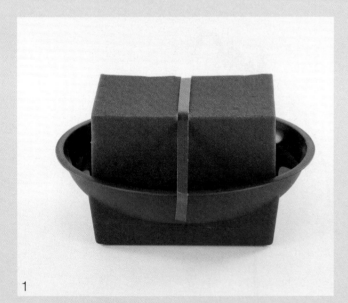

1

Place 1/3 of a block of soaked floral foam into the container, secure with anchor tape and place the dish with the long length side to side.

2

Place the first carnation directly in the middle of the floral foam. Place four carnations around the base. Place the last four carnations on the middle layer, on top of the floral foam at 45° angle, halfway between the top flower and the four around the base. Note: this layer is placed opposite of the bottom layer.

3

Green the arrangement following the same pattern as the carnations.

4

Add the daisy pompons halfway in each area where the carnations form a triangle.

5

Add statice for depth in the arrangement.

6

Finish with adding limonium or another filler, staying within the form of the arrangement.

The same principles and elements used to create a fresh-cut floral design apply to designs made with artificial botanicals. The round arrangement in this Step-by-Step may also be made using artificial plant materials. Choose elements for an artificial arrangement according to qualities such as form, size, color, and texture.

A *Hogarth curve* is an S-shaped curve created by placing two crescents end-to-end so that they curve in opposite directions. Named for an English painter, William Hogarth (1697–1794), the Hogarth curve has a sophisticated pattern with a downward sweeping curved line extending below the lip of the container. For this reason, the Hogarth curve design is constructed in a tall vessel, often with a stem or pedestal style base to display the complete S-shaped appearance of the design. Generally not as popular because it is more difficult to construct, this design shape requires curving floral material and floral foam inserted with additional height to allow for the downward directed insertion of products.

Triangular Styles

Triangular designs may be equilateral, isosceles, or scalene. In equilateral designs, all three sides of the triangle are of equal length. In isosceles designs, two of the sides are of equal length, and in scalene designs, none of the sides are of equal length. Variations include symmetrical and asymmetrical triangles and right triangles, in which one of the angles equals 90°. See **Figure 10-4**. The cone shape has a triangular appearance, but it has a three-dimensional shape, with a circular base narrowing to a point at the top of the arrangement. Long and low centerpieces follow a *double-ended triangle design* when viewed from above as well as from the side.

| Equilateral Triangle | Isosceles Triangle | Right Triangle | Double-Ended Triangle |

Mayovskyy Andrew/Shutterstock.com; Oleg Rodionov/Shutterstock.com; Mayovskyy Andrew/Shutterstock.com; Rob Hainer/Shutterstock.com

Figure 10-4. Types of triangular shapes.

Square Styles

Few floral designs are actually square. Some are rectangular, however, and all of the linear styles are based on the square as well. Linear styles include the basic horizontal and vertical styles, as well as diagonal styles and combinations. For example, the horizontal and vertical styles can be combined to create a T-shaped design or an inverted T-shaped design. See **Figure 10-5**. Parallel and new convention designs use parallel stem placements so they lend themselves to a more square or rectangular appearance. The *hedgerow design*, with its precise upright design of parallel stem placements in which plant materials are aligned or massed in multiple layers to achieve the effect of nearly solid horizontal bands, can even produce a cubed appearance depending on the shape of container. See **Figure 10-6**. This is also known as *garden wall* or by the English term *Beecher's Brook*.

Koehler & Dramm's Institute of Floristry, Minneapolis; Society of American Florists

Figure 10-5. The inverted-T style combines the vertical and horizontal styles.

1000 Words/Shutterstock.com; Dr. Delphinium Designs in Dallas, SAF

Figure 10-6. Numerous floral design styles are inspired by landscape elements or other natural designs around us. Use of the box container and vertically inserted roses mimics the traditional garden hedgerow, a common landscape feature used to mark property boundaries.

Step-by-Step

Asymmetrical Triangle

For this project you will need the following plant materials: six snapdragons (line), eight purple carnations (mass), leather leaf, a dozen lime green spray mums, and a filler flower. You will also need a utility container, 1/3 of a block of soaked floral foam, a floral knife, scissors, anchor tape, and water.

Place 1/3 of a block of soaked floral foam into the container, secure with anchor tape and place the dish with the long length side to side.

Using the snapdragons, begin creating an asymmetrical triangle. Place the first snapdragon in the back, left-hand corner. Place the next snapdragon directly in front of the first, at the base of the container. Insert the third snapdragon on the right side of the foam so that it is horizontal and resting on the lip of the container. Insert the fourth snapdragon in the front left side of the foam so that it is horizontal, lower than the third flower, and resting on the lip of the container. Place the fifth snapdragon toward the back of the container, upright and to the right of the first flower. The sixth snapdragon is inserted horizontally, halfway between the other horizontal flowers, resting on the lower lip of the container.

The snapdragons now form the skeleton of the asymmetrical triangle. Using leatherleaf or greenery, mimic the shape of the line flower placements, reinforcing the asymmetrical triangle.

Insert the purple carnations within the framework of the snapdragons so they help define the asymmetrical form.

Add the lime green spray mums within the framework of the snapdragons to enforce the asymmetrical form. Add the filler within the framework to complete the arrangement.

Step-by-Step

Equilateral Triangle

When creating a design, you must of course first fill the customer's requests. This is easier when the customer knows exactly what he or she wants and can clearly explain his or her wishes. However, as the designer, you must still make some subjective decisions. They key to making the correct decisions, is applying the correct design principles. Does the container match the occasion or does it convey a different intention or a different meaning? Are the flowers formal enough for a ceremonial dinner or do they look childish? If it is not 100% to the customer's liking, can it be easily modified? Will my cost exceed the profit?

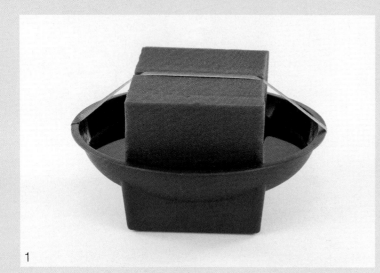

1

To create this arrangement you will need the following plant materials: nine red carnations, seven white spray Chrysanthemums, purple statice, limonium, and leatherleaf. You will also need a utility container, 1/3 a block of floral foam, water, and anchor tape. The meaning and intent of this arrangement could easily be changed by using different colors and/or different plant materials.

Place 1/3 of a block of soaked floral foam into the container, secure with anchor tape and place the dish with the long length front to back.

2

Beginning with the red carnations, place the tallest carnation in the back third, *not the center*, of the floral foam. Make sure the stems are inserted at least 1" into the foam. The tallest flower should be about twice the width of the container. Next, add two carnations in the back half of the floral foam, angled slightly forward to outline the triangle. Remember, the height should be the same as the width. Next place a carnation in the front of the arrangement, resting on the lip of the front of the container. Add two carnations halfway between the top carnation and the side carnations. Add one carnation on the top of the foam, halfway between the tallest carnation and the one in the front of the container. The final two carnations are added on the two front corners of the foam. Look at the arrangement noting the triangle formed by the bottom front, bottom side and the middle carnation. Directly in the middle of that triangle is where you will place these two carnations.

3

Green the arrangement using the same pattern as you did with the carnations. Begin in the back and add to the sides to form the triangle. Move to the front and center.

4

Add the daisy mums between each set of carnations, following the same pattern as the carnations.

5

Add a third texture such as purple statice placed in the same pattern as the carnations but tucked in for some depth to the composition.

6

Finish your arrangement by inserting the limonium or other light filler.

Step-by-Step

Long and Low or Double-Ended Triangle Arrangement

For this project you will need the following plant materials: seven or eight pink carnations, nine purple liatris, sixteen yellow daisies, solidago or baby's breath, leather leaf, and a second green foliage with a different texture than the leather leaf. You will also need a double utility bowl, one block of wet floral foam, anchor tape, water, scissors, a floral knife, and two coordinating pillar candles (optional).

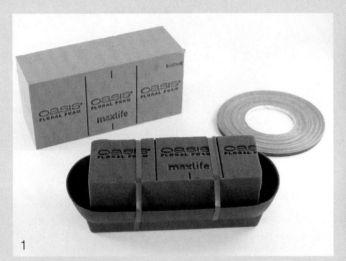

1

Place the fully-soaked floral foam in the utility bowl and secure with anchor tape. If you are using pillar candles, insert them before inserting any greens or flowers. The candles should be inserted first or the stems of the plant materials will interfere with the base of the candles.

2

Insert the leather leaf into the foam to form an outline.

3

The leaf placement will establish the height, width, and length of the double-ended triangle arrangement.

4

Staying within the parameters set by the beginning of the greens, complete greening the arrangement with leather leaf and the second greenery.

5

Inserting the purple larkspur within the same parameters as the greens.

6

Insert the pink carnations following the same pattern as the greens, defining the height, width, and length once again. Note: This is a symmetrical arrangement so what you do to one side, you must do the same to the other.

7

Add yellow daisies throughout the arrangement, maintaining the shape that was outlined by the greens and the pink carnations.

8

Add Monte Cassino aster as a filler. Notice that darker colors will recede and the lighter colors will advance in this arrangement.

Alan49/Shutterstock.com

Figure 10-7. Asian line designs use a few materials in thoughtfully planned flower placement.

Society of American Florists

Figure 10-8. The linear arrangement uses a strong vertical line with all materials leading the eye toward the center of the design.

The Line-Mass Continuum

Another way to classify floral designs is according to the way they use line and mass to achieve an overall effect. In this classification system, the major classes of designs are line (linear), mass, and line-mass. Each of these classes has distinct characteristics and origins. However, they form a *continuum*, or continuous range of designs. For example, some designs may be mostly linear, but with a secondary emphasis on form. These designs fall somewhere between line and line-mass on the continuum.

Line Designs

Asian styles traditionally focus on the beauty and reverence of individual flowers and leaves. They are typically *line designs*—they emphasize lines rather than the plant material grouping as an entire form. In order to keep the focus on the elements within the design, fewer materials are used, and the concept of "less is more" dominates, **Figure 10-7**. Line designs are derived from the traditions of ikebana, Japanese floral design. Ikebana is described later in this chapter.

Line designs have a large amount of negative space. They have more space around the placements than additional flowers or foliage. Another aspect of line designs is the origin and direction of the lines within the pattern. Line directions can be vertical, horizontal, diagonal, pendulous, or curvilinear, **Figure 10-8**. Lines can be parallel to each other, or perpendicular to form a T or an inverted T. Keep in mind that corsages, flowers to carry, and other designs can be linear.

Mass Designs

Mass designs are on the opposite side of the continuum. Form and mass are more important than line in these designs. Their origins can be traced to the wealthy estates of European aristocracy. Dutch and Flemish artists portrayed immense floral arrangements of exotic flowers in their paintings. Although individual flowers and foliage can be seen and admired, the visual impact of mass pattern floral designs is created by the abundance of plant materials used to fill in a geometric form. Mass designs are formed by *massing* flowers, or gathering and placing quantities of flowers together in close proximity.

Mass designs may be constructed as free-standing, all-around arrangements or three-sided arrangements. Free-standing designs are decorative on all sides and are best displayed in the center of a table or room, **Figure 10-9**. Three-sided designs have a definite back and are best displayed against a wall.

Line-Mass Designs

In the center of the continuum between mass and line designs is the line-mass design category. Line-mass design techniques are also of European origin. These designs are a mixture of line and mass designs. They are not fully massed flowers, but neither are they line designs with a large amount of negative space, **Figure 10-10**. In fact, they depend equally on line and mass to achieve their effect. This design category developed with the introduction of floral foams. The various types of foam, discussed in Chapter 3, *Containers, Tools, Mechanics, and Safe Work Practices,* allow for more control over stem placement than the mechanics traditionally used for line and mass style floral arrangements.

Fineart1/Shutterstock.com

Figure 10-9. A round mass design can be admired from all sides.

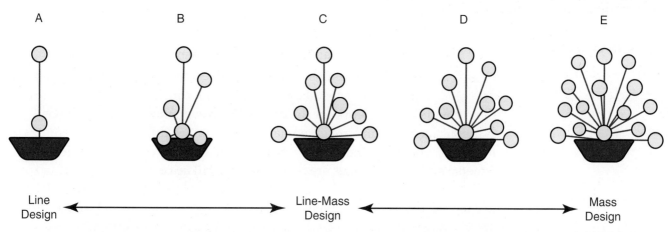

Goodheart-Willcox Publisher

Figure 10-10. Every floral design falls somewhere along the line-mass continuum, from pure line designs to pure mass designs: A—pure linear design; B—mostly linear design with some mass elements; C—equal emphasis on line and mass; D—mostly mass design with some linear elements; E—pure mass design.

Traditional Design Classifications

A more precise way to classify floral designs is to categorize them according to both their regional origin and a historical time frame, or a modern interpretation of that time frame. Culture again is a dominant factor in these categories. Because culture is constantly changing, different styles and techniques become popular over time. *Traditional designs* are generally considered to be those that were developed prior to 1900.

Oriental Design Styles

Historically, Japan and China have provided major influence over Asian design styles. In both of these countries, floral design was closely related to religion and philosophy.

Theodore Scott/Shutterstock.com

Figure 10-11. Ikebana arrangement.

Ikebana

Many experts believe that all of today's formal design styles, both eastern and western, were originally derived from *ikebana*, the traditional Japanese discipline of flower arranging. See **Figure 10-11**. Formalized in the 15th century, ikebana was considered not so much an art form as a method of spiritual development. Today, it is known as the Japanese art of flower arranging, but it remains a highly disciplined process that has specific guidelines.

Over the years, more than 2,000 schools of ikebana have developed. The most active schools today are the Ikenobo, Ohara, and Sogetsu. Although each school of ikebana has its own characteristics, all forms of ikebana also have several characteristics in common:

- Negative space plays a major role in the design.
- All types of plant material may be used, including withered leaves as well as branches, stems, and flowers.
- The design showcases the beauty of individual flowers and leaves.
- All of the materials used in the design, including the container, combine to convey a sense of harmony.
- Designs are highly stylized and have a symbolic meaning.

Most ikebana designs also include three main lines that provide a framework for the design. However, these lines also have symbolic meaning and are given names. The names differ in the different ikebana schools, but their significance remains the same. For example, in the Sogetsu school, the names are Shin, Soe, and Hikae or Tai.

The *Shin* is the longest line and is usually created using a branch that is 1 1/2 to 2 times the width of the container. It represents spiritual truth, or heaven. The second-longest line is the *Soe*, which represents humans, who form a link between heaven and earth. It is also usually a branch, and is typically about 3/4 the length of the Shin. The *Hikae* or *Tai* is the shortest line. It can be created using either a branch or a flower. In either case, it should be 1/2 to 3/4 the length of the Soe.

Chinese Designs

Like Japanese designs, Chinese designs reflect a love of nature and may use few materials. However, the Chinese arrangements emphasize natural features, rather than the stylized designs of ikebana. Designs often feature plant materials that are currently in season, arranged in a way that reflects their positions in nature. The arrangements are balanced, but often asymmetrical, **Figure 10-12**.

Chinese designs are essentially line designs, but the lines are rarely static. Instead, they provide a sense a movement. The flowers in an arrangement are often one color or a few closely related colors. Strongly contrasting colors are rarely used, although the container may contrast sharply with the flower colors.

European Design Styles

As explained earlier in this chapter, European design styles generally fall on the mass side of the line-mass continuum, but many variations have developed over the years. The following sections describe a few of the styles that are still used today.

Della Robbia

Floral designs made mostly or entirely from fruits and vegetables are called *della Robbia designs*, named after a family of Italian sculptors in the Italian Renaissance of the 15th and 16th centuries. A key feature of their sculptures and relief work is the use of fruit and floral motifs. This term can apply to all types of designs, from flowers to wear and carry to centerpieces, garlands, and event floral designs. Della Robbia designs are usually symmetrical and uncluttered, and often mix fresh plant material with dried materials. Fall and winter floral designs often contain fruit, live or artificial, due to their seasonal themes, **Figure 10-13**.

Flemish

The Flemish design style is influenced by the Flemish and Dutch painters of the Renaissance period in Europe. Arrangements in this style are typically large and contain many different types of flowers in bright, vibrant colors and interesting textures. Fruits, vegetables, and other accessories are often included, **Figure 10-14**. Accessories are usually natural items such as shells or stones.

Z.H.CHEN/Shutterstock.com

Figure 10-12. A piece inspired by a Chinese design emphasizes nature in its true form, without stylization.

Malgorzata Kistryn/Shutterstock.com; StacieStauffSmith Photos/Shutterstock.com

Figure 10-13. A relief sculpture inspired by the della Robbia family of the 15th century. Note the prominence of the fruit. The della Robbia floral design style contains many of the same elements.

Society of American Florists, Flower Factor; IgorGolovniov/Shutterstock.com

Figure 10-14. A floral arrangement created in the Flemish design style is inspired by the Dutch and Flemish artists of the Renaissance.

Society of American Florists, HotHouse Design Studio, Birmingham, AL

Figure 10-15. This bouquet with serpentine lines is an interpretation of the Biedermeier design patterning.

Biedermeier

Named after the Biedermeier period in the German Classical Revival of the early 1800s, ***Biedermeier designs*** are patterned arrangements. Concentric rings of floral materials create strong rhythms with no negative space, **Figure 10-15.** In today's American floristry, Biedermeier designs are commonly seen in competitions and exhibitions but may also be used for beautiful wedding arrangements. A Biedermeier wedding bouquet is also made with concentric rings of different flowers, or materials accentuating one type or color in each circular ring or line of pattern.

English Garden

The lush gardens of English estates in the 19th and 20th centuries provided the basis for the ***English garden design*** style. These formal mass designs are usually symmetrical arrangements in a radial or triangular shape. They feature large flowers in many different colors, as well as plenty of foliage, **Figure 10-16.** This style was influenced somewhat by the Chinese style and may include woody branches, bringing individual designs closer to line-mass on the line-mass continuum.

Formalinear

Another European style is the ***formalinear design*** style. This style combines different plant materials arranged in groups emphasizing bold forms and clean lines. Strong use of negative spaces highlights the individual flowers, leaves, stem angles, and material qualities of texture and color. This type of design is sometimes referred to as *high style design*.

Vegetative

In *vegetative designs*, flowers and foliage appear as they would in nature. *Zoning* is used to position like flowers and foliage together, as if they have grown there naturally, **Figure 10-17**. They seem to be growing, as if live plants have been transplanted into the container. The flowers used in an arrangement should be naturally compatible and include stages of development from bud to fully open flowers. That is, they should be from a similar climate and region. Some designers may use only what would be growing in a garden at a particular time or season.

American Design Styles

Traditional styles developed in colonial America, and later the United States, were heavily influenced by European design styles. However, they used locally available materials, which resulted in different overall effects.

Early Colonial

Early American colonists (1600–1699) developed a style known today as *early colonial design*, or simply *colonial*. This is a round style that has elements in common with the European styles of its time. However, many of the plant materials used in the European arrangements were not available in the colonies. The early colonial style is less formal and includes native flowers and grasses.

Hurst Photo/Shutterstock.com

Figure 10-16. The English garden design style is reminiscent of the beauty and variety of flowers used in gardens on English estates.

 Pro Tip

The word *tropical* means that a plant material is related to or situated in areas near the geographic equator. Plants in these regions thrive in warm and humid environments.

Zigzag Mountain Art/Shutterstock.com; nata-lunata/Shutterstock.com

Figure 10-17. Vegetative designs mimic the way plants grow in nature and are grouped within the arrangement like this European garden basket. Tightly massed bouquets of today have been referred to as colonial.

StacieStauffSmith Photos/Shutterstock.com

Figure 10-18. A close-up photo of present day Williamsburg holiday decorations reveal a strong textural combination of materials surrounded by a collar of shiny magnolia leaves with velvety brown backs.

Thinking Green

Soy Candles

Many of today's interpretations of the early colonial style include candles. Using soy candles in recyclable containers is an environmentally responsible alternative to traditional candles.

Gourds, seed pods, and berries are often used as well. Accessories may include candles or candlesticks, inkwells, and other items that were found in colonial households. Many florists refer to a round mass of flowers as a *colonial bouquet*.

Williamsburg

By 1700, as some American settlers became more affluent, their floral designs began to reflect their new wealth. Floral designs in the late colonial style, better known as the **Williamsburg design** style, were closer in appearance to European designs of the time. English and French styles especially were reflected in the Williamsburg style. Designs became more complex and sophisticated and were often triangular or fan-shaped instead of round. Containers were often imported from Europe. See **Figure 10-18**. Today's Williamsburg designs are *interpretive designs*, meaning that they are not necessarily historically accurate, but may contain plant materials, mechanics, or containers typical of the 18th century, **Figure 10-19**.

20th-Century and Contemporary Designs

Floral design styles developed after 1900 were commonly known as *contemporary designs*. However, this term is now used to mean design styles developed more recently, during the late 20th and early 21st centuries.

Steve Heap/Shutterstock.com

Figure 10-19. Today, during Christmas in Williamsburg, buildings are festooned with garlands containing fresh fruits. Magnolia leaves, boxwood, holly and even exotic fruits like pineapple are used extensively.

20th-Century Designs

The early 1900s were a time of dramatic cultural changes based on technological advances in both communication and transportation technology. These changes and others were reflected in design styles for everything from clothes to furniture to floral arrangements. The following styles developed during the 20th century.

Cascade

The Art Nouveau period, which began just before 1900 and lasted into the 1920s, gave rise to several new ideas about fashion and art. The *cascade design* style is a direct reflection of these new ideas. Cascade designs are line designs that include a slightly curvilinear line that falls or hangs from a container. If the arrangement is to be floor-standing, a tall container is needed. However, if the arrangement will flow over the side of a mantel or shelf, any container may be used.

Many florists use the term *cascade design* in reference to a flowers-to-carry design with dominant hanging line, **Figure 10-20**. The term is also used as a synonym for *hanging line*.

Waterfall

A *waterfall design* is a cascade design with the addition of elements that suggest the flow of water, **Figure 10-21**. This type of design uses descending lines, sometimes intentionally crossed to create several layers of different, typically sheer materials with delicate texture. They emphasize depth and create a flowing effect, frequently incorporating materials such as shells, wired beads, buttons, or various other elements of interest. This design style is highly technical and best achieved by an experience designer.

Ekaterina Pokrovskaya/Shutterstock.com

Figure 10-20. The cascade design creates a beautiful and memorable impression as a bridal bouquet. There is no set limit to the length of the bouquet and some are made to flow as long as the bridal gown's hem.

CHAINFOTO24/Shutterstock.com; Daniela Pelazza/Shutterstock.com

Figure 10-21. The waterfall design is a cascade design that represents or calls to mind falling water. The shape of the bouquet replicates the natural waterfall, yet is void of the usual layers of materials to produce the refined waterfall design style.

Alan49/Shutterstock.com

Figure 10-22. The arrangement shown above is done in freestyle. As you look at the design, you can see more than one focal point and the general use of negative space.

Sharon McGukin, SAF

Figure 10-23. An abstract floral object, or flob. Note how the designer uses the roots as well as the flowers and stems as part of the design.

Freestyle

Freestyle designs are 20th-century designs attributed to the Sogetsu school of ikebana. The Sogetsu school allows greater freedom for interpreting the rules of traditional ikebana, **Figure 10-22**. Although still highly stylized, these arrangements may have more than one focal area. Negative space remains an important element of a freestyle design.

Abstract

A floral object or *flob* reflects the Abstract Movement in sculpture. Flobs may contain natural and artificial materials presented in unnatural ways. In fact, the key element of an *abstract design* is that it is completely unnatural or unrealistic. Common materials may be used in uncommon ways, and lines may be used to form unusual shapes completely unlike the usual geometric shapes. Examples of flobs include a stack of bricks with flowers inserted in the cracks, and a wall hanging of wire fencing with foliage woven into it, **Figure 10-23**.

Parallel Systems

The *parallel systems design* is a European style developed in the 1980s in which stems are placed parallel to one another. The lines of the flower stems do not cross. Each placement has its own point of origin, as opposed to radial designs in which all stems emerge from the same point. All of the stems, or groupings of stems, are the same distance apart from each other and are placed in the same vertical direction. The arrangement is created in a low, wide container, usually rectangular, **Figure 10-24**.

Bryan Swan, Karin's Florist, Vienna, VA, Society of American Florists

Figure 10-24. This piece displays basal interest with roses and pepperberries while predominantly using vertical placements of cones and groupings of Norfolk Island pine in parallel systems.

New Convention

A variation of the parallel systems style is the *new convention design*, which includes both horizontal and vertical stem placements. The horizontal stems usually extend from all four sides of the container and are often of the same plant material as the vertical stems, although this is not required.

Millefleur

Many different types and colors of flowers are typical of the *millefleur design* style. The term *millefleur* is a French word that means "1000 flowers." Millefleur arrangements are radial, and no one type of flower is dominant, although all of the flowers are typically about the same size. See **Figure 10-25**.

Phoenix

You may have heard the old story about the phoenix, a mythological Greek bird that dies by fire, then rises from the ashes. The *phoenix design* style is named for this bird. It is a radial arrangement with a burst of long-stemmed plant materials arising from the central vertical axis, **Figure 10-26**. The base of the arrangement is generally a tightly spaced mass, with no negative space. The line materials that rise from the center of the mass are often branches or line materials that represent renewal or rebirth. The mass elements and the line elements are both equally important in this type of design, making it a true line-mass design.

Other Notable Designs

Many other design styles became popular throughout the 20th century. A few of the more notable include:

- Pot-et-fleur design. The floral designer mixes potted plants and a cut flower arrangement in a single container.
- Stacked design. Two or more containers are tiered one on top of the other, often with each container being smaller than the one below it.
- Topiary design. Live plants are clipped and trained into the shapes of human, animal, stylized, or geometric shapes, **Figure 10-27**.

smuay/Shutterstock.com

Figure 10-25. In a mille de fleurs arrangement, no one type of flower is dominant.

The Flower Studio in Austin, TX; Society of American Florists

Figure 10-26. A phoenix design represents rebirth and is named for the mythological Greek bird.

Denis Vrubievski/Shutterstock.com; Lestertair/Shutterstock.com

Figure 10-27. Topiary has been popular for many years. Geometric forms around a central axis are common. Floral designs today often mimic topiary shapes in the landscape around us.

Today's Floral Designs

In the last 20 years, trends in floral design have returned to more naturalistic forms, as opposed to the abstract designs of the 1960s and 1970s. Increased concern about the environment translates into natural, vegetative designs. *Landscape designs* are similar to vegetative designs, but reflect landscapes created by humans, not nature. Combining geometric forms and again taking inspiration from nature, these designs use line as well as mass and often have a slight oriental feel.

Another interesting development is the more extensive use of clear glass containers with or without floral foam. The container may be a cube or another unusual geometric shape, **Figure 10-28**. With clear containers, the stems of the plant material are clearly visible, so the water must be kept pristine. Many of these arrangements are *monochromatic*—they include different types of flowers, but all of the flowers are the same or similar colors. Almost minimalist in appearance, the simple forms

Elena Rostunova/Shutterstock.com

Figure 10-28. Clear glass container.

of circles and squares are grouped into an intentional representation of the external landscape environment with plants of varying shapes and sizes, designed with a modern presentation. Decorative colored floral foams are also used inside the transparent glass, adding a color dimension to the container. In this situation, the mechanics (foam) are purposely displayed. Insertions need to be intentional as any hole in this decorative foam which does not contain a stem, is noticeable and gives the impression of a mistake.

A variation of this style is the ***underwater design***. In this style, part or all of the floral design is contained in a glass or see-through container and is displayed under water, **Figure 10-29**. The container in this type of arrangement should be chosen carefully, because glass distorts the items in the water. For example, a round container tends to enlarge the appearance of the plant materials. Complete submersion of the blossom under water also shortens the life of the bloom.

Like the life of the flower floating in a stream, some trends in design will come and go quickly. Floral design will continue to be influenced by interior design, fashion, and art. In tandem, new floral products and their creative applications will keep a strong designer current with the changing trends in floristry.

Thinking Green

Recycled Glass Containers

Using recycled glass containers for designs that require clear glass is an eco-friendly idea that customers may find very appealing.

Apples Eyes Studio/Shutterstock.com

Figure 10-29. Considerations for an underwater design include the shape of the container as well as the plant materials it contains. This simplistic design makes quite a statement with the leaves wrapped around the inside of the bubble bowl and the single pink orchid.

Summary

- Many professional floral designs are based on geometric forms such as the circle, triangle, and square.
- Line designs use minimal amounts of plant material and emphasize individual lines rather than the arrangement as a whole.
- Line-mass designs have an equal emphasis on line and mass or form.
- Traditional floral designs were developed before 1900 and include Oriental, European, and American styles.
- Many of the floral design styles of the 20th century were related to cultural changes based on technological advances.
- Today's floral designs have returned to more naturalistic forms, including vegetative, landscape, and underwater designs.

Review Questions

Go to www.g-wlearning.com/floraldesign/ to use the fill-in-form.

Answer the following questions using the information provided in this chapter.

1. How is a Hogarth curve created?
2. What is the difference between a line design and a mass design?
3. List at least four characteristics common to all ikebana designs.
4. What is the major difference between traditional Japanese and Chinese floral design?
5. What technique is used in vegetative designs to position flowers and foliage as they would grow naturally?
6. In what way do early colonial designs differ from the European styles of the same period?
7. What is a flob?
8. What is the difference between a parallel systems design and a new convention design?
9. Describe the identifying characteristics of a phoenix design.
10. Explain the differences between vegetative and landscape designs.

Activities

1. Combine a mass pattern with a line pattern in a single design. What are the results? Make one of the patterns more dominant than the other, then switch pattern dominance. How can these designs be practically designed and used?
2. Using a list of specific floral materials provided by your instructor, implement the design process to create a geometric arrangement of your choice. How did the specified floral materials affect your design process?
3. Create a parallel systems arrangement using clusters of vertical stems for the main placements.
4. Form groups of four students and, using real student-designed floral arrangements or images from your portfolios, evaluate your peers' designs in terms of the formal design qualities covered in the text.
5. Visit an art museum with your peers. Evaluate, analyze, and discuss the use of design principles in landscape paintings and how they differ by historical era. Sketch an arrangement based on your discussion.

Critical Thinking

1. A customer brings a rectangular tin container to your flower shop. The tin is a family antique from the Art Nouveau period and has elaborate pressed designs on the sides. She wants you to create an arrangement to showcase the container. What type of arrangement might you suggest to meet this customer's requirements?
2. A young couple has just moved into a townhouse with an L-shaped stairway to the second floor. There is a window at the landing (where the staircase changes direction), and they want an arrangement to place in the window. They want the design to look good from the outside, but also to trail down the wall on the inside. What type of arrangement might you suggest, and what type of container would you use?
3. A local architectural firm has just finished restoring a home that was originally built in 1820 and will now be used to house a museum of local history. The city and the architectural firm are jointly holding an open house to showcase restoration. The architectural firm has hired you to provide five "period" arrangements similar to those that might have been used when the house was new. What type or types of arrangements are appropriate? What might you need to take into consideration when filling this order?

STEM Activities and Academics

1. **Math** Understanding sizes and proportions is important for some types of floral design. Review the size requirements for traditional ikebana, as stated in this chapter. Then perform the necessary calculations to complete the following chart. Round your answers to the nearest tenth of a decimal inch.

Container Width	Maximum Shin Length	Maximum Soe Length	Maximum Hikae (Tai) Length
7″			
9″			
11″			
15″			

2. **Technology.** Conduct research into the advances in communication and travel technology that occurred from 1900 through 1970. Compare these advances with the changing styles of floral design during the same period. What was the effect of technology on floral design during this time period? Provide examples from your research.

3. **Engineering.** With a partner or team, plan a new business devoted to developing new flower specimens to appeal to people based on today's cultural patterns and preferences. Perform the necessary research to explore today's trends and identify how they might impact your new company's work. Specify at least one flower type you think could be created by hybridization or other means. Form a mock company and create a preliminary plan to engineer the new plant type. If resources are available, try your plan. Document your research and methods.

4. **Math.** At a local flower shop or at the website of a retail florist, classify the available floral designs according to their geometric shapes. Tally the number of arrangements based on circle, triangle, and square shapes. Create a bar graph showing your results. Which geometric shape is most popular?

5. **Language Arts.** Write an essay explaining how the selection of floral materials affects the design process.

Communicating about Floral Design

1. **Reading and Writing.** Draw a monochromatic triangular floral arrangement using an orange hue. Use orange daisy-shaped asters, white miniature carnations, small mums, and orange asclepias tuberosa for filler flowers. Draw it in a blue floral bowl. Use real floral materials if available. Create a second arrangement using a different color scheme.

2. **Speaking and Writing.** Choose two design styles or use two styles assigned by your instructor. Find five pictures of floral arrangements created in each of these two styles. Be sure to give the photographers or designers credit for their work. Using two separate 11″ × 14″ poster boards, create a poster for each type of design. Include a description of the design style on each poster. Be prepared to give specific reasons each image is an example of your design style and whether it is a strong or weak representation. Present your project to the class.

3. **Speaking and Reading.** Choose two types of floral designs to compare and contrast. Research each type of design and gather information on its history, who popularized it, and the types of materials used. Obtain at least two illustrations of each design and use a dark marker to outline the basic framework, or skeleton, of each composition. Prepare a presentation for your class. Use a computer to project and explain each design. You may also use poster board and printed images for your presentation.

4. **Speaking and Writing.** Use line drawings on poster board to explain the skeleton and basic shape of at least three types of designs covered in this chapter. Indicate which types of flowers are used to establish the skeletons of each design as well as the types of containers each type may use. Display the drawings as reference tools for the class. Be prepared to explain to the class how and why each type of flower (mass, line, filler, form) contributes to the design.

Chapter

11

Site Assessment and Theme Development

objectives

After reading this chapter, you will be able to:

- Determine the basic information needed to develop or produce a special event.
- Analyze an event site in order to create appropriate floral designs.
- Create thematic designs for large or small spaces or venues.
- Produce an event timeline for the setup, installation, and removal of designs at an event site.
- Discuss budget and pricing considerations for special events.

key terms

event setup	production	site assessment
event timeline	sightline	venue
logistics		

Go to **www.g-wlearning.com/floraldesign/** for online vocabulary activities using key terms from the chapter.

introduction

Floral designers are often asked to provide floral decorations for many different kinds of events. Many customers have an idea for a theme they want to follow. Others may want the designer to provide a selection of ideas from which they can choose. In either case, it is the floral designer's responsibility to develop the chosen theme to satisfy the customer's needs or wants. The entire process of planning or developing an event is known as *production*.

Before you can develop a theme, you must gather information about the purpose of the event, the people who will attend, and the site where the event will be held, **Figure 11-1**. You will need to be able to gather information quickly, assess the purpose of an event or occasion, and then create appropriate floral designs. By asking the correct questions, you can collect the information you need.

Figure 11-1. Gathering information from the client requires good oral communication skills.

Basic Information

When beginning to design for any event, large or small, it is helpful always to ask the same basic questions: Who? What? Where? When? These questions establish the basic information on which you will build the product. You may wish to use a checklist of information and questions when you interview a customer in order to create an appropriate theme for an event.

Who

First, determine "who" your customers are and what defines them. Are they regular flower buyers familiar with floral products, or do they need some guidance on selecting themes as well as flower types? Do they prefer a more contemporary design style or something with a more traditional flair? If the customers have visited your flower shop in the past, you may be able to determine their preferences based on their purchase history, **Figure 11-2**. Is their style preference country or modern? Primitive or techno? By understanding their tastes, you can develop a stronger sense of how to create products they will enjoy. This will also help narrow the range of options.

Figure 11-2. Every customer has personal tastes and preferences that you will need to accommodate in your event planning.

If the event is to be held in honor of a particular person or people, such as a birthday or anniversary, you will need additional information. For a birthday, the person's age and gender will make a difference in the event development. You would not plan the same type of event for a 5-year-old girl as you would for a 25-year-old man. For anniversaries, ask how many years the couple has been married. In all events to honor people, you may want to ask about any favorites the person may have. Try to find out the person's favorite color, type of flower, or even a favorite celebrity. Knowing the person's likes and dislikes will help you design something as an extension of themselves, an event the person will truly enjoy.

Safety Note

Many event venues do not allow open flame candles. Battery operated LED lights are available in numerous shapes, styles, and varying color hues.

What

What is the occasion? Is it a small or large event? When designing pieces for everyday events such as patient hospital visits or the birthday of an administrative professional, think small in size. Arrangements must fit on the tray next to a hospital bed, or on the desk in an office, **Figure 11-3**.

If the occasion is a special birthday, perhaps a significant number such as sixteen, the affair may be larger. It may be held in a dance hall, ballroom, or restaurant party room, and you will need to think of the bigger, overall look of the event. If the theme of the event, perhaps for a *quinceañera* (a coming-out ball for a girl's 15th birthday), is centered around a request for a princess-themed party, you will develop details suiting this overall concept.

Where

Where will the event be held? Will it be held indoors or outside? If an outdoor setting is planned, what are the options if the weather turns poor? A florist needs to have a backup plan for how to secure things in case of high winds, remove things quickly for unexpected storms, and how to transport materials or designs to another location smoothly. In the case of a location change, will the arrangements also be moved? Where will they be placed? Gather as much information as possible about the setting in which the event will take place. Visit the *venue*, or site, and perform a site assessment to determine what will and will not work in your design. If possible, walk through the site with the customer and listen to any ideas he or she may have.

Society of American Florists

Figure 11-3. This bold, colorful phoenix design is a good size for office settings and work spaces with little counter space.

When

Will the occasion occur in the spring, summer, fall, or winter? You can take cues from nature to create seasonal arrangements for both indoor and outdoor events. The dominant colors of a season, for example, autumnal shades in fall, and evergreens with red or white in winter, are beautiful basics to begin an event "look." Another consideration is the time of day. Will the event take place in the morning, afternoon, or evening? Will it be held after dark, and if so, who will be responsible for the lighting?

Site Assessment

Every location has strengths and limitations. Closely related to the basic question of where the event will be held, the *site assessment* is a thorough examination of the venue. On this visit, it is important to gather details about the environment surrounding the location, **Figure 11-4**. Every site has a distinct character, and the most successful designs work with this character, rather than struggling against it to make the space look completely different.

Architecture

What is the architecture of the space? Are the ceilings higher than 12'? Are they lower? Is the ceiling flat or pitched? These spatial details will determine what type of materials you select and the overall height of designs. For example, large vase arrangements filled with tall willow branches are impressive inside a space with high ceilings, but do not work as well if the ceiling is low and flat. In a smaller space, they may feel overbearing.

How is the space decorated? Does it contain a crystal and glass chandelier or rustic oak log rafters? Is there a strong sense of traditional architecture with classic interior wall treatments, or is it a trendier, more modern space with sleek walls and floor coverings? Look around the space for style cues that can give you a sense of what is required to accomplish the theme, **Figure 11-5**.

When a space has interesting architectural features, you may capitalize on this and allow these features to provide the background. This would allow a small-scale design to provide the necessary thematic detail. Your design may capitalize on the existing surroundings while providing visual detail at

Sergey Chirkov/Shutterstock.com; Joshua Rainey Photography/Shutterstock.com

Figure 11-4. Visiting the site of the event allows you to understand the spatial requirements and the overall character of the space. Allow the client to express ideas and thoughts as you go through the site together.

infinity21/Shutterstock.com; iofoto/Shutterstock.com; mambographer/Shutterstock.com

Figure 11-5. Plan the event to blend with the character of the architecture. For this venue, a "by the sea" or nautical theme would be appropriate.

the appropriate level. For example, suppose the event centers on a round table for ten guests. When patrons are seated, their eye is drawn down from the vast and ornate surroundings to a more focused area with dramatic detail in texture, form, and color combinations. See **Figure 11-6**.

Focal Points

Every room or space has at least one *focal point*. As you enter the space, view the setting and note the areas that are natural focal points, or places where your eyes travel first, **Figure 11-7**. Examples include the front door, the main entrance to the reception room, or a head table or main stage. These areas should be developed with floral design or thematic pieces of some type.

pio3/Shutterstock.com

Figure 11-6. For an event that involves a single table, a low, round centerpiece that does not inhibit conversation around the table is a good choice.

The line of vision between a person and an object, called the *sightline*, is another potential area of theme development. Do you notice items at your eye level or higher, toward the ceiling? Pay attention to all focal points and lines of sight. The impact of a floral display can be maximized in these areas.

Daniela Pelazza/Shutterstock.com

Figure 11-7. Framed by the canopy and by the flower stands, aisle runner leads the eye directly to the focal point under the canopy. The color red is a directional color so using red for the aisle runner is a wise decision.

Logistics

Consider the location of the event from a logistical point of view. *Logistics* are the practical organization, planning, and coordination required to make the event run smoothly. What size delivery vehicle will you need? Is the location within a five minute drive from your shop? Will it be close enough to make multiple small trips for arrangements in a smaller delivery vehicle? Or is it a thirty minute drive with no option for returning to your shop if you forget something?

When you are establishing setup times for events, allow enough time for unexpected things, such as traffic and/or weather, along the way. It is also helpful to prepare a toolbox or traveling kit to keep in the delivery vehicle. Stock it with scissors, various weights of wire, wire cutters, ribbon, floral glue, corsage or boutonniere pins, pen, paper, and floral tape, as well as any other items you need on a regular basis, **Figure 11-8**. Having a set of floral tools at the site during setup can help avoid disaster if a problem occurs and you need to make a quick fix. When you are assisting with a wedding ceremony, a few loose cut flowers and greens may also come in handy to quickly construct a boutonniere or corsage the customer forgot to order.

Seregam/Shutterstock.com

Figure 11-8. Florists who focus on more elaborate displays, should carry a tool kit that includes a cordless drill, hammer, tape measure, and basic floral design necessities (tape, wire, pins, etc.).

Thematic Development

The site assessment described earlier forms the basis and the starting point for thematic décor. It sets a foundation on which you can build the design style. It also gives insight into how to construct the floral designs and supporting materials, both the mechanics and design style.

The principles and elements of design apply to all aspects of the event. The components of the theme should be present in all of the materials to gather the most impact. For example, the graphics used on the invitations, the composition of photographic images, the culinary presentation on plates or the buffet, and the floral designs should all have elements in common. When all of the pieces have a solid design and a common design thread, a cohesive look and style is created, resulting in a successful visual experience, **Figure 11-9**.

c12/Shutterstock.com; KMW Photography/Shutterstock.com; popovich_vl/Shutterstock/com; Pavels Rumme/Shutterstock.com; Viktoriiapdb/Shutterstock.com

Figure 11-9. The color purple is a strong design thread that creates a cohesive look and style for this wedding venue.

Color Story

Color is typically the primary source of thematic development. It is the common denominator for all accessories associated with event details. A color might be chosen because of the season of an event or because it is the customer's favorite color. Once chosen, the colors can be introduced with table linens, invitations, ribbon, and fabrics, **Figure 11-10**.

For flowers, use color families to provide more options. See Chapter 7, *Elements of Design*, and Chapter 8, *Flower Selection*, for more information about using color families and color wheels to choose appropriate colors. Keep in mind that some color families provide more options than others. For example, many naturally colored flower varieties are available with the color orange and its family members of yellow and red. Assorted shapes, textures, and sizes are available in line, form, filler, and mass flowers. With the color

Figure 11-10. Young ladies having a *quinceañera* party must make many of the same choices a bride makes when planning a wedding. Everything from the invitation to the flower arrangements tie the color story together.

blue, however, not as many options are available. In this situation, you may suggest using a color that is complementary to the chosen primary color and emphasize that this is also very effective.

Often the invitation for the occasion can provide an inspiration. For example, the invitation for the quinceañera mentioned earlier in this chapter might display details of glitter accompanied by a crown, printed on pink paper. Building on the look of the invitation, you would work with the color pink. Using several types of pink flowers, the color could be used in table centerpieces, door décor, flowers to wear or carry, and party favors. Accents of beads or rhinestones aid in strengthening the princess theme and should coordinate with each other around the main color pink. If heightened color accent is desired, include lime green flowers. The boldness of this color plays well with many other colors while adding an intensity of energy and visual impact.

Audience

The basic information you gathered about who the event will honor can help you create pieces appropriate for the background. The setting for a wedding anniversary for a couple who was married in 1965 might be entirely different from an anniversary for a 21st-century wedding. Research the trends, colors, and events of the wedding year and consider using floral materials similar to those available during that time.

For example, photos from a 1970s wedding that show the decorations or even the bridal bouquet can tell you many things about the color story and style of the couple's big day, their favorite flowers, and what types were available at the time of their wedding. Looking for clues like these may assist you in producing designs that combine the flowers used then with new items available now. Successfully producing designs for this event will help the couple and their family make new memories. It may also create an opportunity for increasing future sales to extended family members and friends. See **Figure 11-11.**

AnnaKostyuk/Shutterstock.com; Karen Grigoryan/Shutterstock.com

Figure 11-11. Viewing photos of a couple's wedding may help you plan for a coordinating anniversary event.

Location

A smart designer also does research into the location and surrounding environment of the event. Will it be located in a largely ethnic community? Are any rituals and customs connected to this community? Take hints for designs from the surrounding area. Is the setting formal? Is the area urban or rural? These questions provide a direction for you to follow in creating the design. It forms a foundation for decisions to best satisfy the customer.

Season

The season in which the event is to be held may also provide ideas for design themes. For example, spring conjures images of flowering trees, blooming bulbs, and a variety of pastel colors in a garden-style display. Both outdoor and indoor settings can reflect the explosion of new birth associated with the look of spring, **Figure 11-12**. Forsythia and other flowering materials are dramatic in large vases. Potted blooming azalea and hydrangea plants, combined with containers of tulip bulbs, give party-goers a sense of spring.

Summer designs can include bold colors such as hot pink, bright orange, sunny yellows, lime green, and bright purples. Designs for receptions or parties held in outdoor venues can incorporate the various greens of surrounding trees, shrubs, and turf, **Figure 11-13**. Daring colors can also be brought indoors to add high energy and a festive feel to an event. Playful props of summer outdoor activities can be combined with the bold colors indoors to beat the heat, but still provide the festive sense of summer.

In the fall, consider including large pumpkins, gourds, and hay bales as signs of the harvest, **Figure 11-14**. These large elements can easily be incorporated into the setting or environment for events held during the fall season.

inifinity21/Shutterstock.com; TravnikovStudio/Shutterstock.com; MicroBeans Studio/iStock/Thinkstock

Figure 11-12. Spring events may showcase budding spring flowers and pastel colors.

Iakiv Pekarskyi/Shutterstock.com; MNStudio/Shutterstock.com; aastock/Shutterstock.com; aastock/Shutterstock.com; Kim Ruoff/Shutterstock.com

Figure 11-13. The color green is used successfully for this outdoor summer event.

Robert Crum/Shutterstock.com; Paul Rich Studio/Shutterstock.com; Symbiot/Shutterstock.com; Don Blais/Shutterstock.com; Paul Rich Studio/Shutterstock.com

Figure 11-14. Fall events often use the yellow-orange-red color families to imitate the colors of autumn leaves.

In the flower shop, you can create arrangements of varying sizes and price points for use in both smaller tabletop merchandising displays and large window displays or events. This allows something for every customer.

For a winter venue, consider using a plant's textural interest as a basis for a concept. Pine cones, short-needled pine branches, and berried branches are excellent choices. Evergreens on a background of white snow, mixed with the intense colors of red holly berries, make a dramatic combination for entry areas. Increase thematic effect by placing objects of interest related to the activities of the season, like sledding and skating, in high visibility locations. Seasonal looks in designs can be used in interior spaces as well. Artificial snow and winter themed accessories work well in combination with fresh cut materials. See **Figure 11-15**. When artificial evergreens are used, design them to resemble the regular combination of fresh materials. Use varying textures and shapes of artificial snowflocked pine, fir, and juniper together with holiday accents of ribbon and glass ornaments.

Spatial Scale

Scale and proportion in floral design are both concerned with size. Scale refers to the size of an object as a whole, in relation to another object. The size of a space will determine the scale of your design. Use visual clues such as ceiling height, table tops, and sightlines to establish a scale for your designs.

Also consider alternative design options. For example, when a small arrangement is used in a space with high ceilings, balloons might be an option to create the illusion of size without the expense. The balloons give the sense of a lower ceiling, bringing the attention of the eye to a lower level within the space. Branching materials such as bundled curly willow can also achieve this effect. When creating arrangements to raise the sightline of a space or make a large space seem more intimate,

Figure 11-15. Most winter events are held indoors, but designs often include "snow."

floral designs in tall vases with branching effects can also do the same. See **Figure 11-16**.

Event Timeline

A critical part of planning an event is developing the *event timeline*, or schedule of when each task will occur so that the event will run smoothly. The events on the timeline include setup, installation, and removal tasks.

Setup and Installation

Event setup includes all of the physical tasks required to install designs and prepare the venue for the event. Depending on the site and the type of event, this may require a floral designer to work with other suppliers, such as lighting consultants or musicians, **Figure 11-17**. If this is the case, communication with these suppliers is important to ensure that the schedule works for everyone.

Vadym Zaitsev/Shutterstock.com; infinity21/Shutterstock.com

Figure 11-16. Adding visual size to a design does not always mean a great additional expense. In this arrangement, the inexpensive balloons give the sense of a lower ceiling. The elegant arrangements make the large space more intimate.

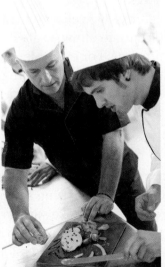

oliveromg/Shutterstock.com; Goodluz/Shutterstock.com; Africa Studio/Shutterstock.com; dotshock/Shutterstock.com

Figure 11-17. When more than one supplier needs to set up equipment or materials, communication between suppliers can help ensure that they do not get in each other's way.

To create an event timeline, you will need to know the answers to these questions:

- What time are the guests arriving?
- How much time will it take to install what has been ordered for the venue?
- How far is the venue from your flower shop?
- Will any items need to be rented, and if so, who will be responsible for transporting the rented items to the event site?
- How much assistance will you need for installation?
- How much time will be needed for installation?
- Will a large number of additional staff be required?
- If the event requires several suppliers, how much of the setup and removal will be your responsibility?
- How long will the event last?

The installation of any event requires much advance planning, and good planning is the key to success. Be sure to consider the time required to set up any rented items, such as columns, stands, or even a tent. If outside help will be required, you may need to begin searching for people with the appropriate skills months in advance. What types of skills should the additional staff possess? Often flower shop drivers can assist with the unloading and placement of items.

The setup portion of the event timeline should specify when staff should begin loading the delivery vehicle, when the vehicle should leave for the event site, and how much time has been allowed for installation at the site. If additional delivery vehicles are rented, incorporate the time necessary and staffing required to acquire the vehicles as well as return them. See **Figure 11-18**. Be sure to allow a safe margin for each item on the timeline. For example, the time allowed for the vehicle to travel from the flower shop to the event site should include extra time for stoplights and potential traffic jams.

Safety Note

Proper Lifting Techniques

Make sure all of your employees understand proper lifting techniques. You should lift using the large muscles in your legs, and carry heavy items close to your body.

Dmitry Kalinovsky/Shutterstock.com

Figure 11-18. It may be necessary to rent a different vehicle with more space, depending on the size of the event and pieces ordered. Loading the items takes time. Be sure to allow enough time for loading to take place without rushing, which could damage some of the items.

 **Pro Tip**

Use removable vehicle magnets with your shop's name and phone number when you rent a vehicle.

Reusable Props

Instead of renting props such as a tent, chuppah, columns, or stands for individual occasions, consider purchasing reusable props that you can transport to and from the event sites. Make sure large items can be broken down into smaller pieces yet are sturdy enough to be used again and again. They should be lightweight, yet give the impression of something permanent. By avoiding the use of throwaway props, you can help the environment, and by buying them, you can save money by avoiding recurring rental fees.

Removal

Once the event has ended, it will be the designer's responsibility to remove some or all of the designs or decorations. When more than one type of supplier is involved, each company generally removes the items it installed. You will be responsible for removing all of the floral designs and associated decorations, unless the customer has arranged to keep them.

Remember that teardown of props and other materials from an event require both time and staffing, **Figure 11-19**. Have cleaning supplies on hand to clean up if necessary. You may want to consider keeping supplies such as a broom and dustpan, cleaning cloths, paper towels, and garbage bags in your delivery or removal vehicle, in case they are needed. The quantity and size of rental elements or support materials should also be considered. If necessary, be sure a large van or panel truck is available at the appropriate time for prop removal as well as installation.

CHANARAT/Shutterstock.com

Figure 11-19. Responsible designers clean up after themselves. In addition to removing your designs from the event site, be sure to clean up any spills or fallen flowers or foliage.

Budget and Pricing

Before you can begin production of any specific event, you will need to know the client's budget. The client's financial concerns will help determine your product selections. Provide ideas to carry out the event theme in many formats and varying price points. If your flower shop does many special events, you may find it convenient to prepare a price sheet that lists various services and props. This information can serve as a springboard for conversations with the customer during planning sessions. Floral product selections can then be made based on the event budget.

When pricing an event, be sure to include all of the expenses associated with the event. In addition to the floral supplies, accessories, and labor, this may include large props and rental of tents or other items. It also includes delivery, setup, and removal of all of the items. Do not forget to include an appropriate markup. Pricing methods are described in more detail in Chapter 18, *Floriculture Marketing, Pricing, and Sales*.

DutchScenery/iStock/Thinkstock; HaraldBiebel/iStock/Thinkstock

The floriculture industry is international, so you will be working with professionals from around the world. The crates are on wheels at a flower auction in the Netherlands. The bundled flowers are for sale in a French market.

Summary

- The basic information needed before you can design for an event include: Who? What? Where? When?
- A thorough assessment of the event site is necessary to gather details that will affect the design and theme for the event.
- The color story is the primary source of thematic development for an event, but the audience, location, season, and spatial scale must also be considered.
- Creating an event timeline for setup, installation, and removal of design elements is an important part of event planning.
- The client's budget is an important factor in determining how a theme is developed.

Review Questions

Go to www.g-wlearning.com/floraldesign/ to use the fill-in-form.

Answer the following questions using the information provided in this chapter.

1. What tasks are included in the production of an event?
2. What basic information would you need to know in order to plan a birthday party?
3. Why is site assessment an important part of the planning process for an event?
4. What is the difference between a focal point and a sightline?
5. When you consider the logistics of an event, what factors should you take into consideration?
6. What one element is generally the primary source of thematic development?
7. How might the age of a couple celebrating an anniversary affect the theme you develop for the event?
8. What colors might work best for an outdoor party that will take place in July?
9. What events should be included on an event timeline?
10. What items should you include in your estimate when you determine the price for an event?

Activities

1. Research architectural styles and design styles appropriate for event venues.
2. Create a storyboard with photographs or magazine clippings depicting color, theme, accents, and areas of floral design for a planned event.
3. Sketch designs that would be appropriate for a birthday party for a 6-year-old boy who was born on October 15. Consider your own experiences when you were a child, and use your imagination to create a fun theme for the event.
4. Visit a local park and identify a site for a fall harvest party. Observe and take notes on the site characteristics, and use your observations to develop ideas for a design theme. Sketch your ideas.
5. Visit an art museum with your peers. Evaluate, analyze, and discuss the use of design principles in landscape paintings and how they differ by historical era. Sketch an arrangement based on your discussion.

Critical Thinking

1. A customer is throwing a holiday party in December, but he does not want to use the colors red and green. He wants something "elegant" for an indoor setting at the ballroom of a local hotel. What season-appropriate color schemes might you propose for this event?
2. A customer is planning an outdoor wedding at a park just outside of town. He wants the wedding to take place next to a waterfall. What should you include in your site assessment for this location? What should you include in your plans to provide safety for the customer, the guests, and the floral designs?

STEM Activities and Academics

1. **Science.** Investigate the science behind the changing color of leaves in the fall. Write a three-page report explaining the chemical reasons for the color changes and why different species turn different colors.

2. **Technology.** Research props that are commonly used for indoor and outdoor events. Choose a prop that has been improved by technology within the last 20 years and prepare a 2-minute oral report to describe the technology and the effect it had on current use of the prop.

3. **Engineering.** Create an event timeline for a dance to be held under a tent at a local park in the summer. The event will have approximately 30 attendees, and will take place from 8 PM until midnight. The theme is to be "summer fun." The venue is 30 minutes from your flower shop. Outline a design for the event and determine what will be needed, including other suppliers, if necessary. Then create the event timeline to accommodate all of these factors.

4. **Math.** Visit an event or meeting room at a local hotel. Use a tape measure to measure the room and identify the location of all focal points, doors, and windows. Then use graph paper or a computer with computer-aided design or architecture software to create a floor plan of the meeting room. Use a scale of $1/4'' = 1'$. Use your floor plan to determine suitable sizes for floral designs for a wedding reception.

5. **Language Arts.** With a partner, role-play the process of gathering basic information from a client for a 4th-of-July party. Each partner should develop a list of appropriate questions to gather important facts. Take turns playing the client and the floral designer. In each case, the floral designer should practice using good communication skills to obtain information from the client.

Communicating about Floral Design

1. **Speaking.** With a peer, role-play the following situation: a client cannot have the floral garlands attached in the archways of the mansion that she wants for her parents' anniversary party due to restrictions by the historical society. The designer must explain why she cannot have the arrangements and present her with an alternative plan. One student plays the role of the designer and the other acts as the client. Discuss reasons why the historical society would place restrictions on flower arrangements. As the designer explains the restrictions and alternatives, the client should ask questions if the explanation is unclear. Switch roles and repeat the activity.

2. **Listening and Speaking.** With a group of three other peers, research three of the following types of venues: country club, public outdoor garden, private estate, historic mansion, historic public building, and a beach front. Each student investigates one of these topics: restrictions for wedding decorations; types of flower arrangements allowed; photography restrictions; types of chairs and tables available; and capacity of venue. Then each group presents their findings to the class, and the other class members take notes on the presentation.

3. **Listening and Speaking.** You are a floral designer, and you have a client with the following requests and restrictions for a special event: primary color red, secondary color yellow, accents of black and white, dark green and lime green or yellow green leaves; no roses, no daisies, no baby's breath, no ferns; clear vases, but no stems showing; no shiny ribbon or tulle, only natural accents; tall table arrangements, floral jewelry for the female guests, matching boutonnieres for the men.

   Draw up a proposal for your client. Your proposal should include the following: types of flowers, black and white accents, greenery, natural accents, vases, method of concealing the stems; type of table arrangements, floral jewelry, and boutonnieres. Create your proposal in the form of a presentation. Share the presentation with the class as though the class were your client. Ask for and answer any questions that your client might have.

Chapter

12 Flowers to Wear and Carry

objectives

After reading this chapter, you will be able to:

- Describe the design considerations that apply to various types of corsages.
- Create various styles of flowers-to-wear designs, including corsages and boutonnieres.
- Produce a floral jewelry design.
- Apply appropriate techniques to mount flowers and foliage on wires.
- Construct various styles of flowers-to-carry designs, including hand-tied bouquets and bouquets with foam holders.

key terms

arm bouquet
boutonniere
cascade design
composite flower
corsage stem
corsage
crescent design
double-spray corsage

duchess rose
floral jewelry
flowers-to-carry design
flowers-to-wear design
glamellia
hand-tied bouquet
hand-wired bouquet
headpiece

hemispherical design
lei
personal flowers
pomander
prayer book adornment
shatter
single-flower corsage
single-spray corsage

Go to www.g-wlearning.com/floraldesign/ for online vocabulary activities using key terms from the chapter.

introduction

In this chapter, we will explore the many ways to create designs for flowers to wear and flowers to carry. Referred to as *personal flowers*, these designs can be used for proms, weddings, and many other occasions, **Figure 12-1**. From single flowers to intricate cascades of blossoms, flowers to wear or carry require technical knowledge and skill to be created correctly.

Flowers to Wear

Flowers can make an outfit more stylish and a special day even more special. *Flowers-to-wear designs* include boutonnieres, corsages, headpieces, and other floral designs that are meant to be worn on the clothing or on the body.

Boutonnieres

The word *boutonniere* is derived from a French term meaning to wear a flower in the buttonhole of a lapel. Boutonniere designs may be made from single flowers or multiple flowers. They may also include variety of plant materials and other non-floral items, such as decorative wire, jewels, and novelties. See **Figure 12-2**.

Today, many boutonnieres are still made in the traditional way using wire and tape mechanics. Others are created using adhesives. A straight stem is always appropriate and does not call attention to the mechanics. However, in a wired and taped boutonniere, the wiring and taping may include small but noticeable touches to enhance the design. See **Figure 12-3**.

bikeriderlondon/Shutterstock.com

Figure 12-1. Flowers-to-wear make special days memorable. Corsages are often designed to complement prom or homecoming dresses.

Stanislav Popov/Shutterstock.com

Figure 12-2. The delicate, silver filigree boutonniere holder provides a dart-like finish below a swirl of silvery wire in this design.

ethanaylett/iStock/Thinkstock; Bribar/iStock/Thinkstock

Figure 12-3. Boutonnieres coordinate with the bride's bouquet and the wedding colors.

When a boutonniere includes multiple materials, each wire may be individually taped, then bound together with a smaller band of tape at the binding point. The individual stems are flared slightly to give the look of a miniature gathered bouquet. Wired and taped stems may be curled or spiraled for interesting effects. Remember that the focal point of boutonniere designs should be on the largest flower used and that good taste should prevail.

Manufacturers offer a wide variety of boutonniere holders and accessories fastened in place with a few drops of adhesive glue. Instead of relying on pins to hold the boutonniere on the lapel, specially-designed holders are backed with strong magnets. They make attaching boutonnieres to lapels simple and fast, with no danger of harming fabric.

Corsages

Corsages are wearable floral arrangements for women, **Figure 12-4**. For a prom, a young woman may receive a corsage from her date that coordinates or contrasts with her formal dress. It is also appropriate for women to wear flowers on their wedding anniversary or for a wedding. A bride may wear a corsage for a small, intimate wedding instead of carrying a bouquet of flowers. This would work well with a tasteful, street-length dress or tailored suit. Mothers, grandmothers, and other women who are special to the bride and groom are given flowers to wear at a wedding ceremony and reception.

beachlane/Shutterstock.com

Figure 12-4. Petite spray roses and small, delicate accents are a nice choice for a traditional young lady's corsage. Three miniature roses and waxflower with foliage and ribbon accents are all that is needed.

Step-by-Step

Simple Rose Boutonniere

1

For this project you will need the following plant materials: one standard rose and two ivy leaves. You will also need #24 or #26 gauge wire, wire cutters, stem wrap, and boutonniere pins.

2

Leave approximately 3/4″ of stem on the rose, do not remove the sepals. Pierce the rose through the ovary with #24 or #26 gauge wire. Gently, pull the wires down so they are parallel to the stem of the flower.

3

Floral tape the wire and the flower, beginning just above the pierce of the wire. Filler could be added if desired, behind and to the side of the rose and floral taped.

4

Ivy leaves may now be placed behind the rose and to the side, using an ivy leaf or other foliage that is already wired makes for easy placement and manipulating the angle of the leaf.

5

Cut the stem to approximately 1 1/2″ making sure no wire is exposed. Add boutonniere pins. Spray boutonniere with finishing spray, let dry, insert into a plastic bag or box and place in the cooler. Cut the wire stem to a length of about 2″–3″. Add boutonniere pins and package for freshness and presentation.

Step-by-Step

Pinning a Boutonniere

1. Ask the gentleman if you may pin a boutonniere to his lapel.
2. Turn the lapel back
3. Insert the pin through the fabric near the center of the widest part of the lapel
4. Hold the boutonniere in place.
5. If mechanics allow, bring the pin through the stem of the boutonniere, or around the stem.
6. Bring the pin through the upper part of the lapel and to the back.
7. If necessary, make slight adjustments so the boutonniere sits squarely in the widest part of the lapel and that the flowers are positioned to their best advantage.
8. If the boutonniere seems unsteady or detached for any reason, repeat the process so it will stay in place.

GáborKucsma/iStock/Thinkstock

A corsage may be presented to women who are recognized for an award or achievement. Also, if a female political leader presents a speech at a high school honor society banquet, a corsage in the school colors, the honor society's colors, or a neutral palette may be presented. Corsages can be worn just about anywhere, but most often they are worn on the wrist, lapel, or on the shoulder, in which case the left shoulder is appropriate, **Figure 12-5**.

Mike Watson Images/Moodboard/Thinkstock; aijohn784/iStock/Thinkstock

Figure 12-5. Corsages may be made with bright, bold analogous colors or with a monochromatic color scheme.

Richard Foote/Shutterstock.com

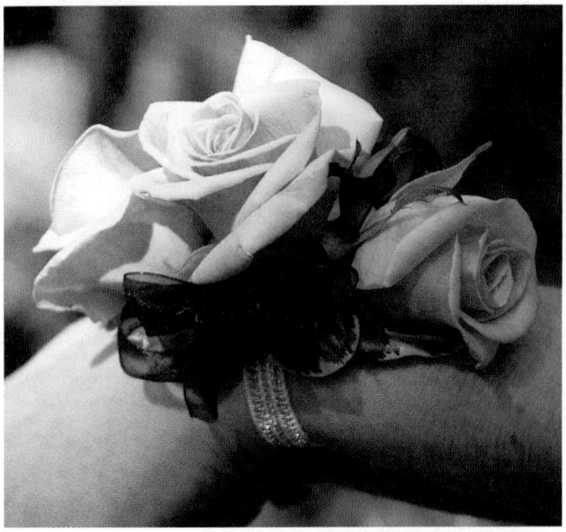

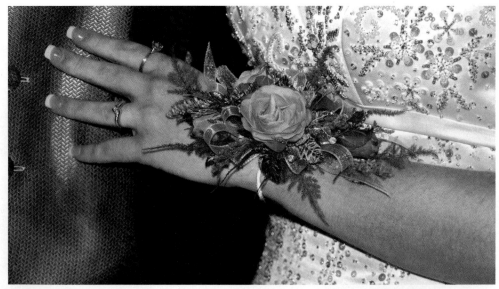

Figure 12-6. A single spray corsage relies on facing flowers in a radiating pattern.

Popular Types of Corsages

Single-flower corsages can be made quickly and can be formal or informal, depending on the materials chosen. When a large number of corsages are required for an event, florists often follow this style using a flower than can stay fresh-looking for several hours.

A ***single-spray corsage***, sometimes called a *garland corsage*, can be made from flowers that are all the same type or from a variety of blooms. This style works well on a woman's shoulder or wrist, **Figure 12-6**. Although the traditional way of wearing a corsage is stem down, this style is often visually pleasing with the stem facing up.

Placing two single-spray corsages end-to-end results in a ***double-spray corsage***. Care should be taken to use very small flowers and leaves for this style or the finished design may be too large.

Designing Flowers to Wear

Flowers to wear should be constructed to work with, not against, the outfit. Flowers to wear should not necessarily match the color of an outfit, but should complement it. If the color of the flowers is exactly the same as the color of the fabric, the flowers will blend in with the fabric. Chapter 7, *Elements of Design*, discusses the various color schemes that floral designers employ. For example, the designer may choose plant materials that are the direct complement of the clothing color, **Figure 12-7**. If a woman's dress is bright blue, the designer might use orange flowers to provide high contrast to the cool blue.

Debbie Page Photography/Shutterstock.com

Figure 12-7. The orange flowers of the corsage are a direct complement to the turquoise gown.

Another design consideration is that many flowers-to-wear designs do not have a water source. It is best to avoid flowers that require large amounts of water to stay fresh. If the customer requests flowers that need a water source, an alternative is to use a manufactured *corsage stem*. This device has absorbent material that can be soaked in water and then used to attach the corsage to a woman's clothing. The absorbent material is wrapped in waterproof floral tape to prevent the moisture from leaking.

Flowers to wear may be subjected to many other hazards that are beyond the designer's control. If an event is held outdoors, the flowers may be subjected to heat, humidity, or wind. People who wear flowers may be hugged, or they may bump into others at receptions and events. Delicate flowers that are prone to quick wilting, crushing or disintegration may not be the best candidates for all corsages and boutonnieres. See **Figure 12-8**.

Finally, flowers-to-wear designs must be lightweight—so light, in fact, that the wearer may forget that it is there. The lighter the arrangement is, the more comfortable it will be to wear. Always choose the lightest gauge of wire necessary for support to mount flowers, greenery, and accessories.

Mariana Rusanovschi/Shutterstock.com

Figure 12-8. Orchids can be delicate and easily smashed, but they make exceptional boutonnieres and corsages.

Wiring Flowers to Wear

For flowers-to-wear designs, floral designers detach flower heads and foliage from their stems and mount them on wires. This allows them to be more easily and artistically positioned. Wiring prevents the bulkiness that would occur from binding natural stems.

In many types of plant material, the weakest area is the stem just below the flower head. For example, when a rose on its stem loses moisture, the first part of the flower to collapse is the neck. If slender, taped wires replace the stem, the design will look better and last longer. See **Figure 12-9**.

Today's floral designers sometimes use new products such as adhesives instead of wiring and taping flowers. However, wiring is still an important skill for all floral designers.

Maria Maarbes/Shutterstock.com

Figure 12-9. The neck of roses is the weakest part of the flower when water stress occurs. Replacement of natural stem with wire helps to extend the flower's display in wearable designs.

Step-by-Step

Wiring Foliage, Stitch Method

For this project you will need the one ivy leaf and one piece of thin wire (28 or 30 gauge). The stitch wiring method is predominately used on foliage. This allows you to add foliage to corsages or boutonnieres and manipulate the foliage into the desired angles.

1

2

3

Turn the leaf to the back where you can see the mid vein more clearly. Make a tiny stitch with your thin wire.

Holding the stitch with your thumb and first finger, gently grab the two wires and pull them down parallel to the mid vein.

Floral tape the stem and the wire together starting at the base of the leaf and work downward toward the ends of the wires.

Step-by-Step

Wiring Standard and Spray Roses, Pierce Method

For this procedure you will need a single rose, #22 or #24 gauge wire (depends on size of rose), wire cutters, and floral tape.

1

2

3

Cut the rose stem approximately 1″ long, leaving the leafy sepals in place.

Cut a 9″ piece of wire and insert it through the calyx of the rose. Bring the wires down on each side.

Wrap the stem with floral tape, covering from the pierce point downward.

Step-by-Step

Wiring Carnations, Cross Pierce Method

The cross pierce method is used for wiring flowers such as carnations.

For this project you will need a standard carnation, two lengths of wire (24–26 gauge) about 4″ long, and a roll of stem wrap.

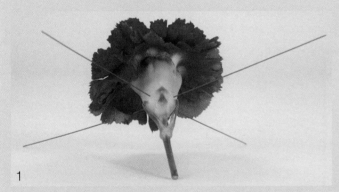

1 Cut the stem of the carnation about 1″ below the calyx. Insert one wire through the carnation at the midpoint of the calyx. This ensures that the wire will stay secure and not pull through the flower. Turn the flower and pierce through the calyx with the second wire. The wires should form an X.

2 Unroll several inches of stem wrap and stretch it out so it will adhere to the wire. It may be necessary to add more tape to the calyx since its rounded form is bulky and a challenge to cover.

3 Gently, pull the wires down so they are parallel to the stem of the flower. Floral tape the wire and the flower, beginning just above the cross pierce of the wires.

4 When you have finished, check to make sure the non-decorative green wire is fully covered and that the tape was firmly stretched during wrapping. Unstretched tape adds bulk to artificial stems and this bulk can add up when other corsage or boutonniere materials are added.

Step-by-Step

Wiring Filler Flowers and Foliage, Clutch Method

The clutch method of wiring is often used for clusters of filler flowers such as waxflower, baby's breath, and caspia. For this project you will need a thin piece of wire (#28 gauge) and one small cluster of flowers.

Hold the thin piece of wire parallel to the stem at the binding point.

Gently pull the wire that you have been wrapping downward so it is parallel to the stem and the other half of the wire. Take the top portion of the wire and wrap it around the stem.

Floral tape the flowers beginning at your binding point to cover your mechanics.

Step-by-Step

Standard Chrysanthemum, Insertion Method

The insertion wire method is helpful for large headed, mass flowers like Football Mums, Dahlias, and Sunflowers.

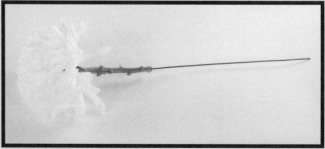

Cut the flower stem to a length of about 4".

Insert a #20 gauge wire into the base of the stem. Carefully drive it into the stem and into the base of the flower head. Stop when the wire tip is just below the petals. The end of the wire should not show through the petals. Add stem wrap.

Step-by-Step

Wiring Daisy Chrysanthemums, Hook Method

The hook wire method is used primarily for gerbera daisies, daisy Chrysanthemums or other flowers that have a stem too small or too weak to pierce.

For this project you will need one daisy Chrysanthemum, a piece of #24 or #26 gauge wire cut to size, floral tape, scissors, and a floral knife.

Cut the daisy Chrysanthemum stem approximately 3/4" to 1" in length. Insert a wire up through the middle of the stem coming out the top of the flower.

Bend the top 1/4" tip of the wire down creating a "hook."

Gently pull the wire back down so it hooks in the center of the flower. Floral tape the stem and the wire directly below the base of the flower head.

Step-by-Step

Wiring Stephanotis, Multiple Methods

A variety of methods may be used to wire stephanotis blossoms. Premade stephanotis stems consist of a wire with a portion of cotton on the top. You may make your own stems by bending wire into a hairpin shape and adding a small portion of cotton at the bend of the wire. The first section addresses premade, commercial stephanotis stems and hook wiring and the second section addresses using wire and cotton.

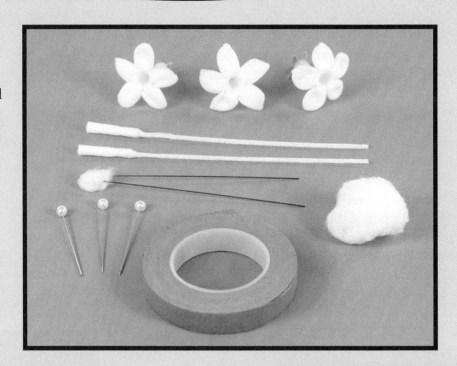

Using Premade Stems

1

Place the cotton portion of the stem in water for a few minutes to ensure the cotton is saturated. Remove the green receptacles from the base of the flower. Insert the soaked stephanotis stem into the basal opening of the flower.

2

Insert a pearl corsage pin into the top of the flower and cover the stem and wire with stem wrap.

Using Wire

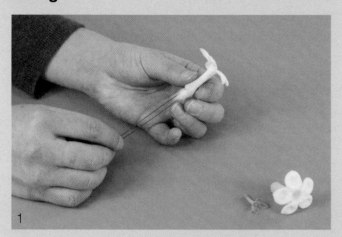

1

2

Draw a hairpin of light gauge wire through the stephanotis blossom from the top. Add a small wad of wet cotton to the base of the flower.

Wrap the green floral tape to secure the wire and hide the mechanics.

Step-by-Step

Cymbidium and Cattleya Orchids, Cross Tandem Wiring

Cymbidium orchids are a good example of needing two wires for stability because of the size of the head of the flower. However, if we cross pierce at exactly the same location, the stem can become severed at this point. For this project you will need thin wire (#26 or #28 gauge), the orchid, scissors, wire cutters, and floral tape.

1

2

3

Using the thin wire, insert the wire through the stem of the orchid about 1/8" down from the base of the petals meeting the stem.

Turn the orchid and place the second wire through the stem approximately 1/8" lower than the first insertion. This will form an "X" but will not sever the stem.

Gently, pull the wires down so they are parallel to the stem of the flower. Floral tape the wire and the flower, beginning just above the tandem cross pierce of the wires.

Step-by-Step

Wiring Phalaeonopsis Orchids

Phalaeonopsis orchids have a heavy head but a thin stem. The stem is too thin to pierce so this flower needs a unique wiring technique. For this project you will need thin wire (#26 or #28 gauge), the orchid, scissors, wire cutters, white floral tape, and green floral tape.

Hold the thin piece of wire and tape only the middle of the wire with white floral tape.

Bend the wire into a hairpin and place the orchid so that the wire is on both sides of the throat of the orchid. Gently pull the hairpin down so the white floral tape is just about resting on the throat of the orchid.

Now the wires are parallel to the stem and ready for floral tape. Tape at the base of the flower head, at the top of the flower stem.

Chrysanthemum Corsages

Football mum corsages are popular for fall homecoming festivities in many parts of the country. Though their styling may be different at various high schools and colleges, they usually signify school spirit through color. Traditionally, these corsages are made using standard incurved Chrysanthemums (*Dendranthema grandiflora*), commonly known as *mums*. In some regions, homecoming corsages may use one, two or even three mums accented with multiple ribbon streamers. The addition of novelties such as paw-print patterns for a school mascot, miniature footballs, or bells make the design more exciting. Some mum corsages also have ribbons personalized with names, initials, jersey numbers, or Greek fraternity letters applied using adhesive stickers, pens, or glitter and glue. See **Figure 12-10**.

www.MelzMumz.com, Custom Homecoming Mums and Garters

Figure 12-10. "Garters" are made for the guys to wear on their arms. Constructed in the same manner as the mum corsages, the accents represent the wearer's interests, clubs, and sports in which he participates.

Chrysanthemums are somewhat fragile flowers. Each "petal" of the mum is an entire flower, not just a petal. If they are bumped or jostled, these flowers may *shatter*—the petals literally fall away. Once this begins, the other petals may lose their integrity. See **Figure 12-11**. A spray adhesive is sold to help prevent mum shattering. It is applied on the back of the flower at the point where the petals join the stem. Apply adhesive sprays in a well-ventilated area or outdoors, according to manufacturer's suggested usage. Some florists prefer to drip melted candle wax in the same or similar color as the mum at the base of the flower to hold the petals in place.

AN NGUYEN/Shutterstock.com

Figure 12-11. Standard Chrysanthemum petal shattering can be prevented by applying wax or adhesives where petals join the receptacle.

Corsage Design Considerations

The floral designer should find out whether the corsage is for an adult or child and create the design in the appropriate size. A common pitfall when learning how to construct corsages is to select too many materials, resulting in a design that is too large and bulky. The amount of material needed varies with the design and the wearer. For example, a corsage for a young girl may have only one or two small flowers, **Figure 12-12**. A finished bow using #3 ribbon for a single flower corsage should be only about 3" across. On the other hand, a homecoming corsage may be very large and showy, with dramatic extensions of ribbon and novelties.

Take time to listen to the client's requests when taking a corsage order. When a customer states that she wants something small or dainty, you can help ensure customer satisfaction by using a ruler or tape measure to determine the corsage's dimensions.

Heidi Brand/Shutterstock.com

Figure 12-12. The correct size for a corsage depends on the size of the person wearing it. Just one or two miniature flowers are all that are needed for children's corsages and boutonnieres.

Safety Note

Melting Candle Wax
If you use melted candle wax to prevent a mum from shattering, hold the candle and flower away from other objects that may catch on fire.

Step-by-Step

Football Mum Corsage

In many states, wearing football mums for the fall season is quite common. However, states like Texas and Missouri really do them BIG, like those on the facing page. Many school floral departments make and sell football mums for a profit to gain practice and help fund the floral program. With your instructor's help, organize a football mum sale. Begin simple the first year or you and your peers may be overwhelmed. Do some research and experiment with materials until you feel confident in yourselves and your product.

For this procedure you will need a Chrysanthemum and 3–6 Salal leaves. You will also need the following materials: mum adhesive or candle wax, bow (school colors), streamers, #22 or #28 wire, floral tape, novelty items, finishing spray, floral knife, and scissors.

1 Mist the back of the Chrysanthemum with mum adhesive following manufacturer's recommendations or drip candle wax on the petals at their attachment point.

2

Prepare #9 florist bow using school colors. Add streamers to the bow for holding novelties or for dramatic flair.

Using #20 or #22 wire, mount and tape 3–6 medium to large Salal leaves to be used as a corsage backing.

3

Cut the Chrysanthemum stem to a length of about 4"–5". Insert #20 gauge wire into the base of the stem. Stop when wire is just about to peek through the petals.

4

Add novelty items such as mini football helmets and megaphones by tying them into the ribbon streamers or gluing them with floral adhesive. Mist only the mum with finishing spray. Package in a large corsage box for freshness and protection.

5

Football Mum Corsages

www.MelzMumz.com, Custom Homecoming Mums and Garters

Corsages should be designed to complement the wearer and her dress style. Often, this is impossible for a customer to communicate, so professional florists keep their designs petite, often in neutral colors such as white, cream, pale yellow, pale green, or blush pink.

Customer expectations vary greatly. Some customers want large, showy corsages. A wrist corsage may extend along the forearm and require two or three wristbands. Other customers insist on keeping corsages small, containing only two or three miniature flowers. Because clients often have high expectations for corsages, it is best to find out exactly what the client wants when the order is placed.

When the corsage will be worn on a dress, knowledge of the fabric and design styling of the dress is helpful. Corsages that are heavy or have protruding wires can damage lightweight fabrics. The fabric must be able to support a corsage. If not, an alternative is to wear the flowers on the wrist.

For wrist corsages, ribbon, flowers, greenery, and accessories are usually attached to a clear plastic rectangle that serves as the base of the design. Some of today's wrist corsage styles use costume jewelry bracelets in various colors and styles as the design base. See **Figure 12-13**.

Preparation and Construction

Whether you are preparing one or a series of corsages, prepare all of the elements in steps to save time. Time- and labor-saving techniques are often needed during peak business periods. For example, sometimes high school proms are scheduled for the same weekend as Mother's Day, a busy floral-gift holiday. If a flower shop has been commissioned to design flowers for a wedding during the same weekend, labor-saving techniques and devices are a necessity.

Following the proper steps to create the corsage will help maintain the overall display freshness of the finished design. If you are organized, work in steps, and use the proper postharvest techniques, your flowers-to-wear designs will remain fresh longer. Tips for organizing and constructing a corsage include:

- Prepare nonperishable items, such as ribbon bows and trims, first.
- Use wet paper toweling or mist a waterproof tabletop to slow down plant material transpiration.
- Organize all leaves and flowers in like groups to facilitate quick assembly.
- Wire foliage first, then flowers.
- Assemble the finished pieces to create the corsage.

If you are making multiple corsages of the same style, follow the same steps, but prepare the materials for all of the corsages before beginning assembly.

Degtiarova Viktoriia/Shutterstock.com;
Monday Morning Flowers and Balloons Co., Princeton, NJ and Yardley, PA

Figure 12-13. This cream colored wrist corsage is made from permanent botanical roses, accented with crystal beads. Some wrist corsages are designed around costume jewelry that serves as the base for the design.

Step-by-Step

Constructing a Corsage

For this procedure, you will need the following plant materials: two placements of Plumosa fern, three placements of waxflower, five spray roses, filler flower, and a main flower. You will also need a #3 satin ribbon bow, wire, tape, floral knife, scissors, and floral adhesive.

Prepare a #3 satin ribbon bow. Using the methods you have learned in this chapter, wire and tape the following materials:

- 2 placements of Plumosa fern, about 1.5"×2" long
- 3 placements of waxflower, clustered
- 5 spray roses, including buds showing color to fully-open flowers. Organize materials from small to large sizes.

Remember to keep flowers misted as you work and when you finish this process.

Select materials for the corsage, greenery, filler flower, bow, and the main flower. Use different sizes of the main flower to add more interest to the corsage. For example, when choosing spray roses and spray carnations in a corsage, choose a couple of buds for the beginning and end of the corsage and more open, larger flowers for the focal area.

Wire and tape materials for the corsage. Add the filler flower to the focal flower and tape together. Add greenery to the focal flowers and tape together. Begin the assembly of the corsage with the smallest bloom, then gradually adding flowers as they get larger in size.

Hold the corsage at one point where three to four blooms will be above the binding point and two to three blooms will be bent downwards, below the binding point. The bow is nestled into the corsage at the binding point. Use floral tape to secure all materials at the binding point. This allows for a very lightweight construction. The ends of the wired and taped flowers can be left exposed, trimmed into a diagonal fashion or curled for a finished look.

Step-by-Step

Pinning a Corsage

1. Ask the woman if you may pin a corsage to her dress at the shoulder line.
2. Holding just the corsage pin, make a stitch into the fabric with the head of the pin toward her neck and the sharp end away from her neck.
3. Bring the pin through the fabric and back out to the top for a distance of about 1/4″.
4. Hold the corsage in place so that the stem is at the bottom and the top slightly curves over the round of the shoulder.
5. If mechanics allow, bring the pin through the stem of the corsage. If not, bring the pin around the stem.
6. Bring the pin through the fabric a second time.
7. If necessary, make slight adjustments so that the corsage's flowers are positioned to their best advantage.
8. If the corsage seems unsteady or detaches for any reason, repeat the process to anchor it more firmly.

Nina Buday/Shutterstock.com

Figure 12-14. An abundant wreath of carnations, freesia, roses and ivy berries adorn this model.

Bird in Paradise/Shutterstock.com

Figure 12-15. Leis can be made from foliage or flowers and may be circular or hang like a garland.

Other Flowers to Wear

Flowers-to-wear designs are limited only by the designer's—or customer's—imagination. For example, *headpieces* are floral designs that are worn on the head. They may consist of a circle of flowers, greenery, or a combination of the two and are often used for events such as weddings or a first communion. Variations of headpieces include headdresses, chaplets, circlets, coronets or crowns, profile hairpieces, and headbands, **Figure 12-14.**

Floral jewelry consists of necklaces, scarves, bracelets, anklets, and even rings made of flowers. One type of floral necklace is the *lei*, a garland of flowers with or without greenery. Originating in Polynesia, leis are used to welcome guests or to identify important people. The plant material is woven together or is strung using needle and durable thread. See **Figure 12-15.**

A floral scarf can be created by weaving flowers into a broad coverlet that can be worn like a shawl. As an alternative, some floral designers attach flowers to an existing shawl or scarf using adhesive, or by weaving the stems into the cloth.

Step-by-Step

Glued Mechanic Wrist Corsage

This corsage is constructed without the use of wire and tape.

For this project you will need flowers, greenery such as ivy leaves, a bow, a wristlet with a plastic platform, and floral adhesive.

Begin by attaching the plastic platform to the wristlet if it is not already attached. You may also secure the flowers with the same ribbon you are going to use for the bow. Put floral adhesive on the back of one leaf and place it directly on the plastic platform. Add the second leaf in the same manner.

Add the bow by placing glue on the leaves and attaching the bow. You may also tie the bow on the platform before you attach the greenery.

Once your glue has set enough, the flowers may be added. Cut the flower stem short as the glue will be placed directly on the cut of the stem. Placing the glue on the cut helps seal it so the flower will not lose as much water and it will last longer.

With the glue on the back of the flower, separate the loops of the bow to nestle the flower in between the loops. After the main flowers are in place, you may add filler or other light greens in the same manner. Let the corsage sit for at least 10 minutes for the adhesive to dry completely. Then spritz with a finishing spray. When dry, place in a corsage bag and place in the cooler.

Step-by-Step

Floral Jewelry Design

There are many types of floral jewelry that can be designed using the new and innovative products the floral industry has to offer. One of these products is aluminum wire, available in many colors and sizes.

Boutonniere

To make the boutonniere, you will need one small spray Chrysanthemum (button mum) and one placement of filler flowers. You will also need needle nose pliers, 12 gauge aluminum wire, anchor tape, scissors, floral adhesive glue, a decorative pearl pin, wire cutters, and a boutonniere pin.

1

Using needle nose pliers, shape the 12 gauge aluminum wire into the desired shape. This will be the background for the boutonniere that will be against the lapel of a jacket. Add some anchor tape to the wire where the floral adhesive glue will be placed. Floral glue works best when it has greater surface area for adhesion. The wire does not have a broad surface so we need to amend that before adding the glue.

2

Insert the decorative pin into the center of the button mum and trim the extra length of the pin so it is flush with the back of the flower. Now you may glue the Chrysanthemum and the small cluster of filler flowers to the wire. When pinning a boutonniere that has a wire background. Use a boutonniere pin to "stitch" over the wire onto the lapel.

Floral Ring

To make the floral ring, you will need the same materials you used to make the boutonniere except for the filler flowers.

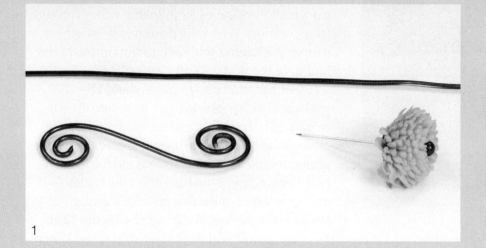

Using a 6″ piece of 12 gauge aluminum wire, use needle nose pliers to shape the wire, leaving a 3″ space in the middle.

1

Use a wooden dowel or a finger to shape the wire to the desired size. Place a decorative pearl head pin into the button mum and trim the extra length of the pin so it is flush with the back of the flower.

2

Prepare the wire for glue by using anchor tape to create a platform base. Glue the button mum to the prepared area of the ring. Let the glued jewelry sit for at least 10 minutes for the adhesive to dry completely. Then spritz with a finishing spray, when dry, place in a corsage bag and place in the cooler.

3

animorphic/iStock/Thinkstock

Figure 12-16. Blowing air into a plastic bag can help protect a corsage or boutonniere by providing a cushion of air around it.

Packaging Flowers to Wear

Packaging is important for flowers to wear because they are perishable gifts. Speedy designing will help these designs to stay fresh longer. As you assemble the flowers into a design, mist them with an antitranspirant spray to seal the stomatal pores. This will help prevent the petals and leaves from losing water through transpiration. When the design is finished, proper packaging will help maintain freshness and give the flowers extra appeal.

Corsages and boutonnieres should be packaged in clear plastic bags. Blow into the bag to expand it, creating a cushion of air around the arrangement. Make sure there is space between the plastic and the flower petals to avoid the growth of *Botrytis*, a fungus that can affect the health and appearance of the flowers. Use a corsage or boutonniere pin to seal the bag. See **Figure 12-16**.

Some stores add pins to the corsage and seal the bag with staples. When placing pins in a corsage prior to client presentation, make sure the pins are parallel to the stem rather than driven through, with sharp points protruding.

If you use a clear plastic box for corsages and boutonnieres, bags are not necessary. However, 1″ to 2″ of a cushioning product in the bottom of the box will keep the design from rolling around or turning upside-down, **Figure 12-17**.

Did You Know?
Boxing Easily Damaged Flowers

Corsages with flowers that are easily damaged, such as Cattleya orchids, should be packaged with shredded wax paper or shredded cellophane around the base of the corsage as a cushion. These materials do not soak up water, so they will not become soggy and messy.

Comstock/Stockbyte/Thinkstock

Figure 12-17. A properly boxed corsage.

It is good practice to finish the outside of the box with an adhesive sticker displaying the company logo, a care card, and ribbon trim. Boxed or bagged flowers should be refrigerated until used.

Flowers to Carry

Florists create *flowers-to-carry designs* mostly for weddings, but they are appropriate for other occasions. They are often called *bouquets*. Homecoming queens and their courts, as well as women in pageants, are presented with flowers-to-carry designs. See **Figure 12-18**. From medal-winning Olympic athletes to young girls in dance recitals, the presentation of flowers is considered a socially appropriate gift. It is the job of the professional florist to make sure the flowers are fresh and expertly designed.

Bouquet Shapes

Flowers-to-carry designs can be classified according to their finished geometric shape. Variations of the basic geometric forms can be used to create an almost infinite number of flowers-to-carry designs. Popular geometric shapes today include variations on the hemisphere, oval, and crescent shapes. The rounded *hemispherical design* has been a popular bouquet style for many years and is still the most popular form today.

bikeriderlondon/Shutterstock.com; Hill Street Studios/Bend Images/Thinkstock

Figure 12-18. Bouquets are often presented to graduates, pageant contestants, and the winners of athletic events or other awards.

It can be small or large, with one type of flower or many different types, **Figure 12-19**.

A *cascade design* has an oval or egg shape, **Figure 12-20**. The elongated end can be made with the design extending downward a few inches or a few feet, depending on the customer's preference. It is used for formal, large-scale weddings in which the bride wears a long gown with or without a long train or veil.

In *crescent designs*, the designer relies on the negative space to define the form, **Figure 12-21**. This design may be made with the points of the crescent directed to the sides or the floor when carried.

Other bouquets of interest include arm bouquets, composite flowers, pomanders, and prayer book adornments. *Arm bouquets* are made to appear as sheaves of flowers and are cradled in the arm, **Figure 12-22**. These designs are commonly used for homecoming court attendants and special presentations for VIPs.

A *composite flower* is a single flower shape constructed from the petals of several flowers. One example of a composite flower is a *duchess rose*, in which the petals of many roses are detached and then formed into a single, large rose, **Figure 12-23**.

Visions/Shutterstock.com

Figure 12-19. This bridal bouquet is a perfect hemisphere of roses accented with pearl beads.

Ekaterina Pokrovskaya/Shutterstock.com

Figure 12-20. A traditional cascade bouquet made with roses, Alstroemeria and red pearl beads.

Gromovataya/Shutterstock.com

Figure 12-21. A crescent-shaped bouquet, hand-tied, awaits presentation to a bride.

dbdavidova/Shutterstock.com

Figure 12-22. An arm bouquet carried by a flower girl. The flower girl's bouquet usually matches the bridesmaids'.

Shmeliova Natalia/Shutterstock.com

Figure 12-23. A type of composite flower, this duchess rose is made from the petals of many fully-opened, mature roses.

Composite flowers can also be made from gladiolus florets. Because these have the appearance of camellias but are made of Gladioli, they are called *glamellias*. Composite flowers are made using adhesives, wire, or a combination of the two.

Pomanders are spherical designs made from various plant materials. They are often referred to as *kissing balls* and are sometimes carried by flower girls in a wedding, **Figure 12-24**. *Prayer book adornments* are sometimes

Olga Ekaterincheva/Shutterstock.com; Iryna Prokofieva/Shutterstock.com

Figure 12-24. A pomander can be made for an adult or scaled down for a flower girl.

used when brides opt to hold a Bible or prayer book. The adornment can be any size, depending on the customer's wishes. Some are dramatic and long, like a standard-sized bridal bouquet. Others consist of a small cluster of miniature flowers that allow the book to be dominant. Designers creating this type of arrangement must take care to not harm the book, which may be a family heirloom.

Bouquet Mechanics

Flowers-to-carry designs also may be classified according to the mechanics used to control the floral placements within the design. *Hand-tied bouquets* are the most popular constructions. These designs include flowers on their natural stems that are bound with a suitable device. In some designs, the stems are embellished or wrapped to make them sturdier. Flowers are added one stem at a time, starting with the center placements. Stems are then added in a spiral pattern to achieve the desired geometric form.

Hand-tied bouquets can be bound with raffia, string, cable ties, rubber bands, or paper-covered wire, floral tape, or cloth, **Figure 12-25**.

T.Scarbrough/Shutterstock.com; Mark Hayes/Shutterstock.com

Figure 12-25. Hand-tied bouquets are loose and more casual than formally-wired bouquets.

The binding must hold the flowers in place without cutting them. Brides often choose a ribbon trim to complement the wedding colors.

When the flowers requested by the customer are especially delicate, the natural stems may be replaced with floral wire. This type of bouquet is known as a **hand-wired bouquet** or a *wired-and-taped bouquet*. Many florists used to construct all of their flowers-to-carry this way, but most use the hand-tying technique today. This technique was developed in the early days of floristry in the 19th century, but is still useful, allowing designers to achieve intricate geometric forms and to present flowers to their best advantage. This technique, if done correctly, will produce a beautiful bouquet, lightweight in appearance and actual weight.

Flowers to carry may also be designed in manufactured bouquet holders. These holders consist of a handle with a small cage of fresh floral foam on top. They are also available with foam suitable for holding silk and dried flowers. These holders are useful because they offer a water source to cut flowers, prolonging their freshness. Adhesives can be used to lock stems in place, thus reducing the chance that flowers will fall out of the bouquet holder.

Flower holders can be constructed using a variety of materials. Referred to in the floral industry as *armatures*, these devices may be purchased pre-made or fabricated by the designer. They can be made from fresh or dried twigs, stems, or heavy-gauge wire. See **Figure 12-26**.

Pefkos/Shutterstock.com

Figure 12-26. Dried twigs tied together into a star shape can control placements for a flowers-to-carry design.

Summary

- Flowers to wear are appropriate for many occasions and should be considered a gift and a fashion accessory by the recipient.
- Men wear boutonnieres, consisting of a single flower or a floral cluster, usually in the left lapel.
- Women wear corsages, usually on the wrist or on the left shoulder.
- The size of a corsage should be proportional to the size of the wearer.
- In addition to corsages and boutonnieres, flowers to wear include various types of headpieces and floral jewelry.
- When possible, personal flower designs should be created using flowers that do not wilt quickly.
- The flowers in flowers-to-wear designs are usually wired so that they can be more easily handled and positioned.
- Flowers-to-carry designs are classified according to their geometric form or the mechanics used to create them.
- Popular bouquet styles include the hemispherical, cascade, and crescent shapes.
- Mechanics for hand-tied flowers-to-carry designs include various binding devices, such as paper-covered wire, string, and cable ties.
- Bouquet holders consist of fresh floral foam in a cage, attached to a handle; they offer flowers a water source.

Review Questions

Go to www.g-wlearning.com/floraldesign/ to use the fill-in-form.

Answer the following questions using the information provided in this chapter.

1. What types of designs are referred to as "personal flowers"?
2. Name two types of mechanics that are commonly used to create boutonnieres.
3. Name three occasions for which a corsage might be appropriate.
4. Why do designers generally avoid using flowers that are the same color as the person's clothing?
5. How can a floral designer provide a water source for a corsage?
6. What gauge of wire should be used for boutonnieres and corsages?
7. Why are flowers to wear usually wired?
8. What special consideration is required for flowers to wear that include Chrysanthemums?
9. When a customer has a specific idea for the size of a corsage, how can you ensure that the customer is satisfied with your design?
10. Explain how to save time and labor when you are preparing a series of corsages.
11. List four types of floral headpieces.
12. What should you do to help keep the flowers fresh while you are assembling flowers to wear?
13. What three shapes are most popular for bouquets?
14. What is a composite flower?
15. What is the difference between a hand-tied bouquet and a hand-wired bouquet?

Activities

1. Create a wrist corsage using adhesive mechanics for a 7-year-old girl.
2. Create an armature with twigs found in landscapes near you.
3. Design a hemispherical flowers-to-carry design in a bouquet holder.
4. List various symbols that could be used in a homecoming corsage style for your favorite school. Then devise three different price levels and "recipes" (sets of instructions) for homecoming corsages that could be sold at schools near you.
5. Hold a contest in which each participant makes and packages a corsage. The type of corsage and information about the corsage will be announced by your instructor, who will act as the contest judge, at the beginning of the practicum. All plant and non-plant materials needed to construct and package the corsage will be provided. Each participant will be allowed 20 minutes to complete the

construction of the corsage and complete an itemized listing of costs for the corsage constructed. The scorecard that will be used to judge the results is shown in the *Appendix*.

Critical Thinking

1. Your coworker is designing a corsage for a 10-year-old girl on the occasion of her first piano recital. The design includes two pink roses and an orchid surrounded by greenery. Evaluate this design. Is it appropriate? Explain your answer.
2. A customer requests a corsage with "pretty blue flowers" to match her daughter's dress. She has even brought in a sample of the fabric for you to match. What should you say to this customer before accepting the order?
3. One concern about many flowers-to-wear designs is that they do not have a water source, and water is important to keep the flowers looking fresh. Why, then, do floral designers avoid using packaging materials that absorb and retain water?

STEM Activities and Academics

1. **Language Arts.** Choose a corsage or boutonniere that you have designed and created. Write a short report justifying the artistic decisions you made in this floral design. Include a photo of the arrangement and a description of the purpose of the design and the person for whom it was created.
2. **Social Studies.** Pomanders were not always merely decorative items. Conduct research on the history of pomanders. What does "pomander" mean? For what purposes did people wear or carry them?
3. **Math.** Design a corsage and matching boutonniere suitable for a prom. List all of the ingredients for the two pieces, as well as their wholesale prices. Add up the cost to make the corsage and boutonniere. You can find the prices using an online wholesale florist. Since wholesale florists generally sell bunches rather than single items, you will need to perform calculations to find the price per piece that you will use. Add a labor charge of $5 and a reasonable profit for the flower shop to find the selling (retail) price of the set. Compare your designs and prices with those of your classmates.
4. **Science.** Obtain at least three different types of cushioning products that are used for packaging corsages and boutonnieres. Devise and perform a test to find out which is the most absorbent and which is the least absorbent. Document your testing methods and the results of your experiment.
5. **Language Arts.** Choose a flowers-to-wear or flowers-to-carry design created by one of your classmates. Study the design carefully to determine the precise intent of your classmate in creating this design. Prepare a 1-minute oral report and deliver it to the class regarding the intent of the design.

Communicating about Floral Design

1. **Speaking and Writing.** Working in a group of three or four students, recall the last time you attended a wedding. Discuss common floral elements (corsage, boutonniere, bouquet, pew decorations, etc.). Write down the five most common elements. Do research and find out how each of these customs came to be part of wedding celebrations. For example, the flower petals strewn about by flower girls were originally used to prevent the bride from stepping on evil spirits. Share your findings with the class.
2. **Speaking and Listening.** Working in small groups, create a poster by drawing a football mum corsage with labels illustrating the basic components. Toward the edges of the poster, draw the types of accessories that are often added to the football mum. Use arrows and labels to indicate where these accessories are usually attached.
   Draw a figure on a second poster with labels illustrating the various positions in which a football mum may be worn. Use different-colored markers to indicate the positions and explain how the design is modified to fit each position. Have a volunteer briefly stand before the class as a "visual" aid to help indicate how a football mum may be worn.
3. **Speaking and Reading.** As a floral designer's assistant, create an informational pamphlet on the types of flowers to wear that are available through the designer's business. Research the history of the types of flowers to wear for some background information. Include images in your pamphlet.

Chapter

13 Wedding Flowers

objectives

After reading this chapter, you will be able to:

- Explain how the site of a wedding affects the wedding floral designer's work.
- Describe the ceremonies and floral needs for various types of weddings.
- List typical wedding attendants and the floral designs often created for each.
- Understand the business aspects of wedding floral design.
- Discuss the information gathered at the initial consultation.
- Design wedding flowers for an altar piece, pew decorations, and a cake topper.

key terms

Anand Karaj	junior bridesmaid	ring bearer
attendant	Kanyadaan	Saptapadi
bema	maid of honor	secular
best man	matron of honor	sourcing
brand	narthex	synagogue
chancel	nave	usher
chuppah	nikah	walima
civil ceremony	officiant	
flower girl	Panigrahana	

Go to **www.g-wlearning.com/floraldesign/** for online vocabulary activities using key terms from the chapter.

introduction

Weddings should be memorable; they should occur in a day full of happy events that create lifelong memories. Whatever the size or budget of the wedding, flowers can help make the occasion a blissful celebration. Flowers are used both in the wedding ceremony and in the reception. They include many different types of arrangements, from bouquets and corsages to room, table, and cake decorations. See **Figure 13-1**.

Wedding floral designers must meet many challenges beyond selecting and designing with the right flowers. They must be skillful in the world of business, and understand accounting practices and marketing and be savvy about using social media to expand their business. They should know design principles as well as post-harvest practices to ensure long-lasting flowers. They must understand and control factors such as temperature, light quality and intensity, water quality, and handling in order to deliver the best products.

Wedding Sites

By the time they consult the floral designer, most couples have chosen their wedding site. Wedding vows can be spoken just about anywhere, including country churches, cathedrals, other places of worship, city ballrooms, desert ranches, and private homes. They may also take place outside in a formal garden, in a tropical forest, or on a seashore or lakeshore. See **Figure 13-2**.

Goncharuk/Shutterstock.com

Figure 13-1. This wedding reception highlights a head table with drapery and flowers while the rose-color theme continues on the guest tables with tall flower arrangements and pink bows tied on the chairs.

Figure 13-2. Floral decorations provide a focal area within the natural beauty of a beachside wedding. Make sure any stands or supports are secured and well-balanced so they do not topple over.

The wedding site may determine many of the characteristics of the wedding decorations and flowers. Established places of worship and existing wedding chapels offer clear-cut guidelines that limit the decisions to be made, including those relating to floral decoration. Other sites, such as open fields, old factories, and other nontraditional sites, require planning that may or may not include the floral designer. When a floral designer is consulted in these cases, he or she should keep in mind delivery, setup, and logistics, as well as focal points associated with wedding floral design. Most standard wedding venues have websites where both the florist and the engaged couple may review regulations and find the name of a contact person. The websites may also include images, capacity, and availability.

Types of Weddings

Weddings can be either religious or *secular* (not religious). Military weddings may be religious or secular. Some weddings are large, formal affairs and take place in large cathedrals, **Figure 13-3**. Others are very small, with only immediate family and close friends present. Most weddings fall somewhere in between. Some couples go as far as to include distant friends and family through an Internet connection. In almost every type of wedding, flowers are used to brighten and help commemorate the day.

Figure 13-3. The design and finish of these pew decorations underscore a formal wedding setting.

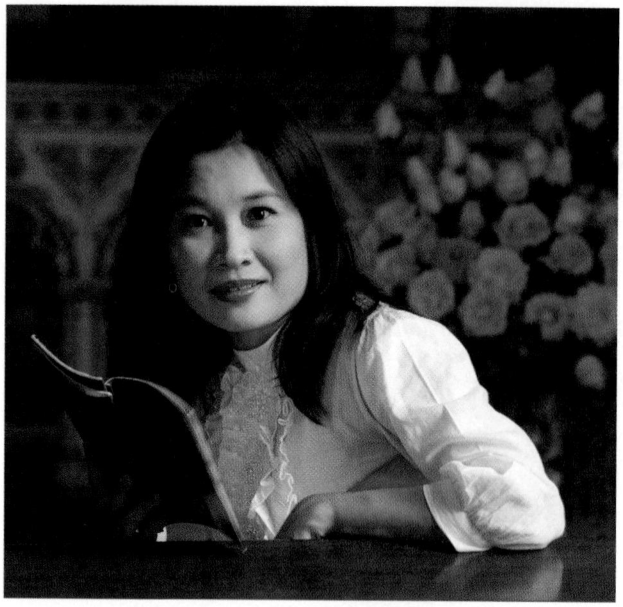

topten22photoMNStudio/Shutterstock.com

Figure 13-4. Wedding celebrants guide florists toward tasteful and appropriate wedding floral decorations.

Religious Weddings

Religious weddings commonly performed in the United States include Christian, Jewish, Buddhist, Hindu, and Muslim weddings, as well as weddings in other religions that may be less well known in this country. The beliefs held in each of these faiths have an effect on wedding floral design. Further, within each faith, individual houses of worship have their own rules and guidelines that may vary greatly.

When a wedding takes place at a place of worship, both religious and practical limitations may apply to the wedding decorations, including floral designs. The best practice is to consult the wedding coordinators and clergy at the chosen house of worship to find out what is (and is not) allowed. See **Figure 13-4**. Then you can suggest and sell only those floral decorations that are acceptable. Consultation, good communication, and positive relations with all parties are essential to avoid problems.

Did You Know?

Tossing the bridal bouquet once represented the passing on of good luck and to ward off evil spirits. Today, whoever catches the bouquet will be the next one to marry.

Some floral designers count on the engaged couple to request floral designs that are acceptable to everyone involved. However, problems occur when wedding planners or floral designers overstep the authority of the wedding ***officiant*** or *celebrant*—the person who performs the ceremony or religious service. It is never worthwhile to do this. The officiant has the authority to limit your involvement at the site, and may even refuse to allow your company to work at that site in the future.

Therefore, when booking a wedding order, if you ever feel unsure about the acceptability or appropriateness of floral decorations discussed, it is always best to consult with the person in charge of the site's floral decoration policies. Do this immediately following the consultation and consult with your customer if his or her ideas are not acceptable for the chosen site. Above all, remember that there is no one set of guidelines for religious wedding ceremonies. Some of the types of religious ceremonies you may encounter are described in the following paragraphs.

Christian Ceremonies

Christian weddings are performed by an ordained minister or priest. They usually take place at a church, but may also take place in a home or other nontraditional setting. The rituals and the specific ceremony performed depend on whether the wedding is Catholic, Eastern Orthodox, or one of the many Protestant denominations.

The entrance of a Catholic church is called a ***narthex***. It is not uncommon for floral designs to be placed in the narthex because this is the space where people are received. The main body of the church is called the ***nave***, and the area behind the nave is the ***chancel***. Focal points in Catholic churches include the altar, pulpit, tabernacle, and baptismal font. Catholic weddings may be large, formal affairs involving many floral arrangements for the site, as well as personal flowers for the bride and groom and the wedding party. See **Figure 13-5**.

MNStudio/Shutterstock.com

Figure 13-5. The celebrant of a Catholic wedding is a priest. He may be assisted by a deacon and several altar servers. Catholic churches are usually very spacious and require large arrangements.

Today's Eastern Orthodox churches include the Greek Orthodox and the Russian Orthodox churches. Layouts and practices of these churches are similar to those in the Catholic Church. The bride and groom may wear floral crowns, symbolizing that they are the king and queen of their new family, **Figure 13-6**. These crowns can be made from metal and adorned with foliage, flowers, or a combination of both.

Protestant churches are often more sparsely designed, with the focus on the pulpit. Although there is sometimes less emphasis on the altar, many Protestant churches decorate the altar with flowers, both for regular services and for special occasions. The bride customarily carries a bouquet, and the groom wears a boutonniere.

Jewish Ceremonies

A Jewish house of worship may be called a synagogue, temple, shul, or house of assembly, depending on the specific type of Judaism, but the most commonly used name is *synagogue*. The sanctuary, where prayer services are performed, contains the ark that holds the Torah, the Jewish code of law. The ark, which is generally a cabinet or indented shelf in a wall, is the most sacred place within the temple.

encrier/iStock/Thinkstock

Figure 13-6. A bride and groom in an Eastern Orthodox wedding.

Figure 13-7. This chuppah is decorated with fabric and flowers, but many attractive variations can be designed.

The wedding officiant is the rabbi. Men wear skullcaps called *yarmulkes* (Yiddish) or *kipot* (Hebrew). The rabbi and the bridal couple stand under a canopy called a **chuppah** that represents the home of the new family. See **Figure 13-7.** The chuppah may be decorated with foliage or flowers, depending on the synagogue guidelines and the celebrant's wishes. Often, a raised platform or stage is part of the synagogue's interior design. This stage, called a **bema**, helps the congregation to see the celebrant, bride, and groom during the ceremony. When floral decorations are to be used in the synagogue, the florist should inquire about who is allowed to enter the synagogue and stand on the bema to install the decorations.

Buddhist Ceremonies

Buddhist marriages are traditionally secular. Buddhist monks do not perform the marriage ceremony, although they do hold separate services to bless the couple. The marriage ceremony itself is not religious. Nevertheless, most Buddhist weddings take place in front of a shrine that has an image of Buddha, **Figure 13-8.** The shrine is decorated with candles and flowers. The couple also offer flowers to the image of Buddha before reciting their vows to one another. A floral designer may be asked to prepare the shrine flowers or the offering flowers, or both.

Figure 13-8. A traditional Buddhist wedding in Thailand. As part of the ceremony, the bride and groom present each other with floral garlands. The parents may also place floral garlands on the couple.

Hindu Ceremonies

Hindu weddings are elaborate affairs that may last for several days, although there is no one standard type of marriage ceremony. Most Hindu weddings involve a minimum of three rituals. The *Kanyadaan* is a ceremony in which the father or guardian of the bride places her hand in the groom's hand and ritual verses are recited. The bride is often adorned with beautiful flowers for this occasion. After the Kanyadaan, the *Panigrahana* ritual is performed. It is symbolic of the union of the bride and groom, and the groom recites verses in which he accepts his responsibility. Finally, the *Saptapadi*, or "seven steps," ritual is performed, **Figure 13-9**. The Saptapadi constitutes the legal marriage. The couple walks around a consecrated fire seven times, reciting vows.

Traditional dress for a Hindu wedding may include a floral garland for the groom and floral decorations for the bride, including a garland or floral shawl. Garlands of flowers or greenery also decorate the wedding site, and flower petals may be strewn over the cloth on which the vows are performed.

Sikh Ceremonies

The Sikh wedding ceremony, called *Anand Karaj*, is traditionally performed by a Sikh priest (*granthi*) at the *gurdwara*, the Sikh place of worship. The wedding hall is decorated with floral arrangements on either side of the main altar, and the area may be decked with floral garlands. Red is one of the traditional colors for a Sikh wedding, along with yellow, gold, pink, blue, and orange.

Did You Know?

In India, flower petals are sprinkled over the couple at the end of the ceremony to ward off evil spirits.

TheFinalMiracle/Shutterstock.com

Figure 13-9. An Indian couple wearing traditional attire for a Hindu marriage ceremony. The bride wears flowers in her hair and both the bride and groom wear flower garlands.

Zurijeta/Shutterstock.com

Figure 13-10. A wedding couple just after the nikah, the Muslim marriage ceremony.

Jupiterimages/Photos.com/Thinkstock

Figure 13-11. The celebrant of this Las Vegas wedding doubles as an Elvis impersonator!

Muslim Ceremonies

The *nikah*, or Muslim marriage, is considered a holy contract between a couple. It can be very simple, but in many cases it becomes a social occasion or celebration, **Figure 13-10**. It may be held in a mosque, but this is often left up to the individuals. If you are asked to provide flowers for the nikah, be aware that in some cases, men and women sit separately. Be sure to ask about the conventions and traditions that are being honored, because they vary.

A florist is more likely to be involved in the *walima*, which is the traditional wedding banquet. It is traditionally held one or more days after the nikah to give family and friends an opportunity to celebrate the new marriage and congratulate the couple. As with all customers, take the time to listen and understand exactly what the customer wants.

Civil Ceremonies

Some couples opt for a *civil ceremony*. A civil ceremony is simple and brief. It is performed by a justice of the peace, judge, or other civil servant authorized by the law to lead the ceremony. The bride might choose a small bouquet or a flower to wear, and perhaps a boutonniere for the groom, but these marriage ceremonies are often spontaneous. They are conducted in state or city office buildings, courthouses, judge's chambers and are of short duration with few, if any, people present other than the civil servant and the required witnesses.

The couple to be married can order any flowers they want over the phone or over the counter at a flower shop just prior to the ceremony. Florists located nearby fill the order with flowers in existing stock. Florists and designers in wedding destinations such as Las Vegas stock finished bouquets and boutonnieres for this purpose, **Figure 13-11**. In fact, the flower shop is often owned by the wedding chapel site, and the flowers are part of a wedding package. Such products and services simplify the process for couples that do not want to spend time organizing sites and vendors.

Military Weddings

When a groom, bride, or both are on active duty or are officers or cadets at a military academy, they may choose to have a military wedding. Military officers wear uniforms, and all other wedding party members wear formal attire. A bride, if in active military, may wear her uniform or traditional bridal attire. Those in uniform do not wear flowers. See **Figure 13-12**.

PhotoWorks/Shutterstock.com

Figure 13-12. A bride or groom in uniform adds a sense of respect for the armed services on their wedding day.

Wedding Attendants

Of course, a wedding is centered on the couple to be married: the bride and groom. However, many other people may also be involved. *Attendants* are the people, both male and female, who participate in the wedding. They help the bride or groom before, during, and immediately after the wedding.

Bridesmaids

Bridesmaids are generally responsible for seeing to the needs of the bride before, during, and after the wedding ceremony and during the reception. For example, if the bride requires help dressing, a needle and thread, or even different shoes, a bridesmaid should offer assistance. See **Figure 13-13**. The average number of attendants in a bridal party is from four to six, although some weddings have fewer and some have more.

Pro Tip

Word of mouth advertising is a powerful tool in the wedding floral business. Florists who are able to delivery quality floral designs and please bridal customers will acquire more bookings within various ethnic and religious communities.

Alex Andrei/Shutterstock.com

Figure 13-13. The traditional role of the bridesmaids is to provide assistance to the bride and her family at the wedding.

Shelllie Jensen/Shutterstock.com

Figure 13-14. The bridesmaids' bouquets emphasize the wedding colors. During the wedding ceremony, the maid or matron of honor will hold the bride's bouquet. Sometimes there are vases with water on the main table to hold the bouquets during dinner and to add more color.

Maid or Matron of Honor

In many weddings, one attendant is designated as the ***maid of honor*** or ***matron of honor***. A maid of honor is an unmarried attendant, and a matron of honor is a married attendant. The maid or matron of honor generally has a special relationship with the bride. She may be a sibling, a college roommate, or a best friend. Honor attendants often have more opportunities to assist the bride. For example, they may help her to choose her wedding gown or collect her clothing and accessories as she changes to leave on her honeymoon. The honor attendant's bouquet may be the same or different from those of the other attendants. See **Figure 13-14**.

Junior Bridesmaids

Some brides include young girls in the wedding. ***Junior bridesmaids*** are usually around 10 years old. They are not quite old enough to be bridesmaids and share in the responsibilities associated with adults. Flowers for junior bridesmaid often resemble those of the bridesmaids, but are scaled down in size. See **Figure 13-15**.

Syda Productions/Shutterstock.com

Figure 13-15. The junior maid in the center carries a slightly smaller bouquet than the adults.

Groomsmen

Groomsmen help before the wedding by greeting and seating guests, handing out programs, and laying an aisle cloth before the processional. They may also remove the aisle cloth after the wedding guests have departed. They are also on hand to take care of any last-minute needs the groom may have.

The *best man* is the leading groomsman, **Figure 13-16**. He has additional duties, such as witnessing the signing of the marriage certificate and helping the groom organize the license, payments and other tasks. In some weddings, additional men are invited to be *ushers* and can be similarly dressed as the groomsmen. All of these men should be provided with boutonnieres. Photographers often begin taking photos with the groomsmen, so the floral designer working on site should be ready to pin their boutonnieres.

Flower Girls and Ring Bearers

Very young children, generally around five years old, may participate in a wedding as a flower girl or a ring bearer. *Flower girls* walk down the aisle just before the bride, carrying a bouquet or loose petals in a basket for scattering in the aisle, **Figure 13-17**.

A *ring bearer* is a young boy who carries the wedding rings. The rings are displayed on a pillow or in a decorative box, often accented with flowers. The ring bearer should wear a boutonniere if he is wearing a tuxedo or suit, **Figure 13-18**. In most cases, the rings he bears are inexpensive reproductions; the actual wedding rings are kept by adult attendants.

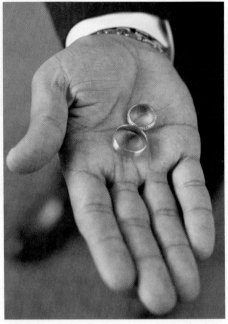

aastock/Shutterstock.com

Figure 13-16. The best man usually keeps the wedding rings until they are needed in the wedding ceremony.

Did You Know?

The tradition of flower girls first appeared in the Middle Ages. Two young girls would dress alike and carry wheat before the bride in the procession. Flower petals replaced the wheat and were strewn in the aisle before the bride as a symbolic gesture wishing her a happy future.

Phaendin/Shutterstock.com

Figure 13-17. Flower girls may scatter petals down the aisle before the bride.

Figure 13-18. A ring bearer with a decorative pillow for wedding rings and a flower girl wait for the beginning of the ceremony.

The Business of Wedding Floral Design

Working as a wedding specialist is fun. Making a sale and pleasing customers is exciting, and providing beautiful flowers to enhance a couple's wedding can be very satisfying. However, it is important to separate the enjoyment of floral design from the profession of floral design. Wedding floral designers earn income through the sales, design, and installation of wedding flowers and related products and services. In order to remain in business, the florist must earn enough income to make the business profitable.

Customer Service

Even the most magnificent floral designs are useless without excellent customer service. The mark of a good floral designer is efficiency. The wedding floral designer must be on time, from the first consultation through removal of props after the wedding. Throughout the process, the designer should be friendly, making the process fun and seemingly effortless for the bride. Today, floral designers must know how to use social media and have an easy to navigate website if they want to stay connected to customers and potential customers.

In order to be successful over time, wedding flower shops focus on excellence. They use quality flowers and provide expert floral designs and superior service. All designs, whether flowers-to-carry, centerpieces, or entryway stunners, must be attractive and remain stable. Good displays generate word-of-mouth advertising. The more people who see your excellent designs, the more potential customers you will attract. Every design should be made on time and in a skillful manner. Staff members must maintain a professional attitude at all times. These attributes build your *brand*, or company identity. As your brand grows, so does your good reputation.

Specialization

Most couples prefer to hire a florist who is familiar with a particular wedding venue and its associated beliefs and practices of a particular faith. Some bridal floral design professionals therefore narrow their focus to cater to brides from a particular religion, social stratum, or ethnicity. This is often the result of having satisfied customers from a particular part of a city, or from a specific congregation or socioeconomic group of people. See **Figure 13-19.** Specialization helps to streamline all aspects of wedding floral design, from the initial consultation and sales through design, installation, and removal. The florist knows most of the customers and, for the most part, what they want.

Kzenon/Shutterstock.com

Figure 13-19. A professional florist knows his customers, from the flowers they demand to the design styles they like.

Communication

Many hours of client contact are necessary to start a company and keep it running. Good communication skills, whether through email, a social medium, or the old-fashioned phone, are therefore extremely important for wedding floral designers. Good communication with clients is extremely important, but floral designers must also be able to communicate with people in the floriculture industry. People in the industry include local growers, warehouse employees, delivery people, and sometimes people from around the world. To be successful, wedding floral designers must be able to convey their own thoughts and ideas while respecting the thoughts and feelings of others.

Profitability

Wedding floral design can be a profitable profession. A successful florist realizes and controls the cost of goods sold. It is easy to lose profitability in the floral business. Underpricing floral designs and services, over-stuffing arrangements with floral products, and inadequate management practices may lead to the failure of the business. Only when the florist keeps a watchful eye on costs, pricing, and customer satisfaction can a wedding flower shop be successful, **Figure 13-20.**

To run a profitable business, the wedding floral designer follows these guidelines:

- Purchase only what is truly necessary at the best price available.
- Purchase good-quality floral products and prepare them using the proper techniques to ensure customer satisfaction.
- Use labor efficiently.
- Sell flowers and designs that meet the customer's needs and budgets.

Hasloo Group Production Studio/Shutterstock.com

Figure 13-20. Careful buying habits contribute to the bottom line of your florist business.

Reliable Sources

A well-made floral design is only as good as the quality of materials used to make it. Floral designers need ready access to high-quality fresh flowers and foliage, as well as good mechanics and accessories. *Sourcing*, the process of finding suitable products at a good price, is a necessary process that takes time and costs money. It is essential for smooth, profitable operation of the company, yet is often overlooked.

A successful florist keeps an eye open for new products, as well as good buys on staple products such as floral containers and mechanics. Do not buy all of your supplies from one vendor. Instead, carefully spread out purchases and establish relationships with several vendors. Then, if one supplier goes out of business, or the relationship is strained, you will have other reliable sources available. You will also have a range of prices; if one of your regular vendors has a sale, you can take advantage of it. The Internet is an extremely valuable resource when you are looking for suppliers. You can visit their websites and look through catalogs, and even check their ratings with the Better Business Bureau or other reputable sites.

Wholesale florists that have supply departments carry the mechanics necessary for design construction. Fresh floral foam, Styrofoam™, waterproof tape, adhesives, wire, stem wrap, and many other types of mechanics can be purchased wholesale. These departments also stock candles, containers, baskets, and sometimes gift items. Some larger wholesale florists carry sizeable props suitable for use in weddings, including arches, chuppahs, gazebos, candelabras, and plant and flower stands.

The Initial Consultation

When a couple is ready to order wedding flowers, they should set an appointment for a consultation with the wedding floral designer. During this consultation, the florist should give the bride his or her undivided attention, avoiding phone calls and distractions, **Figure 13-21**. During the consultation, important information is provided, such as the date, time, and location of the ceremony and reception. The florist should take notes to document these key facts. Listening to the bride and the groom is of utmost importance because it gives the floral designer information in the key moments of the wedding ceremony, offering the opportunity to suggest framing these moments in flowers. A bride is more likely to want floral designs if she sees value in how they highlight important moments.

A good wedding floral designer sees the big picture and steers the client to make decisions that use the floral budget to its best advantage. It is the florist's responsibility to follow the wishes of the officiant as well as the bride in the design, installation, and removal of floral decorations. For best results, a harmonious relationship should be established between all individuals with clear, objective communications. With this in mind, however, the florist's primary responsibility is to the customer.

Fuse/Thinkstock

Figure 13-21. All customers greatly appreciate your undivided attention. When working with an engaged couple, giving your undivided attention will increase your rapport and give you a better understanding of what they would like for their wedding.

Focusing on the Bride

There will be a number of stakeholders involved, so it is important that the wedding florist limit decision making to just a few people per wedding. Parents, friends, and the spouse-to-be can all contribute ideas, but it is very important that the wedding floral designer follow the wishes of a singular client, usually the bride. During the wedding flower consultation, it is easier if the bride comes with one person to make decisions. If several people come with the bride and offer varying opinions, focus on the wants and needs of the bride without dismissing everyone else's opinions.

Wedding consultations can be streamlined if the bride is prepared. When a bride contacts you for an appointment, you may wish to provide a list like the one in **Figure 13-22** to help her organize her thoughts and prepare for the consultation. Many florists provide Internet access to fill in or print forms, make appointments, and make payments. The bride may also send emails with images and ideas to the florist before their initial consultation, so they have an even better idea of what the bride wants for her wedding flowers. Also let her know how long you expect the consultation will last.

Organizing the Consultation

Many floral designers divide the wedding flower consultation into several parts. This makes it easier to concentrate on each topic without forgetting any important information. In fact, some designers use preprinted order forms that are divided into sections according to the order in which the designer wants to cover the topics. See **Figure 13-23**. Internet access also streamlines the process. The customer may be able to fill in and print forms from the florist's website and either email it to the florist or bring in the completed form.

Wedding Flowers Consultation Form

Bride's Name: ____

Groom's Name: ______________________________________

Telephone Number: (_____) _____ – _____ Cellphone: (_____) _____ – _____

Email Address: ______________________________________

Wedding Date: _____ / _____ / _____ Time: ____________

Ceremony location: ___________________________________

Reception location: ___________________________________

Please list your wedding color(s) and theme:

____

____

Please describe your wedding's style:

____

____

Please provide a list of how many people will be receiving flowers, include any special guests along with your wedding party.

____

____

____

____

Please indicate the range of your flower budget:

____ Less than $500

____ $500–$1,000

____ $1,000–$1,500

____ $1,500–$2,500

____ $2,500–$5,000

____ More than $5,000

Please indicate the décor elements you may be interested in consulting about:

____ Wedding Party Flowers (Bouquets, Corsages, Boutonnieres, Headpieces, etc.)

____ Ceremony Flowers (Altar, Aisle, and EntrywayArrangements)

____ Reception Flowers (Cake & Cake Table Flowers, Centerpieces, Entryway and Powder Room Decorations, and Guestbook and Place Setting Card Table Arrangements)

____ Wedding Celebration Flowers (Bachelorette Party, Bridal Shower, and Rehearsal Arrangements)

____ Additional Designs

Goodheart-Willcox Publisher

Figure 13-22. With a well-designed website, you may provide online access to your forms, catalog, and prices. The bride-to-be can print it out at home and bring it in already filled out.

Wedding Flowers Order Form

Name:		**Wedding Date:**	
Address:		**Delivery Time:**	
Phone:		**Ceremony Address:**	
Email:		**Reception Address:**	

Bouquets	Quantity	Price
Bride:		
Bridesmaids:		
Flower girl:		
Toss bouquet:		
Other:		
Corsages		
Mothers:		
Grandmothers:		
Other:		
Boutonnieres		
Groom:		
Groomsmen:		
Fathers:		
Grandfathers:		
Ring bearer:		
Other:		
Ceremony Flowers		
Altar Pieces:		
Aisle & Pew decorations:		
Foliage (Rental greens, Canopy, Altar/Aisle Candelabra):		
Other:		
Reception Flowers		
Cake Flowers:		
Centerpieces:		
Other:		
Wedding Celebration Flowers		
Rehearsal Dinner Centerpieces:		
Bridal Shower Arrangements:		
Bachelorette Party Arrangements:		

Comments		
	Subtotal:	
	Delivery:	
	Sales Tax _______:	
Acceptance by: Date:	**Less Deposit:**	
	Total:	

Goodheart-Willcox Publisher

Figure 13-23. As with your other forms, you may also post organizational charts and helpful hints.

The first major series of questions in an initial consultation involves contact information. This includes cell phone numbers and e-mail addresses of the bride, groom, and any other party who may be responsible for payment.

The second part of the consultation consists of discussions about personal flowers. Bridesmaid's bouquets lead this section because they set the colors of the wedding. Following the bridesmaids, the groomsmen's boutonnieres are discussed. The bride's bouquet is next, followed by the groom's boutonniere, which usually coordinates with the bride's flowers. Gather all of the information needed to create the arrangements. For example, flower girls often wear wreathes in their hair. To fashion an appropriate wreath for a flower girl, you will need to know the size of the child's head.

Also included in the second part of the consultation are the flowers parents, grandparents, and other important people will be wearing. The couple may want boutonnieres and wrist or shoulder corsages for the mother and sisters of the bride and groom, stepmothers and step-siblings and other close family members. Flowers for the extended family may coordinate with the wedding flowers or their clothing.

The third major section of the consultation focuses on floral decorations for the wedding ceremony. Start by discussing flowers for the altar, if they will be needed. If a reading will be given or some other special activity will occur, the spot where the activity takes place during the ceremony can be framed with foliage plants or perhaps a floral design. Pew decorations, cake decorations, entrance arrangements, and any other decorative displays are also discussed at this time. Guide the bride to make practical choices that can be accomplished within the specified time constraints and budget.

Fourth, the party or reception is discussed. Floral centerpieces, buffet designs, cake decorations, and many other ideas can be included in this discussion, **Figure 13-24**. This is the time for the bride to emphasize the wedding's festivity.

DonLand/iStock/Thinkstock; Paul Rich Studio/Shutterstock.com; Eric Limon/Shutterstock.com

Figure 13-24. It is helpful to the bride when a florist can show her examples of flowers and colors that could be used in her wedding. This includes samples of cake decorations, bouquets, and table pieces. A successful florist knows how to stay up on trends in colors and styles and how to keep his or her portfolios up to date.

Although all of the previous steps are essential, the fifth step is the most important from a business perspective: the discussion of payment terms. Most florists ask brides for a percentage of the wedding flower estimate as a down payment. This payment commits the bride to the florist and the florist to the bride. It forms a business agreement between the two parties. The florist should plainly state payment terms so that the bride or the responsible party clearly understands them. Many florists recommend that balances be paid a minimum of two weeks prior to the wedding date. This provides ample time for checks to be fully processed. Wedding flowers must be paid for in advance of the wedding. It is poor business practice to bill the responsible party for flowers and services after the wedding.

Preparing and Installing the Floral Designs

Many wedding floral designers find that the majority of the weddings take place in churches, so the following discussion refers to flowers for church weddings. However, the same principles can be followed for home weddings, outdoor weddings, and even some other religious weddings. In all cases, be sure to check in advance to be sure the planned designs are appropriate and allowable at the chosen wedding site.

Flowers to Wear

The bouquets carried by the bride and bridesmaids, the boutonnieres for the groom and groomsmen, and any floral headpieces may be traditional or contemporary in form, as specified during the consultation. In every case, flowers must appear very fresh during the ceremony. Review Chapter 12, *Flowers to Wear and Carry*, for more information about types of flowers to wear and techniques to keep them looking fresh.

Site Flowers

A formal wedding may require flowers at more than one site on two or more different days. For example, the couple may want table decorations, corsages, and boutonnieres for a rehearsal dinner to be held a day or two before the wedding. Flowers are needed for the wedding ceremony itself and for the reception party or dinner. It is the wedding floral designer's job to coordinate the flowers at all of the various times and places.

At the wedding site, the most important arrangements are installed first, **Figure 13-25**. A different crew of workers may install reception decorations at the same time as those in the ceremony, depending on timing.

CKstockphoto/Shutterstock.com

Figure 13-25. If you are installing wedding flowers by yourself or with a very small crew, always start at the altar because these flowers are the most visible and photographed, proceed with the aisle designs and, finally, exterior florals.

Step-by-Step

Hand-Tied Bouquet

For this procedure you will need the following plant materials: 5–6 stems salal, 3–4 stems limonium, 3 stems purple larkspur, 6–8 hot pink carnations, 3 stems snapdragons, 6–8 stems purple alstroemeria, three stems white snapdragons, three stems blue delphinium, 10 stems yellow spray roses. You will also need binding wire or other materials such as chenille stems, or cable ties, wire cutters, scissors, ribbon, pearl-head pins, water, and a clean vase.

1. Clean all stems and sort according to like materials. A general rule for a hand-tied bouquet would be to work in groups of three. Begin with a form flower, holding three stems in one hand while placing materials with the other, create a teepee effect.

2. Holding the flowers at the binding point, add three stems directly in between each of the first three form flowers.

3. Continue in the same motion by adding another set of flowers directly below the last layer, being careful to not cross stems. Hold the bouquet loosely enough at the binding point that you can add a center flower if desired.

4. Repeat materials if desired but always keeping the stems in the same direction.

5

Greenery can be added at the base for a final step to collar the bouquet and cover any mechanics.

6

Bind the bouquet with binding wire at the binding point.

7

Cut the stems of the bouquet evenly, if you have succeeded at the spiral technique the bouquet should stand on its own!

8

Place the bouquet in a vase for a vase arrangement.

9

For a bouquet, wrap the handle in a ribbon to accent the bouquet. Pearl head pins can be added for decoration and to secure the ribbon.

10

Hand-tied bouquets can be prepared for delivery by placing them in a vase with a small amount of water as to not damage the ribbon.

Step-by-Step

Foam Holder Bouquet

For this project you will need the following plant materials: 14–16 yellow daisies, 12 red spray roses or mini carnations, statice or another filler, leather leaf, and salal or galax leaves. You will also need a bouquet stand, a bouquet holder, wet floral foam, water, and a floral knife.

1

2

When you are designing a bouquet with a foam holder, it is not only convenient, but necessary to have a stand. Remember to use *all* of the holder, from the top all the way to the bottom.

Soak the bouquet holder so the foam is properly hydrated. Begin greening the holder with the leather leaf. Note the greens cover the top and the side surfaces.

3

Set up the parameters of the design with a center daisy for height and four daisies on the top, bottom, and two sides.

4

Place four more daisies in between the parameter daisies to complete the round form. Three daisies can then be placed around the center daisy.

5

Add mini carnations or spray roses in between the daisies. Make sure your design stays within the parameters that have been established by the daisies.

6

Finish with a filler and use galax or salal leaves to finish the back of the bouquet. Note: the round shape is complete with the flowers covering the front of the bouquet holder as well as the sides. When the bridesmaid holds her bouquet and looks down, the top of the bouquet holder should be finished just as the front and sides are.

Jozsa Levente/Shutterstock.com

Figure 13-26. Rehearsal parties may use rustic themes and materials such as fruit, flowers, and baskets on a burlap mat.

The photographer almost always takes photos of the groom and groomsmen first, so their boutonnieres are often the first flowers-to-wear distributed. To learn the proper way to pin a boutonniere to a lapel, see Chapter 12, *Flowers to Wear and Carry*.

The Rehearsal Dinner

Researsal dinners are becoming special events on their own and take on unique styles. Table centerpieces may be rustic or refined, depending on the wishes of the groom's family. Each table should have a similar arrangement, although the bride's table may have a slightly bigger, more complex arrangement, **Figure 13-26**. Coordinating corsages and boutonnieres may be worn by the bride and groom, and sometimes for other members of the wedding party.

Altar Designs

Since the altar is a focal area for a wedding, many brides choose to highlight the area with flowers, plants, and sometimes candlelight. Keep in mind that guests arrive for a wedding and are seated facing the same direction. A luxurious floral design at the front of the church gives them something beautiful to look at while they wait for the wedding to begin.

Altar designs are usually three-sided. The back of the arrangement has few, if any, flowers. It is important that the first placements of flowers in a three-sided design are made two-thirds to three-quarters of the way back in the mechanics, with successive placements made forward into the foam toward the lower, focal area of the design. This helps to maintain the physical balance of the piece. Any visible mechanics are then covered with foliage. See **Figure 13-27**.

Altar arrangements are site-specific; they are made especially for that particular space. When making an altar arrangement, be sure to take into account the viewing point guests will have while seated at the ceremony. If the design is placed on a tall pedestal, ledge or rail, it will be viewed from a different angle than if it rests on a design bench. It may be necessary to provide more floral placements at the lower part of the design in this case.

Pew and Aisle Decorations

Usually, a minimum two pairs of pew decorations are used to mark seating for the bridal party and immediate family. The decorations can be quite simple, consisting of ribbon tied into a bow, or very complex., For example, topiary forms or sculpted, cascading designs may be used.

Pro Tip

Provide Sufficient Water

It is important to add sufficient water to the container of an altar arrangement. Large floral designs containing many stems will drink water fast, quickly depleting reserves in the foam. Maintain sufficient water to keep the flowers looking fresh.

Frances A. Miller/Shutterstock.com

Figure 13-27. This three-sided, mass-patterned floral design highlights a church pulpit.

Step-by-Step

Making an Altar Design

An altar design will be seen from a distance so we want to focus on creating height as well as visual impact from afar. Make sure the design can be viewed from all sides if it is going to be fully visible at the reception.

For this procedure, you will need the following plant materials: five hydrangeas, curly willow stems, 12–15 yellow larkspur stems, and purple larkspur. You will also need a decorative vase or container large enough to hold the taller materials you are using, wet floral foam, water, anchor tape, scissors, and a floral knife.

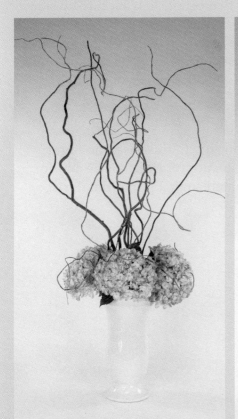

Fill the vase with wet floral foam, leaving an inch or so above the lip of the container. Secure the foam in place with anchor tape. Create a column of curly willow in the center and use fluffy hydrangeas to create strong visual impact. The hydrangeas will cover the mechanics of the floral foam, eliminating the need for greenery.

Add a column of larkspur. This color impact can then be seen better from a distance. Adding a complimentary color such as yellow to the purple also the visual impact of a design stronger when viewed from a distance.

This completed arrangement is a Phoenix Design, where linear materials burst upright from the central vertical axis, arising from a mound of plant material.

Thinking Green

Reusing Wedding Flowers

Reusing flowers from the ceremony at the reception is a good way to recycle wedding flowers. To take the process one step further, donate the flowers to a local hospital or nursing home after the reception.

Make sure that the designs you sell and create can be supported by the type of pew or chair used at the wedding site, **Figure 13-28**.

Many types of pew marker mechanics are sold at wholesale florists, including some that are fitted with floral foam. They can hold fresh flowers, foliage, ribbons, and other decorative items. Although many different types of pew and aisle decorations are quite beautiful, several issues should be considered. Never use a pew decoration that allows moisture to come in contact with wood surfaces. If you are using any type of wire product, take care to curve or curl sharp ends inward so that they do not scratch furniture or snag guests' clothing.

Decorations can be more easily attached to some styles of pew ends than others. Do not use adhesives of any kind to attach these designs. They may leave residues that are difficult to remove, and may mar the finish of the pew or chair. To avoid accidental damage, use floor-stationed pew markers if there is plenty of clearance for two people to walk side-by-side down the aisle.

If candlelight is requested, it should be approved by the wedding venue first. If candles are allowed in the aisles, glass hurricane globes should protect their flames. Many venues allow only artificial candlelight.

The Reception

Sometimes, brides request that flowers used in the wedding ceremony be transported to the reception site. In this case, the floral arrangements can be made so that they are appropriate in size and form for both sites. Delivery must be coordinated so that either the florist or

alexsalcedo/iStock/Thinkstock; Paul Rich Studio/Shutterstock.com; Wolfgang Zwanzger/Shutterstock.com;

Figure 13-28. It is important to know what type of seating will be used before the bride chooses aisle decorations. Wooden pews, open folding chairs, and covered chairs require different types of attachments. The bride may also want to use some type of stand that stakes into the ground.

Step-by-Step

Making a Pew Decoration

To make this arrangement you will need a #40 ribbon, a covered wire or a chenille stem to tie off the bow without scratching the pew, and greenery such as leatherleaf and sprengeri.

Begin with four pieces of leather leaf, with two pieces pointing down and two pieces pointing upward. Repeat with the sprengeri. Bind these materials together so 2/3 of the greenery is below the binding point and 1/3 of the greenery is above the binding point.

Add your #40 bow, attaching at the binding point where the greenery was bound.

Attach the bow to a pew using a pew clip, rubber band or tulle tied around the pew.

Having a 1/3 to 2/3 proportion will ensure that the pew decoration remains stable and is not sitting too high on the pew.

someone associated with the bride can remove, deliver, and set up these flowers, handling them with care, as well as remove them at the end of the reception.

Although this practice helps the bride stretch her budget, it may also be problematic. The person who removes the flowers from the wedding site must wait until nearly every guest leaves the wedding site, then race ahead of them to put the flowers in place at the reception. Most wedding receptions begin immediately following the wedding ceremony so good timing is essential. Many guests forego attending the ceremony and arrive at the reception site well ahead of the bridal party, making the timing even tighter.

If flowers will be placed on buffet tables, the caterer must have an estimate of the amount of space needed for the flowers. Good communication between the caterer and the floral designer is therefore important to ensuring an attractive display.

Florists can also provide floral trims and décor that highlight the wedding cake, **Figure 13-29**. Flowers also decorate the tables upon which the cakes are displayed. Any floral material that comes in contact with the cake should be thoroughly rinsed before application.

Figure 13-29. Fresh flowers, sometimes edible, are often used to adorn the wedding cake.

Step-by-Step

Making a Cake Topper

For this project you will need statice or limonium, ten to twelve pink spray roses, eight to ten pink Peruvian lilies, leather leaf, a secondary type of greenery, wet floral foam, an Iglu™, water, and a floral knife.

1 Using an Iglu™ filled with wet floral foam, check the size of the cake you are designing for and begin greening the Iglu™ with leather leaf or greenery that will not shed on the cake. The Iglu™ will have a plastic base so water will not leak onto the cake.

2 Add a secondary type of greenery for texture.

3 Create the framework for a round arrangement.

4 Add a secondary type of flower and place those flowers in between the framework of the spray roses. Add filler such as statice or limonium to the design. Make sure you do not design on such a large scale for the cake. Keep the floral choices in proportion with the size of the cake.

Note: During delivery, take a towel to dry the base of the cake topper and bring extra flowers to decorate the layers. All flowers should be rinsed ahead of time to make sure there are no chemical residues on the flowers.

Time Management

Time management is one of the most critical issues in wedding floral design. It is important that designers think and work ahead of all deadlines to ensure delivery of the best products possible. The floral designer needs an accurate idea of:

- Timing of flowers, from processing to design to display.
- Duration of the ceremony and duration of reception.
- Time needed for setting up, so that the design work is in place before guests arrive.
- Time for removal of decorations, especially if other, unrelated events will follow in the same location.

The Wedding Ceremony

As the wedding floral designer, you may or may not be present during the wedding ceremony. If you are present, guests may consider you to be an official or knowledgeable source of information. You may be asked questions, so it is good to know the general procedures that are traditionally followed. A brief description of traditional seating and timing for a church wedding is included in this section. See **Figure 13-30**.

Seating

After the flowers are in place and the guests have arrived and have been seated, the immediate families of the wedding couple are seated.

Traditional Positions at Weddings	
Left	**Right**
Bride's family and friends are seated on the left side of the church.	Groom's family and friends are seated on the right side of the church.
Corsages and boutonnieres are worn on the left (over the heart).	Ushers offer their right arm to female guests to be seated, so female guests walk to the right of their escorts.
Wedding rings are worn on the ring finger on the left hand (both bride and groom).	The bride walks down the aisle on the right arm of her father or selected escort.
	Prior to the wedding, the bride often wears the engagement ring on her right ring finger.

Goodheart-Willcox Publisher

Figure 13-30. You may want to include a traditional seating chart in the materials you have prepared for the engaged couple.

The parents of the bride always sit in the first pew on the left, and the groom's parents are on the right when facing the altar. If the church has two aisles, both families are seated in the center section of pews, the bride's on the left and the groom's on the right.

If either of the couple's parents is divorced, the biological mother should be seated in the first pew with her family, as long as the relationship between the bride and groom and their parents is good-natured. Grandparents are then escorted to the pews. An appropriate groomsman or usher seats the mother of the groom with the father of the groom behind them. The mother of the bride is escorted last.

Thanking the Customer

A few days or weeks after the wedding, send the bride or her mother a thank-you note for inviting you to manage the floral arrangements for the wedding, **Figure 13-31**. A nice touch is to include the meanings of some of the flowers in the bride's bouquet or elsewhere in the wedding décor. Refer to the chart of the Victorian meanings of flowers in the Appendix. Small, but meaningful touches like this help to establish your reputation as an exceptional florist.

graletta/Shutterstock.com

Figure 13-31. Sending a thank-you note after the wedding is a small gesture that lets the bride or her mother know you appreciate her business.

Summary

- Weddings can take place almost anywhere: indoors or outdoors, at a place of worship, in a public building, or in a private home.
- Weddings can be religious or secular.
- Different faiths have different guidelines and rules regarding weddings and the placement of wedding decorations.
- Wedding attendants include bridesmaids, including the maid or matron of honor, and groomsmen, including the best man.
- Other wedding participants may include junior bridesmaids, ushers, a ring bearer, and a flower girl.
- Wedding floral design is a business that must make a profit to be successful.
- Wedding consultations have five parts, including include date, time and contact information; personal flowers; floral designs for the wedding site; floral designs for the reception; and payment terms.
- Time management is critical during the installation of flowers for a wedding ceremony and reception.
- The floral designer should have a basic knowledge of the traditional seating and timing for a church wedding.
- The wedding floral designer should send a thank-you note to the client after the wedding.

Review Questions

Go to www.g-wlearning.com/floraldesign/ to use the fill-in-form.

Answer the following questions using the information provided in this chapter.

1. List at least four different sites that are commonly used for wedding ceremonies.
2. When a wedding is to take place at a place of worship, what can the wedding floral designer do to ensure that the planned arrangements are appropriate?
3. What does the chuppah symbolize in a Jewish wedding ceremony?
4. What type of floral arrangements are you most likely to be asked to create for a Buddhist wedding?
5. What three rituals are generally performed in Hindu wedding ceremonies?
6. What special considerations may be present for providing flowers for a nikah or walima?
7. Why do some wedding floral designers choose to specialize in one particular type of wedding?
8. List four guidelines for running a profitable wedding flower shop.
9. Why do some wedding florists send prospective customers a list of things to be done before the initial consultation?
10. What is the maximum number of people who should be included in the initial consultation?
11. Why is a down payment generally required at the time of the initial consultation?
12. What is the usual shape of a floral arrangement designed for an altar?
13. What precautions should you take when you design and install pew decorations?
14. List items a floral designer needs to track in order to manage the timing successfully for a wedding customer.
15. Why is it a good idea to send a thank-you note to the customer after the wedding?

Activities

1. Create an altar arrangement for a low-budget wedding at a church. Present your arrangement to the class and interpret the artistic decisions that allowed you to create a beautiful, but low-cost arrangement.
2. Evaluate an altar arrangement made by a professional wedding floral designer. Interpret and describe your perception of the designer's intent in creating the arrangement.
3. Create a wedding cake top using fresh floral foam mechanics.
4. Create a plan for wedding flowers to decorate a chuppah.
5. Design a bridal bouquet and accompanying bridesmaids' bouquets for a December wedding.
6. Find a photo of a well-designed bridal bouquet. Create a design for boutonnieres that will match the bouquet.
7. Create a floral design to be used for a specific religious ceremony. Evaluate your peers' designs in in terms of cultural tradition and significance.

8. Design table arrangements for a reception dinner. The client wants the arrangements to be completely different from those used at the wedding ceremony, but in the same wedding colors of blue and silver. There will be four tables, and the client wants each arrangement to be slightly different from all the others, but in a unified manner.

Critical Thinking

1. Discuss situations where clients request moving floral designs from the church to the reception, including pros and cons for the designer and for the wedded couple.
2. A young woman requests your help with the decoration for her upcoming wedding. She states that she is Catholic, but her fiancé is a practicing Buddhist. She wants the ceremony and the flowers to be appropriate for her fiancé and his family, without offending her own family. What things should you take into consideration when helping this client?
3. A couple plans to be married at a local hotel. The reserved room at the hotel is a standard, mid-size meeting room, but the bride and her mother want to transform the room into a "lush tropical garden." The wedding is to have a Hawaiian theme. Describe the resources, information, and competencies you will need in order to fulfill this order. Will you need any unusual mechanics or systems of operation?

STEM Activities and Academics

1. **Social Studies.** Refer to the list of noteworthy weddings in history in the Appendix. Make up your own list of noteworthy weddings. Do not include the couples listed in the Appendix, instead, look up the dates of other weddings of famous people, including historical figures and current celebrities. Make a multimedia display to show the people and their wedding dates, along with any interesting information about them. Try to showcase the floral arrangements used in the weddings.
2. **Math.** At the initial consultation for a customer's wedding flowers, the bride has chosen all of the options she wants, and the total price for the wedding flowers is $1,875.00. You will require a percentage of the total price as a down payment. How much will the down payment be if you charge 10% of the total price? 20%? 25%?
3. **Language Arts.** Go to a local wedding flower shop or visit an online wedding flower shop. Obtain the floral designer's portfolio or look at the work shown in the shop. Analyze the arrangements and write a formal report detailing your conclusions about the formal qualities of the designs and any historical or cultural contexts you may detect. Choose one example and describe your conclusions about the designer's intent and the meaning of the arrangement.
4. **Math.** Conduct research to find out the average cost of the following items for a wedding in your area: bride's bouquet, bridesmaids' bouquets, boutonnieres, corsages, altar or other ceremonial arrangements, aisle petals, and table centerpieces (for the reception). Use the figures to put together sample packages for a low budget, a mid-range budget, and a high-end budget for a wedding that will have four bridesmaids, a maid of honor, four groomsmen, a best man, and a flower girl. Create a pricing sheet that shows all three options and breaks out the cost per piece for each option, with total prices at the bottom of the page.
5. **Technology.** Devise a plan for using today's communication technology to facilitate time management for moving floral arrangements from a wedding ceremony to a reception that takes place across town.

Communicating about Floral Design

1. **Speaking.** With a peer, role-play the following situation: a florist must explain to a soon-to-be bride why she cannot have the exotic flowers they planned to use in her wedding arrangements. The flowers were supposed to be flown in the next day, but severe snowstorms have closed several major airports. One student plays the role of the designer; the other acts as the client. Use your own words to explain the situation and the available alternatives. You may use images from your textbook for reference. As the designer explains the situation, the client should ask questions if the explanation is unclear. Switch roles and repeat the activity.

354

Chapter

14

Designing for Special Occasions and Holidays

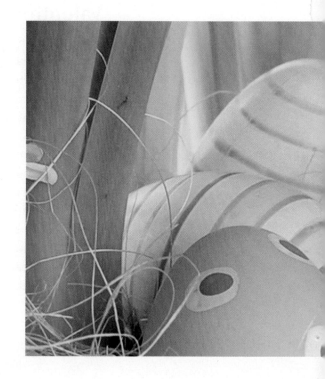

objectives

After reading this chapter, you will be able to:

- Successfully select cut flowers for holiday and special occasion events
- Recognize challenges when ordering materials in high seasonal demand
- Create designs evoking holiday traditions

key terms

cornucopia	monochromatic arrangement
golden anniversary	quinceañera
Hanukkah	silver anniversary
kinara	Spring Festival
Kwanzaa	Tournament of Roses Parade

Go to **www.g-wlearning.com/floraldesign/** for online vocabulary activities using key terms from the chapter.

introduction

Holidays and special occasions are times for people to come together, remember and honor historic events, and celebrate the seasons. Flowers are one of the most popular ways to celebrate holidays and express love, happiness, congratulations and holiday cheer.

Mainstay Holidays

Although individual and personal occasions make up a large part of a florist's business, three major holidays are considered the mainstays: Valentine's Day, Mother's Day, and Christmas.

Valentine's Day

Although it is an unofficial holiday, Valentine's Day is the single busiest day of the year for a florist. The day is celebrated in many countries around the world. The most popular story of origin is that when Valentine of Rome was imprisoned by the Romans, he healed his jailer's blind daughter and, before his execution, he wrote her a letter "from your Valentine" as a farewell. Also according to legend, St. Valentine is said to have cut hearts from parchment to give to the Roman soldiers and persecuted Christians to encourage them to remain faithful Christians.

It wasn't until the High Middle Ages that Valentine's Day was first associated with romantic love. In 18th-century England, it evolved into a day on which lovers expressed their admiration by presenting flowers, offering sweets, and sending cards known as *valentines*. Floral designs for Valentine's Day are typically monochromatic with shades and tints of one color, using pink and white with an emphasis on red, **Figure 14-1**. Accessories such as balloons,

The Flower Studio, Austin TX/SAF; Shirley's Flowers & Gifts, Rogers, AK/SAF

Figure 14-1. Valentine's Day designs may be the traditional bouquet of roses, or something with a modern twist.

Step-by-Step

Valentine Arrangement, Dozen Roses

For this arrangement, you will need the following materials: one dozen red roses, leather leaf, baby's breath or another filler, a thorn remover, waterproof tape, scissors, a clean vase, ribbon, water, and floral food.

1

Begin working on the project by removing foliage and thorns from the rose stems as needed. Clean the stems of the greens and filler flower also. Add water and floral food to the vase. Green the vase with leather leaf interlacing the stems to create a grid or, use a vase with a taped grid.

2

Place one rose in the middle of the vase. Place five roses around the center rose for the middle level and six more around the lowest level. Add baby's breath or filler in between the roses.

3

A bow is optional but can dress up a dozen roses for any occasion—like Valentine's Day!

chocolate, and heart-shaped trinkets are added to an array of products and design styles.

In the past, florists purchased the red flowers needed for Christmas and Valentine's Day through local growers. Due to short growing seasons and costly greenhouse upkeep, supplies were limited and costs were high. In today's global markets, acquiring red flowers, including roses, is much easier and the competitive market keeps the prices stable. Florists may purchase materials from growers in warmer climates who have less overhead expenses and can take advantage of a longer growing season. Shipping has become easier, and production has increased to fill the demand.

Did You Know?

The earliest surviving valentine is a 15th-century *rondeau* (a 13-line poem) written by Charles, Duke of Orleans, to his wife while he was imprisoned in the Tower of London in 1415 AD.

Step-by-Step

Mother's Day Arrangement

A mother's day arrangement is a great opportunity to decorate a container for a keepsake. *All* moms love something homemade. For this project you will need the following plant materials: 2-3 stems purple larkspur, 8–10 pink spray roses, yellow stock, two lilies, leather leaf, and additional greens. You will also need a large, clean vase, decorative ribbon, a rhinestone buckle, glue dots or hot glue, wet floral foam, water, floral food, scissors, and a floral knife.

1

Before preparing the floral materials, decorate the vase. Run the decorative ribbon through the rhinestone buckle and wrap the ribbon around the vase. Secure the ribbon with glue dots or hot glue. Secure the soaked floral foam in the decorated vase. Insert the leather leaf first, adding additional greens as desired to add a variety of textures.

2

Insert the purple larkspur to establish the vertical line of the arrangement.

3

Insert a group of pink spray roses to one side.

Group yellow stock on the side opposite to the roses. Grouping the materials adds more visual weight to each flower.

4

Add the lilies to create a focal point in the arrangement.

5

Mother's Day

The second Sunday in May is Mother's Day in the United States and many other countries. Mother's Day was created to honor mothers and motherhood. It is the busiest weekend of the year for florists. Floral gifts typically include standard arrangements, European gardens, container arrangements, and flowering plants, **Figure 14-2**. The historically popular corsage is still the gift of choice in some regions.

Sunny studio, Igor Yaruta/Shutterstock.com; Goodluz/Shutterstock.com

Figure 14-2. Mother's Day designs may be traditional or contemporary, and often incorporate the colors of spring and early summer.

Christmas

Although Christmas is a religious holiday, it has also become an international cultural and commercial event. For over 2000 years, people have celebrated Christmas with both religious and secular practices. Christmas has not always been the phenomenon that it is today. Easter was the main holiday for Christians, and the birth of Christ was not celebrated. In the fourth century, church officials designated December 25th for the celebration of the birth of Jesus. By the end of the eighth century, the Christmas holiday was celebrated across most of the known world. In the United States, Christmas was declared a federal holiday in 1870.

For the florist, the December holiday season offers endless sale opportunities. People begin decorating right after Thanksgiving, and continue through Christmas and New Year's Eve. Many churches decorate with live poinsettias and evergreen trees. Centerpieces or small floral arrangements are often given as hostess gifts for the numerous parties of the season. Live poinsettias are sent to employees, colleagues, and friends. See **Figure 14-3**.

> **Pro Tip**
>
> **Buying Stock**
>
> Seasonal and holiday stock, including accessories, are often discounted during the nonpeak season of summer. Consider taking advantage of these sales to stock up for next year's holiday.

Busy Floral Holidays

The three mainstay holidays may be the bread and butter of many florists, but there are many other days of the year when a florist will experience a rise in sales. Easter is a busy holiday for many designers and so is Thanksgiving. People have dinners and parties and decorate their homes in honor of the holidays. In the spring, many people order patriotic arrangements for their homes and to place on gravesites on Memorial Day.

Jill Lang/Shutterstock.com; LiliGraphie/Shutterstock.com

Figure 14-3. Florists can sell poinsettias in deluxe containers as well as a decorated version for and added charge.

Step-by-Step

Holiday Mantel Arrangement

A fireplace is the focal point of a room. When creating floral arrangements for the mantel, consider mirror-image, asymmetrical designs. They can provide a frame for what lies between such as a portrait or holiday village collection.

For this arrangement, you will need the following plant materials: ten red roses, five stems white spray chrysanthemums, two white birch branches, pine cones, and mixed evergreens. You will also need a stable, rectangular container not less than 4″ deep, wet floral foam, anchor tape, floral knife, scissors, silver ornaments, and holiday ribbon.

1

If you are making two arrangements, design them together as if they were going to be one. To keep them symmetrical, when you add material to the container on the right, do the mirror image on the left.

2

Continue greening each arrangement as an asymmetrical triangle.

3

When you add flowers, begin at the top, creating the line by sequencing your materials down to the lip of the container and then moving left or right depending on which piece you are putting together. You can create the line by placing materials close enough so the eye connects each flower to the next, but far enough apart to give each flower a distinct and separate space. Fill in between with white pompons and add a grouping of silver balls accent to the focal area of the design.

Step-by-Step

Centerpiece with Hurricane Glass and Candle

This project has been designed with holiday colors but could easily be modified to fit any occasion.

For this project you will need a decorative container large enough to hold a candle (taper or pillar), the hurricane glass (optional), wet floral foam, anchor tape, scissors, wood picks, a floral knife, water, a mix of evergreens, five or six white carnations, ribbons, and berries or silver ornament balls.

1

2

Begin by firmly inserting the soaked floral foam into the container so it sits approximately 1" above the rim of the container. This should fit snugly so the weight of the arrangement will not tip and pull it out easily, allowing enough room for water. Prepare the pillar candle by placing a layer of anchor tape around the base. Place and tape the wood picks evenly around the base of the candle. Use another layer of anchor tape to hold them in place.

Insert the candle into the center of the floral foam. The wood picks will absorb water and expand so they will not slip out of the arrangement.

3

4

Green the arrangement with a mix of evergreens. Start with heaviest evergreens first. Remove 1–2 inches of evergreen needles from stems before placing in the floral foam.

Once the heavier greens have been inserted, add holly stems for contrasting texture.

5

6

Complete the arrangement with carnations, ribbons, and berries or silver ornament balls.

This arrangement may easily be made with a taper candle and hurricane glass.

dvande/Shutterstock.com

Figure 14-4. Extravagant displays of Easter lilies are common in Christian churches to celebrate Easter Sunday.

Easter

A religious holiday, Easter is celebrated by Christians around the world as the day of Jesus Christ's resurrection from the dead. The date varies each year because it is set as the first Sunday after the first full moon after the Vernal Equinox. During the Lenten season, the church is symbolically kept barren except for purple vestments on the altar and sometimes on the walls. On Easter Sunday, the church brings in a display of flowering plants and floral arrangements to celebrate the occasion, **Figure 14-4**. Designs vary from traditional to contemporary, depending on the interior of the church and local preferences.

The Easter lily, *Lilium longiflorum*, is the dominant blooming plant. Its trumpet-shaped flowers symbolize purity, hope, and life—the spiritual essence of Easter. The Easter lily ranks among the top four floriculture crops, along with poinsettias, azaleas, and mums.

Floral designs for homes frequently include accessories of bunnies, chicks, eggs, and novelty containers. Centerpieces for family gatherings are popular, and are created with the pastel colors of spring. Baskets arrangements are also heavily used.

Thanksgiving

The familiar story of the first Thanksgiving took place in Plymouth Colony in 1621. This event was celebrated by the Pilgrims and the Wampanoag Native Americans after The Pilgrims' first harvest in the New World. Native Americans taught the Pilgrims how to cultivate corn, catch fish, extract sap from maple trees, and avoid poisonous plants. When the first corn harvest proved successful, the governor organized a celebratory feast that lasted three days and to which we now refer to as Thanksgiving. Congress made it an official holiday in 1941.

Several types of floral arrangements are popular during this fall holiday. Fall wreaths are made with dried vines, berries and artificial or preserved leaves in bright reds, yellows, and oranges. Accent arragements are made with added dry grasses, preserved flowers and leaves or harvested materials of the season. Perhaps the most popular is the *cornucopia*. First used by the ancient Romans and Greeks, the cornucopia is filled with fruits and vegetables to celebrate the abundance of food and grains gathered during the fall harvest. For a Thanksgiving arrangement, the cornucopia is often filled with bright fall flowers mixed with colorful berries, fall fruits, and foliage, **Figure 14-5**.

Jeanne Hatch/iStock/Thinkstock

Figure 14-5. The cornucopia has become a symbol of Thanksgiving as it signifies a bountiful harvest.

Step-by-Step

Making a Cornucopia, The Mechanics of Attaching Fruit

For this project you will need a cornucopia with a fitted liner, soaked floral foam, green tape, 3–5 pomegranates, pears or apples, wooden picks for the fruit, oregonia and boxwood foliage, leather leaf, 10 yellow spray chrysanthemums, 12 small, orange miniature carnations (red, gold, or maroon flowers may be substituted for a more autumnal look), and 2-4 stems of solidago or similar filler flower.

Add the soaked, fresh floral foam to the rigid plastic liner. Secure the foam in the liner with waterproof tape. Secure the liner to the basket. Prepare the artificial or real fruit for the cornucopia by inserting wooden picks into the base of each piece. If you are using artificial fruit, you may add glue to the pick before inserting it into the fruit.

Make greenery insertions into the foam to create an ovoid form. Green the arrangement, using a variety of greenery such as leather leaf and oregonia. Follow the asymmetrical shape of the basket.

Add spray chrysanthemums and miniature carnations to the design. Keep in mind this arrangement is often used as a centerpiece, so make sure all sides of the design are finished by turning the container as you work.

Tuck the fruit in to add depth to the arrangement and finish with a filler to soften the textures between the flowers and the smoothness of the fruit.

Step-by-Step

Thanksgiving Centerpiece

For this project you will need the following plant materials: five burgundy miniature carnations, 3 stems orange lilies, 3-4 stems burgundy cushion pompons, two stems yellow daisies, solidago, leather leaf, and oregonia, or a second green foliage with a different texture than the leather leaf. You will also need a double utility bowl, one block of wet floral foam, anchor tape, water, scissors, a floral knife, and two coordinating taper candles candles (optional).

1

2

Place the fully-soaked floral foam in the utility bowl and secure with anchor tape. If you are using taper candles, insert them before inserting any greens or flowers. The candles should be inserted first or the stems of the plant materials will interfere with the base of the candles, making it difficult to fully insert them and keep them level.

Insert the leather leaf into the foam to form an outline and establish the height, width, and length of the arrangement.

3

Staying within the parameters set by the first foliage placements, complete greening the arrangement with leather leaf and oregonia or a second greenery with a different texture.

4

Insert the mini carnations following the same pattern as the greens, defining the height, width, and length once again. Note: This is a symmetrical arrangement, so both sides of the design should appear finished. Insert the lilies on diagonal lines, with largest toward the center. The addition of the lilies allows the eye to see some variety in size, color, and texture.

5

Add burgundy cushion pompons throughout the arrangement, maintaining the shape that was outlined by the greens and the mini carnations

6

Add filler like solidago and a touch of yellow daisies to lighten up the analogous color harmony. Notice that darker colors will recede and the lighter colors will advance in this arrangement. If desired, focal materials may be added to the center on both sides (not shown).

Memorial Day

Memorial Day is observed on the last Monday of May and honors all Americans who gave their lives while serving in the United States Armed Forces. Initially, Memorial Day was known as *Decoration Day* and people used flags and flowers to decorate the graves of Confederate and Union soldiers who died in the Civil War. Today, we honor all veterans who have died in the line of duty by decorating their graves with floral wreaths and bouquets, **Figure 14-6**.

Special Occasions

People traditionally celebrate personal occasions in their lives, and these celebrations often include flowers. In addition to weddings, florists are asked to create special designs for occasions such as birthdays, anniversaries, the arrival of new babies, and graduations.

An Van de Wal/Shutterstock.com; Chuck Rausin/Shutterstock.com

Figure 14-6. On occasions such as Memorial Day and Veteran's Day, the President of the United States, or someone appointed by the President, places a wreath at the Tomb of the Unknown Soldier at Arlington National Cemetery. Similar ceremonies are carried out at many other cemeteries, and individuals place bouquets, flags, or wreaths on the graves of family members in remembrance.

Step-by-Step

Patriotic Holiday Arrangement

When creating a patriotic arrangement for a US holiday, nothing could be a more appropriate color scheme than red, white, and blue. The flowers, container, and accessories may use these all-American colors to create a real sense of unity. As you create the following arrangement, keep in mind what the colors mean to Americans. Patriotism is a strong force standing behind the red, white, and blue and a large part of the American culture.

For this project you will need the following plant materials: leatherleaf, three or four stems of blue delphiniums, six red carnations, and 2-3 stems white daisies. You will also need a clean vase, water, floral food, and a floral knife.

1 Begin by greening the vase with leather leaf. Create the triangular form by inserting a bright blue delphinium in the center, one on the left, and then one on the right. The fullness of the delphinium is a real asset in this vase arrangement because it pulls the viewer's eye from the top, all the way down to the lip of the vase.

2 Insert the red carnations with equal intervals to maintain the rhythm of your design.

3 Insert the white daisies. The white flowers provide strong contrast that helps the red carnations and blue delphiniums stand out. Finally, add a flag or other patriotic embellishment.

Ardith Beveridge, AAF, AIFD, PFCI, CAFA, Koehler & Dramm's Institute of Floristry, Minneapolis, MN

Figure 14-7. Beginning students can create this clever and easy arrangement using daisy pomps and decorative gem pins. Finish details with decorative wire.

Birthdays

Birthday bouquets may be constructed in anything from vases to baskets to novelty containers, or even become a shape themselves, **Figure 14-7**. Primary colors of red, yellow, and blue are favorite choices. Today, with global markets selling bold-colored, natural cultivars, bouquets of these mixed colors are extremely popular. *Monochromatic arrangements*, which consist of shades and tints of one color, are also a good choice—especially if it is the recipient's favorite color. Another idea is to use the flower type that is traditionally associated with the person's birth month, **Figure 14-8**. Accessories for this type of gift frequently include birthday horns, thematic accents, and balloons.

Quinceañera

A milestone birthday in the life a young girl in many Spanish-speaking cultures is called a *quinceañera*. This is the celebration of a girl's fifteenth birthday. The fifteenth birthday marks the transition from childhood to young womanhood. The event may begin with a mass of thanksgiving and the church may be decorated as if a wedding were taking place. Depending on the local customs, the birthday girl may

Birth Month Flowers	
January	Carnation
February	Iris, Violet
March	Daffodil
April	Daisy, Peonies
May	Lily, Lily of the Valley
June	Rose
July	Delphinium
August	Dahlia, Gladiolus
September	Aster, Forget-me-not
October	Calendula (aka Marigold)
November	Chrysanthemum
December	Poinsettia, Holly, Narcissus, Paperwhite

Goodheart-Willcox Publisher

Figure 14-8. The flowers associated with a person's birth month may be used in a birthday arrangement.

wear an elaborate white or brightly-colored gown and carry a bouquet, **Figure 14-9**. She may also be accompanied by a number of *chambelanes* (young men) dressed in tuxedos and wearing boutonnieres. Sometimes, there are seven chambelanes and seven *damas* (young girls) accompanying the birthday girl. The damas wear wrist corsages or carry small bouquets.

The reception may be held outdoors or in a hall adorned with floral arrangements and decorations. When the father and daughter enter the reception hall, friends and relatives may line up to give the father a flower (usually roses). A florist contracts flowers for a quinceañera as if a wedding were being planned. The girl chooses a color theme for all aspects of the party, including the flowers to wear, carry, and adorn the hall.

Anniversaries

Every anniversary is special, but some are considered milestones and are often celebrated with family and friends. Many anniversaries are traditionally tied to a particular material. For example, on the fifth wedding anniversary, the traditional gift or gift of recognition is made of wood, **Figure 14-10**. Anniversaries such as the twenty-fifth and fiftieth are special cause for celebration. The 25th wedding anniversary is called the *silver anniversary* and the 50th is called the *golden anniversary*. For the 25th anniversary, the florist could use silver thematic pieces such as silver ribbon, containers, or accessories. For the 50th wedding anniversary, the warm color of golden yellow and gilded or golden accessories may be used to carry out the theme.

Jupiterimages/Stockbyte/Thinkstock

Figure 14-9. A Quinceñera is booked in the same manner as a wedding.

\multicolumn{4}{c}{**Anniversary Flowers and Gifts**}			
Anniversary Year	**Anniversary Flower**	**Traditional Gift**	**Modern Gift**
1st	Red & White Roses, Carnation	Paper	Clock, Plastic, Gold Jewelry
2nd	Carnations (White), Lily of the Valley	Cotton	China, Cotton, Calico, Garnet
3rd	Bird of Paradise, Sunflower	Leather	Crystal, Glass, Pearls
4th	Alstroemeria, Hydrangea	Linen, Silk, Fruit, Flowers	Appliances, Linen, Silk, Nylon, Blue Topaz
5th	Bonsai, Topiary, Daisy	Wood	Silverware, Sapphire
6th	Red Tulips, Calla Lily	Iron, Sugar	Wood, Candy, Amethyst
7th	Ivy Plant, Freesia	Copper, Wool	Stationary, Brass, Desk Sets, Onyx
8th	White Lilies, Lilac	Bronze, Pottery	Linens, Lace, Tourmaline Jewelry
9th	Living Plant, Bird of Paradise	Pottery, China, Willow	Leather, Lapis Jewelry
10th	Pink Rose, Daffodil	Tin, Aluminum	Diamond Jewelry
11th	Daisys (White), Tulip	Steel	Fashion Jewelry, Turquoise Jewelry
12th	Sunflower, Peony	Silk, Linen	Pearls, Jade
13th	Stock, Chrysanthemum	Lace	Textiles, Fur, Citrine
14th	Gladiolas, Dahlia	Ivory	Gold Jewelry, Opal
15th	Stephanotis, Rose	Crystal	Watches, Glass, Ruby
16th	Statice, Rose	Tourmaline, Wax	Silver Hollowware, Peridot
17th	Carnation (Red), Rose	Furniture, Watch, Shell	Furniture, Diamond, Watch
18th	Porcelana Roses, Rose	Turquoise, Feathers	Porcelain, Cat's Eye Jewelry
19th	Bronze Mums, Rose	Aquamarine	Bronze, Aquamarine
20th	Rose (Pink and White), Aster	China	Platinum, Emerald
25th	Roses, Iris	Silver	Sterling Silver
30th	White Rose, Lily (white or yellow)	Pearl	Diamond
35th	African Violet	Coral, Jade	Jade
40th	Red Roses, Gladiolus	Ruby	Ruby, Garnet
45th	Blue Iris	Sapphire	Sapphire
50th	Yellow Roses, Violet	Gold	Gold
55th	Calla	Emerald	Emerald
60th	Orchids	Diamond	Diamond, Gold
75th	Couple's Favorite	Platinum	Star Sapphire, Diamond-like Stones, Gold

Goodheart-Willcox Publisher

Figure 14-10. A list of anniversary flowers by year. However, recall that each type of flower also has a traditional meaning (see *Appendix*). The chart also lists traditional and modern gifts for designated years.

They may also use accessories such as wedding bands or an anniversary bell, as well as white doves to symbolize marriage. Historically, corsages and boutonnieres are worn to these anniversary celebrations by the guests of honor. When consulting with the party arranger, encourage the use of colors and flowers that were used on the couple's wedding day to make the day even more memorable. See **Figure 14-11**.

New Baby

People often send plants and flowers to celebrate the birth of a baby. Floral designers typically use pastel color stories such as mint green, powder blue, light pink, and pale yellow. The scale of materials used is often smaller than in everyday designs. Novelty keepsake containers and accessories are common, **Figure 14-12**. Containers of assorted plants with little gifts or plush animals attached are also an option.

Sarsmis/Shutterstock.com; aastock/Shutterstock.com

Figure 14-11. Anniversary party themes usually match the traditional colors assigned to the occasion. This is especially true of significant anniversaries such as the golden 50th anniversary.

Denise Kappa/Shutterstock.com; liveslow/istock

Figure 14-12. Floral arrangements to celebrate the birth of a baby are smaller designs. Many have accessories that can later be used by the baby, such as a plush toy or a rattle.

Step-by-Step

Vase Arrangement

For this project you will need the following plant materials: leatherleaf, 7 snapdragons, 7 red carnations, and filler. You will also need a glass vase, water, floral food, and a floral knife. Before you begin preparing the plant materials, fill the clean vase with water and add the floral food. By adding a particular, decorative ribbon, the vase arrangement may be used for any occasion, including anniversaries, birthdays, or graduations.

As you and your peers complete the vase arrangement, discuss any problems you may have encountered. Evaluate each other's designs and give a quick oral critique based on the design principles and elements you have learned through this textbook.

Clean the stems of any foliage that will fall below the water line. Begin greening the vase with the leatherleaf. Place the greens so they fall just slightly into the neck of the vase to create a framework to hold the flowers.

1

Place one of the snapdragons in the center and form one triangle around the lip of the vase. Form a second triangle in the middle of the vase, turning the triangle so it is opposite of the bottom triangle.

2

Add carnations between the snapdragons to maintain an even rhythm in the arrangement. Working in triangles helps keep the arrangement round.

3

Add filler to the arrangement.

4

Birth wreaths are a popular gift in some regions. Hung on the door of the hospital or of the household that has the newborn baby, the wreath is traditionally pale pink for baby girls and pale blue for baby boys. Wreaths may include the first initial of the newborn or the full name with the date, weight, length, and time of birth. Lightweight wreaths constructed of ribbon loops are adorned with small flowers. Stems of baby's breath, delphinium florets, and tiny spray roses are excellent floral options.

Graduation

Graduation from high school or college marks a huge milestone in a person's life. Family and friends may hold parties or dinners in honor of the graduates, and the decorations often include floral arrangements, **Figure 14-13**. Floral designers may use the school's colors or the grad's favorite colors. Common accessories include graduation caps and diplomas.

bikeriderlondon/Shutterstock.com

Figure 14-13. Flower bouquets are traditionally given after the graduation ceremony.

Nontraditional Opportunities

In addition to making floral arrangements for the mainstay holidays and other occasions like Easter and Thanksgiving, florists can expand their business by marketing arrangements for many nontraditional holidays. See **Figure 14-14**. Every holiday has its own story, so understanding the origin of other potential flower-giving events is important. With basic knowledge of the historical, religious, patriotic, and cultural significance of the holidays, a smart designer can create suitable arrangements for any occasion. Designers who know the history and culture that surrounds their place of business can use this knowledge to gain more customers. Knowing how the people around you celebrate national and cultural holidays allows you to cater specifically to these customers.

New Year's Day

In 46 BCE, Emperor Julius Caesar introduced the Julian calendar and instituted January 1st as the first day of the year to honor Janus, the Roman god of beginnings. Romans celebrated by offering gifts to Janus, decorating their homes with laurel branches, attending rowdy parties, and exchanging gifts with one another.

Today, New Year's Day is best known for the annual *Tournament of Roses Parade* in Pasadena, California. See **Figure 14-15**. The Tournament of Roses Parade began as a promotional effort by Pasadena's distinguished Valley Hunt Club. In the winter of 1890, the club members invited their former East Coast neighbors to a mid-winter holiday, where they could watch chariot races, jousting, foot races, polo, and tug-of-war under the warm California sun.

Did You Know? 🌿

In some Spanish-speaking countries, people eat a dozen grapes right before midnight to symbolize their hopes and wishes for the months ahead.

Step-by-Step

Mardi Gras Arrangement

Mardi Gras is an occasion with bright colors and to emphasize those colors, we will use the technique of grouping to make a larger impact in this formal linear design.

For this project you will need the following plant materials: four stems of purple (or violet) larkspur, three or four stems of liatris, two or three blue hydrangeas, four or five dark purple carnations, and six green button chrysanthemums. You will also need a bright color cylinder vase, wet floral foam, Mardi Gras beads or other accents, water, floral food, and a floral knife.

1

Place the soaked foam so it sits about 1" above the rim of the vase. Group the liatris line material in the center of the floral foam. Add two horizontal lines of purple (or violet) larkspur. Make sure to sequence the material as it is horizontal so your eye will move to the center of the arrangement.

2

Place the blue hydrangea in the center front of the arrangement for the focal area.

4

To pull the strong vertical line into the focal area, place carnations starting halfway down the vertical line and integrating the carnations into the focal area.

5

Add accents of green cushion pompons and Mardi Gras beads to make your arrangement party ready.

Once the entire class has completed the Mardi Gras arrangement, evaluate each other's designs. Discuss ways in which you could make the design more contemporary and how you could modify the design to include more of your own artistic expression.

The whole city participates in the celebration and floral arrangements are used in hotel lobbies, restaurants, bars, convention halls, and office buildings. Parties for Mardi Gras season begin after January 12 until Fat Tuesday. Many residents also hold their own celebrations, providing yet another opportunity for local florists. Arrangements are typically created using the traditional Mardi Gras colors of purple, gold, and green. Accessories of masks, feathers, beads, and gold doubloons are standard decorating materials.

St. Patrick's Day

The feast day of St. Patrick, the patron saint of Ireland, is celebrated on March 17th. Many cities host parades and people wear green to celebrate. St. Patrick's Day provides many opportunities for the florist. Floral arrangements are used in churches, restaurants, and Irish pubs. Regionally, schools have fund-raisers in which students may buy and send a single green carnation to the person of their choice within the school building.

Did You Know?

The first parade to honor St. Patrick's Day wasn't even in Ireland. It took place in New York on March 17, 1762. Today, the New York parade is the oldest civilian parade with more than 150,000 participants.

Chapter

15 Sympathy Flowers

objectives

After reading this chapter, you will be able to:

- Describe the different types of funeral events and services.
- Explain the challenges of marketing sympathy flowers.
- Understand the aspects and techniques of a sympathy flower consultation.
- Design half-couch and full-couch casket sprays.
- Summarize other types of floral designs for the casket.
- Design various types of memorial arrangements.
- Explain the use of live plants in sympathy arrangements.
- List methods of working efficiently with funeral home personnel.

key terms

casket blanket	eulogy	mausoleum
casket saddle	European dish garden	pall
casket scarf	full-couch casket spray	script
casket spray design	funeral basket	selection guide
cemetery saddle	half-couch casket spray	set piece
cremation urn	inset piece	standing spray
dish garden	interment	visitation

Go to **www.g-wlearning.com/floraldesign/** for online vocabulary activities using key terms from the chapter.

introduction

Flowers provide an excellent way to communicate emotions when someone has lost a loved one. The symbolism expressed by flowers can help people say what cannot easily be spoken. The arrival of flowers and plants at a visitation, a funeral service, or the homes of bereaved loved ones provide a show of support. They show that someone cares.

Research by Drs. Candace Shoemaker and Diane Relf has shown that flowers and plants provide consolation to the bereaved. They are appropriate and fitting tributes to the deceased, and the flowers brighten up a somber environment. People appreciate receiving flowers not only immediately following the death of their loved one, but in the days or weeks afterward, **Figure 15-1**.

Designing appropriate arrangements and plant displays for sympathy flowers requires an understanding of the purpose of various pieces and the special needs associated with them. Funeral flowers must always be fresh and must be able to stand up to extended periods of display in funeral homes and places of worship. Floral designs that are delivered to residences should last as long as possible.

Funeral Customs

Funeral customs vary from faith to faith and within geographic regions, cultures, and families. For example, the Jewish faith does not call for flowers for funeral rites, but some families may welcome and accept them. The florist should always defer to the religious celebrant and the professional funeral director.

Lisa F. Young/Shutterstock.com

Figure 15-1. People appreciate receiving flowers in the days and weeks after the funeral.

All of the decisions made by the family are very personal and must be respected. On a business level, they have many ramifications for the flower shop. The funeral services, locations, and times will affect the types of floral designs to be sold and designed, as well as the duration of the display. Floral designs may be required for visitation, a private viewing, the funeral service, and interment.

Visitation

Visitation, also referred to as *calling hours*, is a time when the loved ones of the deceased receive family and friends, **Figure 15-2**. Visitors pay their respects to the deceased and offer solace to the family. During this time, the deceased's loved ones receive sympathy and support from friends and family.

Visitations may be brief, perhaps just an hour, or may be longer. Sometimes two different visitations may be held. It is not uncommon for a visitation to be held in the afternoon and then again in the evening, with a formal funeral service the next day.

Private Viewing

Often, family members have a private viewing before the published visitation. This time is very important because it gives the family time to grieve privately and to begin to accept the death of their loved one. It should always be the goal of the florist to ensure that the flowers ordered

Did You Know?

The percentage of deaths resulting in cremation is on the rise in the United States. In 1985, about 15% of all deaths resulted in cremations. The Cremation Association of North America predicts that the number will rise to nearly 56% by 2025.

Pics721/Shutterstock.com

Figure 15-2. A visitation provides a time for family and friends to "say good-bye" and pay last respects to the deceased. The casket or urn is placed in the space of the room's focal point and chairs are arranged for quiet contemplation or discussions.

Figure 15-3. Funeral homes stock both urns and boxes, among other types of containers, suitable for cremated remains.

Figure 15-4. The funeral service depends on the faith of the deceased, but often involves someone speaking words of comfort.

by the family are delivered and in place before this first, important viewing. If the flowers are not in place, the family may feel additional stress, wondering if their order will be delivered on time.

Either a casket or cremation urn is the focal point in the funeral parlor. A *cremation urn* is a receptacle for cremated remains, **Figure 15-3**. Caskets are made of metal or wood, while cremation urns are usually made from metal, porcelain, or wood. The casket may be fully open, half-open, or fully closed, depending on family wishes or the request of the deceased. In some cases, the family may hold only a memorial service with no visitation. Sometimes there is no casket or cremation urn at a memorial service. In these cases, an easel spray is often the focal point, as described later in this chapter.

Funeral Services

A funeral service may involve spoken tributes and religious rites. A *eulogy* is a speech written about and delivered on behalf of the deceased person by a relative or friend, but not all funerals have eulogies. Clergy administer religious rites depending on the faith or beliefs of the immediate family. In some cases, friends and family speak informally about the deceased, offering memories and anecdotes about the person. See **Figure 15-4**.

Interment

Following the funeral, the remains of the deceased may be committed to *interment*, which may be ground burial or placement in a *mausoleum*. Sometimes, cremated remains are not interred, but are kept in a single container or several, smaller containers by family members. Some cemeteries also have gardens, niched walls, or other areas where cremation urns can be displayed. See **Figure 15-5**. It is common for families to host a meal at the home or restaurant following these events.

Aron Hsiao/Shutterstock.com; avarand/Shutterstock.com

Figure 15-5. The traditional method of interment is burial in a cemetery or in a mausoleum. Mausoleums can be private (holding one family) or public. In cooler climates, mausoleums may be enclosed, but many are outside.

Marketing Sympathy Flowers

Types of funerals have changed over the decades as has the use of sympathy flowers. Traditionally, friends, family, and colleagues sent flowers or plants to the funeral home for a two-day wake or service. Today, funeral practices vary greatly with shorter viewing times and little or no visitation hours being the norm. Many families opt for one-day memorial services and life celebrations in lieu of standard funeral practices. Flowers serve the same purpose of consolation, respect, and remembrance, but for florists, the challenge is to maintain the tradition, albeit in new ways, of using flowers to express what is often difficult to put into words. Floral design and flower related expressions of love, and their marketing, must evolve to reach potential consumers who simply do not know the power of flowers as a means of expressing emotions at such a difficult and emotional time.

Using Selection Guides

It is a challenge to market sympathy tributes to the public due to the unpleasant feelings associated with funerals. Perhaps the most helpful tool to show clients diverse, creative ideas for casket sprays and cremation designs is to use *selection guides*. These books are filled with tastefully designed arrangements created by talented, experienced florists. They illustrate floral tributes displayed on or within caskets, as well as designs that fit underneath or around cremation urns.

Funeral Home Connections

Funeral homes work closely with florists, so one excellent way to advertise floral products is to visit nearby funeral homes. It is best to call ahead to make an appointment so that there is time to talk about business. Meet with the funeral directors and, if you anticipate doing business with the funeral home frequently, ask for a tour. Ask to include other staff from the flower shop, such as floral designers and delivery staff, on the tour.

Remember that although funeral professionals are constantly handling flowers and plants, they often do not receive them as gifts. Taking a small gift of a plant or some cut flowers to these industry professionals may be greatly appreciated and may help ensure that they remember your flower shop when clients ask them for recommendations. Funeral directors should be a part of every florist's professional friendship circle. Florists should make the funeral director's job easier whenever possible.

Funeral Floral Consultations

When you conduct a sales consultation for funeral flowers, it is courteous to have family members seated at a table, away from the sounds and distractions of flower shop operations, **Figure 15-6**. The consultation should start with the name of the deceased, funeral home name and location, and the days and times of the services.

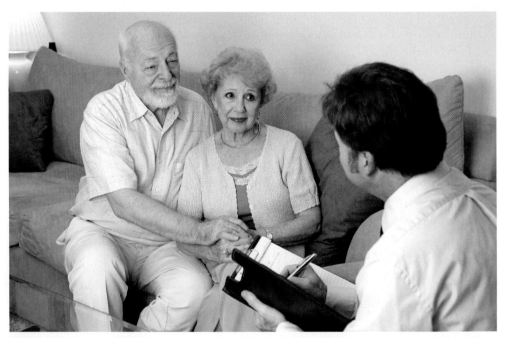

Kzenon/Shutterstock.com

Figure 15-6. Ordering sympathy flowers for a loved one's funeral is a sad and very emotional event. Protect your clients from public view by conducting the consultation in a private space, away from other customers. Selection guides and examples of flowers in stock help sympathy floral clients make important decisions.

Remember that this is an emotional time for the customer. Be sure to listen carefully to the customer rather than allowing yourself to slip into order-taking. Gently point out types of floral designs, colors, and combinations using selection guides. Provide retail examples with three different price points so that the family can choose designs within an appropriate price range.

Generally, the main floral design for the casket is selected first. This design is purchased by the next of kin; for example, a wife whose husband has died. In some areas, *script* is attached to a ribbon and shows the relationship of the giver to the deceased person **Figure 15-7**. In the above example, the script would read "Husband." Customers generally appreciate a florist's effort to personalize funeral floral designs. A favorite flower, color, or activity such as sport or pastime can help the floral designer to tailor an arrangement to an individual.

Once the clients have chosen the main floral design, you may suggest companion designs to create a coordinated look, especially if other family members desire to purchase flowers. Adult children, brothers, sisters, or friends may purchase floral designs to be placed near the casket. Children and grandchildren's love can be expressed with small designs such as inset pieces. Inset pieces are described later in this chapter.

Selling from Available Stock

An important sales technique is to sell funeral flowers from existing stock. This means that during the sales consultation, the florist shows not only selection guides, but also live floral specimens from the shop's cut flower cooler. Selection guides are helpful sales tools to show clients what finished designs will resemble, but clients will appreciate experiencing the color, form, and fragrance of the flowers that will actually be used.

Using flowers from existing stock helps the florist to maintain profitability. For example, customers may want a yellow rose casket spray or may request sunflowers. If these flowers are not in stock, the florist could show alternatives from the shop's cooler, such as coral roses or Asiatic lilies. See **Figure 15-8**. Although these are not the same flowers, they are quite beautiful.

Laurin Rinder/Shutterstock.com; Laurin Rinder/Hemera/Thinkstock

Figure 15-7. Pastel spring flowers and colors are used in these casket sprays, accented with ribbon and script.

Staras/Shutterstock.com

Figure 15-8. Extraordinary flowers may be available in the cooler, so show the customer examples of existing stock.

Monkey Business Images/Shutterstock.com

Figure 15-9. Respectfully present the bill and request payment in full. Politely close the sale with a firm handshake and words of gratitude.

Most of the time, if the flowers are indeed attractive and fresh, customers are satisfied and allow the florist to fill the order using the substitute flowers. In this way, the professional florist can move these perishable commodities through the inventory system and replenish with new stock.

Ordering from Wholesale Florists

Sometimes, it is not possible to sell from existing inventory. A family may truly desire a specific flower or color that is not in stock. While it is best to sell from your cooler, you certainly would not want customers to buy flowers elsewhere. In these cases, having an established relationship with a reliable wholesale florist is especially helpful. The wholesale florist can generally provide exactly what the client wants.

Closing the Sale

When all designs, colors, and flowers have been decided upon, the sale should be closed with complete payment. It is not good business practice to send customers a bill later. All too often, the balance will remain unpaid. Payment should be made up front, before flowers are purchased, arranged, and delivered. A fair exchange of payment for quality goods and services is the foundation of good business, **Figure 15-9**.

Pro Tip

Building Rapport

When you telephone a funeral home for details about an upcoming funeral, identify yourself and your flower shop to the funeral home. This will help you build rapport with the funeral home and may help build business referrals.

Flowers From Friends and Associates

Not every sympathy flower order is sent from an immediate family member. Other family members, friends, and business associates may want to send expressions of sympathy. These clients may not have full information about the funeral service schedule. To help these customers, the florist should have ready access to funeral service information via newspaper or the Internet. When customers call to send flowers or plants to a funeral, the florist will have accurate information and can process the order efficiently. Sometimes it is necessary to call the funeral home for details.

Once an order placed by a friend or associate is finished, an enclosure card and matching envelope should be attached. It is important that the card be legibly handwritten or typed. Some stores having point-of-sale systems can print the card and envelope, but a handwritten card may be more pleasing to the bereaved family than a computer-generated card. Sympathy enclosure cards often have a reverse side printed with several lines for important contact information. Family members generally send thank-you notes for floral tributes, and appreciate it when florists take the time to provide sender contact information. See **Figure 15-10**.

Pro Tip

Write a brief description of the arrangement on the back of the enclosure card as well as the sender's contact information. This will help the family remember who gave each arrangement, which, in turn, will help the family thank the giver more specifically.

JP Floral Designs & Gifts, Inc.

Willcox Lane, Chicago IL (123)456-7890

Dear Aunt Julie and Uncle Dan,

Please accept our condolences for your loss. Our pets also mean the world to us and we pray that Hamlet is in the fields of heaven and running and playing once more.

Love, Scott and Laurie

JP Floral Designs & Gifts, Inc.
Willcox Lane, Chicago IL (123)456-7890

Name of giver: _____

Address: _____

Phone: _____

Email: _____

Goodheart-Willcox.com

Figure 15-10. Enclosure cards should be completed, front and back, to help the family acknowledge floral tributes. A brief description of the arrangement may be included on the back of the card to make it easier for the bereaved to recall the arrangement.

Traditional Casket Sprays

When a casket is present at a memorial service, it is customary for a floral arrangement to be placed on top. These *casket spray designs* are usually radial arrangements of flowers and foliage in mass or line-mass form. See **Figure 15-11**. A casket spray is sometimes referred to as a *casket cover* or *pall*. These terms may be confusing at first, because they may also be used for other types of casket floral designs and accessories explained later in this chapter. Technically, a *pall* is any type of covering for a casket. Experience will help the florist determine when the terms are used to describe casket sprays.

Funeral homes often have stands that can hold a casket spray above the open lid. During visitation, the casket lid may be fully open, half-open, or fully closed. The lower portion of half couch caskets is closed during visitation. The casket lid is permanently closed at the end of the last visitation. At this point, there may be a religious service and the casket spray may or may not be placed on the casket, according to religious customs. Often, there is a final committal when the casket is placed at the gravesite. A brief prayer service or other memorial is made, then the attendees leave before the casket is interred. After the burial, casket sprays are placed on the ground at the burial site. They remain in place for several days, becoming temporary grave markers. For these reasons, there is great emotional value in a well-designed casket spray.

Types of Casket Sprays

The finished size of a casket spray depends on local customs, family preferences, and individual flower shop style. Another major consideration is the style of the casket lid. Some casket lids are all in one piece (full couch), and others are divided in half (half couch). Casket sprays are usually classified according to the type of lid they are designed to fit. A *half-couch casket spray* is about half the length of the casket, and a *full-couch casket spray* runs the entire length or two-thirds of a casket. See **Figure 15-12**.

Rob Hainer/Shutterstock.com

Figure 15-11. This casket spray is accented by a dove, holding delicate ribbons.

Villere's of Metairie, LA/SAF; Robert Hoetink/Shutterstock.com

Figure 15-12. This half-couch casket spray uses zoning technique where like flowers are used in adjacent positions within the overall design. A full couch spray extends two-thirds to the full length of the casket.

Mechanics for Casket Sprays

Traditionally, casket sprays were made using Styrofoam®. A board of Styrofoam was attached to a wire frame. Foliage was then placed directly into the foam or was placed on wooden or steel picks, which were then driven into the Styrofoam. Flower stems were placed in water tubes with pointed ends, providing each flower with a temporary water source and making them easier to impale into the firm Styrofoam base.

Today, *casket saddles* and other commercial casket spray holders are sold in wholesale floral supply departments and can accommodate fresh floral foam, **Figure 15-13**. A casket saddle is shaped to fit the top of a casket. It keeps the arrangement from slipping off the casket and is also waterproof to avoid leaks, which could damage surfaces or carpets at the funeral home. Some casket spray holders are sold complete with a non-scratch, non-skid base, fresh floral foam, and a rigid plastic cage covering the foam. The plastic cage helps keep the mechanic stable and intact.

When making a casket spray, it is important to disguise the mechanics with plant materials. This can be a challenge because the casket spray holder mechanics are somewhat bulky. A wide base is necessary to ensure that the design will be sturdy enough to withstand handling and transport.

Safety Note

Sharp Edges
When creating sympathy pieces, avoid leaving sharp edges or points from picks, wire, or other floral mechanics that can hurt people or damage furniture.

Goodheart-Willcox Publisher

Figure 15-13. Casket saddles are made in many styles to accommodate various designs and types of caskets.

Step-by-Step

Making a Half-Couch Casket Spray

For this symmetrical arrangement you will need tailored emerald, leather leaf, salal, twenty to twenty-five pink carnations, heather or larkspur, and seven to ten stargazer lilies. You will also need a casket saddle, wet floral foam, water, anchor tape or another means of securing the foam, scissors, floral knife, and ribbon.

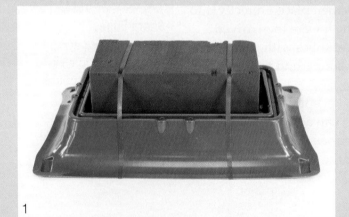

1

Place the soaked floral foam in the casket saddle and secure with anchor tape.

2

Begin greening the outline of the casket spray with the tailored emerald. Insert the first piece in the front, using the lip of the container as a guide to rest the greenery on. Place the emerald hanging down so it will drape down the front of the casket. Next, place two pieces of emerald on either side. Insert a shorter piece in the center for height and one in the back, half as long as the one in the front. Place another set of tailored emerald foliage between the front and sides, between the top and sides, and between the top and back. The placement of the tailored emerald will create the skeleton to guide you as you begin to place the flowers.

3

Using a second type of foliage that is smaller in scale, such as leather leaf, fill in between the skeleton placement of the emerald foliage to cover your mechanics.

4

Finally, complete greening the piece with greenery for texture, such as salal.

5

Begin adding the carnations following the same pattern as the emerald foliage. The carnations are equally spaced to maintain a steady rhythm in the design.

6

A filler such as heather, or a line flower, such as larkspur, can be added between the carnations.

7

Insert the stargazer lilies beginning at the top center of the arrangement and moving forward to draw your eye from the center of the arrangement downward and back up again. Notice that the heaviest focal area is at the top of the arrangement and then the lilies taper and narrow as they descend.

8

A ribbon can be added in the focal area and the tails may hang down or rest to the side. Script can also be added onto the tails of the ribbon.

Military and state funerals may use the United States flag as a casket pall, Figure **15-14**. The flag may be used to fully cover a full couch casket or may be neatly folded in regular pleats for a half couch casket. Casket sprays should not be placed on top of the flag because this is considered disrespectful. Instead, the spray can be placed on a stand above the casket lid. Alternatively, the flag, folded in triangular form, may be placed inside the casket and flowers displayed on the lid.

Other Casket Arrangements

Other types of casket floral adornments provide alternatives to the radial casket spray. The use of tapestries, quilts, or other handmade blankets that cover all or part of the casket comforts many families. Textile decorations look especially nice when combined with floral clusters that repeat some of the colors and adhere to the theme. Examples include a pastel quilt combined with country garden flowers or a religious tapestry beneath a cross made of flowers.

Blankets, Scarves, and Garlands

It is possible to make a blanket, scarf, or garland completely from foliage or flowers. A *casket blanket* is a floral pall that is sometimes used on fully closed or half-open caskets. It covers some or all the top of the casket and drapes over the sides, either sideways or lengthwise. Florists start off with a piece of fabric such as burlap, felt, or other thick, soft textile. High-end blankets may have a tapestry or brocade fabric as a base. Floral adhesive in spray or liquid form is used to adhere leaves, flowers, or both to the fabric base.

Robert Byron/Hemera/Thinkstock; Margie Hurwich/Shutterstock.com

Figure 15-14. When a US flag is draped over the coffin, the casket spray must not be placed on top. It is disrespectful. Instead, the spray may be displayed on a stand near the casket. A memorial wreath is also appropriate and may be placed on a stand near the casket.

A *casket scarf* is smaller than a blanket and is designed to drape over a closed casket or the closed side of a half-open casket. Longer scarves may be designed to run lengthwise down a closed casket. Although the construction of a scarf is similar to that of a blanket, it uses fewer materials and may be a good option for families on a tight budget. A garland, or runner, is a flexible piece that can be shaped to drape gracefully across the casket. Runners are primarily used to cover the hinge of an open or half-open casket.

Inset Pieces

Smaller pieces called *inset pieces*, may be displayed inside the casket or casket lid during visitations. Designs for the casket lid may consist of small floral arrangements, decorative pillows adorned with flowers, or heart- or cross-shaped arrangements that fit in the casket lid, **Figure 15-15**. Families may also want the deceased to wear a boutonniere or corsage, or they may want a nosegay that will fit inside the casket. A floral rosary may be designed if the deceased was Catholic. Suitable pillows, rosary forms, and other accessories are available from wholesale supply departments.

Digital Vision/Photodisc/Thinkstock

Figure 15-15 A heart-shaped inset piece. Inset pieces are typically small and placed in the casket in such a way as to not be obtrusive.

Memorial Arrangements

Not all sympathy arrangements are designed to decorate the casket. Family members, business associates, and close friends of the deceased may want to contribute floral designs to express their sympathy. Many types of designs are suitable for these relationships and expressions.

Standing Sprays

If, for whatever reason, a casket or urn is not displayed at a funeral service, a **standing spray**, or *easel spray*, may become the focal point. These sprays are placed on tripod stands called *easels*, and may include a photograph of the deceased, surrounded by flowers and foliage.

Standing sprays are also appropriate high-end gifts from close friends and associates. If a casket is present, the standing sprays are generally placed near the head or foot of the casket. In these cases, the florist should create the design to coordinate with the casket spray design. See **Figure 15-16**.

Rena Schild/Shutterstock.com

Figure 15-16. A standing (easel) spray usually coordinates with the casket spray. The red, white, and blue theme used here is typical for a military funeral.

The foundation of a standing spray is usually a rigid plastic cage or a foam bar. The cage or bar is affixed to the tripod before the design is built. Designs are usually line-mass arrangements.

Set Pieces

Another type of sympathy floral design that is displayed on an easel is the set piece. *Set pieces* are more symbolic and are based on forms of specific shapes. Crosses, hearts, flags, and wreaths are some of the commonly used set pieces, **Figure 15-17**. These are tailored to the age and gender of the deceased using elements of design such as color, texture, and form. Mechanics for sympathy set pieces are pre-made from Styrofoam, fresh floral foam, papier-mâché, urethane, or combinations of these products.

Baskets

In many parts of the United States, florists market *funeral baskets*. These designs are not necessarily made in wicker baskets unless specified, but they use inexpensive containers made from papier-mâché or plastic, thus allowing more of the retail value of the design to be placed in cut flowers and foliage.

Figure 15-17. Set pieces are built on formed mechanics, such as this heart, and are usually placed on an easel. Most cemeteries have policies on whether silk or fresh flowers must be used.

Step-by-Step

Making a Set Piece

The materials needed
for this set piece are
a Styrofoam® base,
toothpicks, greening pins,
a sturdy greenery such
as salal, and long-lasting
flowers such as cushion
pompons.

1 Begin greening the piece with similar-sized pieces of
salal. Place the salal on the back of the Styrofoam heart
with the front of the leaf laying against the Styrofoam.
Attach each leaf with a greening pin, making sure to
overlap the leaves to create a collar for the heart.

2 Insert half a toothpick into the 1″ stem of the
cushion pompons. Then, insert the toothpick into the
Styrofoam. The cushion pompons will not slide off the
toothpicks as would be the case if wire were used
instead.

The cushion pompons should be placed next
to each other so that the mechanics are not
visible. Place the set piece on an easel, ready
for display.

3

Step-by-Step

Using Wire, Mesh, and Foam

For this project you will need a maché container, wet floral foam, water with floral food, anchor tape, stapler and staples, poultry wire, and wire cutters.

1

2

Place the soaked floral foam in the maché container the long way so the foam sits about 1" above the rim. A second piece of foam may be required to raise the top piece high enough.

You may secure the foam with anchor tape by placing it across the foam and securing it on either side. You must also place a second piece the long way across the foam. A stapler can be used to secure the tape.

3

Place the poultry wire over the floral foam for added security for bulky floral stems that are typically added to large arrangements. Tuck the wire in on all sides so cut ends are not visible.

Step-by-Step

Greening a Maché Container

For this project you will need the prepared maché container from the previous procedure, five stems of tailored Emerald, leather leaf, salal, and a floral knife.

1

Set your framework for the greens by placing the tailored stems of Emerald first. Insert the first piece in the back half of the floral foam, centering the piece of Emerald and angling it slightly back so it does not appear to be leaning forward. Place the next two pieces on either side of the maché container, slightly tilting the Emerald toward the front and inserting the foliage so the stem rests on the lip of the maché container. Insert two more pieces in between the center and the two side insertions. Use your middle insertion and the side insertions as a guide.

2

3

Now your framework is set and you can move to the next foliage such as leather leaf. Start your placements in the center middle of the floral foam. Follow the exact same pattern/framework you set with the Emerald foliage. This time add a couple of additional pieces to the front, arching over the front of the container.

Finish by filling in with the salal foliage. Follow the same pattern and gradually add more foliage in the spaces in between the framework that has been established. Each addition of new foliage should not extend beyond the original framework. Turn your container to the back and use shorter pieces of the leather leaf and salal to cover your mechanics (floral foam and mesh wire).

Other Floral Arrangements

Many other types of floral designs may be chosen for expressions of sympathy designs. Vase arrangements, flowers arranged in baskets, and plant designs can be used not only for special occasions such as birthdays and anniversaries, but also for sympathy offerings. Flower shops generally carry an assortment of containers for both home-style design and traditional arrangements. They style of arrangement is determined by the final destination of the remembrance. Perhaps a church or a bereaved family member's home.

kzenon/iStock/Thinkstock

Figure 15-18. The bereaved may wish to have individual flowers for people to place on the casket at the end of the ceremony.

kzenon/Shutterstock.com

Figure 15-19. A floral designer puts the finishing touch to flowers surrounding a cremation urn prior to a memorial service.

Individual Flowers

It has become common practice for the bereaved to individually place single flowers on the casket when the ceremony is over. The flowers may be removed from a spray but are more likely to be purchased in bunches. Remember to ask the clientele if they will require flowers for this purpose. They may be roses, carnations, or any flower the bereaved chooses. See **Figure 15-18**.

Designs for Cremation Urns

Floral designs are also created to enhance cremation urns. Instead of large sprays or showy baskets, cremation memorial flowers are usually placed underneath or around the cremation urn, **Figure 15-19**. The goal of the floral designer should be to enhance the cremation container rather than obscure it. Floral mechanics designed specifically for urns help to keep the cremation container stable, clean, and dry. Often, family members want to include photos or mementos of the deceased. In these cases, the floral designer considers not only the arrangement of flowers, but also the integration of the objects into a decorative memorial display.

Cemetery Pieces

Whether the deceased is buried in the ground or placed in a mausoleum or cremation urn, family members often remember their loved one on special occasions for many years after the person has passed away. These occasions may include birthdays, wedding anniversaries, or, if the deceased was a military veteran, holidays such as Memorial Day or Veteran's Day.

Cemetery pieces depend on the type of interment, as well as cemetery regulations. You may want to check with the cemetery, or encourage the person purchasing the flowers to check with the cemetery, before designing a cemetery piece.

For graves that have headstones, a *cemetery saddle* may be used to place a floral spray on top of the headstone, **Figure 15-20**. Some grave markers and headstones may have built-in vases for floral arrangements.

However, many cemeteries today do not permit headstones. Graves are marked instead with engraved markers or plaques that lie flush with the ground. Cemetery pieces for these sites should include stakes so that they can be fastened directly to the ground. Some cemeteries provide vases that are compatible with their rules and regulations. Arrangements to fit in a cemetery vase are usually radial, with gathered stems that fit easily into the vase provided.

Thinking Green

Green Burial Cemeteries
A growing number of cemeteries around the world are promoting eco-friendly burial practices that include biodegradable design and avoidance of silk or other artificial flowers. Only live cut flowers and foliage are permitted in these cemeteries.

PinkCandy/Shutterstock.com

Figure 15-20. Cemetery saddles hold headstone pieces firmly in place.

Step-by-Step

Making an Urn-Bearing Floral Design

For this project you will need the following plant materials: hydrangeas, eight stems of purple liatris, seven to ten stems of delphiniums, ten to twelve carnations, five to seven stargazer lilies, limonium, and greens. You will also need a wet floral foam ring, waterproof base, water, floral food, the urn or dimensions of the urn, and a floral knife.

1

Place the soaked floral foam ring in the waterproof base.

2

Place an urn in the center of the ring to gauge the proportions for the composition.

For this design, we are going to emphasize the urn by framing it in the back with a line flower that is taller than the container, such as liatris. Place the liatris stems so the tallest is in the center and the others gradually decrease in height to the left and to the right. Physically balance the wreath by clustering the hydrangeas and carnations in the front and sides of the arrangement. The materials in the front of the arrangement should not cover up or distract from the urn.

Adding another texture, like limonium, in the same color palette will enhance the visual effect of each area of the design.

Adding another linear material behind the urn will strengthen the backdrop of the arrangement and make the urn be showcased as the focal of the arrangement.

Live Plants

Boyan Dimitrov/Shutterstock.com

Figure 15-21. The peace lily is one of the best-known sympathy plants. Fresh flowers with water tubes may be added to accent the plant.

Many customers appreciate the value of live plants as sympathy remembrances. These are popular because the customer often wants something the family can take home and nurture—in essence, a living memorial. See **Figure 15-21**.

Florists stock plants in varying sizes, varieties, and combinations. Flower shops generally market sympathy plants as either foliage plants or blooming plants. Foliage plants, sometimes referred to as *green plants*, are those that are grown and sold for their attractive foliage. Examples of these include *Schefflera arboricola*, dwarf schefflera; *Ficus benjamina*, weeping fig; and Dracaena species.

Smaller versions of green plants are combined in a single container, creating **dish gardens** or planters. In these designs, plants may be placed with additional soil directly in the container or kept in their individual grow pots. Dish gardens are well suited for tabletop display. Blooming plants are often chosen because the blossoms offer a sense of cheer. Spathiphyllum species (including the peace lily), hydrangea, azalea, poinsettia, chrysanthemum, and African violet are often featured in dish gardens. The use of one or more blooming plants in combination with other plants is called a **European dish garden**. These planters are noteworthy because they look like miniature gardens and may suggest the comfort of a heavenly garden, **Figure 15-22**.

Society of American Florists; Rob Hainer/Shutterstock.com

Figure 15-22. A traditional dish garden is a mixture of small, living green or blooming plants. Fresh flowers may be added for presentation. A European garden basket contains plants in their original pots but designed to appear as a miniature garden.

Delivering Sympathy Flowers

The funeral home staff is responsible for accepting sympathy floral tributes and placing them in the funeral home or other location for funeral services. Therefore, flower shop delivery staff, rather than floral design staff, usually transport the designs to the funeral home.

To work efficiently with the funeral home staff, it is a good idea to learn about the flower room practices of the funeral homes your shop services. Some companies want the florist to place flowers in the viewing rooms, while others prefer the use of a flower receiving room. These funeral homes have a designated space to receive flowers from florists. Often, the flower room is located in a place easily and quickly accessible by floral delivery staff.

Florists must make sure that all floral tributes are tagged so that the funeral home supervisors will know for which funeral the flowers are intended. Several funerals may be held at the same time, so clearly-labeled designs are a necessity.

If yours are the only flowers, let a staff member know you have left them before you leave. Busy staff members may not have the time to check the flower room prior to a visitation, thus the floral tribute may not be in place for services.

In some cases, a floral designer may deliver flowers instead of relying on delivery staff. Some designs may need additional, finishing touches that only a florist can provide. Floral designs that include short-lived flowers, such as spring flowers, gardenias, or other wilt-sensitive materials, may require that a floral designer freshen designs between services or visitations.

Work with funeral professionals to make both floral and funeral products and services better. Funeral directors will look favorably on your shop if you do good work that is on-time, fresh, pleasing to the customer, and mechanically stable.

Pro Tip

Funeral homes often run on a tight schedule. When delivering floral designs, especially those purchased from the immediate family, be on time or early.

Pro Tip

Delivery

Before arriving at a funeral home, turn *off* the radio of the delivery vehicle. A funeral service may be occurring. This is respectful of the mourning family and a means of maintaining good business relations with the funeral home staff.

Rob Hainer/Shutterstock.com; Society of American Florists

Planters are popular as sympathy offerings because of their beauty and longevity.

Summary

- Flowers help to express emotions that are not easy to convey in words.
- Funeral customs vary according to the faith and wishes of the deceased and immediate family, but may include visitation, private viewing, a funeral service, and interment.
- Marketing sympathy flowers is often a challenge because of the unpleasant feelings associated with funerals.
- All of the floral and other funeral decisions made by the family are very personal and must be respected.
- Selling flowers from existing stock helps the florist to maintain profitability.
- Casket spray designs are usually classified according to their size; a half-couch design is about half the length of the casket, and a full-couch design is approximately the entire length of the casket.
- Other types of traditional sympathy floral designs include funeral baskets, standing sprays, set pieces, and inset pieces. Vase arrangements, flowers designed in baskets, plants, and planters are also popular sympathy offerings.
- Florists work closely with funeral home personnel to deliver sympathy flowers promptly and in good condition.

Review Questions

Go to www.g-wlearning.com/floraldesign/ to use the fill-in-form.

Answer the following questions using the information provided in this chapter.

1. What requirements must florists understand when working with sympathy flowers?
2. What is the difference between a visitation and a private viewing?
3. What is a eulogy?
4. Name two causes of the decline in sympathy floral sales.
5. Why is it considered good business for a florist to visit any funeral homes that are in the area?
6. What is the purpose of script on a funeral design?
7. Why is it important for a flower shop to have a good relationship with a reliable, local wholesale florist?
8. What information should be included on the back of an enclosure card?
9. What type of mechanics are usually used for casket sprays today?
10. Where should the casket spray be placed in a military funeral in which the casket is covered with a flag?
11. What is the difference between a casket blanket and a casket scarf?
12. List three examples of an inset piece.
13. What mechanics form the foundation of a standing spray?
14. Briefly describe a typical design for a cremation urn.
15. What mechanic or accessory is necessary for a cemetery piece for a grave that does not have a headstone?
16. Why do some people prefer to give live plants as sympathy pieces?
17. What is the difference between a traditional dish garden and a European dish garden?
18. Why do florists tag floral arrangements before leaving them at a funeral home?
19. When might a floral designer deliver flowers to the funeral home instead of relying on delivery staff?
20. List four characteristics of sympathy flowers that may encourage funeral home professionals to work with your flower shop.

Activities

1. With information provided by your instructor, accurately fill out a sympathy enclosure card and envelope.
2. What type of floral design would be a fitting sympathy tribute for a golfer? For a gardener? List items to be used in those designs, then draw a finished casket spray or other sympathy tribute with those themes.
3. Visit the websites of flower shops located in various parts of the country. Note and categorize the various types of sympathy floral designs sold in different areas or regions.

4. Create a floral inset piece. After you finish, interpret and evaluate the artistic decisions you made. Did you use flowers of an appropriate size for the design? Did you use the right amount of floral material, or too much or too little? Record your observations in your floral notebook, along with a photograph of the design, for future reference. Justify any decisions you made that are unusual.

Critical Thinking

1. During your consultation with a bereaved family, the family members are divided on whether to order inset pieces. The grown daughter wants to have a floral rosary and a small heart for the casket lid, but the wife of the deceased insists that her husband (the girl's father) wanted a closed coffin and that inset pieces are a waste of money. What should you do?
2. A bereaved husband in your flower shop in Texas points to a beautiful arrangement in the selection guide and says he wants this arrangement for his wife's casket. However, he wants to substitute koki'o for the irises in the design, because his wife, a native of Honolulu, loved this flower. You know that koki'o is an extremely rare flower that grows only in Hawaii. You place a quick call to your usual wholesale florist, but they do not have koki'o flowers in stock. What should you do?

STEM Activities and Academics

1. **Social Studies.** Choose a civilization from the past and research funeral customs of that civilization. Write a report comparing and contrasting those customs with customs generally followed by people today.
2. **Math.** During sympathy flower consultation, a family chose the following items to be given by various members of the family:

   Casket spray: $399.99, Rosary inset with red spray roses: $124.99, Pillow-shaped heart inset: $49.00, Cross-shaped set piece: $199.99, 2 standing sprays: $179.99 each

   What is the total amount the family will spend on sympathy flowers, before sales tax? If the sales tax is 6.5%, how much sales tax must added? What is the total amount the florist should collect at the end of the consultation?
3. **Language Arts.** Pretend that you are a florist, and you keep a daily journal to help you remember information that you might need later. Today, you held consultations at your flower shop for two different funerals. Write a journal entry about these consultations that includes all of the information you might need in the future.
4. **Technology.** Conduct research regarding mechanics that are designed specifically for funeral arrangements. Write a report describing the benefits of using these mechanics instead of Styrofoam, and explaining how technology has made this possible.
5. **Science.** Conduct research to find out more about biodegradable cremation urns. Of what materials are these urns made? How long does it take them to decompose? Write a short scientific report on your findings. Be sure to include your sources.

Communicating about Floral Design

1. **Reading and Speaking.** Do some research on images of various types of sympathy arrangements. Find one image for each of the following: radial casket spray, half-couch casket spray, full-couch casket spray, casket blanket, casket scarf, inset piece, standing spray, set piece, funeral basket, designs for urns, and a dish garden. Explain how the images are alike and how they are different. Point out specific areas in each arrangement in your explanations.
2. **Listening and Speaking.** In small groups, review the key terms listed at the beginning of the chapter. For each term, discuss the meaning of term and describe the term in simple, everyday language. Record your group's initial description, and then make suggestions to improve your description. Compare your descriptions with those of the other groups in a classroom discussion.

418

Chapter

16 Permanent Botanicals

objectives

After reading this chapter, you will be able to:

- List applications for permanent botanicals.
- Understand the mechanics used to create permanent arrangements.
- Use mechanical techniques specific to designing with permanent and dried materials.
- Apply techniques to preserve or dry fresh materials for use in permanent arrangements.
- Carry out the procedure for pressing flowers and foliage.

key terms

accent moss

banding and bundling

container method

decorative mechanic

dehydrate

desiccant

extension

flat surface method

freeze drying

glycerin

hang-and-dry method

permanent botanical

sheet moss

silica gel

Spanish moss

wire-rack method

Go to **www.g-wlearning.com/floraldesign/** for online vocabulary activities using key terms from the chapter.

introduction

Many commercial and residential spaces benefit from the use of green plants and fresh cut flowers. However, sometimes the fact that they are perishable and need a water source to survive makes using them difficult. When fresh materials are not suitable, *permanent botanicals*—floral designs made from artificial or dried flowers or plants—are used. A professional designer needs to understand both the mechanics behind using a nonliving material and methods for drying or preserving that material.

Applications for Permanent Botanicals

One big difference between artificial and fresh floral design is the mechanics used in their construction. Artificial flowers do not need a permanent water source, so opportunities for design application are almost endless. Their stems can be extended without water tubes, the flowers can be shaped into any stage of development, and the life cycle never ends. See **Figure 16-1.** They do not have to be replaced until the colors begin to fade, the flowers become dusty beyond recognition, or the materials simply rot away.

Tim Farrell; IRC/Shutterstock.com

Figure 16-1. Permanent botanicals are arrangements made with artificial flowers and foliage, dried natural materials, or both.

Commercial Spaces

Reception areas in offices and other commercial buildings use artificial plants and flowers to provide the sense of living material without the cost of maintaining live plants. Because commercial spaces are typically larger than homes, arrangements tend to be on a larger scale to accommodate the size of the space, **Figure 16-2**. They may feature simulated trees constructed with a combination of real and artificial materials. For example, a birch tree branch might act as a trunk. Holes are drilled into the wood and artificial branches are inserted to give the appearance of a larger, living specimen.

Interior spaces such as hotels, offices, and restaurants often decorate with botanically accurate, realistic flowers made of silk or polyester. See **Figure 16-3**. Some companies use fresh materials in the primary focal areas and select permanent flowers for locations of secondary importance or which are difficult to access on a

luxorphoto/Shutterstock.com; Nick_Nick/Shutterstock.com

Figure 16-2. Plants in commercial spaces are usually larger with large containers. Comparing the images above, the larger plants are a good size for the space, and the smaller sized plant container works best for small areas like a desk top.

posztos/Shutterstock.com; Dallas Events Inc/Shutterstock.com

Figure 16-3. Some commercial venues use floral designs as a major component of their interior design. Whether these pieces are replicated in artificial or permanent materials, the necessary design can be achieved. Cost and maintenance accessibility determine the types of materials to be used.

Figure 16-4. More formal arrangements such as the hedgerow may be made small enough for a tabletop, or large enough for the entryway of a large office building.

regular basis. Hospitals may have live plants in common areas like the entrance but use artificial arrangements in areas that do not receive enough light, are restricted (like the intensive care unit), or are near patient rooms.

Like fresh arrangements, permanent botanicals support the theme of a particular space. In high-tech interiors, materials are selected or adapted for a more industrial-looking application. Design styles like the hedgerow can be created out of artificial materials as well as perishable, **Figure 16-4**. Restaurants tailor their floral pieces to the style of their interior. For example, country-style restaurants might use a combination of dried and artificial materials to achieve a homey atmosphere. Sophisticated traditional restaurants might use much more formal designs. Designers should match the style of the floral design to the style of décor.

Residential Spaces

In homes, the style of artificial floral arrangements should follow the interior design of each living area. A good assessment of the living spaces, such as bedrooms, bathrooms, kitchen, and entries, is necessary before you begin to design. Note whether the residence has an English cottage look, a detailed bungalow style, a rustic look, or another design style. The type of dwelling may also be a factor. For example, a design style for a city loft would not be well-suited for most suburban ranch-style homes.

Take into account not only the design style, but also the amount of visual space in each area. For example, tall artificial trees or plants work well in living rooms with vaulted ceilings. Spaces with lower ceilings or tight seating areas do not provide enough room for large specimens; they would make the room feel uncomfortable and crowded.

A combination of artificial and dried materials is also an option for interior spaces. The appearance of dried materials can add a more natural feeling to the overall arrangement when combined with fabric flowers. Dried herbs are fragrant, have quite a bit of texture, and would be a logical selection for a kitchen design. Lavender is textural, with a strong color and a delightful fragrance. It is also said to have calming properties and would be well-suited for a bedroom arrangement. Dried peppers are brightly colored and have interesting shapes, **Figure 16-5**. Designs using clustered grasses with artificial flowers can be dramatic focal points when used in entry areas.

Figure 16-5. Dried materials, like lavender or peppers, may be purchased in bundles from wholesalers and sometimes in small farmer markets.

Sometimes a location needs the size and height of large plants but does not have the appropriate growing conditions. A good option for this situation would be the use of artificial plants combined with fresh foliage and flowers. The artificial plants would be used to fill the height requirements, and fresh floral materials would be used to add color and interest. The most appropriate design style would be determined by the architecture or décor of the home or in which it is located.

The same space may also benefit from a cut flower arrangement which is easily changeable and still provides a focal point. Floral designers can use their knowledge of environment, application, and plant maintenance to determine the best option for their customers. See **Figure 16-6**.

Figure 16-6. Determining the type of design used in someone's home largely depends on space in which it will be placed. Artificial flowers may be well-suited for the coffee table in a home and today look more realistic.

Types of Artificial Flowers

Today, artificial materials used in professional floral designs are made botanically correct. They closely resemble the natural appearance of flowers and foliages because of their covered stems and beautifully made silk or polyester flowers. Top-quality, individually-stemmed artificial flowers have malleable wire inside that allows the designer to bend the stems into natural positions. These artificial stems are the material of choice for design applications.

Step-by-Step

Adding Extensions

Using silk flowers to add color or create a strong line in a planter is very practical. The flowers may be easily changed to coincide with the season or on the owner's whim. For example, replacing the carnations in the following project with a stem or two of silk lilies, and replacing the bow with an Easter-themed accessory, would create a lovely, Easter-themed planter.

For this project you will need two or three silk flower stems, wood picks with attached wire, scissors, wire cutter, and floral tape that matches the stem color. Follow these steps to extend the stems of the silk flowers.

Cut the silk flower stems, leaving a couple of inches at the bottom free of foliage or flowers. Lay a wood pick parallel to the stem of the silk flower.

1

Begin wrapping the wire around the stem, overlapping the wood pick. This will bind the two pieces.

2

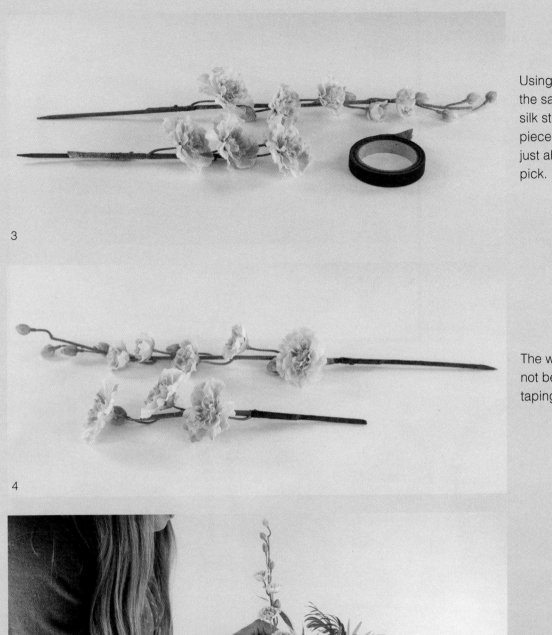

Using floral tape that is the same color as the silk stem, tape the two pieces together, starting just above the wood pick.

3

The wood pick should not be visible when the taping is finished.

4

Insert the "new" stem into your arrangement or planter.

5

Step-by-Step

Covering Mechanics with Sheet Moss

For this project you will need a basket with a liner, dry foam, anchor tape, scissors, sheet moss, water, and greening pins. Prepare your basket or container with floral foam and secure it with anchor tape. Note: This mechanic can be used for wet foam, too, as displayed in the image.

1

To make the moss more pliable, place it in a shallow pan of water. Wring out the extra moisture and separate it slightly with your hands. Be careful not to tear it by pulling too hard. Cover the floral foam with the moss, leaving spaces for flowers and foliage to be inserted.

2

Tuck in the sides of the moss and, using greening pins, secure the moss to the foam so it does not become loose during the design process.

3

Your basket is now ready for the design process. Note: Dry moss should be used with appropriate foam when designing permanent artificial arrangements.

Dried Botanicals

Arrangements made from dried plant materials are long-lasting and need little maintenance. There is a preservation method for almost every type of plant or flower. The only limitation on plant material that can be dried is the amount of time and expense you are willing to commit to the project. Unlike most artificial foliage and flowers, dried plant material is fragile and should always be handled carefully.

Harvesting

The best time to cut flowers is on a dry day or in the late morning after the dew has dried. The stage of development at which a flower is harvested depends partly on the type of flower and partly on the method to be used for drying. In general, however, flowers should be picked at their prime or when they are slightly immature.

For best results, materials need to be fresh, not damaged or bruised, and at the right stage of development for the type of flower, **Figure 16-14**. Do not try to dry materials that are past their prime. Materials will continue to age slightly in appearance as they dry, so a flower will never look better than the day it was harvested. Also, flowers that are past their prime may drop their petals during the drying process. Bruises or damaged margins and petals will appear darker and often become more evident after drying.

Thomas Burli/iStock/Thinkstock; 4Max/Shutterstock.com

Figure 16-14. Harvesting materials at the right time is important to ensure the quality of the finished product.

Cutting Gardens

Starting a cutting garden of your own or a community garden is a great way to acquire flowers and foliage for practicing floral design. The key to a successful cutting garden is careful planning. Do a little research before you begin and your gardening will go much smoother.

You will first need to locate a site with sufficient sunlight, good drainage, and fertile soil. Make a list of flowers and foliage you would like to grow and pare it down to a manageable five or six. Learn what type of conditions suit the plants you'll be growing to make sure they are compatible with your site. The plants may be perennials or annuals and can be started from seed or purchased from a local grower. Plant some for drying and others for fresh arrangements. For a better chance of success, keep your cutting garden small and simple to begin and expand it over time.

> **Pro Tip**
>
> A small space can still yield large harvests! About 20 plants can be squeezed into a 6′ × 8′ raised bed.

Preservation and Care

Fresh flowers and plant materials must be carefully processed before they can be used in permanent arrangements. Methods range from air drying to complex preservation methods. The rest of this chapter describes the various methods and explains which method to use with specific materials.

Air Drying

Air drying is by far the easiest way to preserve flowers. Without chemicals or special equipment, the flower is allowed to *dehydrate*, or dry out, on its own. Methods for air drying plants and flowers include:

- Hang-and-dry method
- Container method
- Flat surface method
- Wire-rack method

The method you choose is often determined by the types of plants you are drying. For instance, flowers with large petals do not dry well using the hang-and-dry method. Flowers with delicate stem structures, such as Queen Anne's lace, should also not be hung to dry. Flowers with high moisture content or a flat, open shape are best dried using a *desiccant*. Others dry best when laid flat on an absorbent surface such as cardboard or newspaper.

The flowers best suited to air drying are the materials that do not wilt readily. Air drying also works well for smaller flower heads such as statice, baby's breath, and solidago, **Figure 16-15**.

Hang-and-Dry Method

The simplest way to dry flowers is to hang them upside-down in a dry place for several weeks. To use this *hang-and-dry method*, first locate a suitable place to hang the materials. A dark, cool place with good air circulation works best. A dry basement or a closet with louvered doors are ideal locations. Install hooks from the wall or ceiling to provide a place to hang the flowers so that they do not touch the wall. Stringing some twine or rope between the hooks will extend your hanging space. The weight of the flowers will determine the type of string or rope to use.

kukuruxa/Shutterstock.com; Kateryna Tsygankova/Shutterstock.com

Figure 16-15. Flowers that do not wilt readily like yarrow, are suitable for air drying. Yarrow and statice are good examples.

Airflow and Temperature

Make sure there is adequate airflow and that the flowers will not be in direct sunlight. If there is high humidity or the specimens are very damp, they will take longer to dry and may not produce satisfactory results. Cool temperatures tend to maintain more of the true color of the materials as they dry. Extra warm temperatures may speed the drying process, but may also cause the materials to become extremely brittle by drying them too quickly.

Positioning the Material to Be Dried

There is no rule saying that material must be hung upside-down, but doing so often works best because the least damage occurs to the materials. See **Figure 16-16**. Hanging the flowers upside-down also puts the stems into the correct position to dry straight. The flowers will dry in the same direction as they are hung, so if you hang the material upside-down, make sure all the buds are facing the ground.

After harvesting your plants and flowers, trim the stems to no shorter than six inches and remove all foliage. The foliage of most plants does not dry well and leaving it on will increase drying time. After removing the foliage, divide the plants by type and gather them in small, loose bundles. Each bundle may be bound with a rubber band or a string using a slip knot. The rubber band and/or slip knot will adjust itself to shrinkage of the stems as they lose moisture. They will also keep the bundle secure without breaking the dried stems. The slip knot makes it easier to remove the dried materials. Make sure to stagger the heads to allow better air circulation. Good airflow will prevent mildew and rot. Large flowers should be hung individually.

Some natural stems that are hung and air-dried will be fairly straight and strong enough to use. Certain flowers, such as strawflowers, have a stem that shrinks so much it can no longer support the weight of its own flower. In these cases, a coated floral wire can be added for additional support.

Mona Makela/Shutterstock.com

Figure 16-16. Hanging flowers upside-down to dry may seem illogical at first, but this positions the flowers for best results. This position takes the weight of the flowers off the stems and helps keep the stems straight.

Air Drying Time

The drying time needed depends on several factors:
- How fast the water evaporates from the plant material.
- The dampness of the area in which the plants are hanging.
- The type of plants and flowers being dried.
- Where and when the plants and flowers were harvested.
- The condition of the materials when they were harvested.
- The stage of growth at which the plants were harvested.
- The part of the plants that you are drying (stems, flowers, fruits, seed pods).

Step-by-Step

Air Drying

Several types of flowers are applicable to air drying. Remove any extra foliage from the stems of the flowers, group several stems together and bundle them with a rubber band.

The rubber band will adjust as the flower stems dry and decrease in size. Create a hook to hang the fresh flower bunches from. Hanging them upside down will help the heads of the flowers remain in the same position as they dry.

As the flowers dry, you will notice the stems and the leaves shrink as moisture is lost.

It can take anywhere from three days to three weeks to complete the drying process. If the stems begin slipping from their binding, you can retie them and hang them back up. Otherwise, try not to touch them until they are completely dry. Remove the flowers from their bundles and spray them with hairspray or a floral sealer to help prevent shredding and shattering, **Figure 16-17**. Dried flowers may be stored in boxes with some type of protection around them, such as shredded newspaper.

Container Drying

Another air drying method is the *container method*. Plants are placed right-side-up in a container with 1/2″ of water, and the water evaporates as the plants dry. This method works well for plants such as ageratum, alliums, hydrangeas, Bells of Ireland, heather, and yarrow. Plants such as baby's breath, poppy seed heads, Chinese lanterns, craspedia, and thistles can be stood upright in dry, tall, cylindrical containers, coffee cans, or wide-mouthed jars that will allow them to bend, resulting in gracefully curving stems as they dry. See **Figure 16-18**.

Isuaneye/Shutterstock.com

Figure 16-17. These strawflowers are fully open and dried. They do not shatter easily. Others, however, should be sprayed with a preservative to retain their appearance and prevent them from picking up excess moisture.

Thinking Green

Aerosols

Many scientists believe that propellants used in traditional aerosol sprays are damaging to the environment. New aerosols are being developed that release few, if any, toxic chemicals into the air. If you use an aerosol product, check the label to see if the product is eco-friendly.

Thomas Klee/Shutterstock.com

Figure 16-18. Seed pods and blossoms of some plants, lavender for example, have different design applications when dried.

Figure 16-19. Drying grasses and moss-like plants flat helps them retain their shape.

Africa Studio/Shutterstock.com

Flat Surface Method

Yet another way to air dry plants is to lay them flat on an absorbent surface such as cardboard or newspaper. This *flat surface method* works well for grasses, moss, lichen, fern fronds, and spiky leaves, **Figure 16-19**. Arrange the material in a single layer without overlapping. Some of the specimens may shrink a little, but will not lose their shape as they would if they were hung upside down or dried upright.

Leaves can be dried on top of a flat screen with newspaper on top to keep them from curling while drying. Grass plumes can be dried the same way, **Figure 16-20**. If arching or twisting stems are desired for design, simply dry materials standing up. Drying times depend on humidity levels surrounding the floral materials, thickness of the stems, and air temperature.

Wire-Rack Method

The *wire-rack method* works especially well with heavy-headed plants. Any type of wire shelf can be used for rack drying. If you do not have a suitable shelving unit, use old refrigerator shelves, oven racks, baker's cooling racks, or a simple shelf made with chicken wire or floral netting. Place the flowers in the rack so that the blossoms rest on top of the rack and the stems hang below. It is important to leave enough room beneath the rack to allow the stems to hang freely.

Pro Tip

Materials that break easily after they are dried such as heather, boxwood and salal leaves can be arranged while they are fresh and left to dry in the arrangement.

Neil Kurtzman/Shutterstock.com

Figure 16-20. When the flowers to be dried are heavy, using the wire-rack method will keep the weight of the flower from bending the stem during the drying process.

The wire-rack method can be used with plants such as globe artichokes, peonies, large onion seed heads, protea, and large thistles.

Freeze Drying

In some cases, a customer may want to preserve a fresh floral arrangement, such as a bridal bouquet. *Freeze drying* is often used in these cases because it can be performed without disturbing the arrangement and rarely results in shrinkage or other disfiguring side effects. However, this method requires special equipment, so it is generally performed only by specialists.

The process of freeze drying quickly removes moisture from material while retaining the majority of its color. Placed into a refrigerated vacuum chamber, any water in the flower changes to ice and then to water vapor quickly. Flowers, fruits, vegetables and herbs can all be freeze-dried, **Figure 16-21**.

Wholesale florists often sell pre-dyed and freeze-dried materials such as roses. These flowers are nice additions to artificial botanical materials, but they should be used in locations with low humidity, because the products will soften if allowed to reabsorb moisture. They should not be used in bathrooms or outdoor locations with high humidity.

Undrey/Shutterstock.com

Figure 16-21. Freeze drying requires special equipment, but dries flowers without shrinkage or distortion. The yellow roses in this image have been dyed and freeze-dried for the sharp color.

Glycerin Foliage Preservation

Because of their fragile and sometimes brittle nature, dried flowers and foliage can be challenging to use in designs. However, the flexibility of some materials can be preserved using a glycerin treatment. Technically named glycerol, *glycerin* is a colorless, odorless, syrupy substance that is used to make certain floral materials, such as foliage, more pliable. Fresh foliage absorbs the glycerin, which replaces the water in the plant's tissues. The glycerin keeps the material supple and smooth.

This method requires the foliage to be either submerged or stood upright in a glycerin and water solution and allowed to absorb the mixture. With this process, foliage maintains the leaf form, texture, and sometimes the color better than air drying. Foliage preserved with glycerin will keep almost indefinitely.

The success of this method depends on the material's ability to absorb the glycerin solution. Foliage should be fresh and fairly mature, but not past its prime, when harvested. Old plants may not absorb the solution. Very young plants that wilt easily may not do well either. The chart in **Figure 16-22** is a list of materials found to preserve well in glycerin.

Safety Note

Protecting Surfaces
Care needs to be taken to limit the amount of moisture surrounding dyed glycerin-treated materials. If allowed to absorb moisture, they will weep drops of color onto surrounding surfaces.

Foliage Recommended for Preserving with Glycerin

Aspidistra	leatherleaf
Beech	Lemon
Cotoneaster	Ligustrum
Dracaena	Magnolia
English Ivy	Maple
Eucalyptus	Mountain Ash
Forsythia	Myrtle
Galax	Nandina
Holly	Oak
Hornbeam	Pittosporum
Huckleberry	Poplar, white or silver
Ivy	Salal
Juniper	Viburnum

Goodheart-Willcox Publisher

Figure 16-22. Candidates for preserving with glycerin.

Pro Tip

Glycerin Uptake

Do not water plants before you harvest them. Plants that have not been watered absorb the glycerin solution faster.

Deciduous materials, such as oak leaves, can be treated with glycerin. These are a staple among florists during the fall-winter decorating season, **Figure 16-23**. They provide an inexpensive way to add interesting form and color to fall centerpieces. Added singly to a design with a wired pick or used in small clusters, leaves add a sense of seasonal interest.

During the winter season, coniferous cut cedar is a good candidate for glycerin treatments. When added to artificial holiday wreaths, the pliable evergreen adds a realistic appearance, especially when used in combination with natural pine cones.

Joyfnp/Shutterstock.com

Figure 16-23. Oak leaves preserved in glycerine must be harvested and processed before they lose green pigments in the fall.

Making the Solution

The most commonly used glycerin mixture is made of 1/3 glycerin and 2/3 water. Adding two tablespoons of bleach, rubbing alcohol, or a disinfectant per cup of mixture will reduce the growth of mold and bacteria. Food coloring or florist's dye may be added to enhance the color of the leaves or to produce special effects. The solution may be adjusted slightly for different leaf textures, **Figure 16-24**.

You will need the following supplies:

- Branches. Branches from beech, maple, oak tulip tree, mulberry, and poplar trees respond well to this preservation method. These branches preserve best in mid to late summer.
- Florist's knife.
- Food coloring or florist's dye.
- Glass container(s).
- Hot water.
- Marker or tape (to mark solution level).
- Measuring cup.
- Mixing utensil.
- Small hammer.
- Small weights (for submersion method).
- Soft, clean cloth.
- Technical grade glycerin (available in drugstores).

Image courtesy of Save On Crafts, www.saveoncrafts.com

Figure 16-24. The type and texture of the foliage being preserved may require a slight adjustment in the glycerin solution.

Step-by-Step

Preserving Upright Materials with Glycerin

Follow the steps below to preserve upright materials using a glycerin solution.

1. Harvest branches up to 18″ long with the desired curves and undamaged foliage.

2. Remove the lower leaves.

3. Heat water just to boiling before mixing in the glycerin. Add food coloring or florist's dye to the solution (optional). Mix well.

4. Pour the glycerin solution into your container. For long stems (max 18″), use a tall glass vase with 6″–10″ of solution. For shorter stems, use 4″–5″ of solution.

5. Recut the stems just before placing the stem end of the branches into the solution. Large, woody stems should be split and some of the bark removed. Mark the solution level on the side of the container.

6. Place the container in a location that has good air circulation.

7. As the materials absorb the solution, add more of the mixture to keep the glycerin at the original marked level.

8. Once the materials have absorbed enough solution to become pliable, remove them and allow them to drain. The branches may be used as they are, or the leaves may be removed and used elsewhere.

Time Needed

Most branches take from one to three weeks to complete the glycerine absorption process. The color of the leaves will gradually change as they absorb the glycerin. The color change may be controlled somewhat by varying the amount of time the branch remains in the solution. Once the foliage has absorbed enough solution to be preserved, you may remove it.

The plant material's texture affects the time it needs to absorb the solution. Coarse-textured leaves take longer to absorb sufficient solution than fine-textured leaves. If the plant material becomes limp after an extended period in the solution, hang the materials upside down for a few days. This will allow the leaves to return to their normal shape.

Coprid/Shutterstock.com

Figure 16-25. This flowing consistency of the sand makes it easier to gently surround flowers without damaging them and still support them until they dry.

Microwave Drying

Another method to dry flowers is to use a microwave oven. Flowers and foliage will dry in minutes instead of weeks, and the flowers may look fresher and more colorful than those preserved by other methods. Depending on the type of material being dried, you can use a container filled with desiccant or dry paper towels.

Surround the flowers with support material to maintain their shape during heating and drying. Without support, the flowers will dry to the shape of the bottom of the container. Options for support material include desiccants with a sand-like consistency, such as *silica gel*, a borax and sand mixture, or kitty litter. See **Figure 16-25**. These will absorb moisture from the flowers while helping to keep their shape.

Preserving with a Desiccant

Before collecting your specimens, gather the following materials:
- Aerosol hair spray, floral sealer, or lacquer.
- Desiccant—silica gel works best.
- Microwave-safe thermometer.
- Microwave-safe container for water.
- Microwave-safe container and lid for plants. Cardboard containers such as shoe boxes or oatmeal boxes work well because they absorb moisture and do not sweat. If you use a food container, do not reuse the dish for food.
- Paper towels.
- Gloves (to prevent extreme dryness of your hands).
- Water.
- Microwave oven.

After using the silica gel for regular or microwave drying, you will need to dry it. **Figure 16-26** lists recommended times for various flowers and foliage. During the process of drying flowers, the silica gel absorbs 1/3 of its weight in water. This moisture needs to be removed from the gel before you can use it again. To dry the silica gel in the microwave, place the gel in a microwave safe container and set the power to medium. Dry for three to five minutes and inspect it for color change. If it is not dry, stir it with a spoon and heat it for another three to five minutes. Stir the gel each time you inspect it. It takes about eight to twelve minutes per pound of gel, but the time will vary according to the microwave. After you have dried the silica gel, store it in an air-tight container to keep it fresh and ready for use. Regular ovens can also be used to dry the silica gel after use. Follow the manufacturer's directions for best results.

Safety Note

Make sure the dish you are using is safe for use in the microwave or oven. Do not use a plastic dish and make sure any glass dish you use can withstand the high temperature of the silica beads as they dry.

Microwave Drying Times		
Flower	**Drying Time* (minutes)**	**Sitting Time (hours)**
Anemone	2 1/2–3	12
Aster	2 1/2	10
Carnation	1–1 1/2*	10
Chrysanthemum	1 1/2–3*	10
Daffodil	2 1/2	10
Dahlia	2 1/2–4	36
Daisy	1 1/2	10
Delphinium	4–5	10
Marigold	1–3	10
Orchid	1–2 1/2*	24
Pansy	2 1/2–3	36
Peony	3–4	36
Poppy	2 1/2–3	24
Rose	1 1/2–2*	10
Salvia	3	24
Zinnia	1 1/2–5	10

*Varies by microwave oven. All times are estimates. Experimentation may be neccessary to achieve the best drying time for each material.

Figure 16-26. Recommended microwave times. Larger flowers may require more drying time. The times listed will also vary for different microwaves.

Step-by-Step

Silica Gel Processing

Keep in mind that every microwave is different so you will have to experiment. The times given here are approximate.
Follow these steps to dry flowers in the microwave using silica gel.

Cover the bottom of the plant container with 1″–2″ of desiccant. You may need more for larger blossoms. Place each flower in the desiccant with the blossom opening upward.

Gently pour the desiccant over the flower until all petals are covered. You will want to hold the flower until there is enough of the medium beneath it to hold it upright. If you are drying more than one flower at a time, do not let the blooms touch in the container. Place the uncovered container in the microwave oven along with a cup of water to prevent excessive drying.

Set the microwave oven on low power and dry for one minute and then check your flowers. If they do not seem to be drying, increase the heat and time accordingly. Since microwave ovens vary in terms of temperature/power level, it is best to begin with a low temperature and short amount of time and work your way up. **Figure 16-26** lists recommended times for various flowers and foliage.

If you can read it from outside the oven, a microwave-safe thermometer can be used to determine how much time is needed to dry flowers. Insert the thermometer into the silica gel 1/2″ from the covered specimens. Most flowers will be finished drying when the temperature of the silica gel reaches 160°F.

When the flowers are finished drying, open the microwave and cover the container immediately. Remove the container from the microwave and slightly crack the lid. Allow the container to cool for 12 to 24 hours before carefully uncovering the flowers. Sufficient cooling helps to preserve the delicate shape of the flowers.

5

Carefully remove the flowers and clean off the petals with a fine brush. Mist the flowers with hairspray or a floral sealer to prevent them from absorbing moisture from the air. Store the dried flowers in an airtight container until ready for use.

6

Pro Tip

Do not use paper towels with a pattern or strong surface texture when pressing plant materials, or you will have marks on your flowers.

Pressed Flowers

For years, botanists have used flower presses to hold specimens collected from the field. Today, pressing flowers is still an option for flower and foliage preservation. The floral materials are gently dried with a paper towel and laid between layers of parchment and an absorbent paper, such as white paper towels. The materials are then sandwiched between two flat surfaces, such as cardboard or wood, and pressed flat.

Dictionaries or large, heavy books are a suitable substitute for the traditional flower press. The drying time depends on the material being preserved and its moisture content, but can be as little as three days.

Flat flowers, as opposed to conical flowers, are best suited for this technique. Violets, delphinium, and pansies are ideal for this method, **Figure 16-27**. Foliage also does well since it is usually flat. Ivy leaves, fern fronds, and dusty miller dry well when pressed.

Pressed materials are nice botanical additions to note cards, bookmarks, and keepsake frames, **Figure 16-28**. Some florists create their own pressed merchandise while others may do custom designs for customers. For example, customers may ask you to create a design around a certificate of remembrance. You should lay out the design on the certificate and then carefully remove the pieces with tweezers. Loosely brush the backs of flowers with adhesive and place them around the certificate. For best results, seal the certificate and flowers in a frame or protective sheath.

Santia/Shutterstock.com

Figure 16-27. Pressed flowers can be used to decorate bookmarks and similar items.

Gordon Swanson/Shutterstock.com; alysta/Shutterstock.com

Figure 16-28. Pressed flowers can be added to craft projects or framed and displayed as art.

Step-by-Step

Flower Pressing

For this project you will need a flower press, absorbent paper, rigid cardboard, and plant materials. Flower presses may come with screws or Velcro to tighten the press.

Choose the plant materials you are going to press. Lay each piece on the absorbent paper the way you would like it to be pressed. Do no overlap the materials.

Close the press carefully, making sure the blooms do not fold over. Secure the straps, or tighten screws, on the outside of the press.

The amount of time it takes for the flowers to be pressed is determined by the size of each piece and its water content.

Summary

- Permanent botanicals are used in both commercial and residential applications.
- Mechanics for permanent botanicals are often different from those for fresh flowers, and may include gluing the foam and/or the floral material in place.
- The same design principles used for fresh flowers are used for permanent botanicals as well.
- One of the most common methods of covering the foundation of a permanent botanical design is to use sheet moss.
- Flowers and foliage to be dried should be harvested while they are in their prime.
- Air drying is the easiest way to preserve fresh floral material.
- Freeze drying provides excellent results, but requires special equipment.
- Glycerin preserves foliage while maintaining its flexibility and texture.
- Flowers can be pressed using a flower press or large, heavy books to supply the necessary pressure.

Review Questions

Go to www.g-wlearning.com/floraldesign/ to use the fill-in-form.

Answer the following questions using the information provided in this chapter.

1. Name at least two major differences between creating fresh floral designs and permanent botanicals.
2. What type of foam is used for the foundation of a permanent botanical design?
3. When is a glue gun preferred instead of a glue pan for working with permanent botanicals?
4. Explain purpose of banding and bundling.
5. When you receive a shipment of high-end silk flowers, what must you do before you can use them effectively in a design?
6. When is it *not* necessary to cover the foundation in a permanent botanical?
7. At what stage of development should flowers be harvested if you intend to dry them?
8. List the four common methods for air drying botanicals.
9. Describe the ideal characteristics of a place for hanging flowers to dry.
10. When is the wire-rack method of air drying used?
11. Name one advantage and one disadvantage of freeze drying.
12. How are items preserved using glycerin different from other dried botanicals?
13. What is the most common formula for a glycerin solution for preserving flowers or foliage?
14. What desiccant is the most commonly used when drying flowers in a microwave?
15. Why is it important to surround flowers with support material when drying them in a microwave?
16. How can you keep leaves from curling when you dry them in a microwave?
17. Briefly describe the process for pressing flowers without using a flower press.

Activities

1. Create a seasonal collage using leaves and floral materials pressed throughout the semester.
2. Harvest hydrangea flowers and allow them to dry. Apply a tint of color; design holiday wreaths or arrangements using the colored florets as accents.
3. Create holiday cards or bookmarks using pressed flowers.
4. Conduct research online to find examples of geometric floral designs. Take screen captures to collect six examples, and evaluate them for effective use of materials and overall design. Then create an original geometric floral design using silk flowers. Display your design as part of a class display.

5. Choose an original design created by a classmate for Activity #4. Analyze the design and make notes about its meaning and formal qualities. Determine whether the design has any historical or cultural meanings or contexts. Discuss your findings with the person who created the design. With the designer, determine a fair price for the design.

6. Enlist the help of your peers and begin a community cutting garden on the school grounds or on some borrowed land (with permission of the owner). Use your cuttings to make bouquets and arrangements to share.

Critical Thinking

1. A customer in coastal South Carolina explains that she is remodeling her bathroom around a nautical theme. She wants a floor-standing dried floral arrangement, with sea grasses and other native grasses, to place beside the shower. How should you handle this request?

2. A summer intern in your flower shop is excited about learning how to preserve fresh flowers. On her own, she attempted to use the container method to air dry six roses. She was very disappointed when the stems bent near the top, so that all of the roses droop and face downward. How can you diplomatically explain what went wrong and what she should do differently next time?

STEM Activities and Academics

1. **Science.** Select a specific flower type and obtain 12 flowers of similar size and stage of development. Divide the flowers into three groups of four flowers each. Use three different drying or preservation methods of your choice to dry the flowers. Evaluate the results. Which method resulted in the best color preservation? Which method caused the least shrinkage? Which method caused the flowers to become most brittle?

2. **Math.** Suppose that you are going to make a batch of glycerin according to the recipe described in this chapter. You want to make 64 ounces of glycerin solution. How much glycerin will you need? How much water will you need? If you add bleach, how much should you add? (21.3 ounces of glycerin; 42.7 ounces of water; 8 tablespoons of bleach)

3. **Technology.** Investigate the principles behind the microwave oven. What are microwaves? How are they used to cook food? What property makes microwaves suitable for drying flowers?

4. **Social Studies.** Dried flowers have been used for many purposes through the centuries. Conduct research to find out how dried flowers were used in ancient Egypt and in Europe during the Middle Ages. When did the use of dried flowers for decoration become popular?

5. **Science.** Pressing flowers naturally distorts their original shape. Yet for centuries, scientists pressed flowers for use in their *herbaria*. Conduct research to find out what a *herbarium* is and why scientists pressed the flowers they gathered for their studies.

6. **Social Studies.** Research the work of Gertrude Jekyll, Frederick Gibberd, or another famous florist of the 20th century. Find descriptions and images of their work. Select one garden or exhibition by this florist. Analyze the garden or exhibition to determine its formal qualities. Try to understand the design decisions within their historical and cultural contexts. Does the design have any particular meaning? What was the intent of the florist?

Communicating about Floral Design

1. **Listening and Speaking.** Working with a partner, compare and contrast permanent botanicals and fresh (living) botanicals. Consider the perspective of the manufacturer/grower, merchandiser, and consumer. In what situations would one product be preferable to the other? Record the key points of your discussion. Hold a class discussion. Compare your responses to those of your classmates.

Dried Botanicals Glossary

The dried botanicals glossary contains materials commonly available on the wholesale market as well as a few products available from local suppliers. To a beginning designer, the wide variety of plant names can be overwhelming. To help you learn both the common names and botanical names, the dried plant materials are alphabetized by the common name used most frequently in the profession and regional locales. The botanical name is listed below the common name and there is a cross-reference chart in the appendix. For the botanical names, major focus is on the Genus name without a specific epithet. Professional florists often use the botanical name as a common name so it is beneficial to learn both. When used in print, the common name is not italicized. *The term botanical name and scientific name may sometimes be used interchangeably. For the sake of consistency, the term botanical name has been used throughout the textbook.*

Go to www.g-wlearning.com/floraldesign/ to use e-flash cards and other activities using the dried botanicals from the illustrated glossary.

AN NGUYEN/Shutterstock.com

Common Name: Austrian Pine Cone
Botanical Name: *Pinus nigra* subsp. *austriaca*

EurngKwan/Shutterstock.com

Common Name: Bamboo, River Cane
Botanical Name: *Phyllostachys* sp.

Susii/Shutterstock.com

Common Name: Billy Balls, Craspedia
Botanical Name: *Craspedia uniflora*

Baisch & Skinner Wholesale, St. Louis MO

Common Name: Birch Branch
Botanical Name: *Betula* sp.

Ignite Lab/Shutterstock.com

Common Name: Bunny Tails
Botanical Name: *Lagurus ovatus*

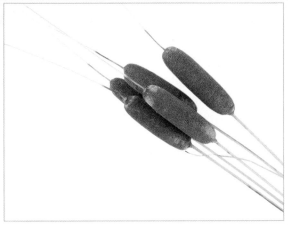

Africa Studio/ Shutterstock.com

Common Name: Cattails
Botanical Name: *Typha* sp.

4Max/Shutterstock.com

Common Name: Chinese Lantern, Physalis
Botanical Name: *Physalis alkekengi*

mladenova/iStock/Thinkstock

Common Name: Cinnamon Sticks
Botanical Name: *Cinnamomum verum*

Baisch & Skinner Wholesale, St. Louis MO

Common Name: Corylus, Contorted Filbert Branch
Botanical Name: *Corylus avellana* 'Contorta'

Discovod/Shutterstock.com

Common Name: Cork
Botanical Name: *Quercus suber*

Images courtesy of Save On Crafts, www.saveoncrafts.com

Common Name: Corkscrew Willow
Botanical Name: *Salix matsudana* 'Tortuosa'

Anna Khomulo/iStock/Thinkstock

Common Name: Cotton
Botanical Name: *Gossypium* sp.

max voran/Shutterstock.com

Common Name: Fountain Grass, Purple
Botanical Name: *Pennisetum setaceum* 'Rubrum'

daizuoxin/iStock/Thinkstock

Common Name: Gomphrena
Botanical Name: *Gomphrena globosa* 'Lavender Lady'

Melinda Fawver/Shutterstock.com

Common Name: Hemlock Cone
Botanical Name: *Tsuga canadensis*

Zoonar RF/Zoonar/Thinkstock

Common Name: Hops
Botanical Name: *Humulus lupulus*

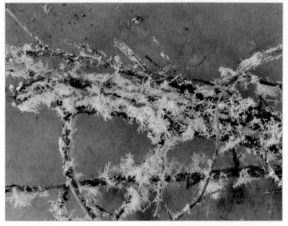

Baisch & Skinner Wholesale, St. Louis MO

Common Name: Lichen Covered Branch, Florist's
Botanical Name: *Usnea* sp.

Melinda Fawver/Shutterstock.com

Common Name: Lichen
Botanical Name: *Hypogymnia* sp.

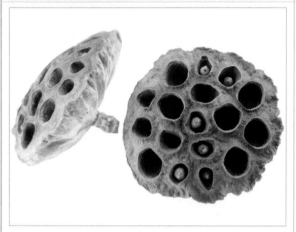

roroto 12p/Shutterstock.com

Common Name: Lotus (large)
Botanical Name: *Nelumbo nucifera*

Medioimages/Photodisc/Thinkstock

Common Name: Lotus (small)
Botanical Name: *Nelumbo nucifera*

Fremme/iStock/ Thinkstock; infinity21/Shutterstock.com

Common Name: Manzanita Branch
Botanical Name: *Arctostaphylos* sp.

Huyangshu/iStock/Thinkstock

Common Name: Millet
Botanical Name: *Setaria* sp.

kamnuan/Shutterstock.com

Common Name: Moss, Florist Sheet
Botanical Name: *Callicladium* sp.

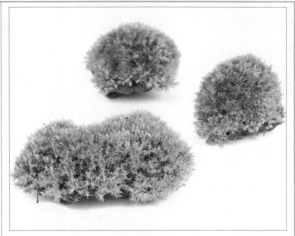

kamnuan/Shutterstock.com

Common Name: Moss, Mood
Botanical Name: *Dicranum* sp.

Madlen/Shutterstock.com

Common Name: Moss, Reindeer
Botanical Name: *Cladina* sp.

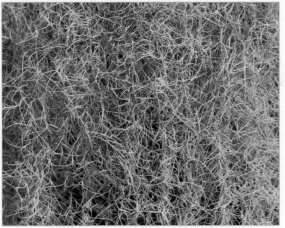

Xerography/Shutterstock.com

Common Name: Moss, Spanish
Botanical Name: *Tillandsia usneoides*

MRS. Siwaporn/Shutterstock.com

Common Name: Okra Pod (dried)
Botanical Name: *Abelmoschus esculentus*

Thilak Piyadigama/iStock/Thinkstock

Common Name: Palmetto Leaf
Botanical Name: *Sabal* sp.

Deyan Georgiev/Shutterstock.com

Common Name: Pampass Grass
Botanical Name: *Cortaderia selloana*

SOMATUSCANI/iStock/Thinkstock

Common Name: Pomegranate
Botanical Name: *Punica* sp.

Coprid/Shutterstock.com

Common Name: Poppy Seed Head
Botanical Name: *Papaver* sp.

2bears/Shutterstock.com

Common Name: Pussy Willow
Botanical Name: *Salix* sp.

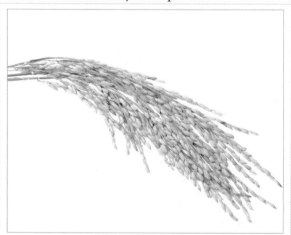

panda3800/Shutterstock.com

Common Name: Rice
Botanical Name: *Oryza sativa*

Eric Krouse/Shutterstock.com

Common Name: Sarracenia, Pitcher Plant
Botanical Name: *Sarracenia* sp.

Common Name: Strawflower
Botanical Name: *Helichrysum* sp.

Common Name: Sugar Cone
Botanical Name: *Pinus taeda*

Common Name: Wheat
Botanical Name: *Triticum* sp.

Common Name: Wheat, Bearded
Botanical Name: *Triticum* sp.

Common Name: White Pine Cone
Botanical Name: *Pinus strobus*

Common Name: Yarrow
Botanical Name: *Achillea* sp.

460

Chapter

17 Maintaining and Decorating Potted Arrangements

objectives

After reading this chapter, you will be able to:

- List the benefits of having living plants indoors.
- Understand the difference between foliage plants, flowering plants, and succulents and cacti.
- Explain how to purchase living plants for resale.
- Describe care and maintenance for tropical plants, succulents, and cacti.
- Identify applications for living plants.
- Design a closed-system or open-system terrarium.
- Create a dish garden.
- Explain the process of acclimation for plants that will be used in areas with low light.

key terms

acclimated	foliage plant	Polyfoil®
all-around design	green wall	pot cover
closed-system terrarium	hardpan	succulent
	interiorscaper	terrarium
dish garden	one-sided design	three-sided design
fairy garden	open-system terrarium	understory plant
flowering plant	planter	volatile organic compound (VOC)

Go to www.g-wlearning.com/floraldesign/ for online vocabulary activities using key terms from the chapter.

introduction

Florists often offer a variety of live plants, and a successful florist uses them in creative ways. The products and services offered by a florist should reflect a wide and varied customer base. To best accommodate such a customer base, you, as a florist, must have a basic understanding of the options available. Giving someone a live plant provides the same joy as giving a cut flower arrangement, whether it's green or blooming, **Figure 17-1**. Therefore, live plants as gift options are an important component of a retail florists' inventory.

GoodMood Photo/Shutterstock.com

Figure 17-1. This bright purple *Cineraria* plant provides a warm welcome.

Benefits of Living Plants

Plants have many benefits to humans. Plants take in carbon dioxide, a necessary component of photosynthesis, and give off pure, clean oxygen. This is the direct opposite of what people do; people take in oxygen and give off carbon dioxide. Because plants produce oxygen and people need oxygen to live, plants and people have an important, ongoing relationship.

Plants can also adjust indoor humidity to comfortable levels between 20% and 60%. This is important because too much humidity encourages mold growth. Too little humidity irritates human nasal passages and can make people more susceptible to infection. Extreme indoor dryness can also damage wood furniture and flooring.

Potted plants have been shown to remove harmful chemicals from the air we breathe. Manufactured products such as carpets, ceiling tiles, floor coverings, paints, particleboard, stains and varnishes, and many other products used and kept indoors give off *volatile organic compounds (VOCs)*. According to the Environmental Protection Agency, repeated or prolonged exposure to some types of VOCs can lead to respiratory irritation, eye irritation, headache, and even memory disorders. Plants take in VOC molecules through leaf stomata and transport them to the root zone. VOCs are also believed to be drawn into the soil by water movement through the soil into root hairs. Within the root zone, living soil microbes use VOCs for food, **Figure 17-2**.

Research has also shown that plants have positive psychological effects on people. For centuries, plants have been given as welcome gifts. They cheer up an interior setting and help people to be more productive.

Apelavi/Shutterstock.com

Figure 17-2. Beneficial soil microbes function in the root zone, aiding in the removal of VOCs.

Types of Floriculture Plants

Most florists carry a selection of potted plants ready for delivery or cash-and-carry sales. These products offer an alternative for clients who do not want cut flowers or arrangements. In earlier days, most florists had their own greenhouses to produce cut flowers and potted plants. With the rise of energy costs, florists found that they could purchase plants wholesale for less than it cost them to grow the plants themselves. Today, most potted plant production occurs in Florida and California. Wholesale florists and greenhouses grow large quantities of hardy, indoor plants and ship them via truck throughout the country, **Figure 17-3**.

Florists classify plants in three broad categories:

- Foliage plants
- Flowering plants
- Succulents and cacti

Pi-Lens/Shutterstock.com

Figure 17-3. A semitruck makes a delivery of greenhouse-grown garden plants to a retail nursery.

Foliage Plants

With the exception of ferns, all indoor plants produce flowers. However, the leaves on many of these plants are more showy and attractive than the flowers. In the floral trade, these are referred to as *foliage plants*, **Figure 17-4**.

Most of the foliage plants that perform well indoors are native to tropical forests. A tropical forest has two basic layers of plants: the treetop layer and the forest floor. *Understory plants* grow on the forest floor, where light does not easily penetrate. Because these understory plants do not need much light, they adapt well to an interior environment. Today's plant breeders continually offer new cultivars with unique and unusual characteristics as options for the consumer.

Did You Know?

Many herbs are interesting foliage plants that have the added advantage of a strong scent. Examples of herbs that can be grown as houseplants include Cuban oregano, sweet bay, and mint.

Moolkum/Shutterstock.com

Figure 17-4. A variety of small green plants in their greenhouse production phase, ready for transplanting to larger pots.

Iakov Filimonov/Shutterstock.com

Figure 17-5. This florist holds a *Cyclamen* plant, which are usually available in the winter and spring.

Flowering Plants

Flowering plants are cultivated and sold because of their showy flowers, **Figure 17-5**. Unlike understory plants, flowering plants need bright light to stay in flower. Even with advances in greenhouse technology, forcing plants, and international shipping, many types of flowering plants are available only during specific seasons. Orchids have become the most popular blooming plant due to their exotic good looks and advances in production techniques. The orchid plants most commonly sold in flower shops are phalaenopsis, dendrobium, and cymbidium species.

Cooler temperatures can prolong the bloom display of flowering plants. Lowering the thermostat even a few degrees can help them stay in flower longer. Spring flowering bulb plants, including tulips, daffodils, hyacinths, Easter lilies, and crocuses can be stored in a florist's cooler for up to two weeks to slow down the blooming process. Even azalea plants can be chilled to slow down the aging process of the flowers.

While flowering plants have more visual impact, foliage plants offer better longevity. A combination of several types can provide a stunning display for both interior and exterior spaces, **Figure 17-6**.

Denise Lett/Shutterstock.com

Figure 17-6. The retail greenhouse display shows the many possibilities for adding color to a home. Spring bulbs, flowering and tropical foliage plants work well together for a strong visual impact.

Succulents and Cacti

Succulents are plants that have thick stems or leaves that can store water. Jade plants and aloe vera are examples of succulents, **Figure 17-7**. Succulents grow in geographic areas where rainfall is low and light intensity is high. The plants use the stored water in times of drought.

Closely related to succulents, cacti are also adapted to life in arid, sunny climates, **Figure 17-8**. Unlike succulents, cacti have spines instead of, or in a few cases in addition to, leaves. Most scientists believe that the spines are modified leaves that have adapted to minimize water loss.

With a large variety of distinct textures and forms, cacti and succulents are popular consumer choices. Cacti and succulents are also commonly used in dish gardens, particularly in warmer climates. Dish gardens are described later in this chapter.

Purchasing Plants

Purchasing healthy plants is key to success. Establishing a good relationship with wholesale growers and distributors is important for acquiring consistently healthy plant material. Different wholesale sources have different strengths so check them out thoroughly. For example, one wholesaler might provide better foliage plants, while another is a good source for succulents. For a florist, finding a wholesale florist greenhouse that provides plant material, from seasonal to standard, and foliage to flowering plants, is a substantial benefit.

Hardin56/iStock/Thinkstock; Akawath/Shutterstock.com

Figure 17-7. Succulent plants can thrive together if placed in full sun and watered when soil becomes dry to the touch.

Did You Know?

Cacti grow natively only in North and South America.

photobac/iStock/Thinkstock

Figure 17-8. Cacti are succulents in the sense that they store water, but horticulturists make a distinction between cacti and other succulent species.

Ingram Publishing/Thinkstock

Figure 17-9. Visiting wholesale growers helps retail buyers see the full range of available plant materials.

Whenever possible, you should visit wholesale operations. This will allow you to see firsthand the various floriculture crops and products available and to choose the best for resale, **Figure 17-9.**

Maintaining Plants

Plants need a certain amount of care whether they are in the flower shop or in the customer's home. Understanding the requirements of individual types of plants for light, water, fertilizer, and other types of general maintenance will help a florist keep plants healthy in the flower shop. When a customer buys a plant, the florist can explain proper care and maintenance.

Light

Most florists purchase their live plants for resale, so their interest is not in producing plants, but in keeping them looking fresh and healthy while on display. Because light is usually the most important factor for healthy indoor plants, it is helpful for florists to understand the three characteristics of light. They are:

- Intensity—the brightness of the light.
- Quality—the colors found in the light.
- Duration—how long the light is available.

Intensity

A window with eastern exposure offers bright, indirect light, and most indoor plants do well in this light intensity, **Figure 17-10.** Western exposures also offer bright light, but the heat energy may overwhelm the plant. Spider plants, hoya, and cactus are good choices for western exposures. Southern exposures offer high light intensity as well as heat energy, so plants that are used to a shady, tropical habitat will not do well. Cacti and succulents do well with southern exposure. Northern exposures are generally dim, but some indoor plants, such as snake plant (sanseviera) and aspidistra, still perform well.

moodboard/moodboard/Thinkstock

Figure 17-10. Bright, but indirect light is best for most indoor plants.

Florist shops without windows must use artificial light. Artificial light can keep plants healthy for extended periods as long as a high enough level of brightness is maintained. See **Figure 17-11**.

Quality

Plants respond best to natural sunlight. For many houseplants, fluorescent tubes provide plenty of light. Both CFL and LED lights are available with different light qualities. You may need to experiment with the various types to determine which type is best for specific types of plants. See **Figure 17-12**.

Duration

Duration is the easiest aspect of light to control. It may not be possible to build a greenhouse or add more windows or skylights, but it is possible to leave lights on in areas of the store where plants are displayed. A longer duration of exposure can compensate for low light intensity.

Water

Watering plants can be tricky. Some people literally drown their plants by overwatering. Roots need a balance between air-filled and water-filled pore spaces. If the soil is constantly wet, roots suffocate. The wet soil environment also invites disease. Other people forget to water their plants, perhaps only watering them when the foliage becomes wilted. An easy test to see if you need to water a plant, is to stick your finger up to the first knuckle into the soil. If any soil particles adhere to your finger when you remove it, the soil contains moisture. If there are no "sticky" particles, it is time to water the plant, **Figure 17-13**.

Take care not to underwater the plant. Allow some water to penetrate throughout the pot so that the entire root ball receives water. However, do not allow plants to stand in water. This is often a problem in flower shops. If the plants stand in water over a long period of time, roots will not survive.

CandyBox Images/Shutterstock.com

Figure 17-11. A good selection of healthy plants can be maintained in a store using artificial light.

AlexMax/istock

Figure 17-12. Choosing the right light quality to provide plants with sufficient artificial light may involve some trial-and-error. Choices include incandescent, compact fluorescent, and LED lightbulbs.

Stephen VanHorn/Shutterstock.com

Figure 17-13. Peace Lily plants wilt if the soil is dry, but may also exhibit wilt if soil remains wet over long periods of time.

Scott Latham/Shutterstock.com

Figure 17-14. Knocking a plant out of its pot will reveal if it is rootbound as seen with this Spider Plant.

Repotting

On occasion, you may need to repot plants that have outgrown their containers, **Figure 17-14**. This may be for a customer, or perhaps a new shipment of plants are top-heavy and ready for repotting. It is good practice to repot a plant in a pot the next size up.

Remove the plant from the old pot and remove and hardpan that has formed. *Hardpan* is hardened organic material on top of the soil that obstructs drainage. Gently tease the soil ball, especially on the top and bottom edges, to loosen the roots. Place some fresh potting mix in the bottom of the new container. Place the plant in the container, centering the root ball and shoots. Then add soil to the sides and top. Gently tamp soil around the sides and top of the root ball. Leave a space between the top of the soil line and the rim of the pot to accommodate watering without spilling. Finally, water the plant thoroughly and allow it to drain. Repeat the watering process to ensure roots have proper moisture to acclimate to the new soil environment. See **Figure 17-15**.

Cleaning

In the rainforest, where many foliage plants originate, rainwater keeps the foliage clean. Plants in a greenhouse may be watered with a hose to simulate rainfall and clean the foliage, however, this method is impractical

Tyler Olson/Shutterstock.com

Figure 17-15. Water newly potted plants until the water runs through the pot drainage holes.

to use in a flower shop. Instead, use a water-moistened, soft towel to clean leaves. Depending on the number of plants you need to clean, this method can take a considerable amount of time and labor, **Figure 17-16**.

Some florists use leaf shine products to provide a glossy finish. Leaf shines do not remove dirt and residue, but coat the leaf with oil. Using leaf shines once or twice when preparing a plant for delivery will not harm it, but repeated use will block the leaf stomata, preventing gas exchange, which is unhealthy for the plant.

Fertilizer

Florists rarely, if ever, use fertilizers because they do not hold plants very long before selling them. *Interiorscapers* sometimes use fertilizers, but only when plants are displayed in areas with high light intensity because these plants are actively growing, producing new roots and leaves. As an interiorscaper, you may use a light fertilizer program in the spring and summer when plants are doing most of their growing. Keep in mind however, that fertilizers encourage growth. If a plant is being maintained at an appropriate size, fertilizers may cause the plant to grow enough to need repotting or even replacement. The goal of interiorscaping is not necessarily new growth, but continual maintenance of a healthy appearance, **Figure 17-17**. Interiorscaping is described in more detail later in this chapter.

Maintenance

Customers may ask for advice when selecting a plant for indoor use. Before recommending a plant, you should first ask them about the type of light exposure the plant will have. Ask them if there are any drafts from exterior doors and if there is a heating/cooling vent nearby that would blow air directly on the plant. You may also want to ask if they prefer a very low-maintenance type of plant. Once you have your answers, you can more readily recommend a plant that will thrive in its environment.

Africa Studio/Shutterstock.com; Olinchuk/Shutterstock.com

Figure 17-16. Avoid getting water on leaves or using leaf shine on fuzzy-leaved plants like African Violets. A damp towel may be used to clean plants with large, smooth leaves.

Foto_by_M/iStock/Thinkstock

Figure 17-17. These plants provide a curtain of green for office windows.

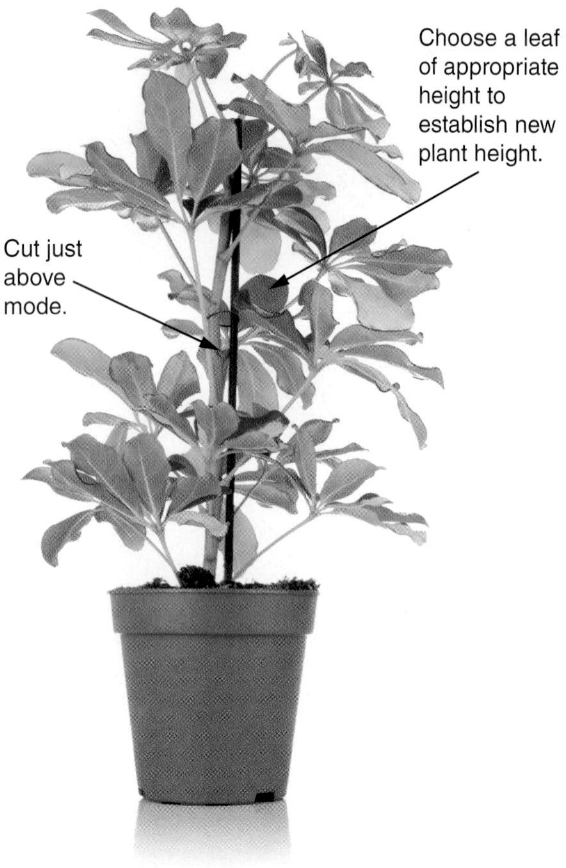

Choose a leaf of appropriate height to establish new plant height.

Cut just above mode.

HomeArt/Shutterstock.com

Figure 17-18. If a plant becomes too leggy, or elongated, trim it to the node nearest to a leaf of appropriate height. The plant above is staked because it is top-heavy. Cutting the plant down will encourage branching to fill out the plant and make it more balanced. Pruning to an outward facing leaf or node will encourage outward growth.

Much of the time, there is not enough light in a home or business to keep a plant looking greenhouse healthy. To avoid this problem, encourage customers to select plants that tolerate low light levels. Also, explain to customers that they should monitor plant locations throughout the day for unexpected shadowing that could minimize a plants' light exposure. Like most indoor environments, light levels are diminished so active plant growth is typically slower, minimizing fertilizer applications.

Whenever a customer buys a live plant, attach a care tag that explains how to maintain the plant. By giving the customer the information necessary to keep the plant healthy, you increase customer satisfaction with the plant and with your flower shop.

Pruning Tropical Plants

Pruning is done for aesthetics and to control growth. As tropical plants begin to grow or elongate, a more compact appearance may be desired or needed. As a guide, trim plants just above the growth node to encourage new branching, **Figure 17-18**. On larger stalks of plant material, such as *Schefflera amate*, an entire stalk may be cut to a short height to encourage the growth of new stems on either side of the main stalk. For pruning more compact plants, such as *Schefflera arboricola*, stagger cuts throughout, maintaining the plant's desired shape. As stated earlier, make sure cuttings are made just above the nodes. Cutting below the nodes will result in leafless stems. For best results, before pruning any plant, do some research to learn its growth patterns and how best to prune it.

Insects and Plant Disease

Florists usually do not have to contend with insect or disease problems associated with indoor plants. U.S. growers are known for producing quality potted plant materials, free of insects and disease. However, insect-infested or diseased plants may occasionally appear in the flower shop.

Insect Control

The best way to control insects is prevention. Florists should inspect every new shipment of fresh potted plants. The most common indoor insect pests are aphids, mealybugs, whiteflies, scale, and spider mites. Most insects are not easily seen, so it is important to inspect the undersides of leaves, leaf axils, and stems. Today's earth-friendly methods of insect removal involve manually removing insects using a cotton swab and water or strong blasts of water. If the plant is completely infested, it should be discarded.

Disease Control

Plant diseases are tricky because they are difficult, if not impossible, to find until the plant is severely affected. Again, prevention is key. Do not overwater indoor plants, and do not allow them to stand in water. As with humans, plants are more susceptible to disease when they are under stress. Over watering or under watering plants, especially on a consistent basis, make plants more vulnerable to insects and disease.

Applications

Potted plants are used for many different purposes in and around homes, offices, hotels, and other buildings. Understanding the many applications for potted plants can help the florist maximize sales and customer satisfaction.

Garden Plants

Some florists offer arrangements in hanging baskets and planters for use on a customer's porch or patio. They combine annual plants based on color, form and texture to create pleasing displays, just as with cut flower designs, **Figure 17-19**. These arrangements are seasonal in warmer climates, offered in the spring months when danger of frost is no longer an issue. Colorful hanging plants are often sold as floral gifts for Easter and Mother's Day.

Ornamental Plants

Plants are sold and displayed in numerous ways to enhance and blend with indoor décor or to express a theme. They provide focal points on tabletops and within rooms. A basic presentation of a potted plant includes a foil wrapping or simple, woven basket and bow. Some florists make creative presentations with potted plants, placing them in various types of decorative containers and adding festive decorative details, **Figure 17-20**. An interesting design can consist of seasonal elements and a contemporary container.

V.J. Matthew/Shutterstock.com

Figure 17-19. Mixed patio planters are popular springtime gifts, especially for Mother's Day.

Julia Zakharova/Shutterstock.com

Figure 17-20. This lavender Campanula plant has added value in a decorated ceramic pot.

Figure 17-25. A well-constructed dish garden has a variety of shapes and textures to hold the viewer's interest. They may contain tall, medium and short or trailing plant materials.

Figure 17-26. This succulent planter would last for an extended period indoors in a southern or western window. Another option its recipient would have is to keep it outdoors in full sun between frost dates.

Dish Gardens

Small plants have more impact when they are grouped together in a single container. The variation of sizes, patterns, and textures make these *dish gardens*, or *planters*, an interesting, long-lasting choice for customers. See **Figure 17-25**.

Typically, dish gardens do not have drainage holes, so that the customer will not have to worry about ruining furniture or the area where the dish garden will be placed. When selling a dish garden, therefore, it is important to educate the customer about proper watering in limited drainage areas.

Making a Dish Garden

When making a dish garden, use a container that is waterproof or that has a waterproof liner. Durable vinyl and glazed ceramic containers are both good choices. Baskets with waterproof liners also make good strong dish garden containers. It is also necessary to use a liner with a metal container if the container has seams. The joining area may appear to be watertight, but it is most likely not and will require a liner.

If a plastic liner is not available, designers sometimes use *Polyfoil*® to make custom-fitted inserts. Polyfoil consists of two layers, one of aluminum foil and the second of plastic film. To ensure durability and the maintenance of a leak-proof liner, many designers use multiple layers of Polyfoil® if there is a possibility that sharp materials may damage the lining.

Planters can be decorative on all sides, suitable for display in the middle of a space, or they can be made for display against a wall. Designs made for the center of a space are *all-around designs*, while those that have a definite back side are called *one-sided designs* or *three-sided designs*. In all-around designs, the taller plants are placed in the middle, with medium and shorter plants at the edges of the container. In three-sided designs, tall plants are placed at the back, the medium plants next, and gradually shorter plants toward the front, with cascading or ground-cover types at the front rim of the container. See **Figure 17-26**.

Making a European Dish Garden

Recall from Chapter 15 that a European dish garden is one that includes flowering plants as well as foliage plants. Unlike the plants in traditional dish gardens, the plants in European dish gardens are usually left in their individual pots.

Step-by-Step

Creating a Dish Garden

The same principles and elements used when creating a floral design apply to dish gardens when selecting materials. Choose elements for dish gardens according to qualities such as form, size, color, and texture. Begin by selecting plant material according to design character color shape, as with creating a floral design.

For this project you will need a decorative container, a liner (if necessary or desired), three or four watered plants, soil, soilless media (soilless potting mix, small pebbles, foam shipping peanuts), decorative stones or moss, twigs, and a decorative accent (optional).

1
To prevent the roots from sitting in pooled water or extremely wet soil, place the soilless media in the bottom of the container or liner. When floral designers create custom dish gardens, they may start off with layers of washed gravel and horticultural grade charcoal, as when making a terrarium. However, these steps are often omitted. The container may be shallow, limiting the amount of soil necessary to sustain plant root health. Most commercial planters do not have these layers, and this is considered standard practice.

2
Remove the plastic pots from the plants by gently pulling the pot off while holding the plant where it meets the top of the soil. Check for healthy roots. Roots should be firm, not brown and mushy.

3
Place your plants in the container and add soil around the plants. Press the soil down gently to secure the plants in place, leaving enough room for watering.

4
Lightly cover the soil with rock, bark, or moss.

Step-by-Step

Creating a European Dish Garden

For this project you will need four or five potted plants (4"–6" pots), a basket with a liner, dry floral foam, a wood pick, ribbon for a bow, wire (#26 or #28 gauge), an accent piece, scissors, dry moss, water, dry branches, and a decorative accent.

It is important to use a basket with a liner so water will not run out.

Choose plants that are in a minimum of a 4" pot. The plants will be staying in their individual pots so to keep them from drying out too quickly, 4"–6" pots work best, depending on the overall size of the basket. Consider the heights of the plants, as well as a variety of colors.

1

Begin by placing the tallest plant toward the back of the basket, then work forward and to the side placing plants in a stair stepping fashion so one plant does not block another. You may need to use the dry foam as risers to vary the plant heights. You may also use the dry foam in between plants to keep them spaced properly. Styrofoam is an ideal material for this because it is lightweight and stable, and does not absorb water.

2

Cover the different pots with moss so the design appears as a single garden. Decorate the basket with branches and an accent piece such as a bird or a bow.

3

If you are adding a bow, attach it to a wood pick and insert it in the soil of one of the plants so it will not fall out.

Decorating Premade Planters

Many wholesale growers create dish gardens and sell them to retail florists. Florists often add finishing touches, such as ribbon bows, seasonal trims, or even fresh flowers in water tubes, before offering them for sale.

Fairy gardens are dish gardens with miniature landscapes. They are completed with the small-scale furniture, figurines, and other accessories that emphasize the fairy theme, **Figure 17-27.** Seemingly simple, fairy gardens take practice, thought, and the right materials in order to achieve the appropriate scale.

Holiday Plants

Specific plants are associated with holiday decorations and gifts by long-standing tradition. **Figure 17-28** lists potted plants that are popular for various holidays. However, because design is dynamic and tastes change, many people look for new and unusual holiday designs. People often want color schemes far from the traditional red and green and may choose complementary or monochromatic colors.

Green Walls

Green walls are becoming more popular as people are more aware of their own carbon footprints. *Green walls* are covered partly or entirely with living plants. They serve as air filters and as art. They may be used indoor or for covering the exterior side of a building. Artists use the plants to create abstract patterns, images, or even corporate logos.

Techniques used to hold the plants in place range from rather simple methods to very complicated methods requiring specialized watering techniques and avid maintenance. The simplest method displays potted plants on an angled frame. These structures allow swift installation or replacement of plants, as needed. The plants may be watered manually from above or with capillary mat strips connecting the root ball to a water reservoir. The plants do not remain in water, but are connected to the watering system which provides a slow and even flow of water.

Warren Price Photography/Shutterstock.com

Figure 17-27. Plant stores and florists may stock small accessories to suit the scale of fairy gardens and terrariums.

Plants for Holidays	
Valentine's Day	Red-, white-, or pink-blooming plants such as Cyclamen, Orchids, Tulip, Miniature Rose, or Kalanchoe
St. Patrick's Day	Oxalis, Shamrock
Easter	Easter lily, Azalea, Hyacinth, Tulip, mixed-bulb dish gardens
Mother's Day	Hydrangea, Miniature rose, Oriental Lily, Geranium, Kalanchoe, Orchids
Thanksgiving	Chrysanthemum
Christmas	Poinsettia, Paperwhite Narcissus, Amaryllis, Cyclamen, Christmas Cactus

Goodheart-Willcox Publisher

Figure 17-28. Plants associated with various holidays.

Step-by-Step

Adding Flowers to Planters

A planter is a collection of plants put together in a decorative container, often a glaze ceramic. Fresh or silk flowers may be added to give the planter added interest and color. If adding fresh flowers, choose flowers that are long-lasting and are in proportion with the size of the planter.

For this project you will need a planter with plants, four to six burgundy carnations, three salmon-colored carnations, a water tube (with pointed bottom) for each carnation stem, water, a floral knife, and any accent pieces you will be using. If you are using silk flowers, you will need wood picks to use as extensions before placing the flower in the planter.

1

First, fill the water tubes with fresh water. You may use water with floral food. Make a fresh cut on each flower before placing them into the water tubes.

2

Once the flowers are in the water tubes, place them securely into the planter.

If you are adding silk flowers to a planter, add a wood pick extension to each stem before placing it in the planter.

3

Complete the planter with a bird or a bow if desired.

4

Some green walls use foam substrates rather than soil. Plants are removed from their grow pots and inserted into slits in pliable foam. These walls have trickle irrigation systems to keep roots moist, **Figure 17-29**. Every type of vertical wall system has positive and negative attributes. Desired visual effect, maintenance needs and growing climate will determine the most appropriate application.

Interiorscaping

Some flower shops offer the design, installation, and maintenance of indoor plants. This requires significant time and effort and is usually a separate department within a company, **Figure 17-30**. Interiorscapers may work with interior designers and architects to create plant placement and displays that will work with the architecture and décor. Some interiorscapers work independently. They may have their own greenhouse or they may contract with a grower. As a self-employed interiorscaper, you would contract with offices and other businesses to maintain and/or replace plant materials throughout the year.

Interiorscapers work with plant materials that have been *acclimated*, or *acclimatized*. Acclimated plants have been placed in successively lower light intensities until they are able to remain healthy in the light levels commonly found in offices and similar commercial environments. It takes longer to produce an acclimated plant, but as a result of this process, the plant stays healthier longer. Its initial cost is higher, but in the long run, it does not need to be replaced as soon as a non-acclimated plant.

Suriyun/Shutterstock.com

Figure 17-29. Green walls are often used to add natural foliage to urban areas. They are also used in office buildings for their beauty and air purification abilities.

cycreation/Shutterstock.com; Jeffery Coleman/Shutterstock.com

Figure 17-30. Indoor plants brighten the work environment and have been proven to boost productivity by providing air purification. A lush and elegant flower garden adds color to the room and the atrium of this exquisite hotel.

Summary

- Plants have many health benefits for humans.
- Florists classify plants in three broad categories: foliage plants, blooming plants, and succulents and cacti.
- Most of the foliage plants that perform well indoors are native to tropical forests, where they grow in dappled sunlight.
- Flowering plants are cultivated and sold because of their showy flowers.
- Florists should seek various sources of potted plants for retail sales.
- Light is usually the most important factor for healthy indoor plants.
- Terrariums consist of a container, usually made of glass, that houses one or more live plants.
- Small plants have more impact when grouped together in a single container, making planters or dish gardens a long-lasting choice for customers.
- Green walls and similar constructions allow plants to grow on walls.
- Interiorscapers install plants to suit the needs of the indoor space and the customer's vision.

Review Questions

Go to www.g-wlearning.com/floraldesign/ to use the fill-in-form.

Answer the following questions using the information provided in this chapter.

1. What important relationship exists between people and plants?
2. What are volatile organic compounds?
3. List the three broad categories of plants sold by florists.
4. What is the difference between a foliage plant and a flowering plant?
5. Name two examples of succulent plants.
6. What are the three characteristics of light that affect plant growth and care?
7. For best light exposure, which way should the front display windows of a flower shop face?
8. What happens to a potted plant if the soil is constantly saturated with water?
9. What is the best way to clean the leaves of a plant?
10. Why should many customers be encouraged to purchase plants that tolerate low light levels?
11. Explain how to help prevent disease in potted plants.
12. *True or False?* Compact plants should be pruned by cutting all the stems to the same height in the desired shape.
13. What is the difference between a closed-system terrarium and an open-system terrarium?
14. What is the purpose of the gravel and charcoal placed in the bottom of a terrarium?
15. What special instructions should be given to a customer who purchases a dish garden without drainage holes?
16. Explain how the plants are arranged in an all-around dish garden.
17. What makes a fairy garden different from other dish gardens?
18. What is a green wall?
19. Explain what an interiorscaper does.
20. Briefly describe the process of acclimating plants.

Activities

1. Using your school's greenhouse, propagate plants suitable for a terrarium.
2. Bring a glass container from home. Use the container to lay out and plant a terrarium using the procedure described in this chapter.

3. Visit local florists and garden centers, noting the date and the types of plants used in dish gardens. Analyze the design of each dish garden. What was the designer's intent? For example, was the planter created with a seasonal theme? Discuss the meaning of each plant or planter.

4. Exchange design portfolios with a classmate. Study the formal qualities of your classmate's portfolio and identify any historical or cultural contexts in individual items. Write a summary statement describing the intent and meaning of at least one item in the portfolio.

5. Select a planter or terrarium created by a classmate. Analyze the design to determine its formal qualities. Does the design have any cultural or historical meaning or context? Does it have any special meaning? What was your classmate's intent in creating the design?

6. Create a dish garden using the procedure described in this chapter.

Critical Thinking

1. A customer is buying a pair of hanging baskets from your flower shop for his front porch. The baskets are nicely balanced now, but he wants the ivy in the baskets to grow and cascade down from the hanging baskets. He asks you what fertilizer he should use to make the ivy grow rapidly. What should you tell him?

2. Three weeks ago, a customer purchased a potted petunia plant at your flower shop. Today, the customer returns with the plant, which is in poor shape. The leaves are wilted, even though the customer states that she has watered the plant every day. The leaves and stalks are an unhealthy-looking light greenish-yellow color. The customer claims that you sold her a "sick plant" and wants her money back. How will you handle this situation?

3. You have just received a shipment of fresh potted plants and notice what appears to be spider mite damage on several of the plants. What steps would you take to make a positive identification of the pest? What steps would you take to manage the pests and prevent infestation of your current inventory?

STEM Activities and Academics

1. **Science.** Search online to find the latest research regarding how plants improve human health. Prepare a multimedia presentation to explain your findings.

2. **Technology.** Investigate the trickle irrigation systems used in some green walls and commercial interiorscapes. Explain how this technology evolved and how it makes plant care easier.

3. **Engineering.** Choose an office or small company in your area. With the permission of the owner or manager, create a plan for an interiorscape for the reception area or showroom of the company. Explain to the owner or manager why you made the choices reflected on your plan.

4. **Math.** Visit the websites of several online wholesale florists or growers. Record the name of each company and the price of each of the following plants: peace lily, English ivy, and geranium. If the plants are offered in different sizes, record the price for each size. Then create a chart showing this information. Include a column in the chart to show the average price for each type and size of plant.

Communicating about Floral Design

1. **Reading and Listening.** In small groups, discuss the main topics in the chapter. Ask questions of other group members to clarify concepts or terms as needed.

2. **Reading and Speaking.** In small groups, discuss the illustrations in chapters. Describe, in your own words, what is being shown in each illustration. Discuss the effectiveness of the illustrations compared to the text description.

Potted Plants Glossary

Whether you are creating a small scale terrarium or designing the floral and plant décor for a large event, a host of potted plant materials are available. In addition to everyday plants, tropical foliage plants and an assortment of blooming potted plants are commercially grown specifically for holidays or for other special events throughout the calendar year. This illustrated glossary highlights the most common materials available today. As a floral designer, you will often be asked about green and flowering plants for the home. To better assist your customers, you should become familiar with the names and availability of these plants and know how to care for them.

To help you learn both the common names and botanical names, the plants are alphabetized by the common name used most frequently in the profession. The botanical name is listed below the common name and there is a cross-reference chart in the appendix. For the botanical names, major focus is on the Genus name without a specific epithet. Professional florists often use the botanical name as a common name so it is beneficial to learn both. When used in print, the common name is not italicized. *The term botanical name and scientific name may sometimes be used interchangeably. For the sake of consistency, the term botanical name has been used throughout the textbook.*

Go to www.g-wlearning.com/floraldesign/ to use e-flash cards and other activities using the potted plants from the illustrated glossary.

Tharakorn Arunothai/Shutterstock.com

Common Name: African Clubmoss, Selaginella
Botanical Name: *Selaginella kraussiana*

godrick/Shutterstock.com

Common Name: African Violet
Botanical Name: *Saintpaulia* sp.

Baisch & Skinner Wholesale, St. Louis MO

Common Name: Agave
Botanical Name: *Agave* sp.

Baisch & Skinner Wholesale, St. Louis MO

Common Name: Aglaonema
Botanical Name: *Aglaonema commutatum*

camelia/Shutterstock.com

Common Name: Aloe Vera
Botanical Name: *Aloe vera*

Steshkin Yevgenly/Shutterstock.com

Common Name: Aphelandra, Zebra Plant
Botanical Name: *Aphelandra squarrosa*

Baisch & Skinner Wholesale, St. Louis MO

Common Name: Areca Palm
Botanical Name: *Chrysalidocarpus lutescens*

Madlen/Shutterstock.com

Common Name: Azalea, Florist's
Botanical Name: *Rhododendron* sp.

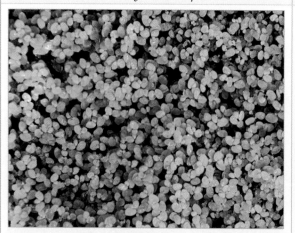

Jahina_Photography/Shutterstock.com

Common Name: Baby's Tears, Mother of Thousands
Botanical Name: *Soleirolia soleirolii*

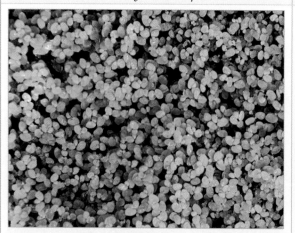

Sakonboon Sansri/Shutterstock.com

Common Name: Bamboo Palm, Lady Palm
Botanical Name: *Rhapis excelsa*

saiko3p/Shutterstock.com

Common Name: Barrel Cactus
Botanical Name: *Echinocactus* sp.

Hvoya/Shutterstock.com

Common Name: Begonia, Iron Cross
Botanical Name: *Begonia masoniana*

Jiri Sebesta/Shutterstock.com

Common Name: Begonia, Rex
Botanical Name: *Begonia Rex-cultorum*

Baisch & Skinner Wholesale, St. Louis MO

Common Name: Begonia, Reiger
Botanical Name: *Begonia x semperflorens-cultorum*

Pekka Nikonen/Shutterstock.com

Common Name: Boston Fern
Botanical Name: *Nephrolepis exaltata*
'Bostoniensis'

Shebeko/Shutterstock.com

Common Name: Bromeliad, Aechmea
Botanical Name: *Aechmea fasciata*

Baisch & Skinner Wholesale, St. Louis MO

Common Name: Burro Tail, Panda Plant
Botanical Name: *Sedum morganianum*

arka38/Shutterstock.com

Common Name: Cactus, Opuntia
Botanical Name: *Opuntia* sp.

Susii/Shutterstock.com

Common Name: Calla
Botanical Name: *Zantedeschia* sp.

Jiri Sebesta/Shutterstock.com

Common Name: Cast Iron Plant, Bar Room Plant
Botanical Name: *Aspidistra elatior*

Irina Borsuchenko/Shutterstock.com

Common Name: Century Plant
Botanical Name: *Agave* sp.

ying/Shutterstock.com

Common Name: Christmas Cactus
Botanical Name: *Zygocactus* sp.

StevenRussellSmithPhotos/Shutterstock.com

Common Name: Clematis
Botanical Name: *Clematis* sp.

S1001/Shutterstock.com

Common Name: Coleus
Botanical Name: *Solenostemon scutellarioides*

Sombat Khamin/Shutterstock.com

Common Name: Creeping Fig
Botanical Name: *Ficus pumila*

Baisch & Skinner Wholesale, St. Louis MO

Common Name: Croton, 'Icetone'
Botanical Name: *Codiaeum variegatum* 'Icetone'

Baisch & Skinner Wholesale, St. Louis MO

Common Name: Croton, 'Red Bananas'
Botanical Name: *Codiaeum variegatum* 'Red Bananas'

WM_idea/Shutterstock.com

Common Name: Dieffenbachia, Dumb Cane
Botanical Name: *Dieffenbachia* sp.

Missouri Botanical Garden

Common Name: Holly Fern
Botanical Name: *Cyrtomium* sp.

Amy Tseng/Shutterstock.com

Common Name: Hosta, Variegated
Botanical Name: *Hosta* sp.

Zygotehaasnobrain/Shutterstock.com

Common Name: Inch Plant
Botanical Name: *Callisia repens*

cynoclub/Shutterstock.com

Common Name: Ivy Geranium
Botanical Name: *Pelargonium peltatum*

LiKar/Shutterstock.com

Common Name: Jade Plant, Dollar Plant
Botanical Name: *Crassula argentea*

Smit/Shutterstock.com

Common Name: Japanese Aralia
Botanical Name: *Fatshedera* sp.

inxti/Shutterstock.com

Common Name: Kalanchoe
Botanical Name: *Kalanchoe* sp.

irabel8/Shutterstock.com

Common Name: Kentia Palm, Thatch Palm
Botanical Name: *Howea forsteriana*

Scisetti Alfio/Shutterstock.com

Common Name: Maidenhair Fern
Botanical Name: *Adiantum raddianum*

Common Name: Money Plant
Botanical Name: *Lunaria* sp.

knin/Shutterstock.com

Baisch & Skinner Wholesale, St. Louis MO

Common Name: Nandina, Green
Botanical Name: *Nandina domestica*

vlabo/Shutterstock.com

Common Name: Nephthytis
Botanical Name: *Syngonium* sp

Melica/Shutterstock.com

Common Name: Nerve Plant
Botanical Name: *Fittonia* sp.

Missouri Botanical Garden

Common Name: Norfolk Island Pine
Botanical Name: *Araucaria heterophylla*

Baisch & Skinner Wholesale, St. Louis MO

Common Name: Parlor Palm
Botanical Name: *Chamaedorea elegans*

WathanyuSowong/Shutterstock.com

Common Name: Peporomia, Emerald Ripple
Peperomia
Botanical Name: *Peperomia* sp.

IakovFilimonov/Shutterstock.com

Common Name: Peporomia obtusifolia
Botanical Name: *Peperomia* sp.

Missouri Botanical Garden

Common Name: Philodendron
Botanical Name: *Schindapsus* sp.

Pinon Road/Shutterstock.com

Common Name: Philodendron
Botanical Name: *Philodendron* sp.

Waddell Images/Shutterstock.com

Common Name: Philodendron Monstera
Botanical Name: *Monstera deliciosa*

41390509/Shutterstock.com

Common Name: Philodendron Selloum
Botanical Name: *Philodendron* sp.

Baisch & Skinner Wholesale, St. Louis MO

Common Name: Phoenix, Pygmy Date Palm
Botanical Name: *Phoenix roebelenii*

EurngKwan/Shutterstock.com

Common Name: Pilea, Aluminum Plant
Botanical Name: *Pilea cadierei*

Missouri Botanical Garden

Common Name: Pilea, Artillery Plant
Botanical Name: *Pilea microphylla*

julie deshaies/Shutterstock.com

Common Name: Polka Dot Plant
Botanical Name: *Hypoestes* sp.

Steshkin Yevgenly/Shutterstock.com

Common Name: Ponytail Palm
Botanical Name: *Beaucarnea recurvata*

Baisch & Skinner Wholesale, St. Louis MO

Common Name: Pothos
Botanical Name: *Epipremnum* sp.

Baisch & Skinner Wholesale, St. Louis MO

Common Name: Pothos, Devil's Ivy
Botanical Name: *Epipremnum* sp.

Missouri Botanical Garden

Common Name: Prayer Plant
Botanical Name: *Maranta leuconeura var. kerchoviana*

matka_Wariatka/Shutterstock.com

Common Name: Primrose
Botanical Name: *Primula* sp.

hd connelly/Shutterstock.com

Common Name: Purple Passion, Velvet Plant
Botanical Name: *Gynura aurantiaca* 'Sarmentosa'

Missouri Botanical Garden

Common Name: Rabbit's Foot Fern
Botanical Name: *Davallia fejeensis*

schab/Shutterstock.com

Common Name: Rosemary
Botanical Name: *Rosmarinus* sp.

Melica/Shutterstock.com

Common Name: Schefflera, Umbrella Plant
Botanical Name: *Schefflera arboricola*

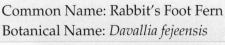

Baisch & Skinner Wholesale, St. Louis MO

Common Name: Sansevieria, Mother-in-Law
Tongue
Botanical Name: *Sansevieria* sp.

Baisch & Skinner Wholesale, St. Louis MO

Common Name: Sansevieria, Mother-in-Law
Tongue
Botanical Name: *Sansevieria* sp.

Baisch & Skinner Wholesale, St. Louis MO

Common Name: Sansevieria, Mother-in-Law Tongue
Botanical Name: *Sansevieria* sp.

Boyan Dimitrov/Shutterstock.com

Common Name: Spathiphyllum, White Anthurium, Peace Lily
Botanical Name: *Spathiphyllum* sp.

Baisch & Skinner Wholesale, St. Louis MO

Common Name: Spider Plant, Airplane Plant
Botanical Name: *Cholorphytum cosmosum*

joloei/Shutterstock.com

Common Name: Staghorn Fern
Botanical Name: *Platycerium bifurcatum*

limn/Shutterstock.com

Common Name: Strawberry Plant
Botanical Name: *Saxifraga stolonifera*

Mamuka Gotsiridze/Shutterstock.com

Common Name: Tradescantia, Purple Wandering Jew
Botanical Name: *Tradescantia pallida*

sritangphoto/Shutterstock.com

Common Name: Umbrella Fern
Botanical Name: *Sticherus* sp.

Fradkin Victoria/Shutterstock.com

Common Name: Wax Plant
Botanical Name: *Hoya carnosa*

tepic/iStock/Thinkstock

Common Name: Yucca, Spanish Dagger
Botanical Name: *Yucca* sp.

Gaby Kooijman/Shutterstock.com

Common Name: Zebra Cactus, Haworthia
Botanical Name: *Haworthia fasciata*

fotoknips/Shutterstock.com

Common Name: Zebra Grass
Botanical Name: *Miscanthus sinensis* 'Zebrinus'

Pekka Nikonen/Shutterstock.com

Common Name: ZZ Plant, Zanzibar Gem
Botanical Name: *Zamioculcas zamiifolia*

Chapter

18 Floriculture Marketing, Pricing, and Sales

objectives

After reading this chapter, you will be able to:

- Explain general principles of financial management.
- Identify methods of purchasing stock that help keep costs at a minimum.
- Calculate retail prices for flower shop merchandise.
- List factors that must be included when estimating and planning wedding flowers.
- Plan a marketing strategy for a flower shop.
- Summarize types of sales in a typical flower shop.

key terms

accounting
assembly line
capital
cash flow
certified public
   accountant (CPA)
cost of goods sold
demographic

financial management
impulse sale
inventory
marketing
marketing plan
markup
markup factor
mass production

operating expense
overhead
preorder
retail price
sales goal
start-up capital
walk-in sale

Go to www.g-wlearning.com/floraldesign/ for online vocabulary activities using key terms from the chapter.

introduction

Flower shops may sell many different types of products and services, depending on the business niche they are trying to fill. Examples include businesses that sell a combination of giftware items and flowers, as well as nurseries that sell landscape materials along with cut flowers. Because of the perishable nature of their products, florists must have the business skills necessary to purchase and sell stock with a minimum of product loss, **Figure 18-1**.

General Retail Operations

The day-to-day operations of a flower shop are the responsibility of the shop's owner or manager. These responsibilities include managing finances, purchasing stock, controlling inventory, and setting the prices for products and services.

Financial Management and Accounting

Some florists believe that a strong designer can successfully run a business without understanding the "business end" of owning a flower shop. Unfortunately, without business skills, flower shop owners rarely succeed. A combination of artistic and financial skill sets is absolutely required for success. An understanding of basic accounting terms and operations is necessary. If the florist does not have financial experience, he or she should seek training or hire an employee who understands financial management.

Vaclav Mach/Shutterstock.com

Figure 18-1. Small, flowering plants, especially the Primrose on the front edge of this display, must sell relatively quickly, when they are at their peak of blooming.

Financial management includes controlling costs, planning purchases, and pricing products correctly. It also includes general *accounting*, which involves keeping records of all costs, expenses, and sales; creating business reports; paying state and local sales taxes, as well as any applicable federal taxes. It is imperative that timely and accurate records be kept by flower shops. Many flower shops hire a *certified public accountant (CPA)* for accounting assistance, **Figure 18-2**. The cost is usually worth the investment, especially if the florist has few business skills.

Capital and Cash Flow

Every company needs *capital*, or money to support its day-to-day operations. A flower shop must have money available to purchase products, pay suppliers, and cover expenses, including payroll. Unless the owner has enough *start-up capital* to cover the initial costs of setting up the business, he or she usually obtains a loan for start-up expenses. The monthly payments on this loan then become part of the shop's overhead expenses. These expenses are described later in this chapter.

When the new flower shop begins making sales, it generates income. *Cash flow* is the income generated by sales in a specific time period, usually a quarter (three months) or a year. This money provides the operating capital for the business.

Since the floral business is centered around holiday sales and special events, cash flow may be slim at times. The term "feast or famine" applies to the income of a flower shop. Sales and income generation are highest for retail flower shops from October through May. The holiday season begins just before Halloween and includes Thanksgiving, Christmas, New Year's Day, and Valentine's day. Spring follows, with excellent floral opportunities from Easter, proms, graduations, and Mother's Day. Summer, on the other hand, contains few major holidays, and sales are typically much weaker. Most florists look for ways to generate income during the slow summer months. See **Figure 18-3**.

Specialty or niche florists—for example, event or wedding florists—often have a more steady cash flow. They can manage the amount of staffing and materials required to accommodate their preplanned occasions. Traditional flower shops that deal with unexpected daily orders, like that of sympathy design work, require

Dusit/Shutterstock.com

Figure 18-2. Your certified public accountant knows all of the latest tax laws and has a firm understanding of the basics of accounting practices.

coronado/Shutterstock.com

Figure 18-3. Many types of floral crops are abundant in the summer, but there are no major floral holidays during this season. Lower demand and greater supply drives price down.

strong management to fulfill those needs of production while keeping their overhead costs at the minimum. Constant review of financial goals and operational plans for the business is required in order to be successful.

Operating Expenses

A flower shop has many *operating expenses*, including *overhead* as well as stock purchases. Overhead expenses include:

- Rent or mortgage payment
- Insurance (both property insurance and liability insurance)
- Utilities (water, gas, electricity)

Depending on the size of the flower shop, employee salaries may make up a large part of the shop's monthly expenses, **Figure 18-4**.

Cost of goods sold is the price you paid for the items you are selling, plus any cost associated with owning that product until it is sold. In the floriculture industry, this includes the cost to keep plants healthy or to keep cut flowers fresh. It is important to track these costs because your products must be priced to cover them and still make a profit.

Purchasing

The shop's profit is greatly affected by purchasing decisions. Smart merchandise buying, along with good planning, helps control the shop's expenses. A good plan is essential. Casual buying on the basis of habit and intuition, rather than on the basis of a plan, can result in excess inventory. This is a primary cause of business failure among retail florists. Flower shops with excess inventory cannot generate maximum profits.

Tyler Olson/Shutterstock.com

Figure 18-4. A businesses' greatest investment is its employees.

For each holiday or event, keep a log of inventory purchases, their cost, and customer demographics. ***Demographics*** include basic information about the types of customers who shop in your store, such as age group and ethnic group. This will help you control your stock.

For instance, for Valentine's Day, create a spreadsheet listing the flowers and accessories ordered and their cost. See **Figure 18-5**. When Valentine's Day is over, tally the number of holiday-specific flowers and hard goods purchased and those left over. Save these numbers and use them to order more accurately for Valentine's Day the following year. You may want to add an estimated amount for increased sales, but the previous year's numbers will give you a good foundation. Many software programs are available to help you manage purchases in this manner.

Accepting Preorders

When purchasing stock for your flower shop, you can use several methods to help control costs. For example, placing ***preorders*** for standard flowers and foliage, such as Christmas greens, can help reduce your costs because wholesale distributors often offer incentives to florists to place orders early, **Figure 18-6**. When retail florists place their orders early, it helps the wholesale florist gauge staffing needs to accommodate their customers during busy periods, which helps reduce their salary costs. Many wholesale florists also pass on discounts they received from growers for ordering early.

Buying in Season

Today's global market has made most types of flowers available throughout the year. Flowers grown in one part of the globe can easily be shipped around the world. Transportation and other costs are higher for doing business this way, but the option is open if a customer wants a specific product that is not in season in your area.

MJTH/Shutterstock.com

Figure 18-5. Good computer skills and technical knowledge are essential to be an effective manager.

Kellis/Shutterstock.com

Figure 18-6. Evergreen growers create wreaths such as this and sell them to wholesale florists. If retail florists order them early in the season, usually in October, wholesalers will in turn offer them early order discounts.

Thinking Green

Buy perishable stock locally and in season to reduce the use of fossil fuels that would otherwise be used to grow and transport crops.

When products are purchased locally during their standard growing season, they are generally less expensive. For example, in the Midwest, summer crops include zinnias, dahlias, and roses, **Figure 18-7**. Transportation costs are minimal because they are grown and sold within a small driving radius. Growers generally pass these savings on to the retail florist. In the winter, these same flowers can be grown only inside heated greenhouses, making them more expensive. To make a profit, the growers must raise their prices to include the cost of fuel to heat the plant's growing environment.

Cut flowers grown from bulbs are another example of seasonal products. Daffodils, amaryllis, ixia, and grape hyacinths are all grown from bulbs to flowers in the spring. Although these products are available year-round, their price becomes higher in summer, fall, and winter.

Tulips are another example. In the spring, tulips are available in large quantities and at competitive prices. A good businessperson takes advantage of this seasonal pricing and availability, incorporating in-season flowers into promotions and everyday designs while saving money on materials.

Also watch for off-season discounts or buying incentives from your suppliers. Holiday décor such as artificial garlands, trees, or ornaments may be discounted during the summer months well in advance of the holiday season. Develop your plans for promotional designs, holiday specials, and gift line promotions during the off-peak season and purchase the items you need when they are on sale.

Buying Patterns

Once the business has been set up for a full year, evaluate the inventory and set up an outline for merchandise purchases. Establish the best times to buy each type of product. Base your decisions on needs, rather than wants.

Hong Vo/Shutterstock.com; Marina Lohrbach/Shutterstock.com

Figure 18-7. A table centerpiece idea using locally grown zinnias and dahlias and a locally-grown mixed bouquet of colorful zinnias and purple ageratum.

For example, needs include basic supply staples such as floral foams, glassware, and everyday office supplies; wants might include trendy lines of products you want to try. See **Figure 18-8.** Purchase items in your "want" category only when you know you have enough cash flow to cover the items you need.

If your demographic analysis shows that your customer base is young, purchase gifts or accessories appropriate for that age group. Supplies for proms, homecomings, and other formal dances include corsage mechanic supplies, wire and floral tape, as well as rhinestone or gem-type details and other items that appeal to that audience.

Vaclav Mach/Shutterstock.com

Figure 18-8. Be careful not to let your wants exceed your shop's needs or you may lose money on hard goods that did not sell.

Inventory Control

Keep good records of all business *inventory*. Your inventory is all of the merchandise, or stock, that a store or company has on hand. This includes fresh flowers, foliage, and plants, as well as supplies and gift items if those are sold separately. Supplies might include floral foams, containers, specialty gift boxes, cards and card holders, and other items for sale to customers. It includes all gift items and holiday-specific merchandise.

Several times throughout the year, take a visual count and an in-depth look at all items on the shelves, **Figure 18-9.** This will keep you from buying unnecessary stock and will remind you to use up what has been on the stock shelves for a length of time. Your accountant will also need your inventory information for tax preparation purposes.

Shop Efficiency

In addition to controlling costs of supplies and merchandise, a smart business owner looks for ways to minimize labor expenses. Floral designers are proud of the fact that they can create one-of-a-kind designs. However, there are times when designs should be created using *mass production* techniques for better efficiency. Examples of designs that should be mass-produced include established holiday designs from a wire service and in-store

Monkey Business Images/Shutterstock.com

Figure 18-9. Floral managers should keep track of merchandise inventory.

Figure 18-10. Most retail florists have design recipes, with exacting varieties and counts of flower stems. These types of designs control costs of goods and labor, and save time, too.

promotions created by the flower shop's own staff. When many arrangements of the same style need to be created in a short time, performing each step for all of the arrangements at once can save time.

Gather the materials for each step of the process and line them up in the order they will be needed to save prep time, **Figure 18-10**. This *assembly line* approach saves steps and time. For example, if you are creating ten corsages, it is more efficient to bring out all of the stems of flowers at once than walking to the cooler ten times for individual flowers. Then perform each step on all of the arrangements before moving to the next step. Although mass production is not preferred by the artist, it is effective in keeping down costs and increasing profits. For orders that require more than one of the same arrangement, this method can also increase consistency among the arrangements.

Pricing Products

The key to any successful retail business is making a profit. To make a profit, the owner or manager must assign fair prices for products and services relative to the shop's expenses. Prices that are too high will drive away sales, but prices that are too low will prevent the shop from being profitable.

The pricing structure is established based on the type of goods or services and the overhead expenses involved. The goal is to find a balance between pricing for profit without overpricing. For some merchandise, a simple markup percentage is sufficient. A *markup* is the difference between the cost of goods sold and the *retail price* you charge to customers. Markup is usually expressed as either a percentage or a markup factor. For example, suppose you carry a line of greeting cards as a sideline in your flower shop. You paid $120 wholesale for a carton that contains 12 boxed sets of decorative cards. First, you must find the wholesale cost of one boxed set by dividing the total amount paid by the number of boxed sets in the carton:

$120 ÷ 12 boxed sets = $10 per boxed set

Now you can calculate how much to charge for an individual boxed set of cards. Suppose your shop's usual markup for incidentals is 15%. To find the retail price, you need to know what 15% of $10 is:

0.15 × $10 = $1.50

So, your markup on one set of boxed cards would be $1.50. To find the retail price for the product, add the original wholesale cost to the markup:

$10 + $1.50 = $11.50

The price of each set of boxed cards would therefore be $11.50.

Not all of your price calculations will be this straightforward. Arrangements designed and created in your shop, for example, are much more complex. You need to know exactly what materials were used in the arrangement, including mechanics, containers, flowers, foliage, and accessories. You also need to know how much time the arrangement took to create. All of these factors must be considered in the final price of the arrangement.

Many shops use markup factors to make these calculations easier. A *markup factor* is a number by which the wholesale cost is multiplied to find the price charged to the customer for that item. For example, all containers might have a markup factor of 2.0. With a 2.0 markup factor, a container that cost $3.60 wholesale would have a retail (customer) cost of $3.60 × 2 = $7.20. **Figure 18-11** shows how markup percentages and markup factors are typically assigned to floral merchandise.

Pro Tip

Calculating Percentages
Change the percentage to a decimal fraction so you can work with it more easily. Percentage is a way of showing parts per hundred. For example, 25% is equal to 25 parts per 100 parts, which can be written as the fraction 25/100. To find the decimal fraction, divide the number of parts by 100: 25 ÷ 100 = 0.25. Multiply the decimal fraction by the number you want to know the percentage of. Example: To calculate what 25% of 50 is, multiply 0.25 × 50. The answer, 12.5, is 25% of 50.

Item	Markup Factor or Percentage
Perishable fresh flower products	3.0
Live plants	2.5
Containers	2.0
Accessories	2.0 + 20% labor/design fee
Hard goods (soil, moss, water tubes, other mechanics)	2.0
Labor	20% of floral material costs

Potted English Ivy in Ceramic Container with Roses and Bow

Item	Wholesale Cost	Markup	Price
Ivy plant	$3.99	2.5	$9.98
3 fresh rose stems @ $1.20 each	$3.60	3.0	$10.80
3 water tubes @ $0.15 each	$0.45	2.0	$0.90
Ceramic container	$5.37	2.0	$10.74
Potting supplies (soil, etc.)	$1.92	2.0	$3.84
Green sheet moss	$2.43	2.0	$4.86
#3 satin ribbon, 1 yard	$1.18	2.0 + 20%	$2.83
Total of floral materials			$43.95
Labor charge (20%)			8.79
Total price			$52.73

Goodheart-Willcox Publisher

Figure 18-11. An example of how markup percentages and factors are assigned to floral merchandise.

Weddings

Weddings are beautiful and memorable events. They are also labor-intensive for the florist in both the design and production stages. Brides frequently choose a florist when the wedding date is set, which may be more than a year in advance. During the months preceding the wedding, the florist spends a considerable amount of time consulting with the bride to plan the theme and color scheme of the floral designs and then to finalize the details.

When pricing floral costs for a wedding, the cost of materials is established with a standard pricing structure for hard goods and flowers. Many wedding-specific factors must be considered. For example, some bridal and bridesmaid bouquets may be labor-intensive because special wiring and construction techniques may be needed to prolong the freshness of the floral materials. Custom wiring may also be needed to create bouquet shapes or designs to match the style of bridal gown. On the other hand, bouquets may take very little time while specialized centerpieces or church decor might require more time than traditional designs, **Figure 18-12**.

maetisa/Shutterstock.com

Figure 18-12. Once the technique of hand-tying bouquets is mastered, a bridal bouquet can be completed in ten to fifteen minutes.

Estimating and Planning

At the initial wedding consultation, the bride explains her wishes and preferences for her wedding flowers. Depending on the religion and customs of the bride and groom, flowers have both different meanings and different applications. See Chapter 13, *Wedding Flowers*, for more information about rules and guidelines for wedding venues. Ethnic groups also follow particular customs, so take the demographics of your customers into account when suggesting custom designs and arrangements. Your job is to find out exactly what each bride and groom prefer, then produce what they want, **Figure 18-13**. With every bride comes a new opportunity to develop, create, and install a thematic environment for their wedding.

Brian Chase/Shutterstock.com

Figure 18-13. For their winter wedding, this couple requested silver accents in the bride's bouquet.

Once a bride has expressed her wishes, you can begin to work up a pricing estimate, **Figure 18-14**. A wedding floral estimate may be built around the couple's preplanned budget. You may first calculate the basic components and then begin adding the price of the flowers the bride has chosen. Quite often, the flowers and arrangements a bride has chosen exceed the floral budget. For some brides, beautiful, fresh flowers are a priority, but merely an obligation for others. This difference of priority may cause a bride to increase the floral budget and do without a limousine or other type of service. As an excited, well-trained florist, you can capture a fair portion of the bride's wedding budget.

Pricing Wedding Orders

Wedding pricing follows the same structure of regular daily sales in a flower shop. The biggest difference is the labor involved. Because floral design is a creative service that requires time and skill, labor costs are generally increased when producing any type of wedding flowers. Just like the services of a good, creative hair stylist, pastry chef, or jewelry designer, a florist charges for skill, ability, and experience. Larger markups of up to 30% are customary in bridal work for anything requiring extra time or skill, **Figure 18-15**.

Ordering

In order to ensure the availability of flowers for a wedding, orders must be placed long in advance. This is especially important for any specialty flowers that will be used. You must also plan ahead for complications and have an alternative plan in place. Production gaps, crop failures, and even shipping complications can affect the availability of the ordered products. Follow up with suppliers and vendors several weeks in advance of the wedding. Even with preordering, allow extra time to acquire materials in case something happens. You must also plan ahead for the hard goods you will need.

Iakov Filimonov/Shutterstock.com

Figure 18-14. Figuring a wedding flower estimate takes time and product knowledge. It is a necessary part of wedding floral consulting and this labor must be compensated within the floral budget.

Konstantin Goldenberg/Shutterstock.com

Figure 18-15. Large-scale glass containers are popular for wedding receptions, but require much labor to clean, fill, and retrieve after the event. Higher labor charges help to cover the cost of sending trained floral designers to work at wedding venues when finished floral designs cannot be transported via delivery vans.

Dallas Events Inc./Shutterstock.com

Figure 18-16. Beautiful designs such as these require special construction, design, installation and removal, all within a tight time frame. Careful planning and staffing make them happen.

Delivery, Installation, and Removal

When pricing for an event, gather as much information as possible about the venue in which the wedding is taking place. How far will a delivery person need to drive to the venue from your store? Will security personnel need to be present to unlock buildings? How complicated will it be to set up altar arrangements, aisle runners, or custom designs at the wedding site? How long will it take to remove and return everything? Will the arrangements be moved to the reception venue? All logistical questions should be answered well in advance of the wedding. Delivery, installation, and removal of equipment after the services must be considered when pricing for weddings. A good understanding of the time involved allows you to charge the customer fairly for your time and labor. See **Figure 18-16**.

If a wedding florist has both the capital and the storage space to purchase and keep commonly-used items like arches and pillars, they may rent the items to their clients for additional revenue. The customer typically pays a deposit against damages, plus an additional rental fee per item. When materials are returned unharmed, the deposit is returned to the customer.

Marketing

Maximizing your sales and earning a profit is an art of its own accord. Keeping a steady increase in sales requires a constant reevaluation of the business, as well as excellent marketing skills. *Marketing* is the process of promoting your products and services to increase sales. It involves advertising, holding special promotions, and offering coupons or discounts occasionally to introduce new products or services. It is vital to your business to establish your own quality web site, set up links to and from national and local organizations, and advertise in local media.

Not every sale has to be a big one. Simple product sales are profit-makers too. Selling small monochromatic flower bouquets, loose bundles of flowers, and small potted plants also will boost your total sales. See **Figure 18-17**.

Elena Rostunova/Shutterstock.com

Figure 18-17. Displays of flowers by the bunch generate impulse sales with little labor and material expense. To be a success, they must always be available so that customers can count on a quick, quality purchase.

Marketing Plan

Every flower shop needs a *marketing plan* to determine which products should be promoted, how they should be promoted, and what type of financial results are expected. In order to develop a marketing plan, first you should set your *sales goals*—the amount of sales you want to reach during a specific period of time. Set this time period as a month or a full quarter. Be realistic in setting the goals for your business. Many florists have gotten into the business with unrealistic or romanticized images of owning a flower shop. Keep in mind the reality of the work, including the physically demanding aspects of working on your feet, heavy lifting, seasonal intensity of long hours, and overall physical demands. Make sure your sales goals take these factors into consideration so that your objectives will not be unrealistic.

After you develop your sales goals, consider your current inventory and any upcoming holidays or events. There are two approaches to promoting merchandise, and you can use one or both. First, you can promote merchandise for an upcoming holiday or event. For example, in January, you might plan a promotion to run for two weeks prior to Valentine's Day. This promotion might be a 10% off coupon for bouquets of mixed flowers, for example.

The other approach is to promote existing stock to move it off your shelves. This may be perishable stock that you will lose if you do not sell it quickly. It may also be gift items that have not sold as well as you had anticipated. It is important to sell this stock so that you will have the space to display other, more sellable items.

You can also combine these two approaches. For example, suppose you have a large number of American Flags left over from a Memorial Day promotion. You might plan a promotion for Veteran's Day to use the flags. This would allow you to use accessories you already have in stock (the flags) for an upcoming holiday. See **Figure 18-18**.

PerseoMedusa/Shutterstock.com

Figure 18-18. Colorful watering cans make whimsical floral containers. Different color containers are easily decorated for different holidays and occasions. A good buy on a large quantity can be profitable in the long run.

Blend Images/Shutterstock.com

Figure 18-21. Many customers feel that arranging the flowers you have received is part of the fun.

Monkey Business Images/Shutterstock.com

Figure 18-22. You should always remain pleasant on the phone. It does not matter if you are speaking with a wire service representative or a customer.

are selected and packaged for a simple design, and dry-shipped to the customer's home. The customer must process the fresh cut materials and create the design so instructions and fresh flower food packets are included. Although many people enjoy arranging their own flowers, these types of purchases are not appropriate to send to someone in the hospital or to a funeral home and lack the strong design quality of a professional florist. See **Figure 18-21**.

Wire Services

During the early days of the floriculture industry, customers wanted a way to send perishable floral products to people in other cities, states, and countries. Before refrigeration was available, shipping fresh flowers a great distance was not possible. To solve the issue, florists created a *wire service*, a system of contracting florists in other areas to deliver the product from their shops.

The first service of this type was offered by Florists' Transworld Delivery Association (FTD) in 1910. Since then, other wire services have been created. Teleflora and FTD are currently the dominant wire services. Members pay a monthly fee to belong to the service in exchange for national advertising and exposure to customers outside of their regular marketing area. The clearinghouse, or head office, of the wire service records transactions and processes payments for the wire service, acting as a bookkeeper between florists. Both the sending florist and the filling florist get a portion of the sale. The wire service provider receives a small percentage. The filling florist is required to provide 100% value. See **Figure 18-22**.

Another type of business is an online-only floral shop. Online-only floral shops do not have brick and mortar shops, nor do they stock flowers and plants. They operate by taking orders and transmitting them to flower shops, paying for the order and delivery with credit cards. They generate revenue by charging service fees. This type of business is controversial in the eyes of the floral industry because many florists feel consumers are unwittingly and unnecessarily paying for services they do not need. Before you join any wire service, be sure to analyze the benefits completely and realistically.

Sales Tax

Sales tax is collected by all except five states in the United States. Every state has different rules about what is taxed, and every state sets its own tax rate. Some cities and counties also have a local sales tax that is added to the state sales tax. As a business owner, you are required by law to collect these taxes and submit them to the proper authorities. Work with your accountant to determine the amounts of these and any other taxes for which your flower shop may be liable. See **Figure 18-23**.

To calculate sales tax, convert the percentage into a decimal fraction. Multiply the decimal fraction by the total amount of the sale to find the amount of tax due. Then add the tax due to the total amount of the sale to find the amount the customer should pay. For example, suppose you live in an area where the state sales tax is 6%, the city sales tax is 1.5%, and the county sales tax is 1%. Altogether, you will need to collect 6% + 1.5% + 1% = 8.5% in sales tax. Written as a decimal fraction, this is 0.085 (because 8.5 ÷ 100 = 0.085).

Suppose a customer purchases an arrangement with a retail price of $58.95. To find the sales tax due, multiply the retail price of the arrangement by 0.085:

$58.95 × 0.085 = $5.01075

You will need to round this number to the nearest hundredth (penny). In this case, the tax due rounds to $5.01. Now add the tax due to the retail price:

$58.95 + 5.01 = $63.96

The total amount to be collected from the customer is $63.96.

Andrey_Popov/Shutterstock.com

Figure 18-23. It is always wise to hire a professional to help you with your finances. Until you learn how to properly deal with taxes, trying to save money by doing it on your own may land your business in financial trouble.

Sales Etiquette

The importance of good salesmanship is priceless. Sales are not automatic or guaranteed when someone walks through the door. An enthusiastic, knowledgeable salesperson can ensure that customers have a good experience, increasing the chance that the customer will return for future floral needs. A bad experience may send the consumer directly to your competition. Train your staff to know the products you sell. Give them the tools and resources they need to provide the best information possible to customers.

Product knowledge is not enough, however. Provide employees with behavioral guidelines as well. Eating, drinking, smoking, and chewing gum on the sales floor should not be allowed. Cell phones should be used only for official flower shop business. Personal telephone calls and loud shop chatter in the presence of customers makes a bad impression.

Working in a flower shop requires professionalism. Presenting yourself through positive body language, verbal communication, and overall good manners is essential to your personal success as well as the success of your business. See **Figure 18-24**. Whether you are working for yourself or for someone else, take pride in what you do. Always present yourself in a business-like manner no matter how large or small a task may be. Carry yourself in a confident, professional manner and your confidence will increase your customers' confidence in you as well as your flower shop.

Mila Supinskaya/Shutterstock.com

Figure 18-24. Buying flowers from a knowledgeable, competent florist makes the shopping experience enjoyable.

Summary

- General retail responsibilities of the flower shop owner or manager include managing finances, purchasing stock, controlling inventory, setting the prices for products and services, and planning marketing strategies.
- Every company needs capital and cash flow to support its day-to-day operations.
- A flower shop's expenses include overhead, employee salaries, and stock purchases.
- Purchasing decisions affect a shop's profit; smart buying and good planning help control expenses.
- Proper inventory control is necessary for tax purposes and also allows you to make better purchasing decisions.
- When more than one of the same arrangement are ordered, mass production techniques can save labor costs.
- Markup can be expressed either as a percentage or as a markup factor by which the wholesale cost is multiplied.
- Weddings are very labor-intensive and generally have a higher markup than other flower shop tasks.
- Marketing is the process of promoting your products and services to increase sales.
- Most flower shops generate walk-in sales, phone sales, wire services sales, and Internet sales.

Review Questions

Go to www.g-wlearning.com/floraldesign/ to use the fill-in-form.

Answer the following questions using the information provided in this chapter.

1. What is the difference between financial management and accounting?
2. Why do many florists need to find ways to generate extra income during the summer months?
3. Name three types of overhead expenses.
4. List three ways to help lower or control the cost of stock purchased for a flower shop.
5. When should florists use mass production techniques?
6. What is markup?
7. How much would you charge a customer for a decorative vase that cost $12.49 wholesale, if your markup is 20%?
8. What is the usual markup for detailed labor on wedding products?
9. What is the purpose of a marketing plan?
10. Describe two approaches to promoting merchandise.
11. What are impulse sales?
12. Name four types of sales generated by most flower shops.
13. What are the advantages and disadvantages of belonging to a wire service?
14. Which government bodies collect sales tax?
15. List three behavioral guidelines that apply to all flower shop employees.

Activities

1. Working with a fellow student, "answer" the phone and conduct a telephone sale. Clearly explain the cost of the arrangement and any other fees associated with the sale.
2. Work in small groups to practice waiting on customers. Take turns being the florist and the customers.
3. Work with a partner to role-play sending and receiving a wire order. Take turns sending and receiving the order.
4. Create bud vases for sale around school; use an assembly line for mass production.
5. Role-play body language skills for walk-in and phone sales.

6. Set up a thematic tablescape or tabletop vignette for a favorite holiday.
7. Plan a sales promotion for Mother's Day. Present your plan to the class.

Critical Thinking

1. You are an employee in a flower shop. A customer comes in with a complaint about the incomplete delivery of a large order of poinsettias. Determine and write the most appropriate response addressing the following: Make sure you obtain a clear understanding of the complaint. Reform the complaint to less negative terms. Change the complaint into a question. Explore alternative solutions. Solve the problem. Use proper grammar and spelling in your writing.
2. Your flower shop has a promotion for a simple springtime arrangement that includes eight dendrobium orchids and a small amount of foliage in a glass vase for $129.99. To prepare for the anticipated sales, your shop purchased 120 stems of orchids for a total price of $249.99. The promotion has been running for a week, but only one order has been placed, so you have 112 stems of perishable orchids left. What are possible reasons for the failure of this promotion? What might you do to correct the problem and sell the remaining orchids?
3. You have received a wire order for a standard arrangement of 12 red roses. Explain how you will process this order.

STEM Activities and Academics

1. **Science.** Research the soil conditions and climate in your area. Find out what flowering and foliage plants grow well in these conditions. Then choose three plants that grow well in your area and find out what would be required to start a nursery operation to provide this plant wholesale to florists. Where would you locate your nursery? What permits or business licenses would you need? How would you obtain your first plants? Would you need soil enhancers or irrigation systems? Write a scientific report to present to the city or town council explaining why you chose these plants, in terms of climate and soil conditions.
2. **Technology.** Research recordkeeping or inventory control software for small businesses. Determine which software might be best suited for a flower shop. If possible, download a free trial of the software and use it to record the materials you have used in activities for this chapter or for the entire course. Evaluate how well the software meets the needs of a flower shop. Then design a recordkeeping or inventory control system, either on paper or using an electronic spreadsheet, that you think would work better than the commercial one for a small flower shop. Use your system to enter the same information you entered using the commercial software. Which system would you choose if you were a flower shop owner?
3. **Engineering.** Design an arrangement that contains at least six irises and six tiger lilies, in a "gift" vase of crystal. Use the markups shown in Figure 18-11, and keep the final retail price less than $80.
4. **Math.** Assuming a sales tax of 7.5%, calculate the sales tax and the total amount to be collected from the customer for each of the following sales.
   a. $85.62
   b. $23.95
   c. $179.04
   d. 56.47
   e. $1,108.52
5. **Social Studies.** Research the sales tax in your area and find out how much of the tax is state sales tax and how much is levied by local taxing authorities, such as the city or county. Research the history of each component of the sales tax. When was it instituted? Has the amount changed over the years? What reasons were given for any increases?

6. **Math.** In January, your flower shop is having a "sidewalk sale" of leftover holiday accessories and arrangements. You place the sale merchandise on tables in front of the store with a sign "Everything 20% off the marked price!" A customer selects three potted poinsettias marked $47.99 each, a floral bookmark marked $3.95, and four flower-shaped tree ornaments marked $6.95, $7.35, $9.95, and $5.45. Calculate the total price for these items, including a 7% sales tax.

Communicating about Floral Design

1. **Reading and Speaking.** Some organizations or associations provide mentoring services for small businesses as a membership benefit. Form a small group with two or three of your peers and collect informational materials from associations that provide these services. Analyze the data in these materials based on the knowledge gained from this chapter. Make inferences about the services available and recommend the best ones to the class.

2. **Speaking and Listening.** Interview a floral shop or warehouse owner. Ask the person to describe a typical day at work. Here are some questions you might ask: How does a person open and run their own floral business? Is it difficult to get financing? What is the work environment like? What are the job duties? What kinds of delivery or storage problems are dealt with? What other types of professionals does he or she work with? Report your findings to the class, giving reasons why you would or would not want to pursue a career similar to that of the person you interviewed.

3. **Reading and Writing.** Working with a partner, research the impact of online marketing, business websites, and online ordering on small floral businesses. What types of Internet applications bestow the greatest benefit? Develop a report for the class on the benefits of using the Internet to develop a small business.

4. **Reading and Writing.** Planning a delivery route. Work with two or three peers on this activity. Each member of the group should choose five local addresses (business and residential), and various types of arrangements to be delivered. Determine a delivery time deadline for each item. Trade your list of deliveries with someone in your group. Using a map of the local area, plan the best delivery route and fill out a delivery schedule. Compare your completed routes and explain why you planned your route the way you did. Repeat the exercise, calculating your delivery times using online maps or a GPS.

Appendix

Floral Design Competitions

Floral design competitions are held at both student and professional levels. These competitions provide participants an opportunity to increase their knowledge about floral products and design and build professional skills through interaction with peers, coaches, advisors, and judges. Competitions provide a platform to spotlight excellence and quality of floriculture products and floral design.

Participating in competitions is an excellent way for you to build your skills in floral design and boost your confidence. Participating in competitions will also give you a tangible use for the skills you are developing in class. Hopefully, participating in healthy competitions will help create a desire for success that you can carry over into your life.

Rules and Regulations

Pro Tip

Silence your cell phone before your event begins. Do not use your cell phone during a competition because it suggests dishonesty and is unprofessional.

Each competition has its own set of rules and regulations that are usually available for review as soon as the contest and registration dates are announced. Most organizations also post rules and restrictions on their website as soon as they are available.

You must know and understand the rules and regulations to lessen the chance of costly errors. For example, a maximum height is often given as a restriction for a particular design. If you are working on a centerpiece and your arrangement exceeds the limit, it may be disqualified and eliminated from the competition. Knowing the rules and, in this instance, using a tape measure, would keep the design in the contest. Unless, of course, the use of a ruler or tape measure is not allowed.

Eligibility requirements, fees, and registration deadlines may also be found online and through your instructor.

Tool Kit

Some competitions allow contestants to bring their own tools kits. The restrictions vary by competition and you will be provided with a list of what is allowed. Care should be taken to follow the competition tool box list to the letter. If you bring items that are not allowed, you may be disqualified. Tools are sometimes provided by the organizers of the competition.

The fresh cut plant materials, along with containers and design mechanics, are typically covered through entry fees or may be underwritten by competition sponsors. Whenever possible, express gratitude to the organizers, sponsors, and others involved in organizing and supporting the event.

Individual and Team Events

Many student competitions include both team and individual events. Participating in team competitions will help you learn how to work effectively with other people. Working with a group of your peers toward a common goal will also improve your communication and socializing skills.

The competition encourages creativity, resourcefulness, and focus while giving real-life experience in a high pressure situation. It also gives AIFD student members an experience that is similar to the AIFD certification process for membership in the Institute. The timing, materials, and rules of the competition are comparable to the practice that florists are subjected to in their steps to certification.

Your instructor can advise you and your peers on which events you should enter. After the contest is over, speak with teammates and advisors to ascertain ways in which your performance in future events can be improved.

Areas Covered

Most floral design competitions use a point system to grade each contestant's work. How the point system is applied will vary, but the areas being graded are fairly standard. In general, points are awarded for the following categories:

- The proper use of design principles and elements
    Balance (visually and mechanically stable)
    Proportion (in proportion with allotted space)
    Scale (components in scale with one another)
    Rhythm (leads the viewer's eye)
    Dominance (dominating element)
    Contrast (interest in the design)
- Mechanical concealment (neatness, technical proficiency)
- Conformance (all requirements for the design have been met)
- Proper interpretation for the category
- Creativity or Artistic Concept
- Deliverability
- Pricing

Design Types

The types of designs contestants are assigned vary from small designs such as boutonnieres or floral napkin rings to casket sprays or complete dinner table settings. The level of skill required will also vary according to the contestant's abilities.

Flower and Plant Recognition

Most student competitions include flower and plant recognition. The manner in which the plant material is presented varies. Some competitions use live specimens while others use color photographs or line drawings. Learn which plant materials will be covered by reviewing information provided by the sponsoring organization. Resources, such as the illustrated glossaries in this text, are useful for reviewing the plant materials you will need to recognize for most competitions. You may be required to write the names or identify the plant materials orally for the judges. Proper pronunciation of both common and botanical names may also be judged and scored.

Judges

Pro Tip

Pay special attention to instructions given before the contest begins and speak only when you are asked a question or you have a relative question.

Judges for floral design competitions are usually seasoned professionals who choose to share their knowledge and be of service to the education field and the floral industry. Depending on the sponsoring organization, in order to participate, judges may need to be certified through programs such as the one offered by the American Institute of Floral Designers (AIFD). Such programs ensure that judges are knowledgeable in every aspect of floral design and are able to objectively evaluate each entry using parameters set by the sponsoring organization.

In addition to scoring entries, judges may be required to provide qualitative comments to the contestants. These comments may be written on score sheets or given orally to contestants. Qualitative comments prove extremely helpful to contestants to improve future designs.

Contest Preparation

The best way to begin preparation for competition is attending class and learning the basics of floral design. This includes both class time and lab time as theory is just as important as the "hands on" portion of your education. Understanding and applying the principles and elements of design to your work is extremely important as these concepts are what will be used to judge the entries.

Evaluating

Judges are given standards by which all entries are to be judged. Quantitative judging is where point values or scores are assigned according to criteria.

A category of judging may be on adherence to theme, for instance, a spring centerpiece for a luncheon party. A design using spring flowers would score higher in this category than a design with golden branches and evergreens.

For many competitors, this is their first foray into designing under competition pressure, with a limited amount of design time and specific restrictions on what they are to make. They do not know what floral materials or containers they will encounter when they walk into the competition space. Every year, competitors are disqualified in a design category for exceeding the size limitations, or not having their piece on the judging table when time is called. They may not have access to all the tools they are accustomed to using in class, and may encounter flower varieties they have never used before.

When the contestant has completed the arrangement and is satisfied with the project and workmanship, the contestant should signal the judge and stop work. At this point, the competitor may be asked to move the finished design to a separate area for judging. Many competitors like to continue working on their designs until time is called. No matter what you do, be aware of the amount of time remaining in each category so that you are not caught with unfinished work. In some contests, an announcer will keep participants aware of how much time remains, but this is not always the case.

Once the contest is finished, it is always courteous to clean the area where you have worked. This is good decompression time, allowing you to calm down from the contest activity. When cleaning a contest area, start high and work your way to the floor. First, any extra flowers you have not used should be recut and placed with like flowers in buckets identified by the contest organizers. Next, turn in any unused hard goods provided by the contest committee such as wire, glue, or unused floral foam. Clean the surface of the table, then sweep the floor last. If other contestants need help cleaning, pitch in if you are permitted to do so. Do not leave the contest space until all areas are clean and the organizers release everyone.

Scoring Rubrics

The following are some score sheets or rubrics which may help you to better understand how a contest can be judged. It is helpful to use these sheets as a judge and as a competitor. Try them out to learn not only about your strengths and weaknesses as a judge or a competitor, but to custom design a rubric suited for a design contest.

To save time, measurements can be made by contest committee members rather than judges. If a design is outside of the appropriate size range, it can be disqualified from point judging, but judges can make time to evaluate the design for helpful comments.

Objective, Quantitative (Point-Scored)
Size Requirement
_____ within size
_____ out of size (disqualified)
Design Principle Adherence (70 points, 10 points each)
_____ balance
_____ proportion
_____ rhythm
_____ scale
_____ unity
_____ dominance
_____ harmony
Mechanics (20 points, 10 points each)
_____ mechanic concealment
_____ mechanic stability
Theme (10 points)
_____ adherence and appropriateness to assigned theme
Total Score:
_____

In this example, judges view all design work on their own, then have private discussion together to arrive at consensus. Their evaluations may be written or verbal once their decisions are made. Verbal delivery can be made via audio recording or face-to-face with contest participants. In this type of evaluation, judges must be respected experts as well as possess the ability to articulate and communicate clear, objective information.

Objective, Qualitative Written/Verbal
Size Requirement _____ within size _____ out of size (disqualified)
Design Principle Adherence _____ balance _____ proportion _____ rhythm _____ scale _____ unity _____ dominance _____ harmony
Mechanics _____ mechanic concealment _____ mechanic stability
Theme _____ adherence and appropriateness to assigned theme
Total Score: _____

State Flowers

A "National Garland of Flowers" created for the 1893 Chicago World's Fair was the inspiration for adopting official state floral emblems. The creators of the garland invited each state to select a flower to represent their state. Minnesota was the first state to choose, followed by Oklahoma. The subject became a heated debate in some state legislatures and few had been chosen by the time of the fair. Some states chose both an official flower and an official wildflower when they could not reach a decision. Some states brought in botany professors to debate on behalf of each candidate and others had school children vote when the adults were at a stalemate. Most of the state flowers have remained the same since the early 1900s. A few have been changed for various reasons, including the fact that they were found to not be native to the state. This selection of state flowers led to the adoption of the other state symbols recognized today.

Ana Marques/Shutterstock.com

Alabama
Camellia
Camellia japonica

Arto Hakola/Shutterstock.com

Alaska
Forget-Me-Not
Myosotis sp.

Darla Hallmark/Shutterstock.com

Arizona
Saguaro Cactus Blossom
Carnegiea gigantea

ekina/Shutterstock.com

Arkansas
Apple Blossom
Pyrus coronaria

Kev Vincent Photogtaphy/Shutterstock.com

California
California Poppy
Eschsholtzia californica

Laura Gangi Pond/Shutterstock.com

Colorado
Rocky Mountain Columbine
Aquilegia caerulas

Melinda Fawver/Shutterstock.com

Piter Ha Son/Shutterstock.com

Jim Parkin/Shutterstock.com

Connecticut
Mountain Laurel
Kalmia latifolia

Delaware
Peach Blossom
Prunus persica

Florida
Orange Blossom
Citrus aurantium var. *amara*

Paul Brennan/Shutterstock.com

tonjakkit/Shutterstock.com

Nazzu/Shutterstock.com

Georgia
Cherokee Rose
Rosa laevigata

Hawaii
Hawaiian Hibiscus
Hibiscus rosa-sinensis

Idaho
Mock Orange
Philadelphus lewisii

Fabio Alcini/Shutterstock.com

Fragolini/Shutterstock.com

freya-photographer/Shutterstock.com

Illinois
Purple Violet
Viola sororia

Indiana
Peony
Paeonia lactiflora

Iowa
Wild Prairie Rose
Rosa acicularis

Nadja Rider/Shutterstock.com

Kansas
Sunflower
Helianthus sp.

Chris Hill/Shutterstock.com

Kentucky
Goldenrod
Solidago sp.

Dustie/Shutterstock.com

Louisiana
Magnolia
Magnolia sp.

mubus7/Shutterstock.com

Maine
White Pine Cone and Tassel
Pinus strobus, linnaeus

tim Elliott/Shutterstock.com

Maryland
Black-Eyed Susan
Rudbeckia hirta

Sarah Jessup/Shutterstock.com

Massachusetts
Mayflower
Epigaea repens

R_Szatkowski/Shutterstock.com

Michigan
Apple Blossom
Pyrus coronaria

Heather Nicaise/Shutterstock.com

Minnesota
Pink and White Lady's Slipper
Cypripedium reginae

toriru/Shutterstock.com

Mississippi
Magnolia
Magnolia sp.

jennyt/Shutterstock.com

Missouri
Hawthorn
Crataegus punctata

6015714281/Shutterstock.com

Montana
Bitterroot
Lewisia rediviva

Chris Hill/Shutterstock.com

Nebraska
Goldenrod
Solidago sp.

Deanna Quinton Larson/Thinkstock

Nevada
Sagebrush
Artemisia tridentata

Roxana Bashyrova/Shutterstock.com

New Hampshire
Purple lilac
Syringa vulgaris

Fabio Alcini/Shutterstock.com

New Jersey
Violet
Viola sororia

Bryan Eastham/Shutterstock.com

New Mexico
Yucca Flower
Yucca glauca

sarayut jun-ngam/Shutterstock.com

New York
Rose
Rosa sp.

Zocchi Roberto/Shutterstock.com

North Carolina
American Dogwood
Cornus florida

T. Smith

scphoto60/Shutterstock.com

T. Smith

North Dakota
Wild Prairie Rose
Rosa arkansana

Ohio
Scarlet Carnation
Dianthus caryophyllus

Oklahoma
Oklahoma Rose
Rosa 'Oklahoma'

Sombra/Shutterstock.com

Maria Komar/Shutterstock.com

Fabio Alcini/Shutterstock.com

Oregon
Oregon Grape
Mahonia aquifolium

Pennsylvania
Mountain Laurel
Kalmia latifolia

Rhode Island
Violet
Viola sororia

Fredlyfish4/Shutterstock.com

LianeM/Shutterstock.com

Roger de Montfort/Shutterstock.com

South Carolina
Yellow Jessamine
Gelsemium sempervirens

South Dakota
Pasque Flower
Anemone patens

Tennessee
Iris
Iris

Richard A McMillin/Shutterstock.com

Texas
Bluebonnet
Lupinus

markwalkersmith/Shutterstock.com

Utah
Sego Lily
Calochortus nuttallii

Neil Webster/Shutterstock.com

Vermont
Red Clover
Trifolium pratense

Phillip W. Kirkland/Shutterstock.com

Virginia
American Dogwood
Cornus florida

tab62/Shutterstock.com

Washington
Coast Rhododendron
Rhododendron macrophyllum

Denys Dolnikov/Shutterstock.com

West Virginia
Rhododendron
Rhododendron atlanticum

Aleksander Bolbot/Shutterstock.com

Wisconsin
Wood Violet
Viola papilionacea

Timothy Epp/Shutterstock.com

Wyoming
Indian Paintbrush
Castilleja linariaefolia

Geometrical Designs

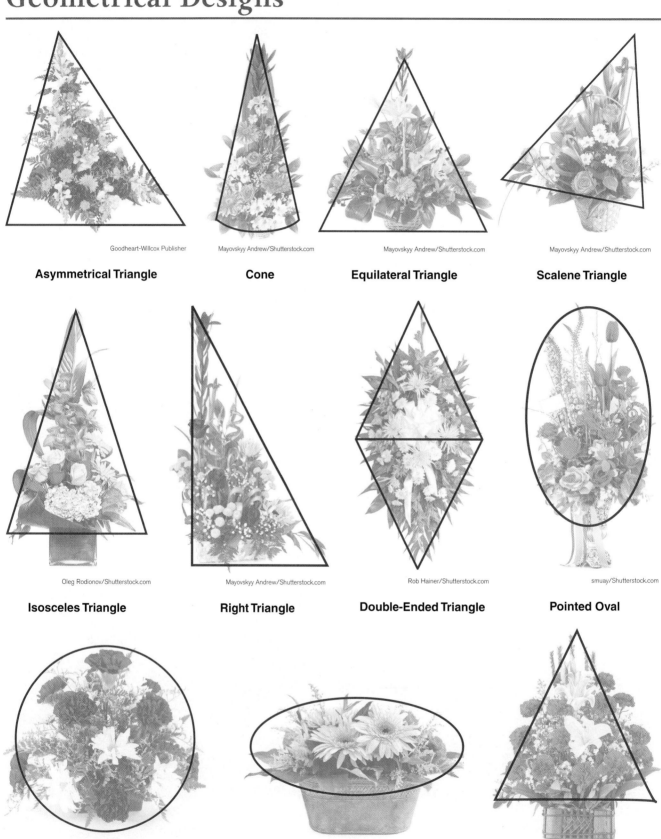

Goodheart-Willcox Publisher

Asymmetrical Triangle

Mayovskyy Andrew/Shutterstock.com

Cone

Mayovskyy Andrew/Shutterstock.com

Equilateral Triangle

Mayovskyy Andrew/Shutterstock.com

Scalene Triangle

Oleg Rodionov/Shutterstock.com

Isosceles Triangle

Mayovskyy Andrew/Shutterstock.com

Right Triangle

Rob Hainer/Shutterstock.com

Double-Ended Triangle

smuay/Shutterstock.com

Pointed Oval

Goodheart-Willcox Publisher

Mound/Round

Elena Elisseeva/Shutterstock.com

Oval

smuay/Shutterstock.com

Symmetrical

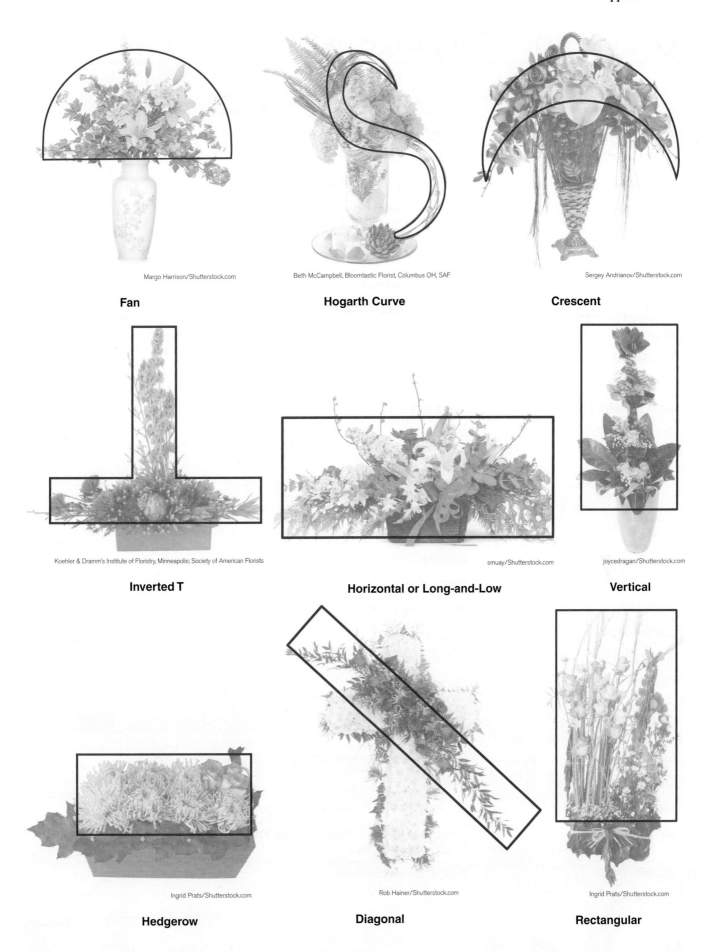

Margo Harrison/Shutterstock.com

Fan

Beth McCampbell, Bloomtastic Florist, Columbus OH, SAF

Hogarth Curve

Sergey Andrianov/Shutterstock.com

Crescent

Koehler & Dramm's Institute of Floristry, Minneapolis; Society of American Florists

Inverted T

smuay/Shutterstock.com

Horizontal or Long-and-Low

joycedragan/Shutterstock.com

Vertical

Ingrid Prats/Shutterstock.com

Hedgerow

Rob Hainer/Shutterstock.com

Diagonal

Ingrid Prats/Shutterstock.com

Rectangular

The Victorian Language of Flowers

Flower	Meaning
Acacia Blossom	Beauty in retirement
Nordic Acorn	Symbol of life and immortality
Aloe	Healing, protection, affection
Alstroemeria	Devotion, friendship
Amaryllis	Pride, pastoral poetry
Ambrosia	Your love is reciprocated
Arbutus	Thee only do I love
Aster	Symbol of love, daintiness
Azalea	Take care of yourself for me, temperance
Bachelor Button	Single blessedness
Basil	Good wishes
Bells of Ireland	Good luck
Bird of Paradise	Magnificence
Bittersweet	Truth
Black-Eyed Susan	Justice
Blue Iris	Faith, wisdom and health
Bluebell	Humility
Bonsai, Topiary	Stability
Cactus	Endurance
Calla Lily	Magnificent beauty
Camellia (pink)	Longing for you
Camellia (red)	You're a flame in my heart
Camellia (white)	You're adorable
Carnation (pink)	I'll never forget you
Carnation (purple)	Capriciousness
Carnation (red)	My heart aches for you, admiration, deep love, passion
Carnation (solid color)	Yes
Carnation (striped)	No, refusal, sorry I cannot be with you, wish I could be with you
Carnation (white)	Sweet and lovely, innocence, pure love, woman's good luck gift , pride, beauty, living for love
Cattail	Peace, prosperity
Chamomile	Patience

(Continued)

Flower	Meaning
Chrysanthemum (red)	I love you
Chrysanthemum (white)	Truth
Chrysanthemum (yellow)	Slighted love
Clover (white)	Think of me
Coreopsis	Always cheerful
Crocus	Cheerfulness, youthful gladness
Daffodil	Regard, unequalled love, you are the only one, the sun is always shining when I am with you
Dahlia	Dignity and elegance, everlasting union
Daisy	Innocence, loyal love, I will never tell, purity
Dandelion	Faithfulness, happiness
Fern	Magic, fascination, confidence and shelter, sincerity
Fern (Maidenhair)	Secret bond of love
Fir	Time
Flax	Domestic symbol
Forget-Me-Not	True love, memories
Forsythia	Anticipation
Freesia	Spirited
Gardenia	You are lovely, secret love, remembrance, strength
Geranium	True friendship
Gladioli	Give me a break, I am really sincere
Gloxinia	Love at first sight
Heather (lavender)	Admiration, solitude
Heather (white)	Protection, wishes will come true
Heliotrope	Eternal love
Holly	Defense, domestic happiness, hope
Hyacinth (blue)	Constancy, fertility
Hyacinth (red or pink)	Play
Hyacinth (white)	Loveliness, I will pray for you
Hydrangea	Perseverance
Iris	Fleur-de-lis, emblem of France, your friendship means so much to me, faith, hope, wisdom and valor, my compliments
Ivy	Wedded love, fidelity, friendship, affection
Ivy (sprig of white tendrils)	Anxious to please, affection
Jasmine (white)	Sweet love

(Continued)

Flower	Meaning
Jonquil	Love me, affection returned, desire, sympathy, desire for affection returned
Lady's Mantle	Comforting
Lilac	First love, joy of youth
Lily (Calla)	Beauty
Lily (Eucharis)	Maiden charms
Lily (white)	It's heavenly to be with you, purity, majesty
Lily (yellow)	I'm walking on air, false
Lily of the Valley	Sweetness, you've made my life complete
Lily, Stargazer	Ambition
Living Plant	Growth, everlasting
Mistletoe	Kiss me, affection, to surmount difficulties
Moss	Maternal love, charity
Mums (bronze)	Joy, long life, truth, wonderful friend
Myrtle	Love, emblem of marriage
Narcissus	Egotism, formality, stay as sweet as you are
Nasturtium	Patriotism
Oak	Strength
Orange Blossom	Innocence, eternal love, marriage and fruitfulness
Orchid	Love, beauty, refinement, beautiful lady, Chinese symbol for many children, mature charm
Pansy	Thoughts
Peony	Happy life, happy marriage
Petunia	Your presence soothes me
Poppy (red)	Pleasure
Poppy (yellow)	Wealth, success
Primrose	I can't live without you
Rose (bouquet of mature blooms)	Gratitude
Rose (bridal)	Happy love
Rose (Hibiscus)	Delicate beauty
Rose (leaf)	You may hope
Rose (pink and white)	I love you still and always will
Rose (pink)	Perfect happiness, to my friend
Rose (Porcelana)	Admiration
Rose (red and white)	Unity

(Continued)

Flower	Meaning
Rose (red)	Love, I love you, perfect love, respect
Rose (single full bloom)	I love you, I still love you
Rose (Tea)	I will remember always
Rose (thornless)	Love at first sight
Rose (white)	Purity, you are heavenly
Rose (yellow)	Joy, gladness and friendship
Rosebud (red)	Pure and lovely, beauty and you, a heart innocent of love
Rosemary	Remembrance
Salvia (blue)	I think of you
Salvia (red)	Forever mine
Smilax	Loveliness
Statice	Lasting beauty
Stephanotis	Happiness in marriage, desire to travel
Stock	Bonds of affection, you will always be beautiful to me
Sunflower	Loyalty
Sweet Pea	Good-bye, departure, blissful pleasure, thank you for a lovely time
Sweet William	Gallantry
Tulip (general)	Perfect lover, fame, flower emblem of Holland
Tulip (red)	Believe me, declaration of love
Tulip (variegated)	Beautiful eyes
Tulip (yellow)	There is sunshine in your smile
Valerian	Readiness
Violet (blue)	Watchfulness, faithfulness, I will always be there
Violet, African	Faithfulness
Viscaria	Will you dance with me?
Willow	Sadness
Yarrow	Everlasting love
Zinnia (Magenta)	Lasting affection
Zinnia (Scarlet)	Constancy
Zinnia (White)	Goodness
Zinnia (Yellow)	Daily remembrance

Anniversary Flowers and Gifts

Anniversary Year	Anniversary Flower	Traditional Gift	Modern Gift
1st	Red & White Roses, Carnation	Paper	Clock, Plastic, Gold Jewelry
2nd	Carnations (White), Lily of the Valley	Cotton	China, Cotton, Calico, Garnet
3rd	Bird of Paradise, Sunflower	Leather	Crystal, Glass, Pearls
4th	Alstroemeria, Hydrangea	Linen, Silk, Fruit, Flowers	Appliances, Linen, Silk, Nylon, Blue Topaz
5th	Bonsai, Topiary, Daisy	Wood	Silverware, Sapphire
6th	Red Tulips, Calla Lily	Iron, Sugar	Wood, Candy, Amethyst
7th	Ivy Plant, Freesia	Copper, Wool	Stationary, Brass, Desk Sets, Onyx
8th	White Lilies, Lilac	Bronze, Pottery	Linens, Lace, Tourmaline Jewelry
9th	Living Plant, Bird of Paradise	Pottery, China, Willow	Leather, Lapis Jewelry
10th	Pink Rose, Daffodil	Tin, Aluminum	Diamond Jewelry
11th	Daisys (White), Tulip	Steel	Fashion Jewelry, Turquoise Jewelry
12th	Sunflower, Peony	Silk, Linen	Pearls, Jade
13th	Stock, Chrysanthemum	Lace	Textiles, Fur, Citrine
14th	Gladiolas, Dahlia	Ivory	Gold Jewelry, Opal
15th	Stephanotis, Rose	Crystal	Watches, Glass, Ruby
16th	Statice, Rose	Tourmaline, Wax	Silver Hollowware, Peridot
17th	Carnation (Red), Rose	Furniture, Watch, Shell	Furniture, Diamond, Watch
18th	Porcelana Roses, Rose	Turquoise, Feathers	Porcelain, Cat's Eye Jewelry
19th	Bronze Mums, Rose	Aquamarine	Bronze, Aquamarine
20th	Rose (Pink and White), Aster	China	Platinum, Emerald
25th	Roses, Iris	Silver	Sterling Silver
30th	White Rose, Lily (white or yellow)	Pearl	Diamond
35th	African Violet	Coral, Jade	Jade
40th	Red Roses, Gladiolus	Ruby	Ruby, Garnet
45th	Blue Iris	Sapphire	Sapphire
50th	Yellow Roses, Violet	Gold	Gold
55th	Calla	Emerald	Emerald
60th	Orchids	Diamond	Diamond, Gold
75th	Couple's Favorite	Platinum	Star Sapphire, Diamond-like Stones, Gold

Noteworthy Weddings

Date	Couple
February 10, 1840	Queen Victoria and Prince Albert
May 21, 1945	Humphrey Bogart and Lauren Bacall
November 7, 1951	Frank Sinatra and Ava Gardner
September 12, 1953	John F. Kennedy and Jacqueline Bouvier
April 18, 1956	Grace Kelly and Prince Rainier
March 15, 1964	Elizabeth Taylor and Richard Burton
May 1, 1967	Priscilla Beaulieu and Elvis Presley
June 12, 1971	Tricia Nixon and Edward Cox
July 29, 1981	Prince Charles and Lady Diana Spencer
September 21, 1996	Carolyn Besette and John Kennedy
July 4, 1999	David Beckham and Victoria Beckham
June 29, 2000	Brad Pitt and Jennifer Anniston
September 14, 2002	Gwen Stefani and Gavin Rossdale
November 18, 2006	Katie Holmes and Tom Cruise
October 23, 2010	Katy Perry and Russell Brand
April 29, 2011	Prince William and Kate Middleton
September 9, 2012	Liv Tyler and Royston Langdon
October 20, 2013	Kelly Clarkson and Brandon Blackstock

Flower Glossary Cross Reference

The following is a cross reference list for the Flower Glossary in Chapter 8. It is alphabetized by botanical name whereas the glossary in Chapter 8 is alphabetized by common name. Both botanical and common names are used in the floral industry. Regionally, common names vary widely but botanical names are universal. The list is useful for reference and for studying and memorizing both common and botanical plant names and their spellings.

Botanical Name	Common Name
Acacia sp.	Mimosa, Acacia
Achillea sp.	Yarrow
Aconitum sp.	True Monkshood
Agapanthus sp.	Lily of the Nile
Ageratum sp.	Ageratum
Alchemilla mollis	Lady's Mantle
Allium sp.	Onion flower
Alpinia sp.	Torch Ginger
Alstroemeria sp.	Alstroemeria, Peruvian Lily
Amaranthus caudatus	Green or Red Tassel Flower
Amaranthus cruentus	Prince's Feather
Amaranthus sp.	Amaranth Fountain Plant
Amaryllis sp.	Amaryllis
Ammi majus	Queen Anne's Lace
Ananas bracteatus	Ornamental Pineapple
Anemone sp.	Anemone, Windflower
Anigozanthos sp.	Kangaroo Paw
Anthurium sp.	Anthurium
Antirrhinum majus	Snapdragon
Aquilegia sp.	Columbine
Argyranthemum sp.	Marguerite Daisy
Asclepias sp.	Milkweed, Butterflyweed

(Continued)

Botanical Name	Common Name
Aster novae belgii	Aster, Novae Belgii
Aster sp.	Aster
Astilbe sp.	Astilbe, Plume Flower
Astrantia major	Masterwort
Atriplex hortensis	Saltbush
Banksia sp.	Banksia
Boronia sp.	Heather Boronia
Bouvardia sp.	Bouvardia
Brassica oleracea	Ornamental Kale
Brunia sp.	Brunia
Buddleja davidii	Butterfly Bush
Bupleurum rotundifolium	Bupleurum
C. sulphureus	Cosmos
Calendula officinalis	Pot Marigold, Calendula
Callicarpa sp.	Beauty Berry
Callistephus chinensis	China Aster
Camellia sp.	Camellia
Camellia sp.	Chinese Rose
Campanula sp.	Bellflower, Chimney Bells
Capsicum annuum	Ornamental Pepper
Carthamus tinctorius	Safflower
Cattleya sp.	Cattleya Orchid Hybrid
Celastrus sp.	Bittersweet
Celosia argentea var. *cristata*	Cockscomb
Centaurea cyanus	Bachelor's Button, Cornflower
Centranthus rubra	Valerian
Chaenomeles sp.	Flowering Quince
Chamelaucium uncinatum	Waxflower
Chelone sp.	Turtlehead
Chrysanthemum sp.	Button Mum

(Continued)

Botanical Name	Common Name
Chrysanthemum sp.	Cushion Mum
Chrysanthemum sp.	Daisy Mum
Chrysanthemum sp.	Spider Mum
Cirsium sp.	Japanese Thistle
Clarkia sp.	Godetia
Clematis sp.	Clematis
Clivia miniata	Clivia, Kaffir Lily
Convallaria majalis	Lily of the Valley
Coreopsis sp.	Tickseed
Cosmos sp.	Cosmos
Craspedia sp.	Craspedia, Billy Balls
Crocosmia sp.	Crocosmia
Cymbidium sp.	Cymbidium Orchid
Cynara sp.	Globe Artichoke
Dahlia sp.	Dahlia
Delphinium sp.	Larkspur
Dendrobium sp.	Dendrobium Orchid
Dianthus sp.	Carnation
Dianthus sp.	Dianthus, Pinks
Dianthus sp.	Spray Carnation
Digitalis purpurea	Purple Foxglove
Echinacea sp.	Cone Flower
Echinops sp.	Globe Thistle
Eremurus sp.	Foxtail Lily
Erica sp.	Heather
Eryngium sp.	Sea Holly
Eucalyptus sp.	Eucalyptus Pods
Eucharis sp.	Eucharis
Euphorbia sp.	Euphorbia
Eustoma grandiflorum	Lisianthus

(Continued)

Botanical Name	Common Name
Forsythia sp.	Forsythia, Golden Bells
Freesia sp.	Freesia
Fuchsia sp.	Fuchsia
Gaillardia sp.	Blanket Flower
Galanthus sp.	Snowdrop
Gardenia jasminoides 'Fortuniana'	Gardenia
Gerbera sp.	Gerbera, African Daisy
Gladiolus sp.	Gladiola, Sword Lily
Gloriosa sp.	Gloriosa, Glory Lily
Gomphocarpus brasiliensis	Milkweed Balloon Plant
Gypsophila sp.	Baby's Breath
Helenium sp.	Helen's Flower
Helianthus sp.	Sunflower
Heliconia sp.	Lobster Claw
Heliconia sp.	Torch Heliconia
Heliopsis sp.	Ox-Eye Daisy
Heuchera sp.	Coral Bells
Hosta sp.	Plantain Hosta
Hydrangea macrophylla sp.	French (Florist's) Hydrangea
Iberis sp.	Candytuft
Iris sp.	Bearded Iris
Iris x xiphium	Dutch Iris
Kniphofia uvaria	Torch-Lily, Red hot poker
Lathyrus sp.	Sweet Pea
Lavandula sp.	Lavender
Leptospermum sp.	Lepto
Leucadendron sp.	Leucadendron, Flame Tip
Leucanthemum sp.	Shasta Daisy
Leucospermum sp.	Pincushion Protea
Liatris sp.	Gayfeather, Liatris

(Continued)

Botanical Name	Common Name
Lilium 'Star Gazer'	Star Gazer Lily
Lilium longiflorum	Trumpet (Easter) Lily
Lilium sp.	Asiatic Lily
Lilium sp.	Oriental Lily
Limonium sp.	Statice, Sea Lavender Statice
Lupinus sp.	Lupine
Lysimachia sp.	Loosestrife
Lysimachia sp.	False Dragonhead, Gooseneck Flower
Malus sp.	Crabapple
Matthiola incana	Flowering Stock
Moluccella laevis	Bells of Ireland
Monarda didyma	Bee-Balm, Fragrant Balm
Mertensia virginica	Blue Bells, Virginia Blue Bells
Muscari sp.	Grape Hyacinth
Myosotis sylvatica	Forget-Me-Not
Narcissus sp.	Daffodil
Nerine sp.	Nerine Lily
Nigella damascena	Love-in-a-Mist
Oncidium sp.	Oncidium Orchid
Ornithogalum sp.	Star of Bethlehem
Paeonia sp.	Peony
Papaver orientalis	Oriental Poppy
Paphiopedilum sp.	Ladyslipper Orchid
Parthenium sp.	Feverfew
Penstemon sp.	Beard Tongue
Phalaenopsis sp.	Butterfly Orchid
Phlox paniculata	Phlox
Platycodon grandiflorus	Balloon Flower
Polianthes tuberosa	Tuberose
Protea cyanoides	King Protea

(Continued)

Botanical Name	Common Name
Protea sp.	Pink Mink Protea
Prunus sp.	Flowering Plum
Ranunculus sp.	Persian Buttercup
Rosa sp.	Spray Rose
Rosa sp.	Sweetheart Rose
Rosa sp.	Tea Rose
Rudbeckia sp.	Black-Eyed Susan
Salix discolor	Pussy Willow
Salvia splendens	Sage, Salvia
Saponaria ocymoides	Saponaria
Sarracenia sp.	Sarracenia, Pitcher Plant
Scabiosa sp.	Scabiosa, Pincushion Flower
Sedum sp.	Stonecrop
Solidago sp.	Solidaster
Stephanotis floribunda	Stephanotis
Strelitzia reginae	Bird of Paradise
Syringa sp.	Lilac
Tagetes erecta	African Marigold
Tricyrtis sp.	Toad Lily
Trollius sp.	Globeflower
Tulipa sp.	Tulip
Vanda sp.	Vanda Orchid
Veronica sp.	Speedwell
Viola odorata	Sweet Violet
Viola x wittrockiana	Pansy
Xeranthemum sp.	Strawflower
Zantedeschia sp.	Calla
Zinnia elegans	Zinnia

Foliage Glossary Cross Reference

The following is a cross reference list for the Foliage Glossary in Chapter 9. It is alphabetized by botanical name whereas the glossary in Chapter 9 is alphabetized by common name. Both botanical and common names are used in the floral industry. Regionally, common names vary widely but botanical names are universal. The list is useful for reference and for studying and memorizing both common and botanical plant names and their spellings.

Botanical Name	Common Name
Adiantum raddianum	Maidenhair Fern
Alocasia amazonica	Alocasia, African Mask
Anthurium sp.	Anthurium
Artemisia sp.	Sagebush
Asparagus densiflorus 'Meyeri'	Foxtail Fern
Asparagus densiflorus 'Sprengeri'	Sprengeri Fern
Asparagus setaceus	Plumosa Fern
Asplenium nidus	Bird's Nest Fern
Aucuba japonica	Aucuba
Brassica oleracea	Ornamental Cabbage, Kale
Buxus sempervirens 'Variegata'	Variegated Boxwood
Buxus sp.	Boxwood
Caladium sp.	Miss Muffet Caladium
Caladium sp.	Pink Caladium
Caladium sp.	Fancy-Leaved Caladium
Calathea lancifolia	Calathea, Rattlesnake Plant
Calathea sp.	Calathea
Calathea sp.	Calathea
Caleocedrus decurrens	California Incense Cedar
Callistemon sp.	Bottle-Brush Plant
Camellia sp.	Camellia
Chamaecyparis lawsoniana	Port Orford Cedar
Chlorophytum cosmosum	Spider Plant, Airplane Plant
Codiaeum sp.	Croton

(Continued)

Botanical Name	Common Name
Codiaeum sp.	Yellow Croton
Codiaeum variegatum 'Icetone'	Icetone Croton
Codiaeum variegatum 'Red Bananas'	Red Bananas Croton
Cordyline sp.	Ti Leaves
Cotinus sp.	Smokebush
Cryptanthus sp.	Cryptanthus
Cycas revolute	Cycad, Sago Palm
Cyperus sp.	Papyrus
Cytisus scoparius	Scotch Broom
Dicranopteris linearis	Fiddleheads
Dracaena marginata 'Tricolor'	Tricolor Dracaena
Dracaena sanderiana	Dracaena, Lucky Bamboo
Echeveria sp.	Hen and Chicks, Echeveria
Equisetum hyemale	Equisetum, Horsetail, Scouring Rush
Eucalyptus sp.	Eucalyptus
Eucalyptus sp.	Knifeblade Eucalyptus
Eucalyptus sp.	Silver Dollar Eucalyptus
Eucalyptus sp.	Willow Eucalyptus
Euonymus sp.	Wintercreeper
Euphorbia marginata	Euphorbia, Snow-on-the-Mountain
Galax urceolata	Galax
Gaultheria shallon	Salal, Lemon Leaf
Guzmania sp.	Guzmania
Hedera helix	English Ivy
Hedera helix 'variegata'	Variegated English Ivy
Hoya sp.	Wax Plant, Hoya
Ilex opaca	American Holly
Ilex sp.	Variegated Holly
Juniperus sp.	Juniper
Juniperus sp.	Berried Juniper

(Continued)

Botanical Name	Common Name
Laurus nobilis	Laurel
Leucadendron sp.	Leucadendron
Liriope sp.	Variegated Lily Turf Grass
Liriope sp.	Lily Grass, Liriope
Magnolia sp.	Magnolia
Mahonia sp.	Mahonia, Oregon Grape
Melaleuca armillaris	Bracelet Honey Myrtle
Mentha sp.	Mint
Monstera deliciosa	Cutleaf Philodendron
Monstera deliciosa 'variegata'	Variegated Cutleaf Philodendron
Murraya paniculata	Orange Jessamine
Myrtus communis	Myrtus, Myrtle
Nandina domestica	Autumn-colored Nandina
Nandina domestica	Green Nandina
Nandina sp.	Berried Nandina
Nephrolepis exaltata 'Bostoniensis'	Boston Fern
Pandanus sp.	Hala
Peperomia obtusifolia 'Variegata'	Variegated Peperomia
Philodendron 'Xanadu'	Philodendron Xanadu
Philodendron pinnatifidum	Selloum
Phormium sp.	New Zealand Flax
Pinus strobus	White Pine
Pittosporum tobira	Pittosporum
Pittosporum tobira 'Variegatum'	Variegated Pittosporum
Platycerium bifurcatum	Staghorn Fern
Podocarpus sp.	Buddhist Pine
Polystichum munitum	Flat Fern
Pseudotsuga menziesii	Douglas Fir
Radermachera sinica	China Doll, Emerald Tree
Rosmarinus officinalis	Rosemary

(Continued)

Botanical Name	Common Name
Rumohra adiantiformis	Leatherleaf Fern
Ruscus sp.	Israeli Ruscus
Ruscus sp.	Italian Ruscus
Sabal sp.	Palmetto
Salvia sp.	Tricolor Sage
Sanseveria sp.	Mother-in-Law Tongue
Schefflera actinophylla	Schefflera, Australian Ivy
Schefflera arboricola	Schefflera
Senecio cineraria 'Diamond'	Dusty Miller Diamond Frost
Senecio rowleyanus	String of Pearls
Senecio sp.	Dusty Miller
Senecio sp.	String of Hearts
Setaria italica	Foxtail Millet
Skimmia japonica	Skimmia
Sorghum sp.	Broom Corn
Stachys byzantina	Lamb's Ear
Strelitzia reginae	Strelitzia, Bird of Paradise
Stromanthe sanguinea 'Triostar'	Triostar Stromanthe
Syngonium podophyllum	Arrowhead
Syngonium sp.	Syngonium
Tillandsia sp.	Tillandsia
Triticum sp.	Green Wheat
Typha sp.	Cattails
Vaccinium ovatum	Vaccinium, Green Huckleberry
Viburnum sp.	Viburnum berries
Xerophyllum tenax	Bear Grass
Zamia pumila	Coontie Fern

Dried Botanicals Glossary Cross Reference

The following is a cross reference list for the Dried Botanicals Glossary in Chapter 16. It is alphabetized by botanical name whereas the glossary in Chapter 16 is alphabetized by common name. Both botanical and common names are used in the floral industry. Regionally, common names vary widely but botanical names are universal. The list is useful for reference and for studying and memorizing both common and botanical plant names and their spellings.

Botanical Name	Common Name
Abelmoschus esculentus	Okra Pod (dried)
Achillea sp.	Yarrow
Arctostaphylos sp.	Manzanita Branch
Betula sp.	Birch Branch
Callicladium sp.	Florist Sheet Moss
Cinnamomum verum	Cinnamon Sticks
Cladina sp.	Reindeer Moss
Cortaderia selloana	Pampass Grass
Corylus avellana 'Contorta'	Clorylus, Contorted Filbert Branch
Craspedia uniflora	Billy Balls, Craspedia
Dicranum sp.	Mood Moss
Eleusine sp.	Millet
Gomphrena globosa 'Lavender Lady'	Gomphrena
Gossypium sp.	Cotton
Helichrysum sp.	Strawflower
Humulus lupulus	Hops
Hypogymnia sp.	Lichen
Lagurus ovatus	Bunny Tails
Nelumbo nucifera	Lotus (large)
Nelumbo nucifera	Lotus (small)
Oryza sativa	Rice
Papaver sp.	Poppy Seed Head
Pennisetum setaceum 'Rubrum'	Purple Fountain Grass
Phyllostachys sp.	Bamboo, River Cane
Physalis alkekengi	Chinese Lantern, Physalis

(Continued)

Botanical Name	Common Name
Pinus nigra subsp. *austriaca*	Austrian Pine Cone
Pinus strobes	White Pine Cone
Pinus taeda	Sugar Cone
Punica sp.	Pomegranate
Quercus suber	Cork
Sabal sp.	Palmetto Leaf
Salix matsudana 'Tortuosa'	Corkscrew Willow
Salix sp.	Pussy Willow
Sarracenia sp.	Sarracenia, Pitcher Plant
Setaria sp.	Millet
Tillandsia usneoides	Spanish Moss
Triticum sp.	Wheat
Triticum sp.	Bearded Wheat
Tsuga canadensis	Hemlock Cone
Typha sp.	Cattails
Usnea sp.	Florist's Lichen Covered Branch

Potted Plants Glossary Cross Reference

The following is a cross reference list for the Potted Plants Glossary in Chapter 17. It is alphabetized by botanical name whereas the glossary in Chapter 17 is alphabetized by common name. Both botanical and common names are used in the floral industry. Regionally, common names vary widely but botanical names are universal. The list is useful for reference and for studying and memorizing both common and botanical plant names and their spellings.

Botanical Name	Common Name
Adiantum raddianum	Maidenhair Fern
Aechmea fasciata	Bromeliad, Aechmea
Agave sp.	Agave
Agave sp.	Century Plant
Aglaonema commutatum	Aglaonema
Aloe vera	Aloe Vera
Aphelandra squarrosa	Aphelandra, Zebra Plant

(Continued)

Botanical Name	Common Name
Araucaria heterophylla	Norfolk Island Pine
Asparagus densiflorus 'Meyeri'	Foxtail Fern
Aspidistra elatior	Cast Iron Plant, Bar Room Plant
Beaucarnea recurvata	Ponytail Palm
Begonia masoniana	Begonia, Iron Cross
Begonia Rex-cultorum	Begonia, Rex
Begonia x semperflorens-cultorum	Begonia, Reiger
Callisia repens	Inch Plant
Caryota mitis	Fishtail Palm
Chamaedorea elegans	Parlor Palm
Cholorphytum cosmosum	Spider Plant, Airplane Plant
Chrysalidocarpus lutescens	Areca Palm
Cissus sp.	Grape Ivy
Clematis sp.	Clematis
Codiaeum variegatum 'Icetone'	Icetone Croton
Codiaeum variegatum 'Red Bananas'	Red Bananas Croton
Crassula argentea	Jade Plant, Dollar Plant
Cyrtomium sp.	Holly Fern
Davallia fejeensis	Rabbit's Foot Fern
Dieffenbachia sp.	Dieffenbachia, Dumb Cane
Dracaena fragrans 'Massangeana'	Dracaena, Corn Plant Dracaena
Dracaena marginata 'Tricolor'	Tricolor Dracaena
Echeveria sp.	Hen and Chicks
Echinocactus sp.	Barrel Cactus
Epipremnum sp.	Pothos
Epipremnum sp.	Pothos, Devil's Ivy
Erica carnea	Heather
Euphorbia tirucallii	Euphorbia, Firestick Plant
Fatshedera sp.	Japanese Aralia
Ficus benjamina	Benjamin Fig Ficus
Ficus binnendijkii 'Alii'	Alii Ficus

(Continued)

Botanical Name	Common Name
Ficus elastica	Ficus Tree, Indian Rubber Tree
Ficus pumila	Creeping Fig
Fittonia sp.	Nerve Plant
Gynura aurantiaca 'Sarmentosa'	Purple Passion, Velvet Plant
Haworthia fasciata	Zebra Cactus, Haworthia
Hosta sp.	Variegated Hosta
Howea forsteriana	Kentia Palm, Thatch Palm
Hoya carnosa	Wax Plant
Hypoestes sp.	Polka Dot Plant
Kalanchoe sp.	Kalanchoe
Lunaria sp.	Money Plant
Maranta leuconeura var. *kerchoviana*	Prayer Plant
Miscanthus sinensis 'Zebrinus'	Zebra Grass
Monstera deliciosa	Philodendron Monstera
Nandina domestica	Green Nandina
Nephrolepis exaltata 'Bostoniensis'	Boston Fern
Opuntia sp.	Opuntia Cactus
Pelargonium peltatum	Ivy Geranium
Peperomia sp.	Peporomia, Emerald Ripple Peperomia
Peperomia sp.	Peporomia obtusifolia
Philodendron sp.	Philodendron Selloum
Philodendron sp.	Philodendron
Phoenix roebelenii	Phoenix, Pygmy Date Palm
Pilea cadierei	Pilea, Aluminum Plant
Pilea microphylla	Pilea, Artillery Plant
Platycerium bifurcatum	Staghorn Fern
Primula sp.	Primrose
Rhapis excelsa	Bamboo Palm, Lady Palm
Rhododendron sp.	Florist's Azalea
Rosmarinus sp.	Rosemary
Saintpaulia sp.	African Violet

(Continued)

Botanical Name	Common Name
Sansevieria sp.	Sansevieria, Mother-in-Law Tongue
Saxifraga stolonifera	Strawberry Plant
Schefflera arboricola	Schefflera, Umbrella Plant
Schefflera arboricola 'Varieagata'	Dwarf Variegated Schefflera, Dwarf Variegated Umbrella Tree
Schindapsus sp.	Philodendron
Sedum morganianum	Burro Tail, Panda Plant
Selaginella kraussiana	African Clubmoss, Selaginella
Soleirolia soleirolii	Baby's Tears, Mother of Thousands
Solenostemon scutellarioides	Coleus
Spathiphyllum sp.	Spathiphyllum, White Anthurium, Peace Lily
Sticherus sp.	Umbrella Fern
Syngonium sp.	Nephthytis
Tradescantia pallid	Tradescantia, Purple Wandering Jew
Yucca sp.	Yucca, Spanish Dagger
Zamioculcas zamiifolia	ZZ Plant, Zanzibar Gem
Zantedeschia sp.	Calla
Zygocactus sp.	Christmas Cactus

Postharvest and Storage Guidelines for Foliage

Florist greens	Botanical Name	Leaf Length	Texture	Storage Temperature	Storage Life	Vase Life
Alocasia	*Alocasia amazonica*	8"–36"	Coarse	60°F (15.5°C)	–	7–14 days
Anthurium	*Anthurium* sp.	8"–12"	Coarse	55°F–40°F (12.5°C–4°C)	1 week	7–14 days
Aspidistra	*Aspidistra elatior*	8"–36"	Coarse	40°F–55°F (4°C–13°C)	2 weeks	14–21 days
Bear Grass	*Xerophyllum tenax*	24"–30"	–	–	–	7–21 days
Bird's Nest Fern	*Asplenium nidus*	4'–6'	–	–	–	7–14 days
Boston Fern	*Nephrolepis exaltata* 'Bostoniensis'	20"–8'	–	–	–	5–10 days
Boxwood	*Buxus* sp.	6"–18"	Fine	35°F–40°F (2°C –4°C)	1–2 months	3–5 weeks
Brake Fern	*Pteridium aquilinum*	3'	Coarse	33°F–40°F (0.5°C–4°C)	3 weeks	2–5 days
Broom Corn	*Sorghum* sp.	8"–24"	–	–	–	7–21 days
Caladium	*Caladium* sp.	6"–18"	–	–	–	5 days
Calathea	*Calathea* sp.	4"–8"	Coarse	–	–	14–21 days
Camellia	*Camellia* sp.	12"–24"	Leathery	40°F (4°C)	4 weeks	3 weeks
Cattails	*Typha* sp.	3'–6'	–	–	–	5–14 days
Cedar	*Cedrus* sp.	18"–30"	Prickly	33°F–40°F (0.5°C–4°C)	4 weeks	3–6 days
Croton	*Codiaeum* sp.	6" or more	Smooth	35°F–40°F (2°C–4°C)	2 weeks	4 weeks
Crypanthus	*Cryptanthus* sp.	4"–24"	–	–	–	–
Cycas	*Cycas revolute*	26"–30"	–	–	–	4 weeks
Cyperus	*Cyperus* sp.	6"–10"	Fine–scaly	–	–	7–10 days
Dagger and Wood Ferns	–	10"–24"	Fine	33°F–40°F (0.5°C–4°C)	2–3 months	10–20 days
Dieffenbachia	*Dieffenbachia* sp.	6"–24"	Smooth	55°F (13°C)	1 week	10–22 days
Douglas Fir	*Pseudotsuga menziesii*	–	–	–	–	–
Dracaena	*Dracaena* sp.	6"–18"	Straplike	35°F–40°F (2°C–4°C)	2 weeks	14–21 days
English Ivy	*Hedera helix* cv.	12"–24"	Smooth	33°F–36°F (0.5°C–2°C)	4 weeks	5–10 days
Equisetum	*Equisetum hyemale*	8"–5'	–	–	–	12 days
Eucalyptus	*Eucalyptus* sp.	Depends on species	Leathery	35°F–40°F (2°C–4°C)	1–3 weeks	10 days

(Continued)

Florist greens	Botanical Name	Leaf Length	Texture	Storage Temperature	Storage Life	Vase Life
Fiddleheads	*Dicranopteris linearis*	–	–	45°F (7°C)	–	10–14 days
Foxtail Fern	*Asparagus densiflorus* 'Meyeri'	1'–2'	–	35°F–50°F (2°C–5°C)	–	6–14 days
Galax	*Galax urceolata*	3"–6"	Smooth	33°F–40°F (0.5°C–4°C)	4 weeks	5–10 days
Ground Pine	*Lycopodium obscurum*	3"–6"	Needles	33°F–40°F (0.5°C–4°C)	4 weeks	5–7 days
Hala, Pandanus	*Pandanus* sp.	2'–3'	–	–	–	10–14 days
Hedera	*Hedera helix*	stems 12"–36" leaves 1"–6"	Smooth	35°F–40°F (2°C–4°C)	2–3 weeks	7–28 days
Huckleberry	*Vaccinium* sp.	18"–30"	Fine	33°F–40°F (0.5°C–4°C)	1–4 weeks	7–14 days
Ilex, Holly	*Ilex opaca*	18"–30"	Prickly	33°F–36°F (0.5°C–2°C)	3–5 weeks	5–14 days
Juniper	*Juniperus* sp.	12"–24"	Needles	33°F–40°F (0.5°C–4°C)	1–2 months	7–14 days
Laurel, Mountain	*Laurus nobilis*	20"–30"	Smooth	33°F–40°F (0.5°C–4°C)	2–4 weeks	7–10 days
Leatherleaf Fern	*Rumohra adiantiformis*	10"–24"	Lacy	34°F–40°F (1°C–4°C)	1–2 months	7–15 days
Leucadendron	*Leucadendron* sp.	3"–6"	Soft, silky	35°F–40°F (2°C–4°C)	–	7–21 days
Leucothoe	*Leucothoe* sp.	12"–40"	Lacy	35°F–40°F (2°C–4°C)	4 weeks	7–21 days
Magnolia	*Magnolia* sp.	18"–36"	Smooth	35°F–40°F (2°C–4°C)	2–4 weeks	5–8 days
Mahonia, Oregon Grape	*Mahonia* sp.	12"	Spiky, leathery	–	–	14–21 days
Maidenhair Fern	*Adiantum raddianum*	8"–20"	Lacy	33°F–40°F (0.5°C–4°C)	1 week	3–7 days
Mistletoe	*Viscum album*	6"–12"	Fine	33°F–36°F (0.5°C–2°C)	3–4 weeks	5–14 days
Monstera	*Monstera deliciosa*	–	Smooth	–	–	18–30 days
Myrtle, Myrtus	*Myrtus communis*	1"–2"	–	–	–	–
Nephthytis	–	6"–14"	–	–	–	–
New Zealand Flax	*Phormium* sp.	–	–	–	–	20–30 days
Palm, Commodore	*Chamaedorea* sp.	18"–40"	Palm	45°F (7°C)	3 weeks	5–7 days
Papyrus	*Cyperus* sp.	Depends on species	–	–	–	7–10 days
Perperomia	*Peperomia* sp.	–	Smooth	35°F–40°F (2°C–4°C)	–	10–14 days

(Continued)

Florist greens	Botanical Name	Leaf Length	Texture	Storage Temperature	Storage Life	Vase Life
Philodendron	*Philodendron* sp.	10"–30"	Smooth	35°F–40°F (2°C–4°C)	1 week	10–14 days
Pittosporum	*Pittosporum tobira*	–	–	40°F (4°C)	–	7–14 days
Plumosa Fern	*Asparagus setaceus*	8"–36"	Fine	35°F–40°F (2°C–4°C)	2–3 weeks	6–14 days
Podocarpus	–	18"–40"	Large needles	45°F (7°C)	4 weeks	7–21 days
Pothos	*Epipremnum* sp.	6"–12"	Smooth	35°F–40°F (2°C–4°C)	1 week	–
Sago Palm	–	18"–40"	Needles	40°F–50°F (4°C–10°C)	4 weeks	21–30 days
Salal, Lemon Leaf	*Gaultheria shallon*	2"–4"	Leathery	35°F–40°F (2°C–4°C)	2–4 weeks	7–21 days
Scotch Broom	*Cytisus scoparius*	24"–40"	Grassy	40°F (4°C)	2–3 weeks	7–21 days
Smilax	*Smilax asparagoides*	36"–72"	Vining	40°F (4°C)	3 weeks	5–14 days
Sprengerii Fern	*Asparagus densiflorus* 'Sprengeri'	8"–36"	Fine	35°F–40°F (2°C–4°C)	2–3 weeks	6–14 days
Staghorn Fern	*Platycerium bifurcatum*	12"–40"	Smooth	55°F (13°C)	1 week	3–7 days
Strelitzia	*Strelitzia reginae*	–	Smooth	55°F (13°C)	1 week	7–14 days
Ti leaves, Palm Lily	*Cordyline* sp.	10"–40"	Smooth	40°F (4°C)	1 week	10–14 days
Wintercreeper	*Euonymus* sp.	–	Smooth	–	–	7–20 days

The above information is from a number of reputable sources. All temperatures, storage life days, and vase life days have been averaged using information from these sources. Keep in mind that cutting methods, cooling devices, packaging materials, water quality, and other factors affect plant materials. Use the information provided as a starting point to determine what works best in your facilities.

Postharvest and Storage Guidelines for Flowers

Common Name	Species	Colors	Height	Harvest Stage	Harvest Tip	Storage Life	Storage Temperature	Ethylene Sensitivity	Vase Life
Agapanthus	*Agapanthus aficanus*	blue, purple, pink, white	15"–5'	one-fourth florets open	–	–	33°F–36°F (0.5°C –2.2°C)	Yes	6–12 days
Ageratum	*Ageratum houstonianum*	blue, pink, white	2'–3'	Center florets fully open	–	–	35°F–40°F (2°C–4°C)	–	7–10 days
Allium, Ornamental Onion	*Allium* sp.	varied	2"–5'	one-fourth to one-third florets open	–	2 weeks, dry; 4 weeks, wet	33°F–36°F (0.5°C –2.2°C)	Yes	10–14 days
Alstroemeria, Peruvian Lily	over 50	yellow, orange, apricot, pink, red, purple	1'–3'	first flowers fully colored	–	2 weeks, wet	38°F–40°F (3.3°C–40°C)	Yes	12–14 days
Anemone	over 100	varied	1'–3'	buds beginning to open	–	2 days	40°F–45°F (4°C–7°C)	Yes	4–8 days
Anemone, Poppy	*Anemone coronaria*	varied	12"–18"	buds beginning to open	–	3–5 days	40°F (4°C)	Yes	3–7 days
Anthurium	*Anthurium* sp.	red, white, pink, orange	15"–20"	spadix is 50%–75% mature	–	2–4 weeks	53°F–63°F (13°C–20°C)	No	10–25 days
Aster, China, Annual Aster	*Callistephus chinensis*	white, yellow, blue, red, green, purple, apricot, magenta	8"–8'	fully open flowers	Cut 1" from the stem	1–3 weeks	33°F–40°F (0.5°C–4°C)	No	5–10 days
Aster, Michelmas Daisy	*Aster* spp.	white, purple, blue, pink	3'–4'	mostly open	–	–	36°F–40°F (2.2°C–4°C)	No	5–10 days
Astilbe	*Astilbe* sp.	White, pink, red, rose, purple	18"–48"	55%–70% open	dries out quickly	1 week	33°F–40°F (0.5°C–4°C)	Yes	5–10 days
Atriplex	Over 200 species	red, green, gray	3'–8'	–	–	–	36°F–40°F (2.2°C–4°C)	Yes	5–7 days
Baby's Breath	*Gypsophila* spp.	white, pink	2'–4'	flowers open but not overly mature	–	1–3 weeks	40°F (4°C)	Yes	5–11 days
Bachelor's Button	*Centaurea* spp.	blue, white, pink, yellow	1'–3'	flowers beginning to open	–	5–14 days	36°F–40°F (2.2°C–4°C)	Yes	5–7 days

(Continued)

Common Name	Species	Colors	Height	Harvest Stage	Harvest Tip	Storage Life	Storage Temperature	Ethylene Sensitivity	Vase Life
Balloon Flower	*Platycodon grandiflorus*	blue, white	2'	2 to 3 flowers open	sear end of stem	–	38°F–40°F (3.3°C–4°C)	–	1–7 days
Beard Tongue	*Penstemon* sp.	various	2'–3'	just opening	–	1–2 weeks	–	Yes	5–7 days
Bellflower	*Campanula* sp.	blue, white	2'–4'	half flowers open	–	–	–	Yes	5–16 days
Bells of Ireland	*Moluccella laevis*	green	2'–3'	bells are fully open	–	–	36°F–40°F (2.2°C–4°C)	Yes	7–14 days
Bird of Paradise	*Strelitzia reginae*	orange-blue	2'–4'	just beginning to open	store upright	–	55°F–70°F (13°C–21°C)	No	7–14 days
Black-eyed Susan, Yellow Oxeye Daisy, English Bulls-eye	*Rudbeckia* spp.	yellow	3'	fully open flowers	100°F for 10 minutes	–	–	Yes	3–10 days
Blanket Flower, Indian Blanket Flower	*Gaillardia pulchella*	orange, red, yellow, gold	2'–3'	fully open flowers	–	3 days	40°F (4°C)	–	6–10 days
Blue	*Scilla siberica*	pink, white, yellow, salmon, red	4"–6"	half open flowers	–	2 weeks	36°F–40°F (2.2°C–4°C)	–	6–10 days
Bouvardia	*Bouvardia* sp.	pink, white, yellow, salmon, red	–	–	–	1 week	36°F–40°F (2.2°C–4°C)	yes	7–14 days
Buddleja	*Campanula* sp.	lilac, orange,	4"–10"	–	–	1–2 days	40°F (4°C)	Yes	1–2 days
Calendula	*Caendula* sp.	yellow, gold, orange	–	fully open flowers	–	3–6 days	40°F (4°C)	–	6–12 days
Calla Lily	*Zantedeschia* sp.	various	8"–3'	mostly open	–	1 week	50°–70°F (10°C–21°C)	No	4–8 days
Candytuft	*Iberis* sp.	white, purple, pink	1'–2'	starting to open	–	3 days	40°F (4°C)	–	5–7 days
Canterbury Bells	*Campanula* spp.	white, pink, blue, purple	–	one-half florets open	–	–	–	Yes	7–14 days
Carnation	*Dianthus caryophyllus*	wide range of colors	–	petals emerged 1/2" above calyx	–	2–4 weeks	36°F–40°F (2.2°C–4°C)	Yes	7–15 days

(Continued)

Common Name	Species	Colors	Height	Harvest Stage	Harvest Tip	Storage Life	Storage Temperature	Ethylene Sensitivity	Vase Life
Cattleya	*Cattleya* sp.	wide range of colors	–	3 to 4 days after opening	–	–	50°F–55°F (10°C–13°C)	Yes	–
Chrysanthemum	*Dendranthema* x *grandiflorum*	wide range of colors	–	outer petals fully elongated	–	2–4 weeks	36°F–40°F (2.2°C–4°C)	–	7–21 days
Clarkia, Farwell to Spring	*Clarkia unquiculata*	wide range of colors	–	one-half florets open	–	3 days	40°F (4°C)	–	5–10 days
Climbing Lily, Glory Lily	*Gloriosa superba*	white, yellow, crimson	–	almost fully open flowers	–	–	46°F (7.7°C)	–	3–8 days
Cockscomb	*Celosia argentea var. cristata*	wide range of colors	–	one-half florets open	–	1–3 weeks	36°F–41°F (2.2°C–5.0°C)	Yes	5–14 days
Columbine	*Aquilegia hybrids*	wide range of colors	1'–2'	one-half florets open	–	2 days	40°F (4°C)	Yes	5–7 days
Columbine, Meadow Rue	*Thalictrum aguilegiifolium*	lilac, blue, yellow	18"+	one-half florets open	–	–	–	Yes	–
Cone Flower	*Rudbeckia* sp.	yellow, other	2'	just opening	–	–	–	Yes	5–7 days
Cone Flower	*Echinacea* sp.	purple, white	2'–3'	petals expanding; 50% of globe is blue	–	2 weeks	40°F (4°C)	Yes	7–10 days
Coral Bells	*Heuchera* sp.	red, pink, white	2'–3'	half florets open	–	–	–	–	5–7 days
Coreopsis, Tickseed, Lance Coreopsis	*Coreopsis grandiflora*	wide range of colors	–	fully open flowers	–	3–4 days	40°F (4°C)	–	–
Cornflower	*Centaurea cyanus*	blue, white, pink	–	–	–	3 days	40°F (4°C)	–	6–10 days
Cosmos	*C. sulphureus*	white, pink, crimson, red, orange, yellow	16"–20"	petals opening but not yet flat	–	3–4 days	36°F–40°F (2.2°C–4°C)	–	4–6 days or 1–3 weeks (depends on species)
Craspedia	*Craspedia* sp.	yellow	–	full colored heads, not shedding pollen	–	–	36°F–40°F (2.2°C–4°C)	No	10–12 days
Cymbidium Orchid	*Cymbidium* sp.	wide range of colors	–	–	–	–	36°F–40°F (2.2°C–4°C)	–	7–20 days
Daffodil, Narcissus, Jonquil	*Narcissus* cvs.	white, yellow, orange, pink	–	goose neck stage	–	1–3 weeks	36°F–40°F (2.2°C–4°C)	–	4–10 days

(Continued)

Common Name	Species	Colors	Height	Harvest Stage	Harvest Tip	Storage Life	Storage Temperature	Ethylene Sensitivity	Vase Life
Dahlia	*Dahlia* cvs.	wide range of colors	–	fully open flowers	–	3–5 days	40°F (4°C)	Yes	7–14 days
Daisy, English	*Bellis perennis*	wide range of colors	–	fully open flowers	–	–	39°F–41°F (4°C–5°C)	–	–
Daisy, Marguerite	*Anthemis* sp.	white, gold	2′–3′	just opening	–	1–2 weeks	36°F–40°F (2.2°C–4°C)	–	5–10 days
Daisy, Ox-eye	*Heliopsis* sp.	yellow, gold	3′–6′	fully open	–	–	–	–	7–10 days
Daisy, Shasta	*Leucanthemum* sp.	white	1′–3′	–	–	–	–	–	–
Daylily	*Hemerocallis* cvs.	variety	–	half-open flowers	–	–	35°F–40°F (2°C–4°C)	–	–
Delphinium	*Delphinium* spp.	blue	–	one-half florets open	–	1–2 days	40°F (4°C)	Yes	5–7 days
Dendrobium	*Dendrobium* sp.	wide range of colors	–	–	–	–	50°F–55°F (10°C–13°C)	No	10–15 days
Eucharis	*Eucharis* sp.	pure white with apple green	–	–	–	7–10 days	45°F–50°F (7°C–10°C)	–	–
False Dragonhead	*Physostegia* sp.	pink, white	1′–3′	florets just opening	–	–	–	Yes	7–14 days
Feverfew	*Parthenium* sp.	white	–	–	–	3 days	40°F (4°C)	–	–
Finger Flower, Purple Foxglove	*Digitalis purpurea*	several	2′–3′	one-half florets open	–	1–2 days	40°F (4°C)	Yes	10–14 days
Fleabane	*Erigeron* hybrids	several	1′–2′	just opening	–	–	–	–	7 days
Sweet Violet	*Viola odorata*	mostly purple	–	almost open flowers	–	–	–	–	–
Forget-Me-Not, Woodland	*Myosotis sylvatica*	mostly blues and whites	–	one-half florets open	–	1–2 days	40°F (4°C)	–	–
Foxglove	*Digitalis purpurea*	pink, red, purple, white, and yellow	–	2 to 3 lower florets open	–	–	35°F–40°F (2°C–4°C)	–	–
Freesia	*Freesia* hybrids	wide range of colors	–	first bud beginning to open	–	10–14 days	36°F–40°F (2.2°C–4°C)	Yes	4–12 days
Gaillardia, annual	*Gaillardia pulchella*	red, yellow, orange	–	fully open flowers	–	–	38°F–40°F (3.3°C–4°C)	–	–

(Continued)

Common Name	Species	Colors	Height	Harvest Stage	Harvest Tip	Storage Life	Storage Temperature	Ethylene Sensitivity	Vase Life
Gaillardia, Blanket (Perennial)	*Gaillardia x grandiflora*	red, yellow	2′–3′	fully open flowers	–	–	–	Yes	7–10 days
Gardenia	*Gardenia* sp.	pure white, creamy white	–	–	–	2 weeks	36°F–40°F (2.2°C–4°C)	–	1–3 days
Gerbera Daisy	*Gerbera jamesonii*	wide range of colors	–	2 outer rows of florets showing pollen	–	1–2 weeks	35°F–40°F (2°C– 4°C)	slight	5–10 days
Gladiolus	*Gladiolus cultivars*	wide range of colors	–	1 to 5 buds showing color	–	5–8 days	35°F–42°F (2°C–5°C)	Yes	6–10 days
Globe Artichoke	*Cynara* sp.	purple, blue	6′	showing color	–	–	36°F–40°F (2.2°C–4°C)	Yes	7–12 days
Globe Flower	*Echinops* sp.	blue	2′–3′	half globe blue	–	–	36°F–40°F (2.2°C–4°C)	Yes	6–12 days
Globe Flower	*Trollius* sp.	yellow, orange	1′–2′	petals opening	–	–	36°F–40°F (2.2°C–4°C)	Yes	5–7 days
Globe Thistle	*Echinops ritro*	blue, violet	2′–4′	half-open flowers	–	–	40°F–45°F (4°C–7°C)	–	–
Godetia	*Clarkia amoena*	white, pink, red, lilac	–	one-half florets open	–	1 week	35°F–41°F (2°C–5°C)	Yes	–
Goldenrod	*Solidago* spp.	gold	2′–4′	one-half florets open	–	–	–	Yes	10 days
Heather	*Erica* sp.	purple	–	one-half florets open	–	–	36°F–40°F (2.2°C–4°C)	–	–
Helen's Flower	*Helenium* sp.	orange, red	3′–5′	mostly open	–	–	–	–	8–10 days
Hyacinth, Common Grape	*Muscari botryoides*	pink, blue, violet, red, yellow, salmon	8″–12″	one-half florets open	Better to not recut stems	3 days	35°F–41°F (2°C–5°C)	somewhat	3–7 days
Hydrangea	*Hydrangea* sp.	large variety of colors	–	one-half florets open	–	–	36°F–40°F (2.2°C–4°C)	–	5–8 days
Iris, Bearded	*Iris* cvs.	various	–	colored buds; pencil stage	Rehydrate in warm water	–	36°F–40°F (2.2°C–4°C)	Yes	2–6 days
Iris, bulbous	*Iris* sp.	several	1′–2′	showing color	–	1–2 weeks	36°F–40°F (2.2°C–4°C)	Yes	3–6 days

(Continued)

Common Name	Species	Colors	Height	Harvest Stage	Harvest Tip	Storage Life	Storage Temperature	Ethylene Sensitivity	Vase Life
Japanese Thistle	Cirsium sp. Cirsium japonicum	pink, red	2'–3'	fully open	–	–	36°F–40°F (2.2°C–4°C)	–	5–7 days
Joseph's Coat, Amaranth Fountain Plant, Tampala	Amaranthus tricolor	pink, yellow, red, purple	–	one-half florets open	–	–	–	–	–
Kaffir, Lily, Clivia	Clivia miniata	variety	–	one-fourth florets open	–	–	–	–	–
Kangaroo Paws	Anigozanthos sp.	variety	–	–	–	–	–	No	8–20 days
Lady's Mantle	Alchemilla sp.	green, yellow	1'–2'	fully open	–	–	–	–	7 days
Larkspur, Annual Delphinium	Consolida ambigua	White, pink, lilac, blue	–	2 to 5 florets open	–	–	36°F–41°F (2.2°C–5°C)	Yes	4–12 days
Larkspur, Perennial	Delphinium sp.	several	3'–6'	half florets open	–	–	–	Yes	6–8 days
Lavender	Lavandula sp.	blue, white	1'–2'	mostly open	–	–	–	–	10–14 days
Leopard's Bane	Doronicum sp.	yellow, gold	2'	flowers almost open	–	–	35°F–40°F (2°C–4°C)	–	5 days
Leptosperum	Leptosperum sp.	pink, red, white, orange, salmon	–	–	–	–	–	yes	3–5 days
Liatris	Liatris spicata	lavender-blue	–	3 to 4 florets open	–	–	33°F–36°F (0.5°C–2.2°C)	–	7–14 days
Lilac	Syringa sp.	–	–	–	–	4–6 days	40°F (4°C)	–	7–10 days
Lily	Lilium sp.	many	2'–4'	buds in color	–	2–3 weeks	36°F–40°F (2.2°C–4°C)	Yes	7–12 days
Lily, Foxtail	Eremurus sp.	gold, other	4'–8'	half florets open	–	–	–	Yes	7 days
Lily, Stargazer	Lilium 'Stargazer'	white with pink/red, various others	–	–	–	–	–	–	7–14 days
Lily-of-the-Valley	Convallaria majalis	white, pale pink	–	one-half florets open	–	2–3 weeks	36°F–40°F (2.2°C–4°C)	–	4–11 days

(Continued)

Common Name	Species	Colors	Height	Harvest Stage	Harvest Tip	Storage Life	Storage Temperature	Ethylene Sensitivity	Vase Life
Lisianthus	Eustoma grandiflorum	pink, white, lavender	–	5 to 6 open flowers	–	–	–	Yes	7–10 days
Lobelia	Lobelia sp.	red	2'–4'	buds in color	–	–	–	–	7–10 days
Loosestrife	Lysimachia sp.	yellow, white	2'	about half open	–	–	–	Yes	5–10 days
Love-in-a-Mist	Nigella damascene	pink, white, lavender, purple	–	open flowers	–	–	36°F–40°F (2.2°C–4°C)	–	–
Lupine	Lupinus cvs. Russell	various	2'–3'	one-half florets open	–	3 days	40°F (4°C)	Yes	7 days
Marigold, African	Tagetes erecta	golden, orange, yellow	–	fully open flowers	–	1–2 weeks	40°F (4°C)	–	–
Masterwort	Astrantia major	red, pink, white	2'	upper flowers open	–	–	34°F–41°F (1°C–5°C)	–	5–7 days
Meadow Rue	Thalictrum sp.	purple	3'–6'	mostly open	–	–	–	Yes	7 days
Mignonette, Common	Reseda odorata	grayish green	–	one-half florets open	–	3–5 days	40°F (4°C)	–	–
Milkweed, Butterflyweed	Asclepias sp.	several	2'–4'	mostly open	cool	–	–	Yes	5–8 days
Monkshood	Aconitum sp.	blue, purple	2'–3'	just opening	don't chill	–	34°F–40°F (1°C–4°C)	Yes	7–10 days
Monkshood, True	Aconitum napellus	dark blue	–	one-half florets open	–	3–7 days	34°F–41°F (1°C–5°C)	–	–
Montebretia	Crocosmia x crocosmiiflora	orange	3'	one-half florets open	–	–	–	–	–
Nasturtium	Tropaeolum majus	variety	–	fully open flowers	–	–	36°F–40°F (2.2°C–4°C)	–	–
Nerine	Nerine bowdenii	pure white, cherry red	2'–3'	oldest buds almost open	–	–	–	–	–
Ornamental Onions	Allium sp.	blue, purple	1'–4'	1/3 florets open	cool	7–8 days	–	Yes	7–14 days
Painted Daisies	Chrysanthemum sp.	many	2'	fully open	–	–	40°F (4°C)	–	4–12 days
Pansy	Viola x wittrockiana	range of colors	–	almost open flowers	–	–	35°F–41°F (2°C–5°C)	Yes	–

(Continued)

Common Name	Species	Colors	Height	Harvest Stage	Harvest Tip	Storage Life	Storage Temperature	Ethylene Sensitivity	Vase Life
Peony	*Paeonia sp.*	pink, red, white	2'–3'	buds just in color	–	2–6 weeks	33°F–36°F (0.5°C–2.2°C)	No	4–10 days
Phalaenopsis	*Phalaenopsis sp.*	wide range of colors	–	3 to 4 days after opening	–	–	45°F–50°F (7°C–10°C)	Yes	–
Phlox	*Phlox paniculata*	various	2'–3'	half flowers open	–	1–3 days	40°F (4°C)	Yes	2–7 days
Pincushion Flower	*Scabiosa spp.*	range of colors	–	half-open flowers	–	–	36°F–40°F (2.2°C–4°C)	Yes	8–14 days
Plantain, Funkia	*Hosta sp.*	white, lilac	2'–4'	showing color	–	–	–	–	7–10 days
Plume flower	*Astilbe hybrids*	wide range of colors	2'–3'	one-half florets open	hot water dip	7–10 days	36°F–40°F (2.2°C–4°C)	Yes	4–12 days
Poppy	*Papaver sp.*	wide range of colors	–	Calyx just starting to open	–	–	35°F–40°F (2°C–4°C)	No	5–7 days
Primose	*Primula sp.*	wide range of colors	–	one-half florets open	–	–	36°F–40°F (2.2°C–4°C)	Yes	–
Ranunculus	*Ranunculus asiaticus*	wide range of colors	–	buds beginning to open	–	7–10 days	33°F–41°F (0.5°C–5°C)	Yes	5–7 days
Rose (dry pack)	*Rosa sp.*	range of colors	–	first 1 to 2 petals beginning to unfold	–	1–2 weeks	33°F–35°F (0.5°C–2°C)	–	3–14 days
Rose (in water)	*Rosa sp.*	range of colors	–	first 1 to 2 petals beginning to unfold	–	4–5 days	33°F–35°F (0.5°C–2°C)	–	3–14 days
Rudebeckia, Black-Eyed Susan	*Rudebeckia sp.*	yellow	–	fully opened flowers, first ring of disk florets open	–	–	36°F–41°F (2.2°C–5°C)	–	–
Sage	*Salvia sp.*	various	1'–2'	just opening	–	–	–	Yes	5–7 days
Scabious	*Scabiosa sp.*	white, pink	1'–2'	just opening	–	–	–	Yes	5–7 days
Sea Holly	*Eryngium sp.*	blue	1'–2'	fully open	–	–	38°F–40°F (3.3°C–4°C)	–	10–12 days
Sea Lavender	*Limonium perezii*	blue	2'	mostly open	–	–	33°F–35°F (0.5°C–2°C)	Yes	10–14 days

(Continued)

vascular bundle. The xylem, phloem, and cambium, which run from the roots throughout the plant to distribute water, minerals, and nutrients. (4)

vase life. The useful life span of cut flowers. (5)

vegetative design. A floral design in which flowers and foliage appear as they would in nature; all plant material is naturally compatible and is from a similar climate and region. (10)

vegetative reproduction. A method of reproducing, or propagating, plants from a cutting taken from a leaf or stem. (4)

venation. Patterns of veins in a leaf. (4)

venue. The site or location of a special event. (11)

vine. Leaves arranged naturally to form a chain along a stem or runner. (9)

visible spectrum. The colors produced by the wavelengths of light energy that make up white light, which is visible to the human eye. (7)

visitation. A time when family and friends gather to pay their respects to the deceased and offer solace to the family; also called *calling hours*. (15)

visual balance. The optical stability of an arrangement. (6)

visual weight. The perceived lightness or heaviness of a design. (6)

volatile organic compound (VOC). Gaseous chemicals in the air that are emitted from many household products and materials, including paints, building materials, and office equipment; many VOCs are known to have short-term or long-term harmful effects on human health. (17)

walima. The traditional wedding banquet held one or more days after the nikah in a Muslim marriage. (13)

walk-in sales. Sales to people who come into the store without first calling to place an order. (18)

water pick. A small tube with a pointed bottom and a cap that is pierced in the middle to accommodate a stem; used to provide a water source for individual stems. (3)

waterfall design. A cascade design with the addition of elements that suggest the flow of water. (10)

wholesale florist. A florist that buys plants and other merchandise in bulk from growers and manufacturers and then sells them to retail florists. (1)

Williamsburg design. A floral design style developed in the American colonies after 1700; similar to the early colonial style, but more complex and sophisticated. (10)

wire service. A company, such as Teleflora or FTD, that handles wire orders between member florists. (1)

wire-rack method. A method of drying flowers in which heavy-headed flowers are placed so the flower head rests on a wire rack; the stem extends through and hangs below the rack. (16)

wood pick. A four-sided stick from 2.5″ to 7″ long that is pointed on one end; used to secure floral items in an arrangement. (3)

xylem. Vessels in a plant stem that conduct water and minerals from the roots of a plant to the leaves and flowers. (4)

zoning. Positioning like flowers and foliage together, as if they have grown there naturally. (10)

Index

A

abstract design, 264
accent moss, 431
accents, 125–126
accounting, 502–503
achromatic, 134
acidifier, 96
additive color system, 137
adhesives, 61–62
Administrative Professionals Day, 383
African club moss, 485
African daisy, 188
African marigold, 194
African violet, 485
agave, 485
ageratum, 177
aglaonema, 485
air drying, 436–441
   container, 439
   flat surface, 440
   hang-and-dry, 436–438
air embolism, 102
all-around design, 476
alocasia, 221
aloe vera, 486
alstroemeria, 177
altar design, 344–345
aluminum plant, 495
amaranth fountain plant, 177
amaryllis, 177
American design styles, 261–262

American Institute of Floral Designers
   (AIFD), 19–21
analogous
   arrangements, 159
   colors, 139–140
Anand Karaj, 327
ancient civilizations, 28–31
anniversaries, 371–373, 556
anther, 82
anthurium, 178, 221
aphelandra, 486
application, 156–157
architecture, 274–275
areca palm, 486
arm bouquet, 314
armature, 67
   adding flowers and greenery, 68–69
arrangement styles. *See* floral design types
arrowhead plant, 221
Art Deco, 41
Art Nouveau, 41
artificial flowers. *See also* permanent botanicals
   natural shaping, 430
   stem extension, 430
   types, 423–424
asiatic lily, 192
assembly line, 508
aster, 178
astilbe, 178
asymmetrical floral design, 117–119
asymmetrical triangle, 250–251
attendant, 329–331

kinara, 386
king protea, 191
kingdom, 78
knifeblade eucalyptus, 228
Kwanzaa, 386

L

lady's mantle, 191
ladyslipper orchid, 197
lamb's ear, 231
landscape design, 266–267
larkspur, 191
laurel, 231
lavender, 191
leaf base, 84
leaf shine products, 469
leatherleaf fern, 232
leaves, 84
    functions, 88
lei, 308
lepto, 192
leucadendron, 186, 232
lichen, 456
lichen covered branch, 456
light, 466–467
lilac, 192
lily grass, 232
lily of the Nile, 193
lily of the valley, 193
lily pollen, 169–170
lily turf grass, 232
limited-service flower shop, 7
line, 146–147
    design, 256
    flower, 144
line-mass continuum, 256–257
line-mass design, 257
lisianthus, 193
lobster claw, 193
location, 280
logistics, 276

loosestrife, 193
lotus, 456
love-in-a-mist, 193
lupine, 194

M

magnolia, 232
mahonia, 232
maid of honor, 330
maidenhair fern, 233, 493
mantel arrangement, 361
manzanita branch, 456
Mardi Gras, 379
    arrangement, 380–381
margin, 84
Marguerite daisy, 185
marigold, 194
marketing, 512–514
marketing plan, 513
markup, 508–509
Martin Luther King, Jr. Day, 377
mass design, 256–257
mass flower, 144
massing, 257
mass production, 507–508
masterwork, 194
matron of honor, 330
mausoleum, 394
meanings of flowers, 170–171
    chart, 40
mechanics, 62–63
    bouquet, 316–317
    covering with sheet moss, 434
    decorative, 431
memorial arrangements, 405–413
Memorial Day, 368
meristem, 86
metal container, 52
microwave drying, 444–445
Middle Ages, 32

milfoil yarrow, 205

military weddings, 329

milkweed, 194

milkweed balloon plant, 194

millefleur design, 265

millet, 456

mimosa, 195

mint, 233

Modern Period, 41

money plant, 493

monkshood, 195

monochromatic
    arrangement, 159–160, 370
    color scheme, 139

monofloral, 8

mood moss, 457

mosaic virus, 34

moss, 457

Mother's Day, 359
    arrangement, 358

mother-in-law tongue, 233, 497–498

movie set floral designer, 14

mum, 195

Muslim ceremonies, 328

myrtle, 233

myrtus, 233

N

nandina, 234
    green, 493

narthex, 324

nave, 324

negative space, 117

nephtytis, 493

nerine lily, 196

nerve plant, 494

nesting, 42

new baby, 373

new convention design, 265

New Year's Day, 375, 377

New Year's Eve, 386–387

New Zealand flax, 234

nikah, 328

node, 86

Norfolk island pine, 494

noteworthy weddings, 563

O

officiant, 324

okra pod, 457

oncidium orchid, 197

One-Methylcyclopropene (1-MCP), 105

one-sided design, 476

onion flower, 196

online and wire service florists, 12–13

open-system terrarium, 473–474

operating expenses, 504

opuntia cactus, 488

orange, 162

orange Jessamine, 234

orangeries, 35

orchid, 196

oriental design styles, 258–259

oriental lily, 192

oriental poppy, 198

ornamental
    cabbage, 234
    kale, 197
    pepper, 197
    pineapple, 197
    plants, 471, 473

overhead, 504

ox-eye daisy, 185

P

packing, 97–98

pall, 400

palmetto, 235

palmetto leaf, 457

spatial scale, 282–283

special occasions, 368–375

specialty florists, 11–14

specialty shop, 8

species, 79

speedwell, 202

spider mum, 195

spider plant, 238, 498

spray carnation, 182

spray tint, 141

sprengeri fern, 238

Spring Festival, 378

square styles, 249

stacked design, 265

staghorn fern, 238, 498

stamen, 82

standing spray, 405–406

star gazer lily, 192

star of Bethlehem, 202

start-up capital, 503

state certification, 18–19

state flowers, 557–562

statice, 202

stem strippers, 58

stems, 86

    functions, 89

stem wrap, 60

stephanotis, 202

    wiring, 300–301

stigma, 82

stipules, 84

stitch wire method, 296

stomata, 88

stonecrop, 202

storage, 103–108

    ethylene sensitivity, 104

    relative humidity and circulation, 104

    temperature, 103

storage life

    flowers (chart), 95, 537–546

    foliage (chart), 109, 547–550

stove house, 38

St. Patrick's Day, 381, 383

    arrangement, 382

strawberry plant, 498

strawflower, 202, 459

strelitzia, 238

string of hearts, 238

string of pearls, 239

STS, 105

style, 82

subordinate, 124

subtractive color system, 136

succulent, 465

sugar cone, 459

sunflower, 203

sustainable, 42

sweetheart rose, 200

sweet pea, 203

sweet violet, 203

sword lily, 188

symmetrical floral design, 117–118

sympathy flowers.

    delivering, 415

    floral arrangements, 410

    friends and associates, 398–399

    marketing, 395–396

sympathy remembrances, live plants, 414

synagogue, 325

syngonium, 239

systemic dyeing, 141–143

T

tape products, 60

taxonomy, 77–79

tea rose, 200

temperature, 103

terrarium, 473–475

    setting up, 475

tertiary color, 138

texture, 149–151